Shelter Security in Urban India

About the Editor

Darshini Mahadevia is a Professor at the Faculty of Planning CEPT University. She currently is the Dean of the Faculty. She has Ph.D. from the Centre for the Study of Regional Development (CSRD), Jawaharlal Nehru University, New Delhi. She was a visiting fellow at the University of California, Los Angeles, McGill University, Montreal, Tsinghua University, Beijing and Tianjin University of Finance and Economics, Tianjin. She has collaborated for research with many national and international academic institutions/universities. She has extensively published on urban development policies, including housing policy, urban poverty, human and gender development. In particular, her research is focused on inclusive urban planning. Her latest publication is 'Handbook of Urban Inequalities', co-authored with Sandip Sarkar and published by Oxford University Press. In 2009 she incepted the Centre for Urban Equity at the CEPT University, which functioned as a National Resource Centre for the Ministry of Housing and Urban Poverty Alleviation, Government of India.

SHELTER SECURITY IN URBAN INDIA

Pathways, Barriers and Outcomes

Editor
Darshini Mahadevia

CONCEPT PUBLISHING COMPANY PVT. LTD.
NEW DELHI-110059

ISBN-13: 978-93-5125-181-1

First Published 2015

Published and Printed by

Concept
Since 1974

Concept Publishing Company Pvt. Ltd.
A/15-16, Commercial Block, Mohan Garden
New Delhi-110059 (India)
T: 25351460, 25351794, *F*: 091-11-25357109
E: publishing@conceptpub.com, W: www.conceptpub.com
Editorial Office: H-13, Bali Nagar, New Delhi-110 015, India.

Cataloging in Publication Data--Courtesy: D.K. Agencies (P) Ltd. <docinfo@dkagencies.com>

Shelter security in urban India : pathways, barriers and outcomes / editor, Darshini Mahadevia.
pages cm
Includes bibliographical references and index.
ISBN 9789351251811

1. Urban poor--Housing--Government policy--India--Ahmadābād--Case studies. 2. Urban poor--Housing--Government policy--India--Case studies. 3. Slums--India--Ahmadābād--Case studies. 4. Slums--India--Case studies. I. Mahadevia, Darshini, editor.

HD7287.96.I4S54 2015 DDC 363.58095475 23

Preface

This book is a collection of articles on shelter security based on the research work undertaken at the Centre for Urban Equity (CUE), CEPT University over the last few years. Inadvertently, the collection represents the journey of CUE since its establishment. The first research at the Centre was on social protection, which argued that the shelter security is the foundation for the social protection in urban areas in the context of India and even the developing countries. The journey then continued with the research on different aspects of low-income housing in different cities in India, for which we drew on the grants of the Ministry of Housing and Urban Poverty Alleviation (MoHUPA), Government of India (GoI), Department of International Development (DoID) funds and some of the Centre's own funds. The MoHUPA had selected CEPT University as one of its National Resource Centre (NRC) and funding was made available to undertake research on urban poor housing. Each chapter was a freestanding article, brought out as the working paper of the Centre.

These researches undertaken over last half a decade have been converted into chapters in this book to present before the wider audience our insights into living conditions in the urban informal settlements in the Indian cities, learning from interventions to change them and efficacy of the public housing programmes. The book reiterates, what Roy (2009) argued that the idiom of urbanization in India has been informality and increase in national income does not mean much as the urban housing continues to remain and will remain informal for a vast majority of the population.

Housing or shelter security is the key to rapid as well as inclusive urbanisation, which many countries have addressed in their own way. Post-Second World War, the Western European countries stressed on shelter security, which acted as an important entry point for social security. The developing countries, that urbanized rapidly, for example, Brazil, which is now 85 per cent urbanized, has addressed shelter security through 'Right to City Charter', which followed 'Right to City' movement. Significant participatory slum upgrading has been carried out in South-east Asian countries, Thailand and Indonesia. The socialist block in Asia, China and Vietnam has provided shelter security to the urban workers of all income groups through employee housing, housing being provided as a wage good. India has just embarked on this path through her first large national public housing programme under the Basic Services for the Urban Poor (BSUP) component of the Jawaharlal Nehru National Urban Renewal Mission (JNNURM) followed by Rajiv Awas Yojana (RAY). At the time of going for print of this book, new national government has come to being and a new urban housing programme is expected to replace the JNNURM's BSUP and (RAY).

The book attempts to answer the following questions taking examples from different cities in the country: (i) What are the processes of development of informal housing in the Indian cities? (ii) What are the living conditions and what are the processes that have led to improvement in the same? (iii) What factors or processes create different levels of tenure security and what are the outcomes of the same? (iv) Have public housing programmes been effective? The chapters are the case studies of a city or a state and may answer one or more of the above mentioned questions. The limitations of the book are that the case studies are embedded within the specific contexts of the state and the city and hence hard to generalise. The state is important as the land legislation and development ideology are specific to each state. The data in the case studies are a bit dated; are about five years old. But, there is not much of difference in the processes now than at the time of the study, although, the actual status may have changed somewhat. We, therefore, decided to continue with publishing the individual chapters, even with slightly old data.

We are grateful for the funds we have received under the Social Protection in Asia (SPA) programme funded by the Ford Foundation and International Development Research Council (IDRC) of Canada and managed by the Institute of Development Studies (IDS), Sussex, United Kingdom (UK) and Institute of Human Development (IHD), New Delhi India. Researches on tenure security in Ahmedabad and Surat have been undertaken through these funds. The MoHUPA's funds have been used for research on Andhra Pradesh, Rajkot and Bhopal. Lastly, the MoHUPA, in partnership with DFID, United Kingdom (UK), started Support to

National Policies for Urban Poverty Reduction (SNPUPR) Programme with the objective of informing and capacity building for RAY. Research on Nagpur and Nanded was taken up under the SNPUPR.

The research team at the CUE, of Tejas Patel, Vishal Darji, Kaushal Jajoo and Tejal Patel have helped us in various ways: organising and undertaking the fieldwork, preparing maps and graphics and also taking photographs of the settlements we have studied. Neha Bhatia has carried out the final editing. Nirmala Khadpekar had undertaken the first editing of some of the chapters in the book. Bijal Bhatt of the Mahila Housing SEWA Trust (MHT) and Rajendra Joshi and Keren Nazereth of Saath, had opened up their doors for us to seek their help. They have helped immensely in putting us in contact with the slum dwellers and their leaders. The leaders in each slum who have given us their time in discussing, in particular Devubhen Niraj Jani, Chinamyeebhen of Saath and Bhartibhen of MHT, without whom we would not have gained insights into the lives of the slum dwellers, we are grateful. The MHT and Navsarjan Trust had helped us in our fieldwork in Surat.

The authors owe this research to large many individuals and organisations. But, they also owe the opinions expressed in the chapter articles. The CUE or CEPT University or the funders are not responsible for the views expressed in the articles in the book.

The book has been made possible also because of the co-authors of the book chapters, the young enthusiastic team at the CUE of Pooja Shah, Trishna Gogoi, Suchita Vyas, Abhijit Datey and Renu Desai. Lastly, we, as a Centre at the CEPT University and also in our individual capacity, do not want us, the urban planning professionals and the society, to forget that the cities are made by the people, for the people and of the people. That housing/shelter is the priority and that the shelter policies should not be coloured and hence dictated by anything else but the interest of the people inhabiting the cities and expected to inhibit the cities. Let us not take away our attention from the issues of shelter in the cities in the race to make cities as 'World Class' or 'Economic Growth Engines'. If they are by products of addressing the shelter issues, we have no quarrel with them.

July, 2015 **Darshini Mahadevia**

Contents

List of Tables

List of Exhibits

List of Figures/Maps/Charts

List of Contributors

Darshini Mahadevia is a Professor at the Faculty of Planning CEPT University. She currently is the Dean of the Faculty. She has Ph.D. from the Centre for the Study of Regional Development (CSRD), Jawaharlal Nehru University, New Delhi. She was a visiting fellow at the University of California, Los Angeles, McGill University, Montreal, Tsinghua University, Beijing and Tianjin University of Finance and Economics, Tianjin. She has collaborated for research with many national and international academic institutions/universities. She has extensively published on urban development policies, including housing policy, urban poverty, human and gender development. In particular, her research is focused on inclusive urban planning. Her latest publication is "*Handbook of Urban Inequalities*", co-authored with Sandip Sarkar and published by Oxford University Press. In 2009 she incepted the Centre for Urban Equity at the CEPT University, which functioned as a National Resource Centre for the Ministry of Housing and Urban Poverty Alleviation, Government of India.

Abhijit Datey is an Architect-Urban Housing Planner who has contributed in research pertaining to shelter security, urban street vending and inclusive urban transport. He is currently pursuing Ph.D. at University of Tokyo. His research focuses housing issues of the urban poor and the changing roles of the government housing institutions.

Bijal Bhatt is currently the Director of Mahila Housing SEWA Trust (MHT). She is a civil engineer by training and is a recognized expert in habitat improvement, community development and housing finance. She has proven experience in conceptualizing planning, managing and providing support for slum upgradation programmes across India. Her professional experience has focused on a range of poverty alleviation issues, particularly with women, entrepreneurship, slum upgradation, Water and Sanitation, income and urban planning, housing finance, housing technology etc.

Keren Nazareth is the Executive Director of SAATH since April, 2011. SAATH is a non-profit in India that works with vulnerable households in urban and rural areas. She holds a Masters in Social Work from the Tata Institute of Social Sciences, Mumbai. Her work includes programmes of livelihoods for youth, women and informal sector workers.

Pavan Kumar Ankinapalli is Associate Vice President at IDFC Institute. His earlier work experiences have been at the IDFC Foundation, the Ministry of Housing and Urban Poverty Alleviation on housing, and High Powered Expert Committee on Urban Infrastructure constituted by the Government of India. He has worked on capacity building in PPP, land management and urban finance issues. Pavan has a Masters in Infrastructure Planning from CEPT University, Ahmedabad. He is the co-author of the book "*India's Reluctant Urbanization: Thinking Beyond*" (forthcoming).

Pooja Shah holds Master's degree in Economics and also Masters in Urban and Regional Planning. As a research associate in CEPT University, she worked on a study concerning social protection for urban poor in India which is her key area of interest. She has also taught Economics at undergraduate level in Ahmedabad University.

Rajendra Joshi, a Schwab and Ashoka Fellow has worked with the urban poor in India since 1989 through the NGO Saath and now incubates social enterprises. His publications include "Recycling of Construction Material in Ahmedabad City", 1996, "Integrated Slum Development in the slums of Pravinnagar-Guptanagar, Ahmedabad", 2002, "Pro Poor Accountability in WATSAN at Ahmedabad, India", 2006 and "The Role of the NGO sector in Slum Rehabilitation", 2008.

Renu Desai is an urban researcher and is currently the coordinator of the Centre for Urban Equity (CUE), CEPT University, Ahmedabad. Prior to joining CUE, she was a research associate at the Department of Geography, Durham University, UK. Her Ph.D. is in Architecture from the University of California, Berkeley. Her research interests centre around urban transformation and urban informality in Indian cities with a focus on equitable development and urban citizenship. She is co-editor of

Urbanizing Citizenship: Contested Spaces in Indian Cities (New Delhi: Sage, 2012).

Rutool Sharma is Assistant Professor at Faculty of Planning at CEPT University. Her focus areas include urban land management, spatial planning, and inclusive development. She has been a founding member of CUE. She currently holds position as coordinator of Centre for Urban Land Policy, CEPT University.

Suchita Vyas is a Research Associate at the Centre for Urban Equity, CEPT University. She holds a Masters in Planning (specialization in Housing) from CEPT University and Bachelors in Architecture from APIED, Sardar Patel University. Her work has spanned research on urban informal housing and the urban informal economy.

Trishna Gogoi is an urban planner currently holding the position of Assistant Director in the Directorate of Town and Country Planning, Government of Assam. She is also pursuing her Ph.D. in Social Science at Tata Institute of Social Science, Guwahati, researching on urban land governance in Assam. She had done her Masters in Urban and Regional Planning from CEPT University.

Glossary and Abbreviations

Terminology

Agarbatti	Fragrance sticks
Ahmedabadi	Resident of Ahmedabad
Ashram	A spiritual hermitage or monastery
Bachat	Saving
Balghar/balwadi	Pre-school/kindergarden
Baniya	Grocer
	Squatter or slum settlements in Delhi; also called as *jhuggi jhompdi*
Bawa	Ascetic
Bharwad	A Gujarati caste predominantly engaged in cattle grazing
Bhil	A tribal community
Bidi	Tobacco rolled in a leaf. Indian version of cigarette
Chawl/chali	An informal settlement in which buildings have rooms organized in rows, as called in Mumbai and Gujarat respectively
Chhagda	Shared auto rickshaw
Chhapra	Huts
Chulha	Hearth
Dais	Mid-wives
Dalit	Outcaste, untouchable, also known as *Harijan*
Ekal batti	Individual light
Ekta	Unity
Goonda	Hooligan/a strong man
Guntha	Unit of land measurement in Maharashtra, 1 acre (43,560 sq.ft.) equals 40 guntha.
Gunthewari	Unauthorised layouts formed on the periphery of towns and cities of Maharashtra through the subdivision, sale

	and development of privately-owned land without taking permission for non-agricultural (NA) use and/or acquiring the necessary planning permissions.
Gurudwara	Religious place of Sikhs
Gyanshala	Primary school
Hajj	Annual pilgrimage to Mecca paid by the Muslim community
Harijan	A lower caste of India. People of this caste are mainly sweepers, rag pickers etc.
Inamdar zameen	Land gifted by the former feudal lord under the Mughal rule
Jada	Fat
Katcha	Temporary
Kathiyawadi	Community from Kathiawar, now called Saurashtra region of Gujarat state
Khakhra	Food item
Khat mahurat	A ceremony of putting the first brick in the base before starting any construction work
Mahila	Woman
Mandal	Association
Marwari	Community originally from Marwar region in Rajasthan
Mehendi	Traditional art of painting hand and feet with application of paste of a shrub, also called Henna
Nallah	Open drain
Navratri	A folk dance festival of state of Gujarat spread over nine days
Olakh-patra	Letter proving identity
Papad	Food item
Parchi	A quasi-legal document of financial transaction with the signatures of the buyer and seller along with that of two witnesses
Parivartaan	Transformation—the name for SNP
Patel	A predominant community in Gujarat, traditionally village-based landowners or farmers
Patta	Land rights
Pramukh	Leader
Pucca	Permanent
Rajashahi	Former princely ruler/royal
Rathod	A clan claiming its descent from mythical Indian Solar dynasty
Sakhi	Female friend
Sheri	Numbered street

Suchit	Informal
Swadisht	Delicious
Taba paavti	A house possession document
Talavadi	Small lake or a pond
Tekro	Small hill
Thika	Lease right
Udaan	Fly
Ummeed	Hope
Utara	Form
Vas	Place of residence
Vikasini	Woman as a developer
Vimo	Insurance
Vishi	Chit fund
Yuvak	Young Man
Zari	Brocade art was introduced by the Parsi community, which came from Iran and settled in Surat

Abbreviations

AEC	Ahmedabad Electricity Company
AMC	Ahmedabad Municipal Corporation
APL	Above Poverty Line
APSHCL	Andhra Pradesh State Housing Corporation Limited
ASAG	Ahmedabad Study Action Group
AUDA	Ahmedabad Urban Development Authority
BDA	Bhopal Development Authority
BHEL	Bharat Heavy Electricals Limited
BIS	Bureau of Indian Standards
BMC	Bhopal Municipal Corporation
BPL	Below Poverty Line
BPMC	Bombay Provincial Municipal Corporation
BSHF	Building and Social Housing Foundation
BSUP	Basic Services for the Urban Poor
BVM	Basti Vikas Samiti
CBO	Community-based Organisation
CIDCO	City and Industrial Development Corporation
CSO	Civil Society Organisation
CUE	Centre for Urban Equity
DDA	Delhi Development Authority
DFID	Department of International Development
DMIC	Delhi-Mumbai Industrial Corridor
DoR	Department of Revenue

DoUW	Department of Urban Welfare
DP	Development Plan
DPR	Detailed Project Report
DU	Dwelling Unit
EMI	Equal Monthly Instalment
EYM	Ekta Yuvak Mandal
FDI	Foreign Direct Investment
FGD	Focus Group Discussion
GHMC	Greater Hyderabad Municipal Corporation
GIDC	Gujarat Industrial Corporation
GoI	Government of India
GSCB	Gujarat Slum Clearance Board
HADA	Hazira Area Development Authority
HDB	Housing and Development Board
HH	Households
HKHA	Hong Kong Housing Authority
HPEC	High Powered Expert Committee
HUDCO	Housing and Urban Development Corporation
IAY	Indira Awas Yojana
IDRC	International Development Research Council
IDS	Institute of Development Studies
IHD	Institute of Human Development
IHSDP	Integrated Housing and Slum Development Programme
ISDP	Integrated Slum Development Programme
JIS	Janta Information System
JNNURM	Jawaharlal Nehru National Urban Renewal Mission
KVP	Kisan Vikas Patra
LFPR	Labour Force Participation Rate
LIG	Low Income Groups
LPCD	Litres Per Capita Per Day
LVN	Lok Vikas Nidhi
MHADA	Maharashtra Housing and Area Development Authority
MHT	Mahila Housing SEWA Trust
MMTS	Multi-Modal Transport System
MoHUPA	Ministry of Housing and Urban Poverty Alleviation
MPCE	Monthly Per Capita Expenditure
MPHIDB	Madhya Pradesh Housing and Infrastructure Development Board
MPR	Monthly Progress Report
MPSCB	Madhya Pradesh Slum Clearance Board
MPUSP	Madhya Pradesh Urban Services for Poor
NA	Non-Agricultural

NBA	Nirmal Bharat Abhiyan
NGO	Non-governmental Organisation
NHFC	National Housing Finance Corporation
NIUA	National Institute of Urban Affairs
NMT	Non-motorised transport
NOC	No Objection Certificate
NRC	National Resource Centre
NREGS	National Rural Employment Guarantee Scheme
NSDP	National Slum Development Programme
NSSO	National Sample Survey Organisation
NTM	Nanded Textile Mill
NUHHP	National Urban Housing and Habitat Policy
NWCMC	Nanded Waghala City Municipal Corporation
PDS	Public Distribution System
PHC	Primary Health Centre
PPP	Public-Private Partnership
PPSA	Poverty Pockets Situation Analysis
PWD	Public Works Department
RAY	Rajiv Awas Yojana
RGK	Rajiv Griha Kalpa
RMC	Rajkot Municipal Corporation
RSBY	Rashtriya Swasthya Bima Yojana
RWA	Resident Welfare Association
SAC	Social Audit Committee
SC	Scheduled Caste
SESI	Slum Environment Sanitation Initiative
SEWA	Self Employed Women Association
SEWS	Socially and Economically Weaker Section
SHG	Self-help Groups
SHHP	State Housing and Habitat Policy
SIHS	Subsidised Industrial Housing Scheme
SJSRY	Swarna Jayanti Shahari Rojgar Yojana
SMC	Surat Municipal Corporation
SMM	Sakhi Mahila Mandal
SNP	Slum Networking Project
SNPUPR	Support to National Policies for Urban Poverty Reduction
SOE	State Owned Enterprise
SPA	Social Protection in Asia
SRS	Slum Redevelopment Scheme
SUDA	Surat Urban Development Authority
SWM	Solid Waste Management
TDO	Town Development Officer

UADD	Urban Administration and Development Department
UCD	Urban Community Development
UDA	Urban Development Authority
UIG	Urban Infrastructure and Governance
UK	United Kingdom
ULB	Urban Local Body
ULCRA	Urban Land Ceiling and Regulation Act
UNCHS	United Nations Centre for Human Settlements
URC	Urban Resource Centre
USAID	United States Agency for International Development
VAMBAY	Valmiki Ambedkar Awas Yojana
WFPR	Work Force Participation Rate
WHO	World Health Organization
YUVA	Youth for Unity and Voluntary Action

1 Informality and Shelter Security in Urban India

Darshini Mahadevia

Although India is at a low level of urbanization; 31.7 per cent of her population living in the urban areas in 2011, there is a significant housing distress in particularly the metropolitan and large cities. The housing shortage calculated for the Twelfth Five Year Plan is 18.8 million (NBO, 2012) households in 2012, which is about 23.8 per cent of the total housing stock in 2010 Census[1]. The Population Census of 2011 gives a figure of 13.36 million households as living in slums, which is 16.9 per cent of the total households[2]. Thus, there are also non-slum households living in cramped and/or unserviced housing, qualifying to be considered as part of housing shortage. A revealing fact of the Housing Census of 2010 is availability of 11 million vacant houses[3], which if put to use could take care of about 85 per cent households living in slums in urban India. The arithmetic does not work and therein is located the housing question; while there is large housing vacancy, there is also housing shortage. This has to do with house prices, affordability for housing, and housing supply mechanisms. A part of the vacant houses are purchases for investment purposes, some of it for the purpose of speculation. Besides, significant proportion of households living in informal housing, which also has developed on account of the same reasons in addition to the distorted regulatory system and its implementation mechanism promotes rent seeking. Development of informal housing is global phenomenon in the developing countries and not just India, making Roy (2009) claim that informality is the paradigm of urbanisation in the developing countries.

John F.C. Turner, long time back, in the context of the developing countries, stated that housing is 'bundle of services'. By implication, housing for the poor is not just a built structure, but also includes land and services, water supply, sewerage, electricity, and access. Housing for the low-income groups is incremental, which begins with squatting (to access land) and then gradually improving it to a permanent dwelling unit. Overtime, they consolidate and move into a formal housing. This process of consolidation is the story of policies and play of different actors in the urban context and is very location specific on one hand and is also linked to dynamics of economic mobility of the households on the other. Articles in this book, located in different contexts, indeed explain that the journey from a temporary shelter of bamboo poles covered by plastic sheets to a permanent household is complex and diverse.

Housing thus created by people themselves is often called informal housing. The term informal means that the settlement does not have a legally clear land title or have not obtained development clearance for construction from the planning authority. In all, informal housing is much larger than the slum housing. This book focuses on the description of the informal housing and in particular the low-income housing in it and its interaction with the policy instruments and institutions, leading to improvement in living conditions.

In spite of the declaration in the first UN-HABITAT Conference at Vancouver in 1976, India did not frame any legislation to extend security of tenure to the residents of informal settlements, with exceptions in some states in India, namely Madhya Pradesh, which promulgated tenure security legislation in 1984, followed by some other states in India. For all the years post-independence, India also did not have any public housing programme of any worthwhile size and what could be observed were fragmented and periodic state government level programmes. With the introduction of the Jawaharlal Nehru National Urban Renewal Mission (JNNURM) in 2005, a serious effort of funding public housing for the urban poor came about under the Basic Services for the Urban Poor (BSUP). The BSUP is for the mission cities, which were about 68 in number, the non-mission cities were covered through Integrated Housing and Slum Development Programme (IHSDP). Up to September 30, 2014, 1.44 million BSUP + IHSDP units were sanctioned, of which 0.85 million were completed, another 0.35 million were under construction and 0.62 million were occupied by then[4]. Under the Rajiv Awas Yojana (RAY), as of September 30, 2014, 0.15 million dwelling units were sanctioned, of which just 1,406 units were completed, another 16,412 were under progress and none occupied[5]. Together, only 1.6 million houses were sanctioned in the mission and non-mission cities, which is just 8.4 per cent of the housing shortage estimated at the beginning of the 12th Five Year Plan. Evidently, the first ever attempt in constructing public housing programme for the poor did not have any large reach and the model of public housing construction adopted by the housing agencies of the state governments has not delivered much in reducing the urban housing shortage. As in the past, even in the coming years, the urban poor households will continue to depend on their own devices to find a shelter for themselves, whether secure or not.

India is a diverse country with diverse levels of state engagement in the welfare of the urban poor, including in extending shelter security. Different case studies in the book illustrate this. Given that we are located in Gujarat, we have cases from three cities of the state, Rajkot, Surat and Ahmedabad. We firstly present the case of informal housing in the city of Rajkot and rental housing within it. This is followed by description of informal housing in Surat. Ahmedabad case studies are description of processes of intervention by the Non-governmental Organizations (NGOs) facilitated by the local state and then analysis of factors that influence tenure security in two wards, Vasna and Amraiwadi in the city. Thereafter, we present assessment of the BSUP and other public housing programmes in Madhya Pradesh and Maharashtra. Andhra Pradesh had introduced its indigenous housing programme followed by the BSUP and IHSDP. In fact, the earlier programmes were converted into BSUP and IHSDP in the state. We have assessed them through household survey. In Madhya Pradesh, we have selected Bhopal case for analysis where we have assessed all the programmes, from tenure regularization to slum upgrading and then BSUP, using household survey as well as social audit methodology. Lastly, we have presented intervention by the local state in the informal housing settlements in Nanded. We do not present any concluding chapter as there is no conclusion on ensuring shelter security to all the urban poor in the Indian cities. The problem is going to be more acute in case the rate of urbanization increases and there is significant inflow of migrant labour to the cities. At the least, the state and city governments would do with not demolishing slum housing/informal housing, and if they need to displace them for infrastructure projects, they would do well with a participatory rehabilitation process.

Informal Housing as a Paradigm of Urbanisation

Urbanisation due to a particular form of growth model of globalisation and liberalisation represented by shift towards privatisation and deficit reduction and state withdrawal pursued globally as well in India, have resulted in two phenomena; various informalities and subversions for survival and development. These contemporary informalities are located on the already existing large urban informal sector in housing, which has developed on account of lack of access to formal sector as well as ease of entry and exit in the informal sector. These informalities provide options as well are roadblocks to sustainable development. The ramifications are on the development of institutions and modes of governance, land and housing markets, labour markets and livelihood strategies, spatial forms and safety and security in the cities.

Informal housing has developed because the people themselves have made efforts to build on their own in face of weak state regarding housing supply and unaffordable housing prices in the formal sector. The UN-HABITAT (2003) states that the "poor are the largest producers of shelter and builders of cities in the world." In India, as in other countries of the Global South, urban poor housing has been largely informal, functioning in the clandestine realms of local politics, which Benjamin (2005) terms as, 'quiet politics'. In the same vein, Bayat (2000) has also described the dynamics of the Third World Cities and the informalities as 'quiet encroachment of the ordinary'. Informal life for Bayat (2007: 579) is typified by flexibility, pragmatism, negotiation, constant struggle for survival and self-development. The urban poor seek to remain invisible as they attempt to gain access to the city's resources and build social and economic lives that allow their survival in the city and even upward mobility sometimes. Although this is not a confrontational politics or one that seeks to make conscious and visible claims on the city, it is through these attempts at survival that the urban poor nonetheless subvert dominant modes of city-making. While Bayat's focus is cities in the Middle East, in Indian cities too one finds the urban poor engaging in the quiet encroachment of the ordinary, as the case studies of Ahmedabad, Rajkot and Surat in this book illustrates. Thus, many squatters improve their housing and services through their own investments, with intermittent or no aid from the state (Neuwirth, 2005). This is true also for the cities of Gujarat presented in the subsequent chapters.

The key questions are: what are the processes that create informal housing in the cities of the developing countries, and are there ways of formalising the informal sector in these cities, if any? In other words, can we in the cities of the Global South, or the developing world, or the emerging economies live without informality or do away with informality in housing? Other term used in urban literature is 'slum', which is not just an informal settlement but one such with no or poor basic services and also semi-permanent or temporary shelter units. Bayat (2007) calls slum as a 'habitus of the dispossessed'.

Slums are looked at as an 'affliction' in the cities for example by High Powered Expert Committee (HPEC Report, 2011: 15). Slums have also been considered as menace. Angotti (2005) states that, thus, planning for them has always been "reactionary, rather than in keeping with the socio-political and economic environment" of the city. But, many have objected to the use of term 'slum' with derogatory connotation. Slums are considered assets for a city. All the chapters in this book describe this phenomenon at great length. In context of the Oscar award to Slumdog Millionaire, some took exception to the word slum used for Dharavi, the settlement which was the locale of the film, calling it a zone of economic enterprise (Echanove and Srivastava, 2009). Even informal housing is an economic activity for the slum dwellers as the study of rental housing in Rajkot, in this book shown. Roy (2011: 226) states that the slums are an example of 'subaltern urbanism'. Taking from Partha Chatterjee's (2004: 40) concept of 'political society', which involves claims to habitation and livelihood by "groups of population whose very livelihood or habitation involve violation of the law". Roy (2011) argues that subaltern has now become an agent of change rather than a phenomenon seeking recognition. Subaltern urbanism, therefore, has become "economies of entrepreneurialism and political agency" (Roy 2011: 227). Is this true in all cases?

Studies have now shown that urban slums are not just places of living for the urban poor but, are also places of work and entrepreneurship. Our own studies in various Indian cities show that there is not only home-based work in the slums and informal settlements but these are also places of small manufactories (Mahadevia *et al.*, 2014), and all types of entrepreneurial activities. These activities are the places of 'development tourism' in locales such as Dharavi. De Soto (2000), seeing this entrepreneurial capital from below, argued to legalise it through removal of regulations (laws) that illegalised the slums, to unleash the capitalism from below.

Contemporary debates on informality focus on the politics through which informality develops, that is, the politics through which the urban poor and low-income residents negotiate access to land, housing and urban services. Vote-bank politics and patron-client relations are also central for the urban poor in negotiating access to land, housing and urban services in India. Taking this vote-bank politics as his starting point, Benjamin

(2008) conceptualizes the politics of poor groups in the Indian city Bangalore as "occupancy urbanism." For Benjamin, "poor groups, claiming public services and safeguarding territorial claims, open up political spaces that appropriate institutions and fuel an economy that builds complex alliances.. While engaging the state, these locality politics remain autonomous of it. … This politics is substantial and poses multiple crises for global capital" (Benjamin, 2008: 719).

It is through these politics—both quiet encroachment of the ordinary as well as occupancy urbanism—that many informal settlements have emerged and developed in Indian cities, providing possibilities for fulfilling the shelter needs of the urban poor and low-income groups. Some of these processes, emerging from our studies, have been summarized in the next section. It is important to mention here that scholars have increasingly critiqued notions of informality that equate it with spaces of poverty. Al Sayaad (2004: 26) has argued that urban informality "does not simply consist of the activities of the poor, or a particular status of labour, or marginality. Rather, it is an organizing logic which emerges under the paradigm of liberalization." Roy (2009) argues that in Indian cities, informality should be understood as an idiom of urbanization and India's planning regime as an informalized entity itself, one that is in "a state of deregulation, ambiguity and exception." Here, the law is "rendered open-ended and subject to multiple interpretations and interests" and informality is "inscribed in the ever-shifting relationship between what is legal and illegal, legitimate and illegitimate, authorized and unauthorized." Some areas thus come to be designated as illegal and worthy of demolition while others are protected and formalized. The informal idiom of urbanization can be found in other contexts as well. For instance, Holston (2007) argues that much of the Brazilian city is occupied and built through the "misrule of law" as legal landholdings in both the wealthy and the poorest of Brazilian families are at base "legalized usurpations."

All forms of land transfer, subdivision or house construction which take place without official approval are part of urban informality. Informal housing is explained by UN-HABITAT (2003) as that which does not conform to the laws and regulatory framework of the city. The majority of housing in Indian cities, be it of the poor, middle-class or elite, has an element of informality by this definition, although not all of it is viewed as such. Thus, Durand-Lasserve (2007) points out that "a given settlement type with particular characteristics regarding land tenure, urban planning, and housing can be considered either formal or informal depending on the local context and public authority interpretations."

Informality can be viewed in the context of two core areas of housing: (i) land and (ii) dwelling unit. The primary land holding rights have different implications on informality. Occupancy by squatting or other processes on public, private or trust/customary lands can mean different kinds of informality and different levels of insecurity. As lands have become an expensive commodity, land grabbing, informal subdivisions, informal sales, etc., have made squatting more and more difficult for the poor. Many private-sector developers acquire land from agriculturalists on urban peripheries, subdivide the land into plots for residential purposes and sell them at whatever cost the market is ready to bear. One of the most common features in these transactions is non-registering of agricultural lands as non-agricultural (NA)[6], as a result of which these are informal subdivisions. Such subdivisions are also characterised by lack of development control regulations and services. The developers of such informal land markets are not concerned about legalities and development and infrastructural standards as they do not want to increase the price of their products to a level beyond the reach of low-income households. They leave it to their clients (land buyers) to take care of the provision of paved roads, water connections, etc. Payne (1989) found that such informal subdivisions have become widespread across developing countries, becoming a solution to the housing problems of the urban poor. However, in many cities—from Cairo to Delhi—such subdivisions also comprise very high-end commercial and residential developments (Soliman, 2004; Ghertner, 2008). The construction of houses that do not follow development control regulations and building norms creates informality in the context of the dwelling unit. Informal land occupation coupled with informal dwellings inhabited by the urban poor generally leads to slum-like situations because of the lack of recognition by urban authorities and consequently, the lack or inadequacy of basic services like water, sanitation, drainage, etc.

Basing on experience from India, Benjamin (2008) differentiates three political arenas in Indian cities in the neo-liberal era; the policy arena operated by the state and penetrated by the real estate and finance capital lobbies, the civil society arena that restricts the political activity to the legitimate citizens and occupancy urbanism through which the urban poor assert their territorial claims through vote-bank politics. Giving example of a settlement in Bangalore, Benjamin *et al.* (2008) have explained the processes of claim-making by the *dalits*, which he then argues is not possible when the corporate real estate enters the urban arena.

Roy (2011: 231) states that narratives of subaltern urbanism (and slum is one such narrative), is a challenge to "apocalyptic and dystopian narratives" of a megacity and it "tends to remain bound to the study of spaces of poverty, of essential forms of popular agency, of the habitus of the dispossessed, of the entrepreneurialism of self-organizing economies." There is indeed very high heterogeneity in the form of cities of developing economies. Informality is one such concept that would explain the urban forms in these cities besides concepts of periphery, zones of exception[7] and grey spaces. Term periphery, rooted in the core-periphery theories, has been used to explain Brazilian city forms by Holston (2008) through what he calls 'autoconstructed peripheries', which are informal settlements, not necessarily of poor alone, developed by the residents alone on account of gentrification of Brazilian cities. Term informality has been called an idiom of urbanisation by Roy and Al Sayaad (2004), which has become a mode of production, outside the organised system (taking from the labour studies where informal is outside the organised labour force). In the earlier studies, informality was taken as synonymous with poverty and Mike Davis (2004), indeed uses the phrase 'informal survivalism' to explain the modes of livelihoods and living of the urban poor. Roy (2009) has expanded the discussion to larger realm of everything that is outside the organised and this phenomenon not necessarily restricted to the poor alone but to even elites, who have built spaces, residential as well as commercial, outside the legal and by that large number of developments in the cities are 'informal'. In context of India, she makes a forceful argument that India's planning regime is itself an informalized entity, one that is a state of deregulation, ambiguity and exception (Roy, 2009). This ambiguity and hence deliberate confusion is permitted to be able to find spaces for rent seeking on one hand and allows spaces for grassroots pressures on the other (Mahadevia, 2011a).

Informal spaces occur on account of violations of existing regulations and there are violations on both sides, by the elites (for examples, see Weinstein 2008 for Mumbai; Ghetner 2008 and Gidwani 2006 for Delhi), by the land owners whose surplus land is to be acquired (Mahadevia 2010 and 2011b for Ahmedabad), and by the poor themselves through encroachments on public lands, with or without the help of colonisers (intermediaries) or other actors (See Payne, 1989 for discussion on actors in informal housing).

Informal housing areas, including slums, are the sites of incremental housing by the people and for the people. This is called housing mobility, which is a process through which families adjust their housing characteristics to changing income and household characteristics in context of the lifecycle of the household (Edwards 1983). John F.C. Turner (1968) used this rational to observe housing mobility among the urban poor households in Latin American countries. Turner also illustrated through this study that not just the housing demand changed with the income and lifecycle of the household, but even their spatial location changed. Early in the life, the new migrants to the city tend to have low incomes and are also young in lifecycle. They are called 'bridgeheaders', seeking to find a toehold in the urban system. They then move on to achieve intermediate status of consolidators, at an advanced stage in their lifecycle when their incomes increase, and move into ownership housing on the city periphery where affordable ownership housing is available. At the advanced stage in their lifecycle, expanded family requires large living space which leads to increased housing demand. The higher value on the need for space to accommodate a growing family and security and independence conferred by the ownership housing are traded against lower value on accessibility. Edwards (1983) challenges this model by providing evidence of Bucaramanga, a city in Columbia, where the housing mobility is as much a function of housing supply as housing demand.

Turner's other research, once again based on Latin American cities, indicated that the low-income households were able to build their own housing through self-help and progressive housing development (Turner, 1967). Research on housing for the urban poor led to Turner's demand-based model and self-help housing concept advanced to frame 'progressive housing development' model (Hansen and Williams, 1988). Struyk and Lynn (1983) call it "the upgradation process", Hamer (1985) "incremental housing investment" and Keare and Parris (1982) "progressive development". Whatever the process is called, this model describes the process by which low-income households make incremental investments in housing as their income permits. The model shows low-income households moving through four stages of housing development: (i) Stage Zero—pre-ownership, (ii) Stage, One—initial settlement, (iii) Stage Two—self-motivated upgrading, and (iv) Stage Three—external-shock-motivated upgrading. Stage Zero is when the rural migrants arrive in the city, rent a room or share a room depending on their affordability and have low incomes. In case the rural migrants have higher income then they can move to Stage One directly by purchasing land in the informal housing market.

When a settlement remains for long duration, the residents in them acquire a sense of tenure security (Mahadevia, 2011; Payne, 2000; Durand-Lasserve and Selod, 2007; Neuwirth, 2005). This is called 'perceived security' (Payne, 2000) or *de facto* security (Mahadevia, 2010 and 2011b). However, in the quest to be 'World Class City', whatever that means in the cities of the developing countries, many cities have launched demolition drives, with the backing of planning legislation, which consider slums and squatter settlements as encroachments. Infrastructure project implementation has also led to displacement of slums and squatters and in some instances they have been entitled to rehabilitation. The state of informality assists such drives, which have halted if at all, in case of India, through judicial activism or subaltern insurgence. Holston (2008) calls citizenship acquired thus, through staking claims on informal settlements, as insurgent citizenship.

Informality in developing country cities has attracted attention of researchers for a long time now but in the recent years of the policy makers as well. Recognition and then policy framing on informalities begun in the decade of 1980s, largely from the Latin American studies, and later discovered in South Asia as well and more recently in the developed countries. The idea of formalising the informal housing begun with the discussion of and then introduction of tenure regularisation legislation in many countries and in India as well, after the 1976 UN-HABITAT Conference held in Vancouver. It stressed the importance of land tenure as being next only to food and water in urban areas (Oberlander, 1985).

Processes Forming Informal Housing

In the Indian context, different local-level histories of development regulations and land legislation, combined with cultural practices around use of land have evolved different forms of informal housing settlements. To these practices, modern period's electoral politics has added newer dimensions to the informal housing. Since the reforms period, an angle of land speculation has also been added to the factors influencing informal settlement formation. Some of the factors contributing to informal settlement formation have been discussed below.

Political patronage: The genesis of many informal settlements is clientalist politics, whereby squatter settlements are formed by encroaching on public lands in urban peripheries by the local powerful lords, who more often are not just connected to one or the other political party and are also local leaders of these parties, or by the people themselves with the help or backing of these local leaders. The residents then are enrolled as voters by the local politicians and the former then act as a vote-bank of that political party. Most of such settlements have no rights on the land they are established on, yet the residents perceive a sense of security on account of the political patronage they enjoy. The political support may ensure that the slum is not evicted, as the local politician might lose his/her vote bank. Vote-bank politics play a very important role in the establishment of informal housing in cities of the developing countries and also in India (more in Benjamin, 2005). In slums in Vasna ward, more than 90 per cent sample households possessed election cards whereas in Amraiwadi ward between 15 to 20 per cent households possessed these cards in Ahmedabad. Thus, our case studies did not establish that all slum households had political patronage.

Squatter settlement on public lands: Informal settlements and slums form when freely available public lands are squatted upon by poor migrants and other homeless dwellers. Such squatters do not have any services or facilities. Many a times, such places are not even liveable being filled with jungles and rats, rodents and scorpions, etc. Dharavi in Mumbai was one such slum, where initial settlers lived on water-logged land around the sea and made it liveable by filling it up little by little. Now that the land is consolidated and living on it possible, the real estate developers have developed an interest for it, and have pushed for a Dharavi Redevelopment Plan, through the state government. The housing rights activists as well as the people have, however, opposed the plan. In the context of liberalization and vision of cities to become "World Class", the slums on public lands have become more vulnerable to evictions than those on private lands, as the chapters on slums in two wards in Ahmedabad, Rajkot and Nanded suggest. In contrast, slums on public lands in Bhopal have benefited from tenure regularization followed by the BSUP housing.

Slums on royally allocated lands have become informal settlements as the original owners who allowed people to stay have long deceased. After royal families have ceased to exist such lands have become disputed, as such land allocations do not have any documentation. In Rajkot, government records show that such lands are called '*rajashahi*' or royal lands, but slums have developed on these as there were no owners available to protect these lands from being squatted. By 1950, all the lands belonging to the royals of pre-independence era, were transferred to the Indian State and in a sense became public lands. These were then squatted upon and the local politicians were not interested in evicting them for their electoral interests.

Many informal developments have come up on the fallow lands of government departments, national or state. The growth of informal lands on railway lands, which belong to the railways ministry of the national government, is a most common case in many cities in India. Vacant land along railway tracks, railway yards, workers colonies have mostly seen huge informal slum developments. For example, about 40 per cent slums in Guwahati are on railway lands and other equal numbers on forest lands (Desai *et al.,* 2014).

Informal settlements on social/religious lands: The state or the local government often gives lands to religious organisations for the use of the latter. Such lands are then given by the latter to their benefactors for the purpose of housing. Often such lands are then subdivided and sold multiple times in the informal market and also encroached upon leading to development of an informal settlement. The religious organisations are more often than not unable to reclaim their lands back from the encroachers. The state or the local government, which is the original owner of the land, is also unable to claim back the land. Such settlements tend to remain informal as no agency is able to intervene in its development.

Squatter settlements on former industrial lands: Informal and slum squatters come up on private lands used for industrial housing. In the middle of the twentieth century, in the early industrial cities, the industrial units had created housing to attract workers to the industries. However, the working quarters of many of these industries have grown into flourishing slums, when the units closed down and no decisions were taken on the lands and left as they were. This is the typical case of the mill lands of Ahmedabad and Mumbai. '*Chawls*' or '*chalis*' as they are called in most of the cities were initially rental accommodations, but without any decision on the mill lands post-closure of the mills, the *chawls/chalis* have remained in these areas and more and more people have built their units in and around such areas, all becoming part of the informal development.

Commercial subdivision of agricultural land: Urban peripheral lands, in situation of high population growth rates result in commercial subdivisions of agricultural lands without taking necessary permissions. In India, for land use change from agricultural to non-agricultural, NA (non-agricultural) permission is required. This process is cumbersome and costly and 'informal developers' bypass that. Case study of Rajkot presented in second chapter and that of Surat and Ahmedabad in the subsequent chapters illustrate these processes in depth. The land parcel available is cheap and clients go for incremental housing. After many years of existence, the local authorities extend basic services to these settlements. The former may also undertake a process to legalise such land parcels and bring them in the ambit of the property tax.

Commercial subdivision of land reserved for public purposes or to be acquired: When lands reserved for public purposes such as green belt, education and health and even low-income housing, are notified for acquisition, these are immediately subdivided and sold by the original land owner or are given away to 'informal developers' to subdivide and sell. Similarly, the lands declared as in access under the Urban Land Ceiling and Regulation Act (ULCRA), 1976 and notified for acquisition, also were informally subdivided and sold. The insecurity arising from the government notification for acquisition of land keeps the land prices low, making them affordable to the low-income households. The formality of land leads to price increase. In case of Ahmedabad, for example, large land parcels in the eastern part of the city came into the informal housing market after the promulgation of the ULCRA (*see* Mehta and Mehta, 1989).

Illegal extensions of public sector housing: This can be seen in numerous cases in Delhi Development Authority's (DDA) flats in Delhi. This is observed also in employee housing provided by public and government agencies.

Illegal transfer of legally acquired housing plots/housing units in sites and services programmes throughout many developing countries (Payne, 1989).

Informal Rental Housing: Informal renting can take many forms, from occupying backyard shacks in public housing in South Africa, to sub-tenants in squatter housing in the *favelas* of Brazil, to pavement dwellers in India who make regular payments to someone in authority in order to keep their position. This group, along with new squatters, have the most fragile housing situation, short of having no shelter. They are able to live where they do until someone moves them along (UN-HABITAT, 2003). Renting in informal housing happens across all informal settlements. In slums studied in Rajkot, nearly 30 per cent households were living in rental housing. In Amraiwadi slums in Ahmedabad, just 10 per cent households were living in rental housing.

Informality and Tenure Security in Urban Housing

Tenure security is seen as, "a complex entity which provides protection to a household or individual against their involuntary removal from their house or land without due process of law. In absence of such security policy, the urban poor and low-income migrants seek to consolidate their urban citizenship through political citizenship in an electoral democracy, welfare interventions by the state, organised grassroots movements and, in the absence of all the above, through their own subversions of urban legalities" (Mahadevia, 2011: 6). Tenure ranges between full property-rights to use and transfer of land and/or housing unit up to limited rights of usage. "Secure tenure is the right of all individuals and groups to effective protection by the State against forced evictions, "the permanent or temporary removal against their will of individuals, families and/or communities from the home and/or the land they occupy, without the provision of, and access to, appropriate forms of legal or other protection" (COHRE, 2003 in Durand-Lasserve, 2007).

We find a diversity of tenures in and across informal housing. Tenure is the mode by which land or a dwelling unit is held or owned, or the set of relationships among people concerning land and dwelling unit (Payne, 2000). In fact, a diversity of tenures is significant in providing a diversity of housing choices to urban residents. Payne (2000) further argues that instead of thinking of tenure as legal or illegal, it should be understood as comprising a continuum of tenure categories. Although this tenure continuum might differ between different cities since each city has its own range of *de jure* and *de facto* tenure systems, Payne illustrates his point through a typical tenure continuum, which shows a gradation of tenure security across a range of tenure categories as shown in Figure 1.1. However, tenure security may also improve over time for either individual households or for entire settlements. For instance, informal settlements formed through squatting usually have no tenure security initially, but when they remain for a long duration, they often acquire a sense of security (Mahadevia, 2011; Payne, 2000; Durand-Lasserve and Selod, 2007; Neuwirth, 2005). This is called "perceived security" (Payne, 2000) or *de facto* security (Mahadevia, 2010 and 2011b). *De facto* security often comes through vote-bank politics, the politics of what Benjamin (2008) calls "occupancy urbanism," and through negotiations in political society (Chatterjee, 2004).

Tenure regularization is approached in policy in two ways: *de jure tenure* and *de facto tenure*. A key aspect of informal settlement is the lack of *de jure* or formal title, although even within this informality the perception of tenure security is different for different informal settlements. "In general, poor people in cities move from informal to quasi-legal (*de facto*) tenure through various processes and then to legal (*de jure*) tenure through public policy interventions legalising property titles" (Mahadevia 2011). *De jure* tenure implies the right to the land or housing unit. This is also called the "Functional Approach". In this, secure tenure is seen as a means of achieving definite objective, like poverty alleviation, creditworthiness for housing loans, and compensation for relocation of squatters. Land rights exist as a part of other rights in society as a whole and one cannot be changed easily without the change in others (Payne, 1997). Rights may cover access, use, development or transfer and as such, exist in parallel with ownership. On this basis, it is clear that the ways in which a society allocates title and rights to land is an important indicator of that society, since rights to land can be held to reflect rights in other areas of public life. There are advantages of it such as full individual rights, and security and access to formal credit system, which together maximize incentives for housing improvements (Payne, 2002). The lack of formal documentation of the land or house generates large costs for residents in terms of buying water, higher priced electricity, etc., as the local authorities do not recognise such settlements to provide them with any facilities.

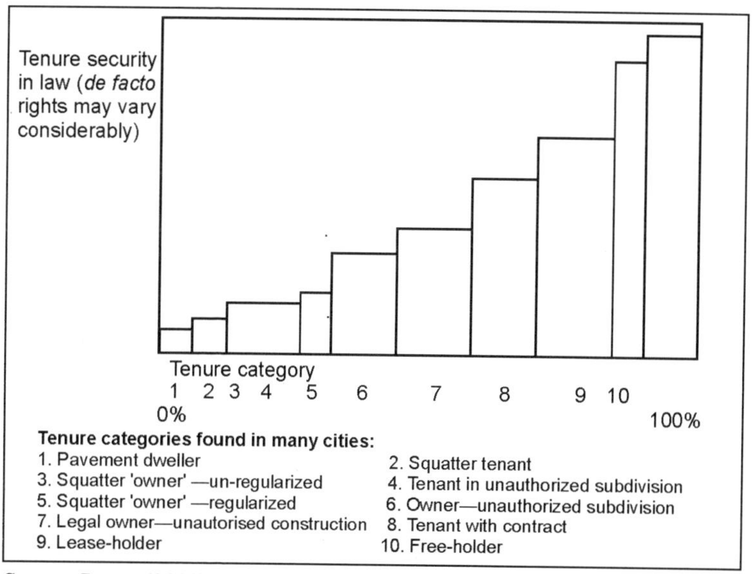

Source: Payne (2000).

Fig. 1.1: Existing Tenure categories in Urban Centres

On the other hand, *de facto* tenure implies protection against evictions ensured through political commitments or administrative practices that lead to a *de facto* recognition of occupancy in informal settlements—without the provision of personal or real rights. This deals with the 'Rights Approach', which says that, "every citizen has the right to a secure place to live." Whichever route is taken, the results are security of tenure in the form of legally valid tenure documents (Durand-Lasserve and Rayston, 2002).

The *Market-based approach* to housing for the poor advocates the clearing of land titles for the poor. It has been largely propounded by Hernando De Soto (2003), in his best seller—The Mystery of Capital, which argues that freeing land titles would ensure that even the poor can have a part to play in capital markets and by that promote capitalism from below. Large many slums are product of informal market sale of land where the sale deeds are not executed or if executed they are not registered with the government. Hence, his argument is that by simply bringing these informal settlements into formal system with registration of their land titles would help to improve their condition. The registration of property rights in squatter settlements is important in making land and house transactions possible and giving occupants' legal protection. It encourages the buying and selling of housing units and makes it possible for households to move to a dwelling that suits their needs and their budgets. It also increases the choice of tenure available to households, allowing them to own or rent as they see fit (World Bank, 1993). This was the idea beneath the RAY reforms of enactment of 'property rights act' by the state government. In many slums, where land is originally bought informally, get into a vicious cycle of informal trade. They cannot trade their property in the formal market because they do not possess any documents or clear land tenure. This creates a land locked kind of a situation for settlements where no legal buying, selling or renting could take place.

The *Welfare Approach* on the other hand counters the idea of giving formal security of tenure. It is argued that nothing additional is gained by providing formal land tenure and that only the perception of tenure rather than formal land tenure helps in people making investments in housing and improving their living conditions. "Empirical evidence points to a continuum of security in illegal settlements that depends less on the exact legal status and more on occupants' perceptions of the probability of eviction and demolition (enforcement); as well as the availability of services and passage of time" (Gilbert, 2001). The right's approach to housing and land tenure emphasizes the right of individuals to secure tenure, which implies, a secure place to live—which is in conformity with international treaties and covenants, guaranteeing social stability and aiming to reduce poverty (Leckie, 2004 in Durand-Lasserve & Selod, 2007). This position argues that the approach of title allocation to the poor can have results which are more damaging to the poor than what they are currently facing. Figure 1.1 shows different categories of land tenure that can exist in any urban area.

Payne's (2000) tenure continuum further shows that the law gives greater tenure security to an owner than to a tenant at each stage. Thus, an owner in an unauthorised subdivision has greater tenure security than a tenant in an unauthorised subdivision. Similarly, a squatter owner, whether in a regularised or unregularized squatter settlement, has greater tenure security than a squatter tenant. Note that Payne (2000) does not define an owner by his/her legal ownership and defines them broadly, as "those with the legal or *de facto* right to occupy, let, use or dispose of their dwelling" (UN-HABITAT, 2003: 3-4). Concept of tenure continuum further explains that ownership always relates to the tenure of a dwelling but not always to the land on which it is built. It sees ownership as a broad continuum of rights, with owners including those who hold full legal title to a serviced dwelling in a formally planned settlement, those who now possess a legal title to a house built on land that was acquired illegally, as well as those with *de facto* rights such as those who own the structure but not the land on which it is built as in the case of land invasions (UN-HABITAT, 2003). In this study, we define ownership even more broadly, including squatters who might not even have *de facto* rights; they are owners simply by virtue of not being tenants and having built their own dwelling, however, impermanent it might be in the face of eviction threats.

Although tenants have lower tenure security than owners at each stage, rental housing nonetheless plays a significant role in meeting the shelter needs of many amongst the urban poor, especially new migrants to the city, for whom ownership housing, even in the informal sector, is unaffordable. For them, rental housing is important for gaining a foothold in the city. It lessens the burden on a migrant to invest in shelter till he/she can find a stable job and save enough to invest in ownership housing. Scholars have, therefore, discussed rental housing as providing a much needed "room for manoeuvre" or flexibility in tenure arrangements during the lifetime of an urban poor household.

The key to improving tenure security in the slum settlements is to make certain periodic interventions that would make providing secure land tenure a process rather than a sudden gift. Also, there is a need of a tenure policy that will incorporate a wide range of informal settlements into a more formal land market in ways which do not create adverse impacts on the poor, particularly tenants and women. It is suggested by Payne (2005) that there should be a five-stage approach to tenure security and strengthening property rights along with incorporating good governance criteria.

Issues in Informal Housing

Definition of informal: The ambiguity in defining informality (as discussed in beginning of this chapter) has relegated many settlements into being informal. A formally undertaken house sale can be termed informal if it builds an extension without permission. Informality can be at diverse levels and would have different standards at different places. Within the ambit of informal also fall the colonies of the rich, who have built their properties on illegally captured and subdivided lands, like the large informal colonies in Delhi built on erstwhile agricultural lands without taking N.A. permission, or without following the development control regulations, or obtained clearance for the land use from the planning authority. When regulations are passed to recognise and provide services to informal settlements, many a times, the rich get the highest benefits out of it. In Jaipur, when *pattas* were given to the occupants of the informal colonies, large many middle and high-income colonies were regularised.

Lack of tenure security: Lack of formal sale, lease or ownership documents can deprive a household from secure tenure. Such households cannot use their land or property as their asset for collateral purposes.

Threats of eviction: Lack of tenure security is directly related to higher threats of eviction.

Lack of basic services and infrastructure: Lack of tenure security is also directly related to the availability of services from the local authorities. In most cases, slum dwellers have to arrange for their own services and that would cost them a lot on their regular expenses, much higher than their formal counterparts.

Poor quality structures: Being on informal lands, the housing provided is of the lowest quality to keep the prices low. Due to lack of tenure security, the residents do not invest much in the improvement of house structures.

Over-crowding: Informal settlements may be overcrowded, especially if they are in prime locations of the city. There is high renting which creates over-crowding. The locational advantage also attracts joint or extended family members to share living quarters, which then can lead to over-crowding. However, informal settlements on the urban periphery do not tend to have over-crowding.

Low investments in housing: This is largely related to level of tenure security; lower the level of security lower is the investments.

Complex government procedures to get legal/formal status: Since the lands are governed by large number of regulations, process of formalisation requires getting clearances from all these regulatory agencies. In particular, the process is complex if the land is under private ownership (Figure 1.2). Clearances are required from the revenue department of the state government, which gives N.A. permission and assures that the stamp-duty is paid for the change in land ownership in the land records. Thereafter, clearance is also required from the ULCRA authority, even though the legislation is repealed. Lastly, the urban planning administration has to give clearance for land use as well as building codes. Every stage of clearance adds to the cost of transaction. Needless to mention, informal land developers avoid getting into these transactions to save costs and increase profits. If all the clearances are obtained, the price of the land increases. In case if a slum manages to get all these clearances, the land price goes up to such an extent that the original dwellers are induced to sell them off leading to gentrification. Hence, answer to addressing the question of informality in housing is not simple.

Extent and Diversity of Rental Housing in Informal Markets

It is a popular belief that all households aspire to own house, and many studies have also proven this assumption to be true. Governments have therefore, usually designed their housing programmes to provide ownership housing, be it in public housing provision as well as resettlement programmes or now in the private sector under the "Affordable Housing" policy of the Government of India (GoI). However, as Kumar (2001) argues, the largely single-minded emphasis on ownership housing in policy has only created a mismatch between policy and lived reality. The crucial question is not whether poor households aspire to ownership housing but whether ownership housing is accessible to them. Kumar argues that it is necessary to put rental housing onto the agendas of multilateral institutions and governments, and they should be encouraged to form "tenure-neutral housing policies." Support for rental housing should be regarded as a complement to home-ownership, and not as a form of competition for it.

The single-minded emphasis on home-ownership, UN-HABITAT argues, is mainly ideological, formed by misplaced notions that owners make better citizens than tenants and that owners contribute to the economy more (UN-HABITAT 2003: 2-3). UNHABITAT has thus increasingly emphasized the importance of bringing rental housing onto housing policy agenda. It further argues that the upgrading programmes must embrace tenants because so many of them live in informal settlements. It states that the governments should formulate rules, credit programmes and forms of assistance to create more rental housing and to improve the existing stock. However, housing policies need to address tenants in other ways as well. For instance, there is very little discussion on including tenants in resettlement and rehabilitation programmes. Hence, it is likely that they are being forced to vacate the unit by owners in case of rehabilitation of the settlement. Anecdotally, we know that landlords who construct housing units for rental purposes tend to push out their tenants if the settlement is to be rehabilitated. To overcome this situation, the RAY guidelines mention that the current occupants (whether owner or tenants) need to be covered under the programme, but does not mention how to do so.

Rental housing can also be explored to meet the shelter needs of the homeless. A Supreme Court judgement on the homeless of 2012, using Article 21 of the Constitution of India, which articulates the Right to Life, states that: "The State owes to the homeless people to ensure at least minimum shelter as part of the State obligation under Article 21."[8] The Supreme Court has ordered the Urban Local Bodies (ULBs) to construct night shelters for the homeless to be rented out on affordable charges. However, there is no policy on who should provide this and how to make this work for the homeless.

Historically, rental housing was supported in India through the Rent Control Act, which put a ceiling on the rents that could be charged to the tenants and also protected the tenants against eviction. Large numbers of industrial housing in the industrial cities of Gujarat and Maharashtra came up in this way. But the Rent Control legislation then froze the rents in the eternity, making even upkeep of such housing impossible for the unit owners. Subsequently, such rental industrial housing deteriorated into slums. This housing is called *chawls* and *chalis* in Mumbai and Ahmedabad, respectively. The early Subsidised Industrial Housing Scheme (SIHS) in some cities also provided incentives to industry owners to create rental or ownership housing for their workers. Up to the Third Five Year Plan (1961-1966), urban housing programmes consisted of: (i) rental housing for slum dwellers and specific low income groups such as plantation labour and dock labour, (ii) rental housing in the public sector townships and for the employees of public sector undertakings, (iii) rental housing for private sector industrial employees, wherein it was made mandatory for private industrial units with a paid-up capital above certain limits to construct housing for at least half their employees. The financial crunch after the Third Plan led to the government discontinuing rental housing programmes for the low-income population such as slum dwellers, industrial workers, plantation labour etc. (Mahadevia, 2003).

With the onset of reforms, policy rhetoric of doing away with Rent Control Act began and this is still being debated today. The JNNURM reforms and then the RAY reforms have made amendment of the Rent Control Act mandatory and a Model Rent legislation has been created by the MoHUPA to assist the states in amending their legislation. This proposed legislation states that the "rent of a housing unit should be fixed by mutual agreement between the landlord and the tenant for a stipulated lease period prior to which, the tenant will not be allowed to be evicted and after the expiry of the said lease period, the tenant will not be permitted to continue in the said housing unit" (MoHUPA, 2007). Thus, rental housing has been recognised as an important area by the National Urban Housing & Habitat Policy (NUHHP), which however does not state who should provide it.

In India, besides the Model Rent legislation created by MoHUPA, there are also existing legislations that can be explored for supporting the rental housing sector. After independence, tenancy laws were promulgated in the states to give ownership rights to the tenants of former landlords. While these laws were largely for rural lands, in Kolkata, rights were given to the *Thika* tenants of the erstwhile landlords who had given their plots of lands or buildings in the urban area to tenants. This legislation is called the West Bengal Thika Tenancy Act and is currently applicable to 100 wards in Kolkata City. The *Thika* tenants were given occupancy rights of the properties they were living in, while the lands were transferred to the State government. Research into the experience of the Thika Tenancy Act could shed light on the possibilities and limitations this kind of legislation holds for expanding tenant rights and improving housing conditions for tenants.

Among public housing programmes, Singapore's large public housing programme, which also has a social housing component, is well-known.

The Singapore Housing and Development Board (HDB) has constructed one and two-room housing units for households unable to afford either rental or ownership housing in the private market (Yuen, 2007). However, in this city-state, 95 per cent of the occupants of the public housing, which constitutes 85 per cent of the total housing stock, are on ownership basis (Yuen, 2007). Hong Kong, on the other hand, has a large public rental housing programme by the Hong Kong Housing Authority (HKHA). In 2011, it provided housing to 30 per cent of the total population of the city.[9] However, this subsidised rental housing programme is now facing a huge backlog of supply. It is not surprising that in developing countries, which have fewer resources, public housing programmes creating rental housing have faced the problem of not being able to match the demand with supply. These programmes—implemented in countries like Kenya, South Africa, Mexico, Venezuala, etc.,—have also faced other challenges such as clientalism in the allocation of the housing which has often meant that the poorest (and true beneficiaries) have been excluded, defaulting on rent payments by tenants, low maintenance and dilapidation of the rental housing units, etc. (UN-HABITAT, 2003: 30). In fact, as the orthodoxy in the 1980s and 1990s tilted in favour of home-ownership, and the World Bank and USAID discredited public rental housing by arguing that governments were inherently inefficient landlords, many of these public rental housing programmes were terminated (UN-HABITAT, 2003: 32).

Even in the former socialist countries like China, rental housing provision has declined. Employer-provided housing, which is in a sense rental housing, was the main approach to housing in these countries. But, since 1997, China has shifted towards commercial housing provided by the private sector and has been encouraging the occupants of the employer-provided housing to purchase the same (Mahadevia, Liu and Yuan, 2012). The increasingly wealthier urban population now prefers to move to modern, large commercial housing from the former employer-provided housing that was small and also deteriorating.

Despite the heightened emphasis on rental housing by institutions like UN-HABITAT, its resuscitation in housing policy has been taking place only in a few countries such as South Africa where it was recognized in 1998 that "expanding homeownership alone could not cope with the sheer scale of the housing deficit" (UN-HABITAT, 2003: 217). A Rental Housing Act was formulated in 1999 and a massive increase in rental accommodation in the form of social housing was planned. A pilot project of 15,000 units was inaugurated in 2002 with private companies building the accommodation, social housing foundations running the projects and the Central Government, through the National Housing Finance Corporation (NHFC) and the Building and Social Housing Foundation helping to finance new projects and improving the performance of the NGOs. However, there have been various problems such as the financial viability of running the projects for the social housing foundations, the housing not really catering to the poor (UN-HABITAT, 2003: 221). The problems facing large-scale public rental housing provision have also led to proposals to support small-scale landlords who are in any case the predominant suppliers of rental housing to the urban poor (in the formal and informal sector) in South African cities. However, "the idea of offering financial help to private landlords and to enhance the quality of private accommodation of the flimsy shelter in the townships was felt to hold too many political risks" (UN-HABITAT, 2003: 223).

A high level of rental housing has been found in many cities around the world, both in developed countries and developing countries. A wide diversity of rental housing is found across cities and within cities. In cities of the developing world, rental housing is found across different formal and informal housing sub-markets. As Payne's (2000) typical tenure continuum diagram shows, tenants are found in formal housing, unauthorized subdivisions and squatter settlements (both regularised and unregularized). Lim (1987) also writes that rental housing is found in various housing sub-markets such as the regular housing market, the invasion housing market, the slum housing market and the squatter housing market. The literature on rental housing further reveals that there is a wide range of rental housing types that cater to the affordability and choices of different tenant groups. Rental housing may vary within and between cities in terms of its size, construction quality, ownership, kind of contract, rental period, rent levels, location, profitability and so on (UNCHS, 2003). For example, Ballestores (2004) identifies six rental housing types in the Philippines—single house in a private sub-division/ slum, shack on rented plot, row-house in private subdivision, room/bed in multiunit buildings, room/bed in houses and room/bed in commercial/ industrial establishments—and also identifies the kind of size, ownership, rent, rent contract, quality and legality for each of these types.

In India, rental housing sub-markets have been categorized on the basis of location (city periphery, industrial unit, commercial areas, along important routes, etc.), type of supplier (private individual/household, trust, employer, government, etc.), housing type (single room, dwelling unit, bed, etc.) and government policies (contractual, leasing, sub-letting, etc.) (NIUA, 1989). Rental housing sub-markets can also be categorized by the income group of tenants, by production and exchange systems, or by type of settlement and provider (Kumar, 2001). In a study on rental housing in Guwahati, different housing sub-markets differentiated by the formal and informal processes of land and housing development, paying attention also to landownership and topography have been identified (Desai *et al.,* 2013). Rental housing is found across all the different sub-markets, and most of these sub-markets also comprise more than one type of rental housing.

Determinants of Rental Housing

Rental housing is influenced by and responds to various local conditions. It is influenced by conditions that are exogenous to the sector, such as local economy, politics, land and finance systems and varied social networks, as well as conditions that are endogenous to landlords and tenants (Kumar, 2001). However, the literature on such determinants is scarce, and thus our understanding of rental housing determinants is still lacking on this front.

One of the basic determinants of rental housing is the rate of migration into a city since rental housing is often the first type of shelter for migrants. If there is a high rate of migration into a city, then the demand for rental housing is likely to be higher, spurring the production of rental housing. If there is no demand for new rental housing, the production of rental housing is likely to slow down. The waves of migrants into cities constitute the majority of tenants in cities. Thus, local opportunities for livelihood influences migration, and consequently rental housing. Cities with a great demand for unskilled labour tend to attract single male migrants, who generally look to rental housing—and shared arrangements within rental housing—to satisfy their shelter needs. Changes in the nature and form of local employment have a "domino" effect on rental housing markets, resulting in either upgrading to fetch higher rents, peripheral relocation of rental housing, or conversion to ownership (Kumar, 2001: 4). Land market dynamics are another important determinant of rental housing. Escalating land prices and increasing land speculation lead to narrowing opportunities for ownership amongst urban residents, even in the informal sector, and the rental housing market may, therefore, expand to fulfil the demand for shelter.

There are also various factors endogenous to tenants and landlords that influence rental housing. This includes the stage in the life-cycle of tenants. For instance, single male migrants who are yet to establish themselves in the city as well as younger couples with younger/fewer children tend to rent. As economic stability increases, such tenants might seek to invest in ownership housing, although this mobility to ownership depends upon the feasibility of becoming owners in a particular city. The affordability of households—that is, the income they have available for expenditure on housing, be it rental housing or ownership housing—influences the rental housing sector. The stage in the life-cycle of owner households also influences rental housing. Owners turn to landlordism for a variety of reasons. Sometimes, this is linked to the stage in the life-cycle of their household and the possibilities that the development of rental housing offers for meeting certain needs and priorities. For instance, owners might turn to landlordism to raise money for housing consolidation (construction and improvement), especially when other ways of raising housing finance are difficult (Kumar, 2001). Incomes from rent have been found to be important source of investments in incremental housing (Hansen and Williams, 1988).

Kumar (2001) also shows how the nature of state intervention shapes the production of rental housing. This is not confined to whether the state invests in directly producing a rental housing stock. For example, land acquisition by the state leading to loss of livelihoods may force farmers to find alternative livelihoods, including renting out of housing. Another example of state intervention shaping rental housing is the nature of the state's squatter resettlement schemes. Kumar (2001) found that in Bangalore larger resettlement plots allowed for constructing and renting out of one room. This was not possible in the smaller resettlement plots in Surat. Also, poorer households could also become landlords in Bangalore since larger plots meant that the owner did not need to expand vertically (a more expensive proposition) to build extra rooms. Rental housing is also dependent on how easily ownership housing is accessible, and in particular, whether there is finance availability for ownership housing. If ownership housing is unaffordable on account of lack of finance, renting is preferred.

Supply and Demand of Rental Housing

In some countries such as the former communist countries of Europe, the public sector has played a large role in supplying rental housing. This rental housing has largely been employer-provided housing. For example, in China, urban residents were largely employees of the State Owned Enterprises (SOE), which provided housing to their respective employees charging minimal rent per month. In most countries of the capitalist developing world, however, the majority of rental housing is supplied by individual owners. Rental housing for the urban poor and low-income groups is supplied largely by individual owners in the informal sector. Some scholars, notably Sunil Kumar, have thus focused their research on landlordism to better understand the supply of rental housing as well as the role that rental housing plays in the lives on its suppliers. Kumar (2001) argues that landlords are often viewed as exploitative accumulators of capital in the form of landed property, while tenants are viewed as disenfranchised individuals and households whose social and economic mobility is hampered by their tenure. He goes on to argue that pitting landlord against tenant in this manner is unproductive, and rather we must analyse their relations as well as the role that rental housing plays in their life-cycle, and thus, in the livelihood responses and strategies of both landlords and tenants.

Different kinds of landlords in the informal sector have thus been identified by Kumar (2011) petty-capitalist landlords, petty-bourgeois landlords and petty-subsistence landlords. At the richer end are petty-capitalist landlords who either possess a large number of rental properties or seek to expand their ownership of landed property. At the poorer end are subsistence landlords who develop rental housing to supplement their income and meet basic consumption needs. In between are petty-bourgeois landlords who do not need rental income to survive but are unable to make improvements to their dwelling or the material quality of their lives without supplementing household income with rental income (Kumar, 2001: 11-12). Kumar, moreover, argues that these landlords are located on a continuum of petty-capitalist, petty-bourgeois and subsistence landlords. Thus, landlords might also move along this continuum as a result of various factors.

On the other side, our understanding into the demand of rental housing comes partly from the existing literature on tenants. As mentioned earlier, the rate of migration is an important determinant of rental housing. However, the nature of demand for rental housing also depends on the kind of migrant groups in the city. A study by Mahadevia, Liu and Yuan (2012) identifies three main types of migrant groups in Indian cities: (i) long-term or permanent migrants who intend to settle down in the city, many getting into regular employment but keeping strong ties with their native town/village; (ii) seasonal migrants who stay in the city for more than 60 days a year but return to their native town/village for some period; and (iii) migrants who are tied to employers who move from one place of employment to another. This study also indicates that migrants' cultural backgrounds influence their rental housing demand. Invariably, recent migrants prefer rental housing and then shift to ownership housing after some years. But, migrants from some of the Northern states in India leave behind their wife and children in their home village and migrate singly. Such migrants prefer to stay in rental housing, mostly shared housing and then go back to their villages after years of stay in the urban areas. This study further finds that migrants employed in the construction sector are more likely to stay in rental housing than those who are self-employed as they move within the city with the construction sites. Many permanent migrants come to the city as single male migrants and then call their families once they are reasonably secure, financially, socially and shelter-wise. The nature of demand for rental housing by these different groups of migrants and by families who migrate *versus* single-male migrants, might vary in terms of the locations in the city where they seek rental housing, the type of rental housing they seek, their affordability given their income and expenditure, etc. Besides new migrants, the National Institute of Urban Affairs (NIUA, 1989) mentions that rental housing is also a preferred alternative for the floating population in the city and the population segment which finds ownership unaffordable (NIUA, 1989). Thus, tenants also include those who have been living in the city for long periods of time but are unable or unwilling to move to ownership housing.

Rental housing constitutes a significant proportion of housing in many cities around the world. In cities of developing countries, rental housing is crucial in fulfilling the shelter needs of the urban poor. For poor migrants, there are limited shelter options, and rental housing, particularly in informal settlements, offers an important option. In some cities, rental housing is also significant for older residents amongst the urban poor as they are unable to make the shift to home ownership because of politico-economic factors that shape their household economic conditions and also unavailability of housing loan at this age making ownership housing unaffordable. New migrants to cities are also often undecided about their long-term plans and many come without the intention of settling down in the city for long. In recent years, regional parochialism, wherein low income migrants in particular have become the target of parochial politics, has resulted in further indecisiveness amongst migrants about their long-term plans regarding settling down in the city. Rental housing is significant for migrants for this reason as well.

Policy Implications

Urban India is replete with informal housing to a great extent, provided by the people themselves. They are called differently, in different places; unauthorized colonies in Delhi, *gunthewari* layouts in Nagpur and Nanded, *suchit* societies in Rajkot and Surat, *chalis* in Gujarat or *chawls* in Maharashtra, *paras* or *gaons* in Guwahati, etc. Besides these, there are squatters and slum settlements, name *bastis*, *jhuggi jhompdi* colonies in Delhi and north Indian cities, and so on. The term informal housing subsumes all these categories and hence has been used in this book to represent the diversity of housing options of the urban poor and low-income households. The supply of informal housing is dependent on many factors and varies from city to city. The factors that can influence informal housing supply in a city are related to land legislation, development plan provisions, settlement-specific and owner-specific processes, land ownership pattern, land prices, processes of land sub-divisions and transfer, historic trajectory of city growth, actors and ecological factors. Their regularisation efforts have to keep these in mind.

The case studies of the informal settlements present a story of the residents' perseverance with patience to make a life for themselves and their families in the cities. There are a few generalizable learnings from these case studies. First of all, the slum development and living conditions' improvement in them is incremental. Rental housing plays an important role in improving the living conditions of the house-owners. In situation where the microfinance is available, women access it to invest incrementally in housing and recover the investments through rents. Many slums, in particular in the cities in Gujarat and Maharashtra have developed on the private lands, either because the land was earmarked for acquisition and then the enterprising owner sub-divided it without any legal procedures and sold plots to the low-income households was a land with disputed ownership. There is a third process of supply of such housing, sub-plotting of agricultural lands on the city's periphery, without taking any necessary statutory permissions. In three cases, the low-income households have been able to access housing, firstly they accessed the land plot on which they constructed and then incrementally improved their house. Today such households sit smugly in their *pucca* houses, with a strong perceived tenure security. In contrast, the squatters who have encroached on the public lands, have been living under the threat of demolitions. Many such squatter settlements are inhabited by the socially and economically vulnerable households, who then enter a vicious cycle of evictions and poverty.

The informal settlements' residents have multiple livelihood strategies and for many of them their house is the workplace, in particular for the women, who multi-task and take care of their house and family and also earn a living. There is high incidence of engagement in home-based work in the informal settlements in Ahmedabad and Surat. In Rajkot, small manufacturing units are located in such settlements, particularly those located in the industrial segments of the city.

The fourth generalisation from these case studies is the provision of basic services in these informal settlements by the respective local authorities irrespective of their tenure status, with exception of a few slums in Ahmedabad that are on public lands.

Lastly, any development in the informal settlement through NGO intervention is a long drawn process, which first requires building of mutual trust and respect, which takes a long time. But, slum redevelopment is best done through community participation than not as we see in the case of Bhopal wherein the BSUP housing has failed in absence of community mobilisation and engagement.

Time and again, efforts have been made to bring them into the official planning system through regularising or formalising them. The terms used also vary from city to city. In Delhi, unauthorised colonies are regularised. In some cities, the informal housing colonies are given *pattas* or land rights, largely on leasehold basis. In some instances, the slums are redeveloped. The two national urban housing programmes, the BSUP under the JNNURM and the RAY have different approach to slums, the former has laid stress on relocating the slums in newly constructed public housing whereas the latter on *in situ* development of slums, either through extending the services (called slum upgrading) or redevelopment into a multi-storey housing. Question of tenure is central to both the approaches of *in situ* development. There is also a difference in level of engagement of the slum communities themselves or the NGOs in the redevelopment of slums or rehabilitating slum communities on new housing sites. The different experiences with regards to formation of informal housing, living conditions within them and their formalisation processes need to be documented for their historical value and policy learnings.

The earlier chapters in the book describe the living conditions in the informal housing settlements in Rajkot, Surat and Ahmedabad. Thereafter, experiences of redevelopment of the slums through efforts of different actors/agencies have been presented in details. Lastly, assessment of the public housing programmes in Bhopal has been presented. There is no uniformity in the content of each of the chapters. They have developed as independent cases on their own over time, but, brought together in a volume for broader audience.

These chapters indicate that the slums are formed through various processes and individual households have made significant efforts to attain their shelter security. In Ahmedabad, where there has been historical orientation towards philanthropy and hence NGOs have taken up development of slums, there has been a successful public-NGO partnership for slum development. In other cities of Gujarat, Rajkot and Surat, whose cases are presented here, there has been solely people-driven and informal actor driven housing for the poor. Same is the case in Nanded in Maharashtra where the housing process is entirely people driven, where, local state actors have intervened to implement the BSUP in an innovative way. The housing in Madhya Pradesh is very much state driven and top-down with poor outcomes due to lack of people's ownership of the same. However, prior to the BSUP, which became a top-down programme in Madhya Pradesh, there were successful participatory programmes, which were abandoned for the BSUP.

The chapters in this book also show that massive investments in housing have been made by the people themselves, although, the authors have not estimated the total value. People's own investments have been followed-up by the public investments in basic infrastructure. At the same time, much more investment needs to be made to improve living conditions in the informal housing settlements that exists. People's own investments are, in a sense, through the markets but not corporate sector but decentralised informal markets. This is how capitalism penetrates down to the grassroots. If the policy makers are pushing for a strategy to assist penetration of corporate real estate sector down to the lowest economic strata, it might be disservice to the local private sector actors and the people themselves, who may be priced out of the corporate sector driven housing market. The affordable housing policy of the GoI is beyond the reach of the low income households and the private sector driven housing is beyond the reach of a household with average income. Hence, under such conditions, the state has to play a facilitative role in promoting people driven housing and create programmes that would lead to further investments in improving living conditions. Besides, access to land for people-driven housing is also necessary and public land supply should be maintained through available instruments of urban planning. Leaving housing to corporate real estate sector would be at our own peril.

NOTES

1. Proportion calculated with total housing stock data of Housing Census of 2010, undertaken as a part of Population Census 2011 enumeration. Housing census data available from http://www.censusindia.gov.in/2011census/hlo/hlo_highlights.html, accessed on February 15, 2014.
2. The number of households living in slums is from http://www.censusindia.gov.in/2011census/hlo/Slum_table/hl-slum/SHH0101-crc.pdf, accessed on February 15, 2014.
3. Data from http://www.censusindia.gov.in/2011census/hlo/hlo_highlights.html, accessed on February 15, 2014.
4. Source: http://mhupa.gov.in/W_new/DMU_REPORT_JNNURM.pdf, accessed on October 22, 2014.
5. Source: http://mhupa.gov.in/W_new/DMU_REPORT_RAY.pdf, accessed on October 22, 2014.
6. For case study of urban land transactions in Ahmedabad, see Mahadevia (2003).
7. By zones of exceptions she means special incentives given to different economic zones and townships that are emerging as economic growth centers in many developing countries. This trend started with China, which wanted to have 'one country two systems', but, then was taken up in many other countries, because of the same idea emerging on account of dualistic economic system.
8. Source: http://supremecourtofindia.nic.in/outtoday/wc19601.pdf (accessed on May 6, 2012). This is from an order of 23/01/2012 for writ petition (civil) no. 196 OF 2001.
9. Hong Kong: the Facts, Source: http://www.gov.hk/en/about/abouthk/factsheets/docs/housing.pdf (accessed on May 6, 2012).

2
Informal Housing—Rajkot[1,2]

Darshini Mahadevia, Trishna Gogoi and *Suchita Vyas*

Introduction

This chapter presents diversity of informal housing situations in Rajkot City, from the squatter settlements to informal land subdivisions and rental housing within them through study of seven settlements. It explores the supply dynamics in these settlements, presents details of tenure arrangements and living conditions within them, contrasting, wherever necessary, the occupants of the self-owned housing and the renters. The entire study is primary survey based and the survey was conducted in 2012.

Rajkot is the fourth largest city in Gujarat state and had a population of a little more than 1 million in 2001[3], which increased to 1.4 million in 2011[4], registering a population growth rate of 3.3 per cent per annum (p.a). This is higher than the national urbanisation rate of 2.2 per cent p.a. in the same period. The city is located in Saurashtra region of the state amidst high growth agriculture region. Rajkot's population growth is on account of small-scale industries manufacturing machine tools, agriculture equipment, automotive parts, watch parts, diesel engines, kitchen knives and other cutting gadgets, and bearings, and casting and forging industries. The industries are concentrated in four main industrial areas: (i) Bhaktinagar Industrial Estate (GIDC), (ii) Aji Industrial Estate (GIDC), (iii) Industrial area around National Textile Mill, and (iv) Sorathiawadi Private Industrial Area (Map 2.1) and spread over the slums and the informal settlements. The city has nearly 20 per cent land under industrial activities.

The study begun by obtaining a list of slums from the Rajkot Municipal Corporation (RMC) and then a visit to many of these settlements to understand the processes of their formation and tenure arrangements. The RMC list contained 84 notified and 104 non-notified slums[5], spread across 23 wards in the city housing 42,585 households and population of 240,179 (Annexure 2.1). The settlements for detailed study were identified after discussions with the RMC officials, so as to represent different geographic locations in the city, such as the industrial areas, commercial and high-income residential areas and peri-urban areas. Seven informal settlements; namely, Khodiyarpara, Kubaliyapara, Lohanagar, Chhotunagar, Amarnagar, Shreenathji society and Rukhadiyapara (Map 2.1), were selected. The sample size was 15 per cent and in the smallest slum we ensured that at the least 30 samples were covered (Table 2.1). Lanes acted as strata for sampling. In many settlements, we had to face antagonism of the dwellers, who were apprehensive of demolitions, on account of the spate of demolitions in the city in the recent past.

Table 2.1: Sample surveyed in informal settlements, Rajkot

Settlement	*Ward No.*	*Total house-holds**	*Sample surveyed*	*Sample size (%)*	*Status*	*Predominant land ownership*
Kubaliyapara	17	401	61	15	Notified	*Rajashahi*
Khodiyarpara	16	274	43	16	Notified	Public
Rukhadiyapara	23	612	99	16	Notified	Railways
Lohanagar	19	310	51	16	Notified	Largely public
Chhotunagar	11	467	77	16	Non-notified	Public
Amarnagar	14	255	48	19	*Suchit*** society	Private
Shreenathji society	21	778	123	16	*Suchit*** society	Private
Total		3,097	502	16		

Note: Rajashahi means of former princely ruler.

* As per the list provided by the RMC.

** *Suchit* Society is informal settlement but with proper layout and all basic services.

Source: Data from the RMC and the primary survey.

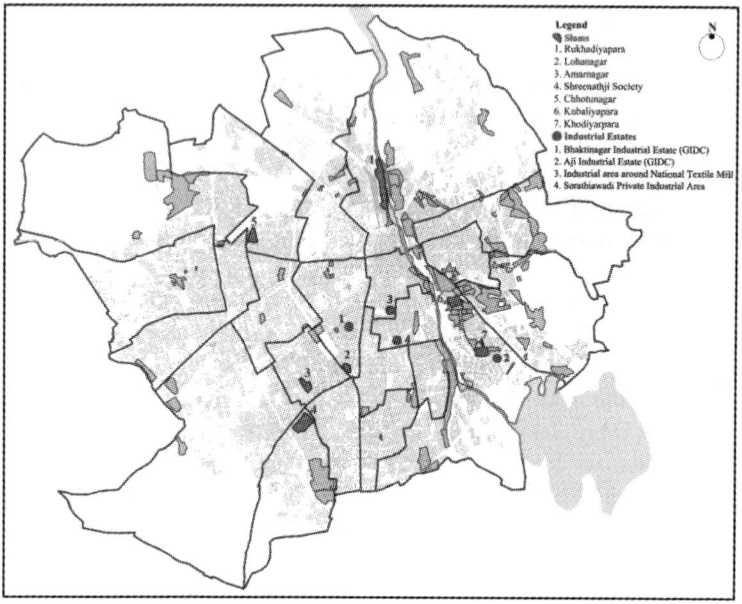

Source: Map prepared by CUE.

Map 2.1: Location of slum clusters in Rajkot and locations of surveyed slum settlements

The informal settlements in Rajkot can be classified into three categories based on three distinguishing characteristics of (i) land ownership and tenure documents, (ii) housing conditions, and (iii) basic services. Based on the combination of these factors, the following categories of informal settlements have been identified in Rajkot:

(i) *Informal settlement on public lands*: In this category, large part of the land is owned by the central, state or local government and the dwellers do not possess any document of use rights to land. These settlements normally come up through illegal land invasions and then incremental house construction, without adhering to any land and planning legislation. Ironically, and contrary to the general understanding, the public agencies are not interested in giving up their lands and hence do not want the settlers of such lands to experience a sense of tenure security, which is achieved through not providing basic services on such lands. Mahadevia (2011) also finds a similar situation in the study of Ahmedabad slums. Hence, majority of the dwelling units in these slums have poor basic services such as water supply, drainage and toilet facilities. Rukhadiyapara, Khodiyarpara and Chhotunagar fall within this category.

(ii) *Informal settlement on private lands*: These are on private lands owned by one or more than one individuals, whose name/names are in the land ownership document. But, the occupants are different, who hold a land-sale agreement done on a stamp-paper, which is a quasi-legal document of financial transaction with the signatures of the buyer and seller along with that of two witnesses. In colloquial language it is called a *parchi*. This, however, is not a land ownership document. There are two sub-categories here:

(a) Those which are on lands that have been earmarked as reserved or no-development land in the Master Plan or notified for acquisition under the Urban Land Ceiling and Regulation Act (ULCRA), 1976. The legal owners, instead of surrendering the land to the planning authority, subdivide it into smaller plots and sell them to individuals who then become occupants of the land. The transaction is through a *parchi*. It is difficult to formalize such land transactions as the original land owner's consent is required. If the land was notified for acquisition then a denotification notice has to be sent. Since neither happen and these processes are not easy, informal occupancy remains almost in perpetuity. The residents of such settlements do perceive some security of tenure and hence they invest in their houses and also spend on obtaining household level basic facilities such as water supply, toilets, bathrooms and sewerage connection. Kubaliyapara and Lohanagar, of the surveyed settlements, fall within this category.

(b) Those which are on private lands and developed through private initiatives, but without adhering to any legal development process, such as procuring Non-Agricultural (NA) development permission from the revenue department and development permissions from the planning authorities. These are called *suchit* societies in Rajkot. The tenure security is high and the occupants invest in housing and individual services. Thus, these houses tend to be *pucca* with household-level toilet and water connections. Since the RMC has put trunk water supply and sewerage network into such settlements, the occupants plug into them. The Gujarat State Government has found a way to legalise/ formalise such colonies after collecting pre-decided penalty through a notification called the Impact Fee Notification. Amarnagar and Shreenathji society are such informal *suchit* societies. The occupants in such settlements are dominantly regular middle class families.

Description of Settlements

Rukhadiyapara (Exhibit 2.1) located close to the railway track has estimated 550 households living on 6.49 hectares (ha) of land at a density of 85 households per ha, which is very low. Of them, 30 per cent are tenants; majority are self-employed, vending vegetables on street and others working as wage labour as those carrying passengers' luggage to and from trains and assistants on food stall on railway platforms. Those selling vegetables are called *Devipujaks* and are local residents but others are migrants from South India and Rajasthan. The RMC has provided this settlement with individual taps as well as common water points, concrete internal roads, open drainage and electricity. Subsidy has been provided for construction of toilets. The perceived security of tenure due to provision of services by the RMC has encouraged the growth of this

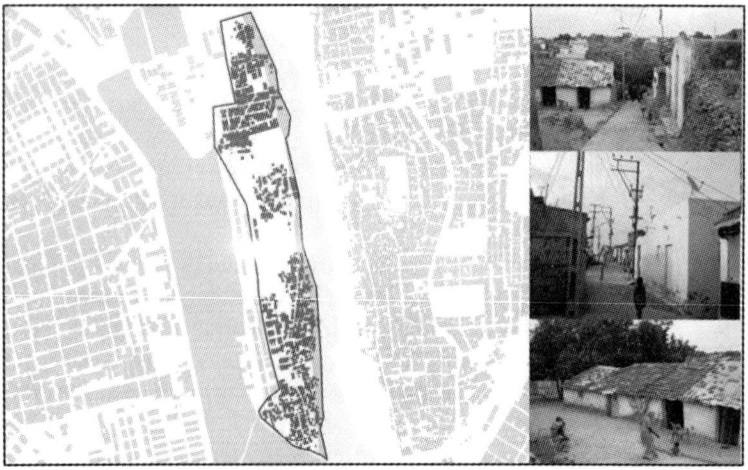

Source: Map prepared by CUE. Photo Credit: CUE.

Exhibit 2.1: Location map and photos of Rukhadiyapara

slum. The undulating land causes inundation of parts in monsoons. During the year prior to the survey, some of the households received a dwelling unit allotment under the BSUP and they were then asked to vacate the slum units. It was alleged that the rumour of sale of land to a private developer was floated to create panic among the dwellers to force them to accept the BSUP units and move out. However, this land belongs to the railways (i.e. primarily Central Government) and cannot be sold.

Chhotunagar slum (Exhibit 2.2) is located close to the airport and covers an area of 2.72 ha. The area is densely populated with a complex network of narrow internal alleys with unhygienic living conditions. Since the slum has developed as a gradual encroachment on the government land, the RMC has not provided any basic services in it. Houses along the road were demolished when the road was widened. The residents are forced to purchase water and electricity from informal suppliers on monthly payments basis. Those unable to afford purchasing water have to fetch water from a distance. Residents are engaged in construction work and vegetable selling. Some are also engaged in brewing local liquor illegally and collecting and selling scrap. The rents vary from Rs. 500 to Rs. 1,500 per month.

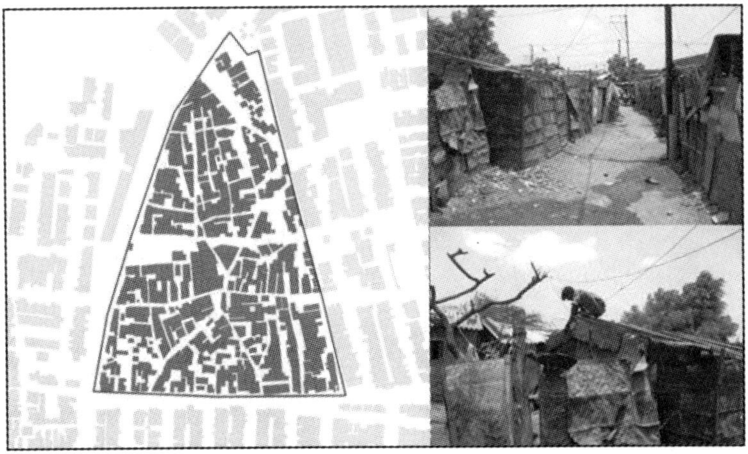

Source: Map prepared by CUE. Photo Credit: CUE.

Exhibit 2.2: Location map and photos of Chhotunagar

Khodiyarpara (Exhibit 2.3) has an area of 3.34 ha. The residents are workers, largely migrants, working in the nearby industries that employ both skilled and unskilled labour. Besides employment in the nearby industries, some are self-employed as drivers and in other personal services and have petty businesses such as food stalls. Some households also have government jobs. This settlement was developed by 'informal developers', who sold land to households who then constructed dwelling units on it. The transactions are through a stamp-paper document or *parchi*. Many have re-purchased dwelling units from the previous occupiers, once again with the document of transaction done on a stamp paper. Some do not have any document. There is presence of strong land mafia in the development of this settlement. The settlement has grown to its current strength due to the perceived security derived from the provision of water connection, paved internal roads, and receipt of property tax bills in the last few years and also due to the RMC-assisted individual toilet construction, connected to a sewerage line. The settlement has grid-pattern development, with well-defined and numbered streets (known as *sheri)*. The *sheris* are alternatively used for purposes like cooking, socialising, sleeping, keeping livestock and doing other household activities throughout the day.

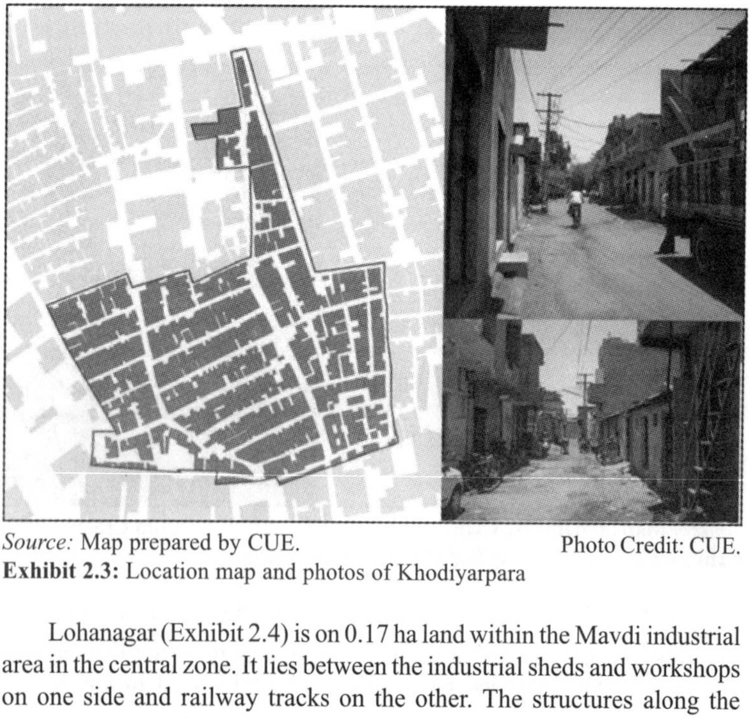

Source: Map prepared by CUE. Photo Credit: CUE.

Exhibit 2.3: Location map and photos of Khodiyarpara

Lohanagar (Exhibit 2.4) is on 0.17 ha land within the Mavdi industrial area in the central zone. It lies between the industrial sheds and workshops on one side and railway tracks on the other. The structures along the

Source: Map prepared by CUE. Photo Credit: CUE.
Exhibit 2.4: Location map and photos of Lohanagar

railway tracks are temporary (of bamboo and jute). Although it lacks in basic services, the settlement is marked by long rows of single rooms for the tenants. Freely available public land, cheap rents, proximity to work areas and an existing social network of family and friends are the pull factors for migrants. Many households in the settlements are engaged in idol making, hawking, and scrap collecting. Since the demand of idols is seasonal, these idol makers become daily wage labourers during rest of the year. On questioning, the residents responded that they would like to shift to new housing if made available, because in their current location basic services are lacking and the living conditions are unhygienic.

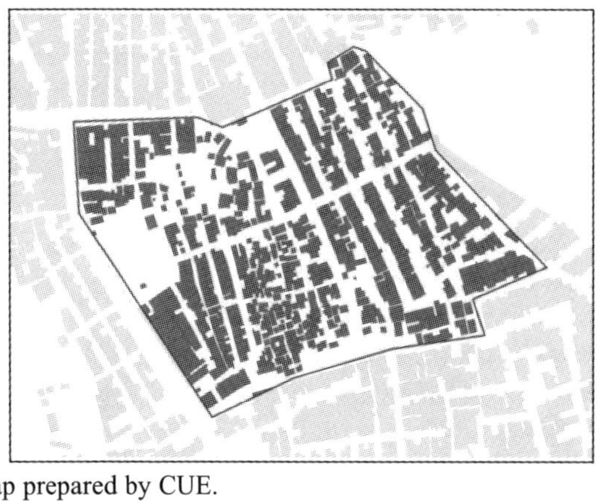

Source: Map prepared by CUE.
Exhibit 2.5: Location map of Kubaliyapara

Kubaliyapara (Exhibit 2.5) is on an area of 4.46 ha with 612 households, and has a density of 137 households per ha. Royal land, called *rajashahi* land along the river was given to a few families in the past, who then sub-divided and sold it through *parchi*. It lacks basic amenities and has degraded housing conditions. Very few houses have individual toilets and also there are no community toilets available here. Tenants in particular do not have access to basic facilities. Some households pay property tax while some do not. The settlement has certain undesirable activities such as brewing and selling of country liquor, prostitution, thefts, etc. Besides, there are itinerant waste collectors, idol makers, wood suppliers, fishermen, and daily wage labour in the settlement. It was found that households of the same caste and occupational group cluster together in the same lane.

Amarnagar, a *suchit* society (Exhibit 2.6), is situated near Mavdi industrial area, on an area of about 0.51 ha. The RMC has provided sufficient basic services like water, electricity, roads, etc. and has proposed to the dwellers that they pay some charges to the revenue department for obtaining NA permission and legalise their holdings. While, reportedly, some of the residents have paid approximately Rs. 29,000 per house, many have entered into litigation, which was on-going at the time of our survey. The settlement is characterised by mixed land use, of residential and industrial use. Over time, the settlement has become an extension of

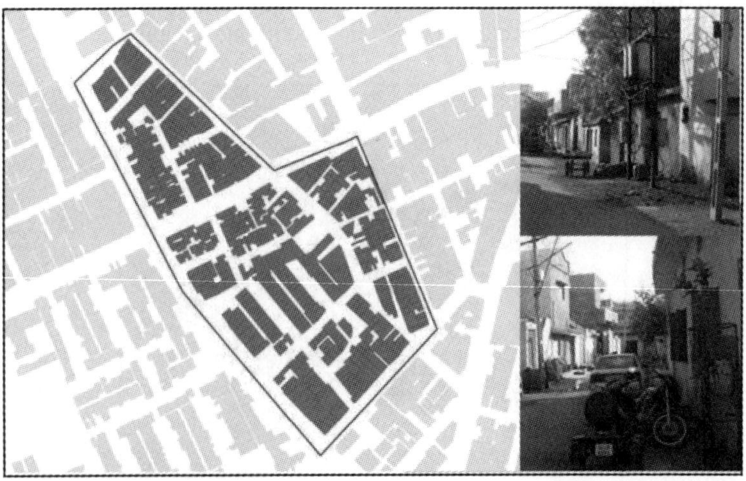

Source: Map prepared by CUE. Photo Credit: CUE.

Exhibit 2.6: Location map and photos of Amarnagar

Source: Map prepared by CUE. Photo Credit: CUE.

Exhibit 2.7: Location map and photos of Shreenathji society

the Mavdi industrial estate as many residential plots have been converted into use for small-scale industries such as of foundry products, automobile spare parts, machine bearings, etc. Mavdi road divides the settlement into two parts, with the small-scale industries on one side and the residential part on the other. People are employed mainly in industries and services. The small-scale industries' owners have provided housing to their employees on the upper floors of the industry/workshop units, very much like in medieval European cities. The price of land/houses as well as the rents is high due to the greater tenure security as well as demand from commercial establishments. It was reported to us that units measuring 40 sq.mt. to 50 sq.mt. were sold for between Rs. 1.8 to Rs. 2.0 million, the property rates coming to about Rs. 40,000 to Rs. 45,000 per sq.mt., which is very high for a city of the size of Rajkot.

Shreenathji society (Exhibit 2.7) is another *suchit* society in the study, with *pucca* houses ranging from single room tenements to large individual bungalows. It is well provided with all basic services. Residents have converted their temporary houses into permanent ones over the years and gradually many households have become owners from tenants by informally buying or constructing their own houses. The area has provision of water supply and electricity and thus the house values and rents are higher here compared to the other surveyed settlements. Due to its recognition by the RMC, owners and tenants have a higher sense of tenure security. Rental housing is informal as no rent agreements or transactions are registered. Generally, the rent is inclusive of the property tax and electricity bills.

Tenure Security

There are various factors affecting sense of security of the slum dwellers in informal settlements and they are: land ownership, type of land transaction registration, property tax assessment of the dwelling unit and receipt of property tax bill, any official document such as election card, ration card, driving licence, bank passbook, etc., carrying the dwelling unit address of the occupant, external agency intervention such as by a NGO and lastly duration of stay in the settlement (Mahadevia, 2010 and 2011). Contrary to general understanding, many slum settlements tend to be on multiple land parcels, each likely to have a different owner. For example, in Chhotunagar, Khodiyarpara and Rukhadiyapara, more than four-fifths of the households live on government land and remaining live on private lands; in Amarnagar and Shreenathji society, 71 per cent and 85 per cent respectively live on private lands (Table 2.2). In case of Amarnagar, the households have right to *rajashahi* land, which is a government land, but, the households living here for long periods consider it as private and 44 per cent of them claim it to be their own land. These complexities of land ownership for a slum should be kept in mind in any settlement upgrading and tenure regularising programme.

Table 2.2: Information on land ownership and documents (% households)

Settlement	*Land ownership*		*Proof of occupancy*			*Those receiving property tax bill*
	Government	*Private*	*Stamp paper document*	*Land registry*	*None*	
Kubaliyapara	55.7	44.3	32.8	1.6	65.6	88.5
Khodiyarpara	90.7	9.3	7.0	0.0	93.0	97.7
Rukhadiyapara	98.0	2.0	5.1	0.0	94.9	57.6
Lohanagar	76.5	23.5	11.8	3.9	84.3	68.6
Chhotunagar	88.3	11.7	1.3	0.0	98.7	29.9
Amarnagar	29.2	70.8	45.8	2.1	52.1	93.8
Shreenathji society	15.4	84.6	42.3	4.9	52.8	92.7
Average	61.8	38.2	21.7	2.0	76.3	73.7

Source: Primary Survey.

Studies have shown that dwellers on publicly owned lands are more vulnerable to evictions as compared to privately owned land; owing to the frequent evictions on government land in the name of land acquisition under reservations in the Master or Development Plans and zonal or local plans (Mahadevia, 2010 and 2011). Thus, settlements on private lands are assumed to have a higher level of tenure security, since the ULB does not have a direct control over such lands and hence cannot evict the dwellers unless it sends a notice for land acquisition under a stated purpose. The fear of demolition was observed during the surveys, amongst dwellers staying on public lands such as Lohanagar, Chhotunagar, etc., as a result of slum demolition drives in Rajkot in the recent past. In case of a slum on dual land ownership, public and private, the segment on the public land is more vulnerable to eviction than that on the private land. This, however, is an observation from the cities in Gujarat and needs to be tested in other states in India.

Other than land ownership, tenure security is also defined at individual household level depending on the documents available with each household. Tenure documents vary; they can be registered documents (legal document), stamp papers (that certify the transaction of money but do not state anything about the land ownership), property tax receipts (evidence of occupancy), electricity bills, election card or voter's ID card and ration card, etc. These documents give *de facto* tenure status to the household.

Slums develop on government lands through squatting and the dwellers do not have any evidence to claim use right on the land or of the dwelling unit. If the water supply has been extended in such slums, the dwellers might receive property tax bill from the ULB, which is used for staking claim to rehabilitation in case of eviction. Property tax bill is an important *de facto* identity held by slum dwellers. However, the data in Table 2.2 shows that the dwellers on both public and private lands were paying property tax. It was found that on the whole 74 per cent of the respondents were receiving property tax bills, even though 76 per cent of the households did not own any document regarding ownership of their land and/or house. Lack of stamp paper document or registered document was seen in settlements on public lands such as Chhotunagar, Khodiyarpara, Rukhadiyapara and Lohanagar. In Chhotunagar settlement, which is marked by seasonal migrants only 30 per cent of the residents receive property tax bill. Rukhadiyapara, which is on railway land, had 40 per cent households without receiving any property tax bill. On the whole, nearly 22 per cent of the households held stamp paper document. In Amarnagar and Shreenathji society established on private lands, nearly 45 per cent of the dwellers have these documents, indicating perception of high *de facto* tenure status. This has resulted in investments in improving housing conditions which will be seen later in the chapter.

Table 2.3: Duration of stay in the settlements, by tenure, Rajkot

Settlement	*Duration of stay in settlement (in years)*									
	All households				*Owners*			*Tenants*		
	< 15	*15 - 30*	*> 30*	*Average*	*< 15*	*15 - 30*	*> 30*	*< 15*	*15 - 30*	*> 30*
Kubaliyapara	24.6	29.5	45.9	29	2	16	81	28	17	56
Khodiyarpara	41.9	46.5	11.6	17	9	38	53	100	0	0
Rukhadiyapara	37.4	26.3	36.4	23	14	25	62	39	43	17
Lohanagar	33.3	27.5	39.2	25	3	22	75	34	27	40
Chhotunagar	41.6	45.5	13.0	17	15	56	29	40	28	32
Amarnagar	35.4	41.7	22.9	20	13	37	50	40	40	20
Shreenathji society	60.2	35.0	4.9	11	25	49	25	53	25	23
Average	41.8	35.1	23.1	19	14	36	50	46	27	27

Source: Primary Survey.

Studies have shown that longer duration of stay in the settlements also gives a perceived security to the dwellers, which then has a positive relation with the variables of living condition, such as economic status, housing investments etc., which is discussed later. Legally they are protected through easement rights as well as households' own efforts to procure documents such as a ration card, an electricity bill, election voter card and so on to prove their residency in the city.

The average duration of stay of all the households surveyed is 19 years (Table 2.3). Only in Shreenathji society, the average years of stay is 11 years, indicating that this is a new settlement. Average duration of stay in Chhotunagar and Khodiyarpara is 17 years, as the former is a settlement of seasonal migrants and latter, that of industrial workers. Kubaliyapara is the oldest settlement of all, with 29 years of average stay by the residents and about 46 per cent staying more than 30 years in the settlement. As already discussed earlier, this settlement has very poor basic facilities although it is the oldest and the largest settlement among our surveyed settlements.

However, there is a difference between the owner-occupants, referred to as owners from here on and tenant-occupants, referred as tenants from here on, in terms of duration of stay. On an average, the owners have stayed in the city for longer duration of time as compared to the tenants. More than 50 per cent of owners have settled in the city for more than 30 years, whereas only 27 per cent tenants are in the city for that long period (Table 2.3). Further, 86 per cent owners have been in the city for more than 15 years, whereas only 54 per cent tenants have been Rajkot residents for that long.

It is important to note that nearly 20 per cent of the tenants have come to the city very recently, that is, in the last five years, while only 1 per cent of the owners fall in this time span. This indicates that access to ownership housing is not available and also not feasible for the new migrants in a city. Hence, rental housing fulfils an important social purpose of providing shelter security to the new migrants of the city. This is true for all the settlements studied. Exception is of Kubaliyapara, which is an old established slum and has 56 per cent of the surveyed tenant households as residents for more than 30 years. This is because Kubaliyapara, being in the industrial area and in a relatively central part of the city, has attracted tenants who are working in the industrial areas. Lohanagar is the second oldest settlement in our study and here 40 per cent of the tenants are living for more than 30 years in the city. This settlement is in Mavdi industrial area and hence has industrial workers who also prefer to stay on rent, than purchase their own house like in Kubaliyapara. In contrast, Shreenathji society is a new settlement and it has the second largest proportion of recent migrants among the tenants. Self-ownership or renting thus is a function of not just age but also location of the settlement. The Turner model of linear relationship between renting/ownership and duration of stay is not observed in Rajkot, but, instead, the relationship is mediated by the land use of the surrounding region.

Methods of Accessing Housing

The governments in developing countries are faced with increasing informal housing development in their cities. This increase is a result of increasing population with limited serviced and planned land for housing development. However, poor policy enforcement, outdated laws, inadequate capacity of local authorities to provide planned and serviced land are widely discussed among influencing factors (Christian, 1995; Kombe, 1995; Kreibich *et al.*, 2002; Topfer, 2002), besides now, speculative housing markets. With this inability of the local government, vast majority of shelter and housing for low-income groups is continued to be provided through the individual effort of people to develop their own houses (Kamau, 2002). The low-income groups tend to seek land in informal market by encroaching and squatting on whatever vacant land (mainly public lands) is available in the city such as railway land, road reservations, land along the drains, etc. and then gradually constructing shelter units, incrementally improving them. Thus their access to housing is through squatting, making unauthorised construction by purchasing piece of private land and building on it without going through legal procedures; inheritance especially in case of old settlements, where two to three generations have been living in the same settlement; and renting such as a room, a house or a piece of land (Gilbert, 1983; DeWandeler *et al.,* 1992; Coccato, 1996).

Table 2.4: Settlement-wise methods to access housing, Rajkot

Settlement	*Access to housing*				
	Inherited	*Bought land & built*	*Squatted & built*	*Purchased*	*Renting*
Kubaliyapara	42.6	11.5	9.8	6.6	29.5
Khodiyarpara	11.6	18.6	25.6	18.6	25.6
Rukhadiyapara	15.2	8.1	43.4	10.1	23.2
Lohanagar	21.6	7.8	33.3	7.8	29.4
Chhotunagar	7.8	5.2	49.4	5.2	32.5
Amarnagar	16.7	31.3	6.3	25.0	20.8
Shreenathji society	4.1	28.5	0.8	34.1	32.5
Average	15.1	16.1	23.7	16.7	28.3

Source: Primary Survey.

In three settlements, Chhotunagar, Lohanagar and Rukhadiyapara, 50 per cent, 33 per cent and 43 per cent households, respectively, have accessed housing through first, squatting on public lands and then incrementally improving their housing (Table 2.4). Some households here have also purchased their houses, which indicates that the original squatters sold their house and moved away or some middleman had built a house on the encroached land and then sold it off. Interestingly, middlemen have constructed housing units on encroached land and rented them out and thus, 33 per cent, 29 per cent and 23 per cent households are living as tenants respectively in these three settlements. These settlements being on public land are under a permanent threat of eviction. Even then, there are households willing to stay as tenants and pay rent to informal middlemen due to lack of alternatives.

As the city expands it becomes increasingly difficult for the poor to find vacant land to squat and build dwellings, and this scarcity results in a market of unauthorized land occupation. This market develops on the city periphery. Since the demand for new housing is more and the supply through legal route, that is, through obtaining all clearances, is extremely cumbersome and time and resource consuming, local entrepreneurs, sub-divide the private lands and put them up for sale to those who can afford these. Lesser the extent of services, lower are the prices and more easily accessible to low-income groups. In fact, households of low to middle-income groups opt for such housing access. Subsequently, the settlement is provided with basic services by the ULB and then sometimes even regularised after taking some charges. Overall, it is seen that nearly 32 per cent of the households have either purchased houses or have bought land and built houses in the settlements under study. Slums established on private lands such as Amarnagar and Shreenathji society show that nearly 56 per cent and 62 per cent households respectively, have either purchased houses or have bought land and built houses. In these two settlements, 20 per cent and 33 per cent households respectively are tenants. This is an illustration of housing not only becoming an asset for the household but also an investment asset for the households with entrepreneurial capabilities. Such a large presence of tenants also shows the demand for rental housing in the cities, which is largely met by the private individual house owners.

In all, 28 per cent households in our sample are tenants. It is close to the national average of 30 per cent rental housing in India as shown by latest National Sample Survey Organisation (NSSO) data (NSSO, 2010). Amongst the surveyed settlements, Shreenathji society has the highest incidence of renting, i.e. 33 per cent. This is a *suchit* society, which designates it as recognised by the RMC. This recognition has made it a popular location for the upwardly mobile low income working class, as well as long-staying migrant families who can afford to stay in better rental housing (if not own one) to shift to this location. Its location in the central part of the city has made it attractive also to middle income groups looking for rental units. Chhotunagar is the other surveyed settlement which has high rental households. It is a slum settlement located near the airport on the 150 feet Ring Road. Unlike the theory of intra-city residential mobility model of Turner, Chhotunagar provides evidence of migrants settling down on city peripheries on their arrival to the city. Recent migrants are finding rental housing on the periphery in Indian cities because commercialisation of the city centre does not allow development of low-rent rental market.

Amarnagar had the lowest presence of rental housing, as the very nature of the settlement is fast changing from residential to industrial. The Bhaktinagar industrial area extends to one side of the Amarnagar slum. As the settlement is a *suchit* society, the selling of land for industrial development has led to the gradual transformation of the landuse to industrial. There are cases, of households selling their 25 sq.mt. dwelling unit at nearly Rs. 2.2 million in the year 2012. Lohanagar is in the industrial suburb, having many small-scale industrial units, where seasonal migrants find rental housing.

Inheritance is another form of access to housing in these settlements. About 15 per cent of the households have inherited their houses. Inheritance of the house in case of owners is from ancestors who might have originally squatted and built their house. For this to happen, the settlement has to be old. Kubaliyapara is one such settlement, which, as mentioned above, is a very old settlement, where 42 per cent of the surveyed households had inherited the houses from their parents. In this settlement, which has very poor quality services, 30 per cent of the households are tenants. The settlement is old and hence this is the reason for higher level of perceived security of tenure, which might have promoted the owners to expand and provide rental housing.

Rental Housing—Types and Supply

Rajkot has different types of rental housing, distinguished through supply process and size. The rental housing category is classified into four types: (i) single-room tenements, (ii) part dwelling unit on rent, (iii) full dwelling unit on rent, and (iv) employer provided housing. Each one of them is discussed below briefly.

Single-room tenements: This type of rental housing was found in almost all the settlements, wherein single rooms are built in a row to be rented out either to single male migrants (who share it with other single male migrants) or to migrant families. The room size generally is about 10 sq.mt. and rooms are not well lit or ventilated. The services such as water supply, bathing space and toilets are common. In some settlements there were common toilets provided by the RMC. There is no separate kitchen and cooking is either outside or in a corner of the room. Some may make a bathing corner inside the dwelling unit. Such tenements are not meant for long-term occupation as there is little or no scope to expand and are often suitable only for single male migrants who share a room while working at nearby places. The landlord/owner are often found to be staying within the settlement, but in a larger dwelling unit than that of the tenants. Sometimes, the small units for renting are constructed in the land demarcated as a compound owned by the owner. In that case, the open courtyard is shared by the owner as well as tenants for activities such as cooking, cutting vegetables, washing, etc. (Exhibit 2.8).

Sometimes the row of single room houses open out on the road, which gives each rental unit a separate access from the main road.

Photo Credit: CUE.
Exhibit 2.8: Tenant sharing common space with owner

Part of house given on rent: Many owners tend to rent part of their house (Exhibit 2.9), as a strategy to enhance their income and recover the costs of their investment in housing. Such rented rooms tend to have a separate entry for the tenant. Families renting a part of their house prefer families over single male migrants as tenants, as the former are considered safer than the latter in behaviour and habits. The owner and tenant(s) mostly share toilet and bathroom.

Such an owner was Karshanbhai, a *chhagda* (shared auto rickshaw) driver staying in Khodiyarpara for last 35 years. He was originally a farmer in Chotila, on the outskirts of Rajkot, but later shifted to Rajkot looking for better employment opportunities. He started staying on rent in a small single-room tenement near his current owned plot. Over the last 30 years, he managed to own a sizeable property by purchasing a house on a 50 sq.mt. plot for Rs. 35,000 in 1980, and then extending it to a 3-room house with separate kitchen and bathroom. Subsequently, he constructed small tenements within his plot for renting, without additional facility for cooking or bathing. At the time of survey, three single male migrants from Uttar Pradesh were renting his tenement since last eight months on a shared rent of Rs. 1,200 per month. While the migrants cook inside their room, they have to resort to open defecation or use the community toilets. Karshanbhai looks after the maintenance of the room. He raises the rent annually, or when the electricity bill increases beyond his affordability. He prefers to give his room out on rent to people from other states because they do not stay on for too long and have fewer demands. Niraliben is another migrant in Rajkot from Chotila. Her two sons have been working in the city as industrial workers for 10 years, staying as tenants in Chandreshwar with steady monthly incomes. After her husband's death in 2009, she sold their ancestral property in Chotila and purchased a house in Shreenathji society at Rs. 80,000. Her sons spent another Rs. 20,000 in renovating this house. They have rented the upper floor of the house to a family from their own community. The tenant-family women keep Niraliben company and she is also not a complete burden on her sons because of the monthly rent she earns.

It was seen that renting not only provides additional income to the household, but also provides funds to improve the property in terms of infrastructure and services. It may be also deduced that additional incomes help access to municipal services, which in turn strengthens their tenure-status.

Photo Credit: CUE.

Exhibit 2.9: House extension rented out

Full house given on rent: Many households with increasing affordability, move out of the slum or informal settlements into formal housing and in turn rent out their houses in the slums and informal settlements. Many households use the rent from their informal houses to support the monthly instalments for their new house. In many cases, the owner of the slum-house stays in another house within the same locality. Free land is encroached upon to build not just self-help housing but also rental housing. In Rukhadiyapara, which is railway land, many employees of the railways have encroached upon the open land next to the railway colony which was originally a crematorium ground, to build own housing. Overtime as the settlement started growing, the original encroachers whose perceived sense of security increased, built rental housing on their plots and have become part of the informal housing suppliers.

Employer provided rental housing: This was seen in small number of cases, wherein the owners of small-scale industries built single room units to house their employees. One such example was found in Khodiyarnagar wherein the owner of a small metal workshop had built single room tenements above his workshop to house the workers. In spite of large industrial activity in Rajkot, employer provided housing is missing in the Rajkot housing market, giving impetus to large-scale informal settlements and rental housing.

Owner-Tenant Relations

Tenants tend to have good relations with their landlords and hence the latter allow for flexibility in rent payment, which was reported by 67 per cent of the surveyed tenant households. The landlords, who are usually residents of the same settlement, understand that it is not convenient for tenants to pay regular rent and hence allow for flexibility in terms of rent amount and payment timings. Kubaliyapara which is one of the oldest slum settlements in Rajkot has a very strong and well-established rental market for the low-income industrial workers, where nearly 83 per cent tenants reported that they will not be asked to vacate if they cannot pay the rent on time. This proportion in Rukhadiyapara was 78 per cent and in Shreenathji society was 75 per cent. For many tenants, paying a fixed amount is not possible and they tend to pay their rent in instalments as per their capacity. Of the total, only one-third of the tenant households reported insecurity in terms of eviction due to non-timely rent payments. In Khodiyarnagar which is an industrial informal settlement, the fear of eviction was the highest. The reason for it could be a higher demand for rental housing by industrial workers due to which owners expect to find a tenant replacement quickly.

Individual households are the major suppliers of rental housing in the informal settlements, which is also found to be the case in the formal housing market. The suppliers (or owners) are found to have lifestyles similar to that of their tenants, but they are marked by regular paid job or better self-employment. As mentioned earlier, in many instances, the rented units or rooms are extension of the owner's house thereby depicting a continuum of housing mobility within the informal housing market.

Socio-economic Profile of Dwellers

Migration

The study shows that 77 per cent of the surveyed households are migrants (Table 2.5), defined by their place of birth. Amarnagar, Khodiyarpara and Shreenathji society have nearly 90 per cent of migrants households, owing to their location close to the industrial estates, which are the main employment centres in the city. Kubaliyapara has shown the least proportion of migrants among the surveyed settlements on account of it being the oldest settlement and many of its households having lived here for more than a generation and have purchased their own dwellings in the course of time. Among the migrants, majority, i.e. 86 per cent are intra-state movers (Table 2.5), and are from the surrounding rural areas as well as nearby talukas of Amreli, Gondal and Dhadhuka, thereby indicating importance of Rajkot as a regional hub and a growth centre. The composition of migrants in our sample is close to the national level average of 87 per cent as intrastate migrants in the decade of 1991-2001. Inter-state migration was high in industrial slums such as Amarnagar and Khodiyarpara, with more than 20 per cent in this category.

Rajkot has provided employment opportunities and services which has increased the attractiveness of settling in the city. Owners have created the housing stock which now serves the tenants' housing needs. Most of the owner households (93%) who have settled in Rajkot are largely from surrounding areas of the city and majority from within Gujarat itself (Table 2.5). Even amongst the tenants, nearly 70 per cent of the households are from in and around the city and from within Gujarat state. However, as compared to owners, there is much higher proportion of inter-state migrants among the tenants. While, only 7 per cent are inter-state migrants among the owners, the share is 30 per cent inter-state migrants among the tenants (Table 2.5). The inter-state migrants are from Uttar Pradesh, Bihar, Maharashtra and the southern states of India. Migrants from outside Gujarat have provided unskilled cheap labour for the industries. These out-of-state migrants are also mostly single-male migrants. Khodiyarpara and Amarnagar have attracted the highest inter-state migrants as they are industrial settlements which have developed around the Aji and Bhaktinagar industrial areas.

Table 2.5: Settlement-wise type of migrants (%), Rajkot

Settlement	*Overall*			*Owners*		*Tenants*	
	Proportion of migrants	*Intra-state*	*Inter-state*	*Intra-state*	*Inter-state*	*Intra-state*	*Inter-state*
Kubaliyapara	51	84	16	95	5	64	36
Khodiyarpara	88	76	24	100	0	18	82
Rukhadiyapara	73	85	15	80	20	100	0
Lohanagar	67	91	9	92	8	89	11
Chhotunagar	77	97	3	94	6	22	78
Amarnagar	90	79	21	97	3	95	5
Shreenathji society	89	87	13	97	3	66	34
Average	77	86	14	93	7	70	30

Source: Primary Survey.

Household Characteristics

The average household size of the surveyed population is 5.2 (Table 2.6), which is lower than that of the city's, which is 5.6. This means that the informal settlements tend to have more single-male migrants than families compared to the formal settlements. These single-male migrants do not, in sociological sense, make a household, although, they do share a common kitchen. The average sex ratio of the informal settlements was 852 females per 1000 males, which is lower than the city's sex ratio of 902 in 2011, corroborating the same fact of significant presence of single male migrant households. Khodiyarnagar, Chhotunagar, Shreenathji society and Amarnagar have the lowest sex ratio. Kubaliyapara, which is the oldest settlement among all, has sex ratio of 944 and a household size of 5.7, both higher than that of Rajkot. Lohanagar is a squatter settlement and seems to be housing the poorest of the households in our sample. In general, poor households have larger family size and hence, this settlement has the largest household size among the settlements in the survey.

Table 2.6: Settlement-wise household size and sex ratio, Rajkot

Settlement	*All tenures*		*Owners*		*Tenants*	
	Sex ratio	*HH size*	*Sex ratio*	*HH size*	*Sex ratio*	*HH size*
Kubaliyapara	944	5.7	963	6.2	881	4.4
Khodiyarpara	694	4.8	758	5.2	462	3.5
Rukhadiyapara	889	5.0	883	5.1	911	4.7
Lohanagar	1,047	6.0	957	6.4	1,364	5.2
Chhotunagar	799	5.0	801	5.4	793	4.2
Amarnagar	809	5.7	935	6.3	276	3.7
Shreenathji society	798	4.9	840	5.4	691	4.0
Average	852	5.2	875	5.6	781	4.2

Source: Primary Survey.

The sex ratio among the tenant households was most skewed, with 781 women per 1000 men, while the same among the owner households was 875. The average household size among tenants was far lower at 4.2, as compared to the owners, which was 5.6. It is evident that more single male migrants tend to live as tenants. Ownership housing is preferred by families and hence owners have large household size and high sex ratio. Amongst tenant households, Amarnagar and Khodiyarpara had the poorest sex ratio on account of these being industrial settlements, with higher instances of young couples and single male migrants, as compared to other settlements. Hence, these had very low sex ratio at 276 and 462, respectively and low household size of 3.7 and 3.5, respectively. Lohanagar was a unique case of high sex ratio, where the sample included tenant households with multiple girl children. These two settlements also had the highest proportion of inter-state migrants among all the settlements. Among the inter-state migrants, those from Bihar were keen to permanently settle in Rajkot, as they do not have sustainable income opportunities back in their home-state. While the migrants from Uttar Pradesh considered Rajkot as a place for alternative source of income during agriculturally lean period in their home state. Migrants who come from in and around Gujarat are more likely to bring in their spouse, children and parents to the city over time, as do the inter-state migrants from the far-off Southern states, who do not plan to return to their villages.

Employment

The Labour Force Participation Rate (LFPR) is related to poverty. Participation in the labour force keeps the households out of poverty;

consequently, the LFPRs are high in poor households as more members of the family tend to work to keep the household out of poverty. In such households, women too have high LFPR. Thus hereby, we would expect that the LFPRs would also be high in our study settlements. This, however, is not the case. The LFPR of the total surveyed population is 53 per cent, with female LFPR of 17 per cent and male LFPR 84 per cent (Table 2.7). The female LFPRs are unusually low. Rukhadiyapara, Lohanagar and Amarnagar, have more than 20 per cent LFPRs among the women, while in all others, less than 20 per cent. The characteristics in all the three settlements are different; the first one has a community where women are engaged in selling vegetables on the streets, the second one has larger number of seasonal migrants and the last one is a *suchit* society with high security of tenure. There is very small difference of male LFPR across the settlements. Work Force Participation Rate (WFPR) follows the same pattern as the LFPRs. The overall female WFPR is quite low, 13 per cent, which is close to national female WFPR in the metros in India (which is 12.4%) and slightly lower than that of metro Gujarat (which is 14.1%) in 2009-10 (Mahadevia and Sarkar, 2012: Table A6.1).

Table 2.7: Settlement-wise labour force participation, Rajkot

Settlement	*Workforce participation rate (%)*			*Labour force participation rate (age 15-59 yrs) (%)*		
	Male	*Female*	*Persons*	*Male*	*Female*	*Total*
Kubaliyapara	62	8	36	85	11	51
Khodiyarpara	60	7	39	79	9	49
Rukhadiyapara	61	19	42	87	27	59
Lohanagar	56	13	34	87	22	55
Chhotunagar	53	9	34	88	13	52
Amarnagar	66	17	44	86	21	56
Shreenathji society	61	10	39	82	13	50
Average	60	13	38	84	17	53

Source: Primary Survey.

There is a marked difference in the economic participation among owners and tenants. The WFPRs among the tenants is higher (43%) as compared to that among the owners (37%) (Table 2.8). This is true for males as well as females. The exception is Kubaliyapara, the oldest settlement among the sample, where the WFPR among owners is higher than that among the tenants in case of males. Among males, again, in Amarnagar and Chhotunagar, the WFPRs of the owners are nearly equal

Table 2.8: Comparison of WFPR between owners and tenants, Rajkot

Settlement	*Owners*			*Tenants*		
	Male	*Female*	*Persons*	*Male*	*Female*	*Persons*
Kubaliyapara	63	6	35	57	16	38
Khodiyarpara	54	7	34	85	8	61
Rukhadiyapara	60	18	40	66	24	56
Lohanagar	56	15	36	58	9	29
Amarnagar	67	17	42	66	25	57
Chhotunagar	53	7	33	52	15	36
Shreenathji society	59	6	35	67	23	49
Average	59	11	37	63	18	43

Source: Primary Survey.

to the tenants. Among the female members, the exception is in case of Lohanagar, wherein owners have higher WFPR than the tenants. The tenants tend to be younger generation whereas the owners are settled families with elderly members and hence, it is obvious that the tenants have higher WFPR than the owners.

Table 2.9: Settlement-wise employment details, Rajkot

Settlement	*Total*			*Owners*			*Tenants*		
	Regular/ salaried	*Casual labour*	*Self-employed*	*Regular/ salaried*	*Casual labour*	*Self-employed*	*Regular/ salaried*	*Casual labour*	*Self-employed*
Kubaliyapara	15	14	71	14	15	71	20	10	70
Khodiyarpara	48	16	36	41	16	43	65	17	17
Rukhadiyapara	28	32	40	26	34	39	35	22	43
Lohanagar	20	30	50	18	29	52	26	30	43
Chhotunagar	13	5	82	11	5	84	19	5	76
Amarnagar	46	20	34	46	18	36	48	29	24
Shreenathji society	44	15	41	39	13	48	53	21	27
Average	31	19	49	28	20	52	39	19	42

Source: Primary Survey.

On the whole, 49 per cent of the workers in the surveyed settlements are self-employed and another 31 per cent are regular employed (Table 2.9). Self-employment includes vending, home-based work by women and petty businesses. The incidence of casual labour is only 19 per cent. However, self-employment among the owners is higher (52%) than among the tenants (42%) and the latter have more regular/salaried work (39%) as compared to owners (28%). Incidence of casual work among the owners as well as tenants is nearly the same. If overall self-employment in a settlement is high, as in case of Kubaliyapara (71%) and Chhotunagar (82%) then it is high among owners as well as tenants. Even then, the owners have higher proportion of self-employed as compared to tenants. Regular/salaried employment is higher in the *suchit* societies, Amarnagar and Shreenathji for owners and the tenants. In fact, the tenants have much higher proportion of regular employment than the owners. Even, Khodiyarpara, which is in the industrial area, has very large proportion of regular/salaried workers, especially among the tenants, who have come to the city only for work. Rukhadiyapara and Lohanagar, former in the residential area and the latter in the industrial area, have high proportion of casual labour, and that is the case among the owners as well as tenants.

Table 2.10: Duration of stay *versus* employment type, Rajkot

Duration of stay	*Total*			*Owners*			*Tenants*		
	Regular/ salaried	*Casual labour*	*Self-employed*	*Regular/ salaried*	*Casual labour*	*Self-employed*	*Regular/ salaried*	*Casual labour*	*Self-employed*
< 5 yrs	46	18	36	9	36	55	47	18	35
5 –14 yrs	38	21	41						
15 – 30 yrs	32	18	49	27	15	58	34	9	57
> 30 yrs	27	20	53	22	14	64	22	14	65

Source: Primary Survey.

A new entrant in the city either gets absorbed as a casual labour or in regular employment in the industrial sector but often without any social security benefits. In case of Rajkot city, numerous small and big industries engage a large number of the new entrants. This can be seen in Table 2.10 where 46 per cent of the dwellers staying in the city for less than five years were regular employed (mainly in the industries) with average monthly incomes of Rs. 4,825. Many migrants may also choose to work as casual labour, which is largely daily wage labour. This type of employment is resorted to if one does not have any skill and/or not being able to find any work. But, just 18 per cent of the workers are employed as casual labour. The largest proportion of workers are engaged as regular workers on coming to the city but gradually shift to self-employment as their stay period in the city increases. This trend can also be seen among the tenants. But, among the owners, the predominant employment is as regular workers. It is interesting to note that engagement as casual labour which is expected in the case of the tenant workforce is not very high. Instead it is the owner households which are engaged as casual labour, at least in the first 15 years of their stay in the city. The shift of tenants from regular salaried workers to self-employed over time is probably due to shifting out from industrial employment into their own small businesses. The intra-state migrants are more engaged as self-employed as compared to inter-state migrants, of which nearly half are regularly employed (Table 2.11).

Table 2.11: Employment by migrant type (in %), Rajkot

Employment category	*Intra-state*	*Inter-state*
Regular/salaried	24	47
Casual labour	17	14
Self-employment	60	39
Total	100	100

Source: Primary Survey.

The highest employment is in trade, hotels and restaurants (37%), followed by manufacturing (26%) and then in construction (15%) (Table 2.12). Chhotunagar has about 80 per cent of workers in trade, hotels and restaurants and are classified as self-employed indicating that they are operating tea-stalls, small eateries, etc. On closer enquiry, we were told that some residents here brewed illicit liquor and customers came to the brewery site to drink. Kubaliyapara, the oldest settlement also has high self-employment, about 62 per cent engaged in the same activity. 26 per cent of the surveyed workers are in manufacturing and stay in the two *suchit* societies of Amarnagar and Shreenathji society and Khodiyarpara. Those employed in manufacturing have the highest incomes, as evident in the two *suchit* societies which have highest household incomes, as discussed later. Although, just 15 per cent of the total workers are engaged in construction, Rukhadiyapara and Lohanagar, have slightly less than a quarter of their workers in this sector.

This analysis shows that the owners tend to be more self-employed and hence are involved in petty businesses and trades, including illicit trades, as compared to tenants. The tenants employed in regular work are earning salaries, as they are to great extent migrants, and many of them may have better education than the owners and hence, are employed in services such as water supply and electricity supply. At the same time, there are low-income unskilled workers among the tenants who are employed in construction activities as well as manufacturing.

Table 2.12: Settlement-wise employment classification by industries, Rajkot

Settlement	Industry-wise employment distribution (%)							
	Agriculture & Fishing	Manu-facturing	Elec., gas & water supply	Constru-ction	Trade, hotels & restaurant	Transpor, storage & communi-cation	Real estate & business services	Commu-nity, social & personnel services
Kubaliyapara	1.6	17.7	0.8	12.9	62.1	1.6	0.0	3.2
Khodiyarnagar	5.1	43.0	0.0	13.9	17.7	10.1	0.0	10.1
Rukhadiyapara	0.0	11.7	1.0	24.3	35.0	6.8	0.0	21.4
Lohanagar	0.0	23.8	0.0	23.8	36.2	6.7	0.0	9.0
Chhotunagar	0.0	5.4	0.0	3.9	80.0	1.6	0.0	8.5
Amarnagar	0.0	45.1	0.0	13.1	12.3	8.0	0.0	22.1
Shreenathji society	2.1	40.2	1.3	11.5	20.9	8.5	0.4	15.0
Total	1.1	26.1	0.6	15.0	36.9	6.2	0.1	13.9

Source: Primary Survey.

Income

The duration of migration and type of work are two important factors that determine income. For both, inter-state as well as intra-state migrants, household income increases with increase in duration of stay (Table 2.13). The household incomes are lowest among the recent migrants (less than 5 years stay). Highest household incomes are of those living in the city between 15 to 30 years. It is indicated that a longer duration of stay in the city helps in elevating the economic status of the migrants as they can escape the poverty trap by improving their employment conditions and thereby wages. Also, the intra-state migrants have an advantage as compared to the inter-state migrants when they arrive in the city and hence they have higher household income as compared to the latter. However, with time, household income of the inter-state migrants increase as probably the better endowed tend to stay back. Also, they tend to work harder than the intra-state migrants to be able to send back money to their families as well as survive in the city. In all surveyed settlements, the household income of the inter-state migrants increases with time, and was found to be some of the highest incomes in the settlement. Lastly, many inter-state migrants are single-male migrants and tend to share an accommodation. As a result, they form a household wherein all members work, leading to high reported income of the household. On the whole, the inter-state migrants' household income was Rs. 8,395, which was higher than that of the intra-state migrants, whose monthly household income was Rs. 7,625 (Table 2.13).

Table 2.13: Duration of stay-wise average monthly incomes of migrants, Rajkot

Years of stay of migrants	*Avg. monthly HH income of intra-state migrants (Rs.)*	*Avg. monthly HH income of inter-state migrants (Rs.)*
Less than 5 years	6,430	4,800
5 - 14 years	7,265	7,705
15 - 30 years	8,100	11,355
More than 30 years	7,435	7,055
Average	7,625	8,395

Note: The survey was carried out in May-June 2012.
Source: Primary Survey.

Table 2.14: Average monthly household and per capita incomes, Rajkot

Settlement	*Household income*				*Per capita income*		
	Average per month in Rs.			*Ratio of tenant to owner*	*Average per month in Rs.*		*Ratio of tenant to owner*
	All	*Owners*	*Tenants*		*Owners*	*Tenants*	
Kubaliyapara	7,100	7,850	5,300	0.68	1,266	1,205	0.95
Khodiyarpara	7,820	7,680	8,335	1.09	1,477	2,381	1.61
Rukhadiyapara	7,115	7,345	6,350	0.86	1,440	1,351	0.94
Lohanagar	6,530	6,845	5,770	0.84	1,070	1,110	1.04
Chhotunagar	5,635	6,035	4,800	0.80	1,118	1,143	1.02
Amarnagar	11,190	11,965	7,915	0.66	1,899	2,139	1.13
Shreenathji society	8,500	9,025	7,420	0.82	1,671	1,855	1.11
Total	7,670	8,110	6,555	0.81	1,448	1,561	1.08

Note: The survey was carried out in May-June 2012.
Source: Primary Survey.

It is seen that owners have higher monthly household income (Rs. 8,110) than the tenants (Rs. 6,555), resulting in tenant's household income ratio to be 81 per cent of the owner's (Table 2.14). This is the case in all the settlements except Khodiyarpara, where the per capita incomes of the tenant households are higher by 8 per cent than the owners, which is on account of lower household size. As explained earlier, many of the tenant households are not a family and instead comprise of single-male migrants and hence they are not typical households. This needs to be kept in mind while analysing the data in Table 2.14. The average per capita income of the owner-households is Rs. 1,448 and that of the tenant-households is Rs. 1,561.

Among the owner-households, Amarnagar, which is a *suchit* society, has reported the highest average household income of around Rs. 11,965, which is 34 per cent more than the average tenant-household income in the same settlement (Table 2.14). Incomes when linked to employment show that Amarnagar has the highest proportion of the owner-households workers in the category of regular salaried employment. Unlike other settlements where the regular salaried are working in small industrial offices, the household heads in Amarnagar are employed in well-paying government and private company jobs, which explains their highest average income. Likewise is the case of the next highest salary-grossing settlement, Shreenathji society, which again is a *suchit* society, and has an average monthly income of Rs. 9,025. The owner-households with the lowest average monthly salary are in Chhotunagar, who are self-employed as vegetable vendors, scrap-collectors, etc.

Among the tenant-households, Khodiyarpara has the highest average monthly household income. This is an old, well-established industrial settlement and has the highest regular salaried workers among the tenant-households. The tenants here are in well-paid, regular salaried jobs, mostly in the nearby GIDC industries and private offices. Closely following are the tenants of Amarnagar and Shreenathji society who are mostly employed in salaried jobs. The poorest tenants are in Chhotunagar, who are largely self-employed like the owner-households. The *suchit* societies, Amarnagar and Shreenathji society have the highest per household incomes of Rs. 11,190 and Rs. 8,500 per month respectively (Table 2.14).

Saving is an important variable in understanding the socio-economic status of a household and it was found in this survey that households living in informal housing are able to save. In our sample, savings as a proportion of the total household income varies from 12 per cent to 21 per

Table 2.15: Settlement-wise average monthly income, expenditure and savings, Rajkot

Settlement	*Avg. HH expenditure (Rs.)*	*Avg. HH saving (Rs.)*	*Savings as % of income*
Kubaliyapara	5,940	1,160	16.3
Khodiyarpara	6,420	1,400	17.9
Rukhadiyapara	5,680	1,435	20.2
Lohanagar	5,720	810	12.4
Chhotunagar	4,950	685	12.2
Amarnagar	8,855	2,335	20.9
Shreenathji society	6,825	1,675	19.7

Source: Primary Survey.

cent (Table 2.15). Savings rate are highest in the *suchit* societies, Amarnagar and Shreenathji society and in Rukhadiyapara as well. In these three settlements, the proportion of income saved is about 20 per cent. Lohanagar and Chhotunagar, the two poorest settlements, have the lowest savings rate of about 12 per cent of the total household income.

Table 2.16: Average household and per capita monthly expenditure by settlement and tenure, Rajkot

Settlement	*Monthly HH expenditure*			*Monthly per capita expenditure (MPCE)*		
	Owners (Rs.)	*Tenants (Rs.)*	*Ratio of tenants to owners*	*Owners (Rs.)*	*Tenants (Rs.)*	*Ratio of tenants to owners*
Kubaliyapara	6,465	4,800	0.74	1,043	1,091	1.05
Khodiyarpara	6,495	6,165	0.95	1,249	1,761	1.41
Rukhadiyapara	5,710	5,700	1.00	1,120	1,213	1.08
Lohanagar	5,780	5,665	0.98	903	1,089	1.21
Chhotunagar	5,205	4,540	0.87	964	1,081	1.12
Amarnagar	9,325	8,000	0.86	1,480	2,162	1.46
Shreenathji society	7,085	6,280	0.89	1,312	1,570	1.20
Average	6,580	5,865	0.89	1,175	1,396	1.19

Source: Primary Survey.

The average monthly household expenditure of the surveyed owner households (Rs. 6,580) is higher than that of the surveyed tenant households (Rs. 5,865) (Table 2.16). The tenant household's monthly expenditure is 89 per cent of that of the owners. This difference is observed in all the settlements. In contrast, the Monthly Per Capita Expenditure (MPCE) is higher in the tenant-households as compared to owner-households (the ratio of tenant to owner is 1.19) because the tenants tend to send back money to their families or pay for services which are otherwise cheaply available to owners. Although there is a 19 per cent differential in the average income levels of the owners and tenants, the average expenditure difference between the two groups is only about 11 per cent. Amongst the owners, Amarnagar has the highest average expenditure per month at Rs. 9,325, while owners at Chhotunagar have reported the lowest expenditures (Rs. 5,205). Amongst the surveyed tenant households, the tenants in Amarnagar have reported the highest average monthly expenditures of Rs. 8,000, while again Chhotunagar has the lowest, at Rs. 4,540 per month.

The expenditure pattern of the tenants and the owners is somewhat different. There are two additional items in the household expenditures of the tenants, which are rent (17%) and remittances (12%) to family members. Together, these two items take up 29 per cent of the household expenditure of the tenants and hence their food expenditure's share is only 55 per cent whereas among the owners the food expenditure is 71 per cent of the total. Both owner and tenant households are engaged in similar kind of work and require similar kind of calories. It seems that the tenants are not incurring as much expenditure on food as they should, in quest for sending remittances back home. Further, the rent and remittances back home has drastically reduced expenditures on education, health and transport as compared to that by the owners. The tenants were spending 1 per cent, 3 per cent and 5 per cent of their total expenditure on education, health and transport respectively whereas the owners were spending 3 per cent, 3 per cent and 10 per cent respectively on these heads of the total household expenditure. Thus, there is also disadvantage to live as a tenant as it leads to trading-off of rents with other expenditure items.

Housing Conditions and Physical Infrastructure

The definition of housing is much wider than just a dwelling structure. Access to basic services such as water supply, sewerage system, electricity connections, roads and street lights is equally essential to lead a better quality of life. Thus alleviation of housing poverty would imply access to basic services. This section looks at the condition of physical infrastructure in these informal settlements and how the provision of basic services differs with the ownership of land and duration of stay. It will also examine the impact of provision of basic services on investment in housing.

Physical Infrastructure Status

It was found that the settlements on private lands such as Amarnagar and Shreenathji society, which are *suchit* societies, are better provided in physical services. As argued earlier, these settlements have higher perceived security, even though they do not have legal tenure, and hence the house-owners have invested in housing and physical infrastructure at the household level. Moreover, these settlements house relatively higher income groups as seen in the previous section. There is, therefore, a strong link between level of tenure security, level of services and household income. Since the households have invested in their housing and individual level infrastructure, the RMC has also extended settlement level infrastructure. Because these societies are on private lands, the RMC is unconcerned if the households perceive high tenure security and settle down permanently on them. Thus, these two settlements have the highest proportion of the households with individual water tap connections, household level toilets and legal electricity connections (Table 2.17).

Table 2.17: Settlement-wise provision of basic services, Rajkot

Settlement	*%age Households having services*		
	HH water connection	*HH level toilets*	*Legal electricity connection*
Kubaliyapara	57.4	50.8	86.9
Khodiyarpara	79.1	83.0	100.0
Rukhadiyapara	29.3	29.3	87.9
Lohanagar	51.0	19.6	90.2
Chhotunagar	5.2	14.3	92.2
Amarnagar	83.3	87.0	100.0
Shreenathji society	88.6	85.4	100.0
Average	55.2	52.6	93.8

Source: Primary Survey.

In contrast, the settlements on the government land have the lowest proportion of households with access to these individual services. In particular, the households residing in Chhotunagar, which is a squatter settlement, have very poor level of services. Majority of the households here are using community toilets and taps. Chhotunagar had the poorest condition among all the settlements because of its non-notified status. Majority of households in this settlement had to purchase water on daily basis and had the least number of household toilets. Chotunagar is followed by Rukhadiyapara, which is on railway land, in poor housing. Dwellers in settlements like Chhotunagar and Rukhadiyapara reported willingness to move out to other areas due to lack low level of tenure security and basic infrastructure.

Overall, it is seen that merely 55 per cent of the households had individual water tap connections and household level toilets. This low penetration of public amenities is due to lack of provision of basic services by the RMC to informal settlements. Also, merely 53 per cent households had individual toilet at household level. It is to be noted that the penetration of electricity connection is, however, quite high; about 94 per cent households had legal electricity connection. Although, there is low tenure security in some settlements such as Chhotunagar and Rukhadiyapara, nearly 90 per cent of their households had legal electricity connection. As mentioned earlier, payment of electricity bill is an important evidence of legal address proof and hence if the households can afford, they prefer to pay their electricity bill and secure their housing status. Thus it was found that the electricity companies have, in the last decade, extended more connections to the households in the informal settlements as the legal status of the settlement is not their concern while gaining clientele.

Duration of Stay and Infrastructure

As seen above, the duration of stay to a great extent affects the economic condition of the households. It also strongly influences the access to household level services such as water supply and toilets. Those living in the city for less than 5 years, find it hard to get household level facilities. For example, while 55 per cent of all the households had household level water connection, for those who have migrated to the city in the last 5 years, only 41 per cent had such water facility (Table 2.18). Availability of household level toilet is lowest among the recent migrants; only 34.5 per cent had this access, while for all households this figure was 52.6 per cent. Recent migrants may not have incomes to provide themselves with individual facilities at household level, but as time passes and they decide to continue living in the city, they also begin to invest in housing. However, this argument holds true only if their houses are not demolished by the authorities. If they face demolition then, they have to start afresh and their willingness to invest in basic services and incremental housing decreases. If in absence of policy on universal coverage of these facilities the households can manage these on their own, which they do, then longer a household stays in the city, the more capable they become in accessing

Table 2.18: Duration of stay *versus* provision of basic services, Rajkot

Years of stay	*%age Households having services*		
	HH water connection	*HH level toilets*	*Legal electricity connection*
Less than 5 years	41.4	34.5	96.6
5-14 years	53.3	50.7	94.7
15-30 years	55.5	57.1	96.2
More than 30 years	57.4	51.9	93.5

Source: Primary Survey.

these services on their own. This improvement in basic services with increase in duration of stay in the city indicates the absence of proactive public policy for water and sanitation provision.

Table 2.19: Income, tenure and provision of basic services, Rajkot

HH income (Rs.)	*%age Households having services*		
	HH water connection	*Having HH toilet*	*HH electricity connection*
up to 4000	39	32	90
4001-8000	53	51	95
8001-12000	66	64	98
12001-16000	74	78	98
above 16000	89	85	100
Owner	61	61	94
Tenant	39	32	96

Source: Primary Survey.

Income and Basic Services

It is tautological to state that with the increase in income, availability of household level services improves. This can be seen in Table 2.19. This again is an outcome of an absence of public policy for basic services, when the households themselves have to invest to access them. They will invest when they have the income to do so. It can also be stated that income increases with increase in duration of stay in a city.

Tenure and Basic Services

The availability of basic services at the household level for the tenants is lower in comparison to owners and the former's length of stay in the city does not improve its access to household level services. Electricity is available to nearly all households in Gujarat because of low connection charges offered by the private electricity companies to the slum households. In case of Ahmedabad, a few NGOs had collectively advocated for the private company to lower connection charges, which it did, resulting in increased coverage of the slum areas with regard to electricity (Joshi *et al.*, 2010). Except electricity, in case of all other services, access is lower for the tenant households than the owner households. For example, 39 per cent households had access to individual water supply and 32 per cent access to individual toilet among the tenants whereas among the owners the proportion was 61 per cent for both services (Table 2.19). Thus, the tenants have to live with poorer access to basic infrastructure in comparison to the owners.

Table 2.20: Source of water by settlements and tenure (%) , Rajkot

Settlement	*Owners*			*Tenants*		
	HH connection	*Community tap*	*Purchased*	*HH connection*	*Community tap*	*Purchased*
Kubaliyapara	63	37	0	44	56	0
Khodiyarpara	97	3	0	27	73	0
Rukhadiyapara	30	70	0	26	74	0
Lohanagar	64	36	0	20	80	0
Chhotunagar	6	50	44	4	48	48
Amarnagar	89	11	0	60	40	0
Shreenathji society	96	4	0	73	28	0
Total	61	32	6	39	52	8

Source: Primary Survey.

Since household level water connection is available to only 61 per cent of the owners, 32 per cent of them use community tap and 6 per cent purchase water (Table 2.20). Purchasing water is observed only in Chhotunagar, where 44 per cent of owners and 48 per cent of tenants purchased water every week, as the RMC has not provided this settlement with any basic services. Thus, the residents of this settlement were the worst-placed in access to water supply and the poor service provision impacted both, the owners as well as tenants. The owners of the rental units are not able to charge higher rents in Chhotunagar. All the residents have to spend on buying water along with incurring expenditures on house rent and fixed electricity charges. This proves that the formal recognition, in other words, notification of a settlement by the local authority is important even in the low-income informal settlements for the owners to realise higher rents and tenants to obtain affordable shelter.

Among the tenants, 39 per cent of the surveyed households reported household level tap connection, and the remaining households depend on community taps (52%) and purchased water (8%). Dependence on community taps is higher among the tenants as compared to owners. Same is the case with regard to purchasing water, more proportion of tenants are forced to purchase water as compared to owners. Amarnagar and Shreenathji society, two *suchit* societies, fared better for the tenants in our survey, due to their recognition by the RMC and public services provision. These two settlements, along with Khodiyarpara, fared better even amongst the owners.

Provision for sanitation was found to be very poor in the informal settlements of Rajkot. Overall, 14 per cent owners and 18 per cent tenants reported defecating in the open as they did not have access to any type of toilet (Table 2.21). In Lohanagar, none of the tenants had household sanitation facilities, while in Chhotunagar only 4 per cent households had access to individual toilet. Amongst the tenant households Kubaliyapara reported the highest case of open defecation (22%). This can be explained by the fact that it was located adjoining the Aji River and was not notified by the RMC and hence the settlement does not have sanitation services. Most people tend to go to the river for their needs. Tenants in Amarnagar and Shreenathji society, the *suchit* societies, reported the maximum household level toilets. Use of community toilet was higher (51%) among the tenants as compared to among the owners (25%). In all settlements, proportion of households having individual toilet was higher among the owners as compared to the tenants. Hence, proportion of households using community toilets and defecating in the open was higher among the tenants as compared to the owners.

Table 2.21: Type of toilet by settlements and tenure (per cent), Rajkot

Settlement	*Owners*			*Tenants*		
	HH toilet	*Community toilet*	*None*	*HH toilet*	*Community toilet*	*None*
Kubaliyapara	56	33	12	39	39	22
Khodiyarpara	100	0	0	36	45	18
Rukhadiyapara	32	13	55	22	4	74
Lohanagar	28	69	3	0	87	13
Chhotunagar	19	77	4	4	96	0
Amarnagar	95	5	0	60	40	0
Shreenathji society	100	0	0	55	45	0
Total	61	25	14	32	51	18

Source: Primary Survey.

Majority of the households of both tenants as well as owners, have electricity connections. However, individual connection among the owners is 90 per cent whereas among the tenants it is 53 per cent (Table 2.22). Thus, a very large proportion, which is 45 per cent of the tenants reported borrowing electricity as compared to only 7 per cent among the owners. Typically, the tenants use the connection of the owner and hence borrow from them or from their neighbours. As seen earlier, some of the rental units are adjacent to that of the owners and in such cases the owners are the neighbours of the tenants. *Suchit* societies have good electricity connection and hence while the owners have universal access, the large proportion of tenants (70% in Shreenathji society and 50% in Amarnagar) also have individual connection. Lohanagar reported the lowest individual connections (only 40%) among tenant households. Khodiyarnagar tenants reported the highest borrowing of electricity (82% households), followed by 60 per cent tenant households of Lohanagar. In case of borrowed electricity, tenants either pay their share of electricity bill to the owner or their rent includes the component of electricity bill. It was reported in Chhotunagar that fixed electricity charge was taken from the tenants by the owners for electricity. The fixed rate was Rs. 200 per month, irrespective of the actual usage.

Table 2.22: Type of electricity connection by settlements and tenure (per cent), Rajkot

Settlement	*Owners*			*Tenants*		
	Legal HH connection	*Borrowed*	*Illegal*	*Legal HH connection*	*Borrowed*	*Illegal*
Kubaliyapara	85	8	8	53	40	7
Khodiyarpara	100	0	0	9	82	9
Rukhadiyapara	79	9	12	62	38	0
Lohanagar	82	18	0	40	60	0
Chhotunagar	83	17	0	44	52	4
Amarnagar	100	0	0	50	50	0
Shreenathji society	99	1	0	70	30	0
Total	90	7	3	53	45	2

Source: Primary Survey.

Housing Condition—Overall

Undoubtedly, Amarnagar and Shreenathji society have the best living conditions amongst all the settlements, with the largest carpet area of 41 sq.mt. and 35 sq.mt. respectively and per capita carpet area of 7.2 sq.mt. and 7.0 sq.mt. respectively (Table 2.23). These two settlements also have the highest average rooms per household. In contrast, Lohanagar followed by Chhotunagar and Rukhadiyapara are the worst, with total carpet area of 24 sq.mt. and per capita carpet area of 4.0 sq.mt., 4.7 sq.mt. and 4.7 sq.mt. respectively. Those having large carpet area also have large plot size. The main explanation of dwelling unit size is the household income. Thus, *suchit* societies have large houses and large per capita dwelling unit space whereas the squatter settlements of Chhotunagar and Lohanagar have small dwelling units and the least per capita dwelling space.

Table 2.23: Settlement-wise dwelling unit size, Rajkot

Settlement	*Average no. of rooms per hh*	*Avg. carpet area (sq.mt.)*	*Avg. plot area (sq.mt.)*	*Per capita carpet area (sq.mt.)*
Kubaliyapara	1.9	33	39	5.8
Khodiyarpara	1.9	31	50	6.6
Rukhadiyapara	1.7	24	33	4.7
Lohanagar	1.5	24	28	4.0
Chhotunagar	1.6	24	31	4.7
Amarnagar	2.5	41	57	7.2
Shreenathji society	2.1	35	47	7.0
Average	1.9	30	41	5.7

Source: Primary Survey.

Table 2.24: Duration of stay and per capita area, Rajkot

Years of stay	*Avg. HH carpet area (sq.mt.)*	*Avg. per capita area (sq.mt.)*
Less than 5 years	18	5.0
5 - 14 years	23	5.7
15 - 30 years	33	6.9
More than 30 years	32	6.5

Source: Primary Survey.

Duration of stay has a strong positive link with the dwelling unit size much in the same way as it is linked to economic situation and physical infrastructure. With the increase in duration of stay, household's economic condition improves. If the settlement has relatively high security of tenure, it leads to investments in housing and infrastructure. This can be seen in Table 2.24, where the average dwelling unit size is just 18 sq.mt. for a recent migrant household, which doubles when the household stays for more than 15 years in the city. It is not just the dwelling unit size that increases but even per capita dwelling space that increases.

Dwelling unit size and per capita living space increases with income. However, in the following Table 2.25, the households with less than

Rs. 4,000 monthly income have larger per capita living space on account of small household size. When the household income increases four times, the total dwelling unit size increase 2.5 times (Table 2.25).

Table 2.25: Settlement-wise dwelling unit size, Rajkot

HH income (Rs.)	*Avg. HH carpet area (sq.mt.)*	*Avg. per capita area (sq.mt.)*
Up to 4000	22	6.8
4001-8000	28	6.2
8001-12000	36	6.4
12001-16000	36	6.1
Above 16000	53	7.0

Source: Primary Survey.

Tenure and Area

There is no differentiation among the rental and owned housing in the settlements that were studied in terms of their quality of housing. However, we find significant difference between the two groups in terms of size of housing (Table 2.26). The owners, on an average, have double the built-up area and more than double the plot area than that of the tenant. For example, the average built-up area of a house where the owners live is 35 sq.mt. whereas that of the tenants' house is 18 sq.mt. Hence, tenants live in smaller housing and overcrowded conditions. The per capita built up for owners is 6.3 sq.mt. whereas that for the tenants is 4.2 sq.mt. (Table 2.26). In fact, in Khodiyarpara, the built up area of a dwelling unit of the tenants is, on an average, just 37 per cent of that of the owners. The inequality between the tenants and the owners is further larger with regard to the plot area. Dwelling units rented by single-male migrants and poorer migrants families are single rooms.

Owners have added additional rooms to their houses and the average number of rooms per dwelling unit is 2.2 for them. In case of tenants, the average rooms per household is just 1.2, which means that some of the tenants have an extra room, whereas most of them live in one room unit, as already mentioned above.

Affordability of the Tenants

Housing affordability is directly a function of household income and house

Table 2.26: Dwelling unit size by tenure and settlement

Settlement	*Average built-up area per household (sq.mt.)*			*Average plot area (sq.mt.)*			*Average no. of rooms per house*			*Per capita built-up (sq.mt.)*		
	Owner	*Tenant*	*Ratio of tenants to owners*	*Owner*	*Tenant*	*Ratio of tenants to owners*	*Owner*	*Tenant*	*Ratio of tenants to owners*	*Owner*	*Tenant*	*Ratio of tenants to owners*
Kubaliyapara	37.0	22.0	0.59	47.0	23.0	0.49	2.3	1.1	0.48	6.0	5.0	0.84
Khodiyarpara	38.0	14.0	0.37	64.0	14.0	0.22	2.3	1.0	0.43	7.3	4.0	0.55
Rukhadiyapara	25.0	20.0	0.80	35.0	27.0	0.77	1.8	1.3	0.72	4.9	4.3	0.87
Lohanagar	29.0	14.0	0.48	33.0	16.0	0.48	1.7	1.2	0.71	4.5	2.7	0.59
Chhotunagar	28.0	15.0	0.54	36.0	19.0	0.53	1.8	1.2	0.67	5.2	3.6	0.69
Amarnagar	47.0	19.0	0.40	68.0	22.0	0.32	2.9	1.2	0.41	7.5	5.1	0.69
Shreenathji society	43.0	19.0	0.44	59.0	23.0	0.39	2.5	1.3	0.52	8.0	4.8	0.60
Average	35.3	17.6	0.50	48.9	20.6	0.42	2.2	1.2	0.55	6.3	4.2	0.66

Source: Primary Survey.

prices in the market. Those who cannot afford formal housing tend to look for an option in the informal housing, where also, income determines the affordability. The low income migrants, who are unable to arrange funds for down payment for purchasing a house, even in the informal sector, tend to live in rental housing. Among those living in rental housing, the ones who cannot afford to pay high rents tend to share a dwelling unit. At the same time, those not intending to stay back in the city also stay in rental housing and the poorer among them tend to share a dwelling unit. Those living as single-male migrants also tend to rent, either an individual dwelling unit or a shared one. In this section we analyse the housing affordability of the tenant-households, which is measured as proportion of income spent on rent.

Table 2.27: Housing affordability, tenants, Rajkot

Income range (Rs.)	*Avg. rent paid (Rs.)*	*Rent as per cent of income*
Up to 4,000	815	40.8
4,001-8,000	1,020	17.0
8,001-12,000	1,245	12.5
Above 12,000	1,340	11.2

Source: Primary Survey.

The average rent paid increases with the income. The households with monthly income of up to Rs. 4,000 paid average monthly rent of Rs. 815 and those above Rs. 12,000 monthly income, paid average monthly rent of Rs. 1,340 (Table 2.27). However, as a proportion of household income, those with monthly income up to Rs. 4,000 spend 41 per cent as rent and those with monthly income above Rs. 12,000 per month spend only 11 per cent of their income on housing. Proportion of income spent on rent declines with increase in income indicating that this is an inelastic expenditure. Consequently, there is also a case for subsidising housing for the urban poor.

Availability (or non-availability) of individual services was to some extent linked to the rent per sq.mt. of area. For example, in Amarnagar, the rent rate was Rs. 78 per sq.mt., and had the largest proportion of households with individual water supply and toilet connection (both figures are 60%) (Table 2.28). Same was true for Shreenathji society. But Kubaliyapara, which had the lowest rate of rent, did not have lowest level of access to individual services. Kubaliyapara is better placed than other surveyed settlements which have higher rents but lower levels of

Table 2.28: Rent rate and availability of household-level facilities, Rajkot

Settlement	*Rent per sq. mt. (Rs.)*	*HH level water connections (%)*	*HH Toilet (%)*	*HH electricity connection (%)*
Kubaliyapara	30	44	39	53
Khodiyarpara	59	27	36	9
Rukhadiyapara	48	26	22	62
Lohanagar	64	20	0	40
Chhotunagar	49	4	4	44
Amarnagar	78	60	60	50
Shreenathji society	72	73	55	70
Average	56	39	32	53

Source: Primary Survey.

facilities, like Rukhadiyapara, Khodiyarpara and Chhotunagar. Also, Chhotunagar is the worst placed in terms of availability of water and toilets at the household level, while the average rent in the settlement is higher than the rents paid in Kubaliyapara and Rukhadiyapara. Lohanagar residents prefer to pay higher rent on account of its nearness to the industrial area, as its location would reduce their daily commuting expenses. But, their access to services is poor (Table 2.28). Thus, other than the level of services in a dwelling unit, locational factors such as closeness to place of work and commercial use of areas have also influenced determination of the rent rates.

Housing Mobility

Housing mobility by definition means movement of residents from one house to another or from one neighbourhood to another. The high rate of mobility is not only driven by economic mobility (increase in affordability) but also due to housing insecurity or need for secure tenure. Table 2.29 shows that nearly 56 per cent of the households surveyed had shifted their residence. Maximum mobility was found in Khodiyarpara (%) followed by Shreenathji society (69%) and Amarnagar (56%). The reason behind higher mobility rate in the latter two settlements could be due to higher tenure security levels in them as already discussed. Mobility in Khodiyarpara is on account of land use conversions as discussed before.

Table 2.29 also gives reasons for the housing mobility, which shows that overall 37 per cent of the residents in these settlements had shifted to

Table 2.29: Housing mobility and reasons for shifting, Rajkot

Settlement	*% HH shifted*	*Reasons for shifting house (%)*					
		Larger house	*Cheaper*	*Closer to work*	*Increase in affordability*	*Had to vacate*	*Other*
Kubaliyapara	44.3	11.1	14.8	11.1	18.5	18.5	25.9
Khodiyarpara	79.1	17.6	5.9	14.7	26.5	17.6	17.6
Rukhadiyapara	45.5	2.2	15.6	4.4	37.8	11.1	28.9
Lohanagar	49.0	12.0	0.0	12.0	16.0	16.0	44.0
Chhotunagar	48.1	10.8	16.2	21.6	18.9	2.7	29.7
Amarnagar	56.3	11.1	11.1	0.0	25.9	18.5	33.3
Shreenathji society	69.1	18.8	7.1	16.5	22.4	15.3	20.0
Total	55.8	12.9	10.0	12.5	24.3	13.9	26.4

Source: Primary Survey.

their present location due to increase in their affordability or need for a larger dwelling size; in contrast to the 10 per cent residents who had shifted to a cheaper accommodation due to lack of affordability. Also, nearly 14 per cent of the residents had to vacate possibly on the demand of the owners to empty the house.

In case of Khodiyarnagar and Amarnagar (the industrial settlements), because of increasing property values, residences were converted into small commercial or industrial workshops. This led to a large number of tenants vacating their present house and to search for new housing. About 14 per cent stated that they had to vacate their earlier house under pressure.

Conclusion

This chapter on Rajkot's informal housing describes variety of ways through which such housing comes up; experience changes in status and security, and provides the low and even middle income households with access to housing. This is the normal way of life of the poorer people in the city. They choose where to stay depending on their employment and affordability. They trade-off closeness to employment to quality of housing, they also trade-off housing expenditures with savings and sending remittances back to their home villages/towns. A mid-sized metro such as Rajkot caters to the regional economy while also attracting long distance migrants. The regional migrants prefer to settle down in Rajkot and be part of the transition process to urbanization. The long distance migrants, in particular from the states in North India, prefer to return back to their native places and do not intend to invest in housing in the city. Housing mobility is linked to the economic mobility of the households. State intervention is minimal in this welfare space and at best the local state has extended them basic services if these settlements are not on lands belonging to the former. In case the settlements are on the lands belonging to the local state, the slum is vulnerable to eviction. Informal settlements' dwellers, in spite of all these odds tend to invest in housing as soon as there is a somewhat increased perception of tenure security. They invest to earn from housing and themselves become small landlords and providers of housing. The process is dynamic and is hard to be captured within any models that have been developed, for example the Turner model of housing mobility. In such a scenario, the best policy option is for the local state to facilitate such households for improving their living conditions and the key to that is by improving their tenure security.

Annexure 2.1

Ward-wise Number of Slum Details

Ward number	*Number of slums*	*Number of slum households*	*Slum population*
1	2	746	4,208
2	2	192	1,083
3	10	1806	10,186
4	3	326	1,838
5	7	4,088	23,057
6	7	1,345	7,586
7	15	2,143	12,087
8	0	0	0
9	4	524	2,955
10	16	2,142	12,082
11	6	511	12,082
12	3	787	2,883
13	10	958	4,439
14	7	1,328	5,403
15	2	230	7,489
16	6	2,388	1,297
17	18	4,320	13,468
18	10	2,572	24,365
19	13	4,414	14,506
20	19	3,111	24,864
21	13	3,457	17,548
22	4	956	5,392
23	11	4,241	23,918
Total	188	42,585	240,179

Source: RMC, based on HH slum Survey.

NOTES

1. This study was undertaken through the funding of the MoHUPA under their funding given to the National Resource Centres in 2009-10. We will like to acknowledge the contribution of Abhijit Datey, Kaushal Jajoo in fieldwork and data analysis and Tejas Patel and Vishal Darji in making of maps and other graphic materials in the text.
2. Our gratitude to the officials of the RMC in facilitating this study. We would like to thank the then Commissioner of the RMC, Mr. Ajay Bhadoo and the town planning officers, Mr. Rupani and Mitesh Joshi.
3. Population Census, 2001.
4. *Ibid.*
5. Notified slums are those which have been acknowledged/notified for the provision of basic services.

3
Informal Housing—Surat[1]

Darshini Mahadevia and *Pooja Shah*

This chapter presents an infrequent case of welfare extension by the local state in improving the living conditions of the urban poor in the city of Surat through qualitative analyses. Firstly, Surat city with its geography, demography, economic history and its current importance in the Indian economy have been discussed. Thereafter, overall slum and land tenure situation in Surat have been presented. The field study is presented in two parts—the first part deals with the eight selected slums for the study in Varachha ward and the second part includes case studies and interviews of slum and pavement dwellers from different parts of the city. The chapter attempts to illustrate that there is diversity in the housing needs of the low-income segment of urban population. It also argues that there is one single important intervention that will change the lives of those at the bottom-end of the urban population; this is, if the basic services are provided by the local authorities, slum dwellers are willing to invest in their houses to improve their standard of life and try to come out of the vicious circle of poverty. The chapter also raises the concern about housing needs of the seasonal workers in a high growth city, whose economic progress is based on these workers. Wherever possible, the 2011 population census data has been used.

Introducing Surat

Surat is situated on the bank of River Tapi, which is one of the perennial rivers of South Gujarat. It is one of the oldest mercantile centres of Gujarat, which first developed as a factory (trading) town of the British in the 17th century on account of its coastal location on the mouth of a delta. The city has about 6 kilometres long coastal belt along the Arabian Sea.

The importance of the city declined after the British developed Mumbai as their base. However, the city gained prominence in Gujarat again when it emerged as a manufacturing hub of the State post 1960, when Gujarat was formed as a separate State. It is also known as Silk city, Diamond city and after the epidemic of September 1994, as Plague City. After the incidence of plague, within two years Surat transformed from one of the filthiest cities to the second cleanest city in the country, as claimed by the media reports. This, however, was not evident during our fieldwork.

The city has many advantages due to its location; it is located midway on the 500 kilometres long Ahmedabad-Mumbai Western Railway corridor; large natural gas reserves have been found in a region 50 kilometres to the north of the city; as many as, 40 express, mail and passenger trains pass through it; National Highway No. 8, which is one of the busiest inter-state trunk routes in the country, passes within 16 kms of the Surat Municipal Corporation (SMC) boundary and the city is a pivotal centre on the Ahmedabad-Mumbai regional corridor. There is a 225 kilometres long industrial belt, starting from Vapi in south Gujarat to Mehsana in north Gujarat and Surat is at the centre of it. It will also fall within the upcoming Delhi-Mumbai Industrial Corridor (DMIC), funded through Japanese investment.

The Shrunken Glory—From International to Dickensian City

Surat used to be an eminent port of the country in the 16th, 17th and 18th centuries. Ships docking at Surat port had their country's flags flying on the harbour and there was a time when flags of 84 countries could be observed at her port. Muslim pilgrims from all over India used Surat port for their journey to Mecca for *Hajj*[2]. Traders from many countries came here to purchase garments, spices, art pieces etc., and thus Surat was an important international trading port. This is the reason why British, French, Danish and Portuguese people made their warehouses in Surat.

One of the key commodities exported from Surat was textiles. In the 19th century, when Europe started to produce her own cloth for which they could not find markets, they restricted the import of textiles from India. Thus, the exports from Surat port declined and the importance of the city as a port begun to diminish. There were other reasons as well like flood, fire and insolvency of Arabian traders which were responsible for decline in the fame of Surat. The development of Mumbai as a port city, finally led to shifting out of the trade and businesses from the city and hence led to decline of the city as an economic hub of India.

After the decline of business at Surat port, as discussed above, the entrepreneurs of Surat started looking for other options for economic revitalisation through technological modernisation. One such first attempt was in modernisation textiles, through setting up of the first textile mill in the city in 1861. The city shifted from manufacturing fabric in the home-looms to a modern textile mill. While this change was underway, the city revived its traditional industry of brocade (*zari*)[3], a hand-woven fabric with silver and golden threads embedded in the weave. The *zari* industry was modernised in 1960s through import of machinery from abroad. Later manufacturing of machinery for *zari* also started in Surat, which continues till today. Thus from 1800 to 1947 there were two major industries in Surat, textile and *zari*. During the British rule in India, the market of *zari* declined because even France started manufacturing brocade textiles which were moderately cheaper than that of Surat. Surat's brocade was out of real gold and silver. After the fall of demand in *zari* market, the workers of this industry stared making brocade textiles out of copper. After this change, Surat again captured the market.

After independence, since the small-scale industries are employment-intensive, the Second Five Year Plan of the Government of India (GoI) provided a key role to village and small-scale industries. The Central and State governments extended a number of fiscal incentives for the growth of small scale industries. On the basis of recommendations of the Textile Enquiry Committee (1954), a programme of conversion of the ordinary looms into improved semi-automatic looms or into decentralised power-looms was encouraged. The weavers of Surat began to take advantage of these incentives and replaced handlooms with power-looms. Like elsewhere, in the initial stage, the growth of power-looms was slow. It was confined to traditional weavers. With government support and credit facilities from banks, others entered the industry. The number of looms increased from 8,105 in 1960 to 19,025 in 1970 with a growth rate of nearly 14 per cent per year (Shah, 1997). Bank nationalisation in the year 1969, further opened avenues for getting bank finance, which led to expansion of small-scale industries in the city. The State government had set up industrial estates by that time, namely the *Udhana Udhyog Nagar* (Udhana Industrial Hub) in Udhana ward in the south zone of the city and Katargam, Sachin and Pandesara in the periphery of the city in the 1960s after the formation of Gujarat State and the Government of Gujarat's (GoG's) thrust towards industrialisation and economic growth. A year-long textile workers' strike in Mumbai in 1982 provided further push to the power-loom industry in Surat. With the expansion of power-looms, the processing industry also developed. Though many of the textile processing units were established in Ahmedabad and Mumbai, Surat also attracted entrepreneurs and workers in for textile processing.

Another important addition to the industrial activity of the city since the 1950s is the diamond and polishing industry. Surat is one of the world's largest centres for diamond polishing. The foundation of the industry in the region which had difficulties in raw material, markets and labour, and majority of the entrepreneurs were from outside the city, is a significant feat. Initially, the industry started as an initiative of few individuals belonging to a particular community which has now expanded to large section of society. Under the Import Replenishment Scheme introduced by the GoI in 1958, diamond traders were allowed to import roughs from the Diamond Trading Corporation, London and other sources abroad and export cut and polished diamonds. Additional support came from the encouragement offered to small-scale industries during this time. By the late 1950s, about 100 diamond cutting and polishing units had been set up[4]. Together with the ease of establishing small-scale industries and various government policies which aimed at increasing the export of polished diamonds helped the growth of such units in the city. Barring a few big units which have recently come up, diamond cutting and processing was also confined to small enterprises. Even now a majority of the diamond processing units are in the small sector.

The city has made a key position in the national economy and world diamond and textile business. The textile and diamond units of Surat region contribute to[5]:

- 42 per cent of the world's total rough diamond cutting and polishing.
- 70 per cent of the nation's total rough diamond cutting and polishing.
- 40 per cent of the nation's total diamond exports.
- 40 per cent of the nation's total man made fabric production.
- 28 per cent of the nation's total manmade fibre production.
- 18 per cent of the nation's total manmade fibre export.
- 12 per cent of the nation's total fabric production.

Hazira, an area 20 kilometres from Surat city across the river Tapi, was like any other village till a few years ago. Hazira Area Development Authority (HADA) was constituted in 1985 under Gujarat Town Planning and Area Development Act of 1976 for planned industrial development.

Nine villages, Hazira, Sunvali, Rajgari, Mora, Bhatlai, Damka, Vansva, Kavas and Limla, spread over 86 square kilometres come under HADA's jurisdiction. Seeing the potential of industrial development in the region due to easy availability of natural gas and proximity to the coast, the State government decided to develop it as an industrial zone. Hazira is now one of the major multi-cargo ports of India. After the economic reforms in India in 1991, with the liberalisation policy, Surat has been very successful in attracting a sizable amount of Foreign Direct Investment (FDI) in various sectors like energy, oil and petroleum. Hazira has mega industrial units. Massive investments have led to inflow of migrant labour to the city, particularly in the construction sector. The level of unemployment is low. However, the wages are also low and the workers are generally deprived of social and other benefits.

Not only within the state of Gujarat, but also at the all India level, Surat has registered high population growth. Surat is Gujarat's second and India's twelfth most populous city. From 0.47 million in 1971 its population increased to 1.48 million in 1991 and almost doubled to 2.8 million in 2001 which has reached to 4.4 million in the year 2011. An outstanding decadal population growth rate of 83.3 per cent was registered in 2001-2011. The literacy rate has gone up from 63 per cent in 1991 to 82 per cent in 2001 to 89 per cent in 2011 and the figures are well above that of the state and the country. The male and female literacy rate of Surat in the year 2011 is 93 per cent and 84 per cent respectively. There is a large migration of single-male migrants into the city for employment and hence the sex ratio in the city is significantly low at 758 as compared to the state and the national average in the year 2011. The sex ratio of the city is constantly declining from 839 in 1991 to 764 in 2001 to 758 in the recent years.

The city's population growth is on account of the migration of industrial workers, particularly in the small-scale sector. The power-loom industry has the maximum number of migrant workers from other states of India, while the workers in diamond industries are by and large from within the state. It is estimated that the total migrants formed 58 per cent of the total population of the city in 1991 and in the slums this proportion was 80 per cent (Swamy, Vyas and Narang, 1997). Migrants are mainly from the adjoining state of Maharashtra and then from Orissa, Uttar Pradesh and Bihar. Since the foundation of Surat Urban Development Authority (SUDA) in late 1970s, the city is growing at a fast pace; though the development in the peripheral areas was not that rapid until 2001. Decadal population growth rate in 1991-2001, did not result in the urban sprawl; on the contrary, it resulted into densification of the core city areas, which were already part of the municipal corporation. With this the municipal area in Surat reached a density of 8,812 persons per square kilometre in 2001 to 13,666 persons per square kilometre in the year 2011. It is believed that the future development will take place outside the municipal limits in the urban development authority areas. Surat as a district reports second highest level of urbanisation in Gujarat (at 79.68%) after Ahmedabad district (84.05%) in Census 2011. However, the rate of urbanisation in Surat district (5.17%) is higher than that of Ahmedabad district (2.65%) in last decade (2001-2011).

Slums and Tenure Situation in Surat

The word slum gives a negative connotation depicted by the images of filth, misery, non-tax paying residents, etc. But, realistically, slums are the housing solutions dwellers themselves have found in response to the state's as well as market's failures in providing the same and that the slums and their dwellers are integral part of the urban system. They contribute significantly to the urban economy through their labour market contributions and informal production activities. The poor represent an extremely important section of the urban labour force and contribute substantially to total productivity and labour market competitiveness. In Surat, the poor migrants and slum dwellers contribute immensely in running lucrative industries like that of diamond and power-looms.

The SMC area is divided into seven zones; viz central, north, south, east, west, south-west and south-east. The maximum slums are in the zones where industries are located. These zones are south-east, where 31.5 per cent households are living in slums, west (22.0%) and south zone (20.1%) (Table 3.1). There are a total of 322 slums in the SMC limit out of which 71 slums are located on Central or State Government lands, 106 slums are on private lands and 145 slums are situated on municipal land (Table 3.2). Thus, a one-third of the slums are on private lands while 22 per cent are on the state government lands where the problems of giving land tenure would be higher than giving tenure to slums on the SMC lands.

Of the total households in the city, 14.4 per cent live in the slums and comprise 17.2 per cent of the city's total population. Of the total slum dwellers, about 80 per cent are migrants; 81 per cent are Hindus and 18 per cent are Muslims. Hindus live mostly in the north-east and south-west. Muslims live mostly in the north-west and east. Small proportion

Table 3.1: Slums in Surat, 2005-06[6]

Zone	*Area (in sq. km.)*	*% population in slums*	*% households in slums*
Central	8.1	7.8	6.0
North	36.4	6.8	6.9
East	37.5	9.6	9.3
West	51.3	24.0	22.0
South	61.8	23.5	20.1
South-west	111.9	17.3	13.5
South-east	19.5	39.7	31.5
Total	326.4	17.2	14.4

Source: SMC.

of slum dwellers are Buddhists, who are concentrated in five slum pockets in the east zone. Forty-one per cent of slum dwellers live in the Udhna-Pandesara industrial area. Of the total slum dwellers, 11 per cent belong to higher castes, of which 47 per cent live in the south-eastern industrial area; 9 per cent are tribals from Dangs district and other parts of Surat district, of which as many as 75 per cent live in the south-east and east. About 20 per cent are Gujarati speaking and 19 per cent speak Hindi (Das, 2006).

Table 3.2: Land ownership in slums, Surat

Zone	*Ownership of Land*		
	Government	*Private*	*SMC*
Central	7	11	7
North	15	14	23
East	5	15	37
West	20	4	16
South	6	31	9
South-west	10	2	13
South-east	8	29	40
Total	71	106	145
% of total slums	22	33	45

Source: SMC, Slum survey 2005-2006.

Generally, when the poor migrants come to a city, their first abode is any footpath, vacant lands along a railway track or in industrial area of the city periphery where they can easily squat upon. Gradually, when the migrants get familiar with the city and get a source of livelihood, they go in for a rented dwelling in an already established slum or continue to live as squatters. With time, the squatter shack is upgraded and as more migrants squat around them, a slum is formed.

We see similar processes in Surat. The poorest migrants from different parts of the country who have come to Surat in search of some casual labour, generally squat upon the pavements. Some of them continued to live on the footpath, till the SMC evicted them to widen the roads. Even if some of them have been evicted occasionally, they return to the same spot if there is no development on the evicted space or in absence of any alternative. This process of attrition goes on till a slum is formed on both sides of the road. These dwellers throughout their life span live without any amenities which is the right of any citizen. The pavement dwellers are, therefore, the least secure residents of the city. But, in the recent years, those evicted are being provided a subsidised public housing, constructed under the Basic Services for the Urban Poor (BSUP) of the Jawaharlal Nehru National Urban Renewal Mission (JNNURM). The same is the situation along the railway tracks. But, they do not get evicted as easily as the pavement dwellers.

The slums within city limits generally start as squatter settlement on vacant plots. These plots generally belong to the ULB, state government, or a charity trust. There are slums also on the private lands, but, they largely develop through informal sub-plotting by the owner or a developer. In Surat, the SMC has provided water supply and sewage services to most of these slums. The slum dwellers have built toilets in their homes according to their affordability. In some of the settlements, NGO like Mahila Housing SEWA Trust (MHT) has helped slum dwellers to construct common toilets in the slum.

Table 3.3: Zone-wise housing condition in slums of Surat

Zone	*Housing Condition in slums in percentage*		
	Pucca	*Semi-pucca*	*Katcha*
Central	10.2	12.3	77.5
North	5.8	38.3	55.8
East	12.4	16.6	71.1
West	6.5	43.1	50.2
South	15.5	15.9	68.5
South-west	24.4	30.3	45.3
South-east	10.0	40.5	49.5
Total	12.1	29.0	58.8

Source: SMC, Slum Survey 2005-2006.

The existing housing condition in the slums in Surat city is pitiable; overall only 12 per cent houses are *pucca* (Table 3.3). South-west zone has 24.4 per cent *pucca* houses and 30.3 per cent semi-*pucca* houses because many of the slums in these zones are now being considered as socially and economically weaker societies about which detailed explanation has been given later in this section. In all other zones, majority houses are *katcha*, of which maximum are concentrated in the central zone (77.5%) and eastern zone (71%) of the city (Table 3.3).

Some slums have been demolished in the city and there is a plan to demolish 69 more slums (Table 3.4) to implement infrastructure projects such as road widening, bridges, other transport projects etc. Generally, the rehabilitation provided is on the periphery of the city. There are cases that the SMC has rehabilitated the slum dwellers on the lands reserved for the Economically Weaker Section (EWS) in the city plans. On completion of the BSUP Dwelling Units (DUs) about 20,000 households would be shifted in them. Rehabilitation leads to improvement in shelter security as well as quality of dwelling unit and basic infrastructure than before. SMC has listed out some of the slums for eviction (Table 3.4), and these dwellers could be rehabilitated in the BSUP houses.

Table 3.4: Slums to be displaced by SMC

Zone	*Total No. of Slums*	*Slums to be displaced*	*Total households to be displaced*	*Total population to be displaced*
West	44	17	7,986	47,873
Central	30	12	2,594	11,653
North	40	7	1,020	5,017
East	58	22	6,617	32,628
South-east	75	11	4,448	27,752
South-west	55	0	0	0
South	25	0	0	0
Total	327	69	22,665	124,923

Source: SMC, 2008.

Slums come up on the urban periphery because as a city sprawls, which is the case with Surat, the land on the city periphery does not get Non-Agricultural (NA) use permission or the land is under any reservation and the owner does not get the benefit of selling the land at a higher price. Thus illegal selling of the land takes place through the local actors.

These actors are called 'land agents' in the local parlance. These land agents divide the land into small plots and sell or rent it to the newly arrived migrants or other low-income people who want to own a house. The documents available with these residents are stamp papers on which the sale agreement has been signed. This document is about the money transaction; it is not about the land plot ownership. The land ownership document is *7-12 utara* (a 7/12 form), which has the name or names of the past and current owners and the tenant cultivators holding rights over it. To own a plot of land means to get one's name entered into this document. The informal land transactions do not involve the buyers' name being registered in this document. Sometimes, after selling the land the agents of the informal land developers would collect rent from the residents. These settlements are not considered as slums, but they are, named 'Socially and Economically Weaker Section (SEWS) colonies'. A case study of one such SEWS, namely Apekshanagar is presented in the following section. Some of the residents have begun receiving property tax bills from SMC. The condition of houses, internal roads and other basic infrastructure in these SEWS colonies are comparatively better than other slums. Such settlements are called *suchit* societies in Gujarat.

The infrastructure in the SEWS colonies as well as slums has been provided by the SMC under 63/2 section of Bombay Provincial Municipal Corporation Act, 1949 (BPMC Act)[7], which provides for reservation of 10 per cent of its annual income (other than the income from the proceeds of the transport undertaking and any other specified items of income as the State Government may from time to time determine and notify in the official Gazettes) for expending in slums and SEWS colonies for the purpose of providing basic facilities like water supply, drainage, sanitation, street lights, medical aid, slum clearance and such other matters if these areas are predominantly populated by members of schedule castes, schedule tribes, and other socially and economically backward sections. The Act further says that if the expenditure thus provided for is not fully utilised in the year then the remaining amount can be carried forward in the budget of the succeeding year. The SMC has been using this provision for extending individual household level services to the slums and SEWS colonies. Thus, the situation regarding basic services in these settlements in the city is good.

The SMC has also been constructing individual toilets at the household level if the settlement is eligible for coverage under the 63/2 section of the BPMC and the household is living in non-*pucca* house. It is possible that a household may not qualify for support for constructing an individual facility then the households may not construct a toilet and a bath space but may construct an extra room to rent out and earn Rs. 600 to Rs. 900 per month and continue to defecate in open.

The SMC has provided water supply and sanitation to many slums in recent years with the help of the MHT, an affiliate of the Self Employed Women's Association (SEWA). The MHT has also helped slum dwellers to get an individual toilet and in the cases where individual toilets are not possible, common toilets have been constructed by this organisation. In the year 1992, only 19 per cent of the slum households had private water taps which increased by only 1 per cent in 2001, but by 2005, 72 per cent slum households in the Surat city had a private water tap (Table 3.5). Around 21 per cent slum households had individual toilets in the year 1992 which has increased to 35 per cent in 2005. The number of public toilets has increased from 558 to 1,914 within these 13 years which means in 1992 there was one public toilet for 168 households, while in 2005 there is one public toilet for 27 households. The ratio is still very high but the progress is significant. Drainage facility is available to 80 per cent households; the proportion having doubled in a span of 13 years. According to 2005 survey of SMC, only 45 per cent households have separate electricity connections. The SMC has done remarkable effort to improve living conditions in the slums.

Table 3.5: Amenities available in the slums of Surat City

Amenities	*1992*	*2001*	*2005*
Private water taps available with slum households (%)	19	20	72
Private latrines available with slum households (%)	20.9	27.5	35.0
Public toilets (No.)	558	NA	1914
Households per public toilet	168.0	NA	27.2
Drainage facilities available with slum households (%)	40	68	80
Separate electricity connections	25	32	45

Source: SMC.

Profile of Slums

This section discusses the primary survey conducted in the slums. In the initial stage, multiple municipal wards were visited which included Pandesara, Bamroli, Udhana, Limbayat, Varachha and Bhatar wards. All of which had large proportion of slums. Discussions with the NGOs working in the slums and slum residents were also held. The survey was conducted in 2010, when only two NGOs of the city, the MHT and the

Navsarjan Trust, were engaged with shelter and basic services schemes. The latter is an organisation for legal aid for the poor and the marginal sections and was involved in the housing issue through the women's rights movement. Finally, Varachha ward was selected, as it had a large slum population as well as interventions by the MHT in providing basic services on behalf of the SMC. All the slums in this ward had water supply, sanitation and electricity access. Total of eight slums were selected for detailed study (Table 3.6), among which in three the MHT was involved in extending these services on behalf of the SMC. In two of the slums, dwellers from other parts of the city were resettled through sites and services schemes. None of the slums were facing eviction threat and in case of one slum on private land, residents of the slum had proceeded with litigation against the owner who wanted to evict them. Three slums in the study area were on municipal lands, of which two were rehabilitated slums. A total of 375 households were covered in the structured questionnaire survey.

In Surat, one cannot evaluate the tenure security on the basis of land ownership, years of existence of the slum or intervention of an external agency for development purposes as argued by Mahadevia (2010 and 2011) for Ahmedabad (discussed in other chapters in this book). The SMC has prepared a list of slums to be evicted for developmental projects and city beautification purposes, irrespective of the years of its existence or land ownership of the slum and most dwellers are expected to get a BSUP house (the summary of which is given in Table 3.4).

Table 3.6: Settlement description, Varachha ward, Surat

Slum Name	*Population*	*Households*	*Land ownership*	*Internal roads*	*NGO intervention*	*Micro-finance*
Krishnanagar	2,028	472	Municipal-EWS	None	Yes	Yes
Dindayalnagar	2,956	764	Municipal-EWS	Paved	No	Yes
Jadabawa No. Tekro	774	123	Private	Paved	No	No
Bombay Colony 1	333	54	Private	None	No	No
Bombay Colony 2	1,450	250	Municipal	*Pucca* Road	Yes	Yes
Gulabchand Ni Chali	291	68	Private	None	No	No
Tas Ni Vadi	693	130	Private	On side of main road	Yes	Yes
Rawaliya Faliya	820	128	Private	*Pucca* Road	Yes	Yes

Source: SMC Survey of 2005 and primary survey in 2010.

Rehabilitation Sites—Krishnanagar and Dindayalnagar

Krishnanagar and Dindalyalnagar slums are on plots reserved for the Economically Weaker Sections (EWS) of the SMC, having 472 households (2,028 residents) and 734 households (2,956 residents) respectively as per SMC survey of 2005. Majority of the males members are working in either power-looms or diamond industry. The current residents of these settlements were relocated here in 1998 after their former squatter settlement was demolished for the purpose of road widening. Residents of Krishnanagar come from the same ward whereas those in Dindayalnagar are from Adajan Patiya area in the nearby ward. Relocated occupants were issued a card by the Land and Property Department of the SMC, giving them right of the occupying the plot (Exhibit 3.1). This card also entitled the occupants for an alternate housing in case of any further eviction. When people were shifted to this location they were provided only open plots. Initially, they constructed dwellings using temporary materials like plastic sheets, mud, wooden sheets, tin etc. Gradually they invested in their housing. Four years after they shifted to this location, the SMC provided them individual water supply and sewerage line. All the dwellings also have electricity. At the time of the survey, a few *katcha* houses were found in both the slums. Many of the residents had mortgaged their card to the informal money lender

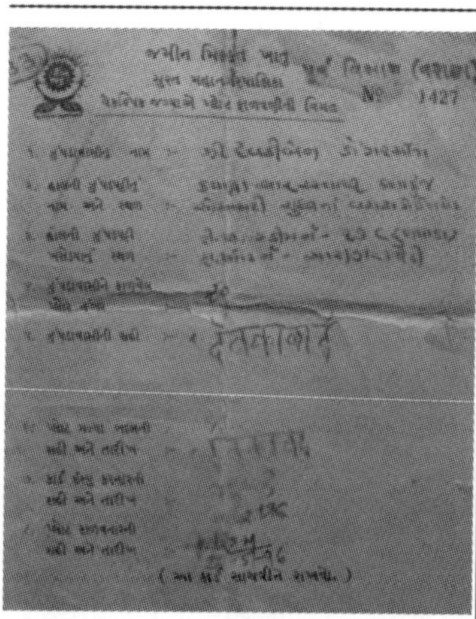

Land and Property Department
(East Zone Varachha)
Surat Municipal Corporation
Details of allotting the plot at alternate place

1. Name of the slum dweller: *Devkiben Dongarsing*
2. Name of the current slum and area: *From Kapadra cross roads to Kalakunj, Varachha main road*
3. Area of the allotted slum: *T.P. Scheme number 17, Plot no. R/7/21*
4. Allotted plot no.: *20*
5. Signature of the slum dweller:
6. Signature and date on receiving the plot:
7. Signature of the officer who issued the card and date:
8. Signature of the person who allotted he plot and date:

(Preserve this card)

Source: Primary Survey.

Exhibit 3.1: Card issued to the slum dwellers rehabilitated on EWS sites

for borrowing money for house construction. This indicates that the SMC's rehabilitation should have included a financial package as well.

Majority of the houses in Krishnanagar are three storied *pucca* housing, including ground floor (hereafter referred to as G+2) (Exhibit 3.2). All the houses have been given an individual number for property tax purposes. The settlement has water supply and sewerage line, which was not laid at the time of shifting the households. Residents paid Rs. 750 for connecting their toilets to main sewerage line. Thereafter, the MHT stepped in to provide support for individual toilet construction for those who wanted to. The physical condition of both Krishnanagar and Dindayalnagar (Exhibit 3.3) are more or less similar except that the latter has streets paved by the MHT and so the settlement is not as filthy as the former. There are cases where households have constructed an additional floor to be given out on rent for supplementary income.

Photo Credit: CUE.

Exhibit 3.2: Living conditions, Krishnanagar[8]

Photo Credit: CUE.

Exhibit 3.3: Living conditions, Dindayalnagar

There is much to be desired from the SMC as far as the maintenance of the settlement is concerned. People complain that the gutter lines get choked every now and then and the SMC workers come for repairs only after repeated complaints. Most of the internal roads in the settlement are not paved resulting into unhygienic, filthy conditions especially during rains. Lack of regular cleaning in the area also aggravates this situation. A dustbin was placed on the road but there was no waste management system within the settlement and residents are not involved in improving the situation.

The MHT has introduced micro finance services of the SEWA Bank in these slums. However, few residents have saved money with and fewer have taken loan from SEWA Bank for the purpose of either constructing additional floors to their house or toilet. In Dindayalnagar, only two households had taken a loan from the SEWA bank for expanding their small business.

During the floods in the year 2006, both the settlements were badly affected. The SMC had shifted these residents to the nearby high rise buildings and schools. The residents lost their furniture and other belongings. Many of them also lost their residential proofs such as the property tax bills, the ration card, and the occupancy right card given by the SMC for the plot post-rehabilitation.

Jada Bawa No Tekro

Jada Bawa No Tekro is situated near the railway line on Varachha road, close to the diamond industries and is one of the oldest slum settlements of Surat city. The residents put its age as 70 years, which could be an exaggeration. It is likely to have come up during the 1960s. This slum was on a small hill (and hence called a *tekro*) below which there was an underpass. There is a temple adjacent to the mount, of one *bawa* named *jada* bawa (*bawa* is an ascetic, *jada* means fat). The temple was built by or for an ascetic, who lived there and from then on, the mount has been called Jada Bawa No Tekro (fat ascetic's hill—if one translates verbatim). According to the residents, the land belongs to a Trust. But, the SMC records state that it is on private land. Residents reported that earlier they paid a rent of Re. 1 to the owner of the land but after getting property tax bill in their name they have stopped paying rent.

The slum has 123 households and a population of 774 persons. Community comprises mostly of Gujarati *Patel*, *Rathod* and people from Uttar Pradesh. Slum dwellers, who could afford, have upgraded their housing to *pucca* and the remaining live in semi-*pucca* houses (Exhibit 3.4). The basic amenities like individual water supply and sewerage have been provided by the SMC since the year 1977. Water supply line had to be changed because of its breakdown. Dwellers paid about Rs. 1,500 to Rs. 2,700 for relaying the water pipes. Households who could not pay this amount are without these facilities. At the time of the survey, the sewerage lines were choked and the SMC had not cleaned them. Internal roads have been paved by SMC. Some dwelling units did not have individual toilets as their occupants could not afford to have one. Many of the households were found to have bath space in their houses. SMC has provided street lights, which were not functioning for two years prior to the survey. A garbage pickup truck collected solid waste from a community dustbin nearby every morning at 7.00 am.

Photo Credit: CUE.

Exhibit 3.4: Living conditions, Jada Bawa No Tekro

Though the settlement is situated on a hill it was still affected by the flood of 2006, when the residents had to move to the railway station for safety. The SMC did provide monetary relief of Rs. 2,400 per household but it was reported that it did not reach everybody in the community; only a few families benefitted. Recession has made a big impact on the livelihood, many male factory workers who were working in power-looms lost their jobs and those who did not lose their jobs, were forced to reduce working hours. On asking them whether some of them had left Surat for their home villages, they replied, "We are staying in Surat from birth. Almost every family is staying here over three to four generations. Many of us even do not know our original village. Now Surat is our home. Where do we go from here?"

Bombay Colony-1

Bombay Colony-1 is a slum located on private land and has 54 households and 333 residents as per 2005 survey of the SMC. Overall, this slum houses a mixed community with the *Bharwad*, Gujaratis and Marathis. Most of the houses are *katcha* type (Exhibit 3.5). Everyone receives property tax bill which is duly paid. The SMC has made all the basic services available at common level while individual household-level water supply connection has been made available on payment of Rs. 400. The MHT has constructed common toilets in the settlement on behalf of the SMC. No house has an individual toilet. Internal roads have not been paved. The environment of the slum is very unhygienic due to poor waste management and garbage collection. Waste from the household is left on the roads from where the waste collection truck picks up every morning. But, many households continue to dump the waste behind the settlement. Malaria is a common disease which affects most of the occupants in the slum which is obvious from the condition of the slum.

Photo Credit: CUE.

Exhibit 3.5: Living conditions, Bombay Colony-1

Most of the men work in diamond cutting factory as well as power-looms and women engage in thread cutting at home or work as domestic help in nearby societies to earn their livelihood. Recession has a huge impact on their livelihood as some of the diamond workers lost their job and others had reduction in either working hours or wages. During the floods in 2006 in Surat city, residents shifted to nearby higher storey buildings for safety. In this time of distress, food relief was provided by the MHT and a monetary help of Rs. 1500 was provided by the SMC.

Bombay Colony-2

Bombay Colony-2 has a population of 1,450 persons in 250 households as per the SMC survey of 2005. The slum is on municipal land. During the tenure of the celebrated Municipal Commissioner of Surat, Mr. S.R. Rao (from May 1995 to December 1997), Varachha road was widened and all the pavement dwellers shifted to different municipal lands. Bombay Colony-2 received some of the evictees and thus expanded in this period. Before this, some families were already staying here who were giving rent to informal encroachers from the *Bharwad*[9] community. The new settlers too begun to give rent to the *Bharwads*. This arrangement was prevailing even during the survey. This is a case of capture of municipal land by a powerful community (the *Bharwad)*, which has wherewithal to engage in physical violence if need be, and then renting out the plots or constructed dwelling units to the households, all outside the purview of the legal system. *Bharwad* community encroached upon the municipal land and then gave it on a rent to some of the current residents illegally. Those evicted from Varachha road rented

Photo Credit: CUE.

Exhibit 3.6: Living conditions, Bombay Colony-2

katcha huts constructed by the *Bharwads*. But, the SMC stepped in and gave an occupancy certificate to these rehabilitees, which had details of their eviction, name and address of allotted slum, allotted plot number and signature of the occupant as well as the sign of SMC official who allotted the plot, much the same way as done for the residents of Krishnanagar and Dindayalnagar (Exhibit 3.1). Unlike other rehabilitation sites, the rehabilitation in this site was in *katcha* housing. Earlier Muslim community used to live in the area but during communal riots of 2002 they were relocated for their safety and they have not returned back settlement since.

Occupants are entitled for alternate housing in case of eviction on the basis of the card received from the SMC. Based on this card, occupants are mortgaging their house and land to access finance. Those who were already staying in the area paid Rs. 700 for documents to establish their right on the property. This document has names of both the parties (buyer and seller), area of the dwelling, and photographs of both the parties.

Most of the housing in Bombay Colony-2 is semi-*pucca* (Exhibit 3.6) and those who could afford have extended one additional floor but such cases are very few since vertical growth is restricted in the area due to high tension electricity line passing through the slum. Therefore, residents are ready for further rehabilitation if they get bigger houses. Earlier when people started building their houses on this land, no services had been provided by the SMC. Slowly, services were made available to the residents. For water they were dependent on the nearby settlements and for which they had to pay Rs. 50 per month. Later on, individual water taps were provided at the cost Rs. 420 per household but only after constant pursuance with SMC with the help of MHT. Afterwards all the remaining basic services, i.e. sanitation, roads and electricity, were provided by the SMC. The toilets are shared. Waste from the households is collected by a pickup truck at 10:00 am. Street cleaning is done by the locals themselves.

For livelihood, the men work either as vendors, casual labour, factory worker or own small shops and women work as domestic help in nearby residential societies, run small shops outside their homes or work as vegetable vendors. Access to micro finance has been provided by the SEWA Bank in this area and people have taken this opportunity and acquired loans either to expand their business or start a new one.

There is a big problem of gambling and consumption of alcohol in the area. This has resulted in an additional burden on the women as men do not contribute their income to the family. From 2008 onwards, recession had serious impacts on the livelihood of the dwellers in this slum. Diamond industry and power-loom sector have been hit the most because of the recession. Inflation also has resulted in increase in the cost of the living. Those who had even a small plot of land have returned to their ancestral home. During the Surat floods, this area was highly inundated and was under about four feet high water, thereby damaged their possessions and stored grains. Relief came from MHT in the form of medicine and food and the local government provided monetary help of Rs. 1,500 to Rs. 2,300 depending on the number of members in the family.

Gulabchand Ni Chali

Gulabchand Ni Chali is situated on a private land. As per 2005 survey of SMC there are about 68 households (currently about 85) and 291 people living in it. The *chawl* consists of mostly Gujarati and Marathi communities and people from Uttar Pradesh, a state in northern India. Housing type in the *chawl* is semi-*pucca* with few *katcha* (Exhibit 3.7). The overall condition of the housing is very poor. The original owner of the land was a person named Gulabchand who had subdivided his land and rented it to the slum dwellers. Occupants of the slum claim to be living on the land for about 80 years. Slum dwellers paid rent varying from Rs. 4 to Rs. 10 depending on the size of the plot. They stopped paying rent when they started receiving property tax bills from the SMC since the land is situated on a prime location—near the railway station. Gulabchand's nephew sold this land to a private builder who then

Photo Credit: CUE.
Exhibit 3.7: Living conditions, Gulabchand Ni Chali

tried to evict the slum dwellers. As a result, the residents filed a law suit against the builder and the court case has been ongoing for the past 14 years. Residents of the *chawl* are waiting for the court case to be in their favour to upgrade their housing to *pucca* structure. All the basic services have been provided to the settlement by the SMC. Thirty years ago, as per the residents, the SMC had provided two common tap water connections. During the survey, everybody had their individual water connection, paying an amount varying from Rs. 1,000 to Rs. 5,000 depending upon the distance from the main water supply line. Drainage line was extended by the SMC without any charges. Very few households have individual toilets and all residents use four common toilets resulting in long queues everyday and occasional disputes. Open plot in the settlement is used for holding social functions.

Tas Ni Vadi

Tas Ni Vadi is located near the Surat railway station. There are 130 households and population of this settlement is 693. All the houses are on two sides of a main road. This settlement is on private land but there is a public road passing through the settlement. Residents claim that they were staying there for over 30 years. The residents have reported that the road existed at this location from the very beginning. When they came and settled here it was a *katcha* road and some years ago a tarred road was laid. The settlement did not begin as a pavement squatting, but today it does appear like pavement dwellings.

Water supply and sewerage have been provided since last few years. MHT has constructed some common and some individual toilets in this settlement (Exhibit 3.8). Water supply is for three hours daily, which is adequate according to the residents. The quality of water is good. This slum does not receive property tax bill. The residents mentioned that

Photo Credit: CUE.
Exhibit 3.8: Living conditions, Tas Ni Vadi

they were contemplating to approach the SMC for property tax bills, arguing that many other slums on private lands were receiving the tax bills. Receiving tax bills would ensure formalisation of their slum in the official records and would spare them from potential evictions. On the other hand, they feared that if they made too many demands, the SMC may evict them. Thus, many of the residents opined of not approaching the SMC.

In terms, of occupational activities, some of the male workers were in the power-looms but most of them do not work. Level of alcohol consumption is very high here among both male and female members. Female work participation is higher than male. Women work as domestic help and also conduct thread cutting work from home. Many of the women complained about domestic violence due to their husbands' alcoholism. Besides, residents brew alcohol themselves and also sell it in surrounding settlements. Field team was asked by some of the women dwellers, not to visit the slum in the evenings because of such activities. Continuous alcohol consumption has deteriorated the health condition of the slum dwellers.

Photo Credit: CUE.
Exhibit 3.9: Living conditions, Rawaliya Falia

Rawaliya Faliya

Rawaliya Faliya is an old slum situated on a private land along the bank of river Tapi. People have been living there for more than three generations and the residents report it to be more than 100 years old settlement. As per the survey done by the SMC in 2005 there were about 820 residents living in

128 households in this slum. Dwelling units in the slum are *pucca* or semi-*pucca* (Exhibit 3.9), and the living conditions are better than the other selected slums for the study. People have upgraded their houses over the years. Everybody in the slum receives property tax bills. Basic services have been made available and individual water taps have been provided by the SMC, but there is problem of insufficient water supply. Occupants make use of the nearby river for cleaning purposes. The SMC provided sewerage line about four years prior to the survey. Toilets have been constructed with financial help from the MHT. Monetary aid of Rs. 1,500 was provided to households who did not own one and of Rs. 500 for repairing the existing toilets. SMC has also constructed an internal road within the slum. For solid waste disposal, a pickup truck comes in the morning and the entire area is cleaned once in a month by the SMC.

The slum being close to river, the residents face high risk of water borne diseases like jaundice, cholera, typhoid, etc. and also vector borne diseases such as malaria, etc. The residents reported high incidence of these diseases. The slum has been repeatedly affected by the floods, of which the 2006 was the worst. During our survey, many respondents had tears in their eyes recalling the 2006 floods, in which they lost all their belongings. The SMC provided monetary help of Rs. 2,375 per household, while the MHT provided food supply to the slum dwellers. Impact of

Table 3.7: Socio-economic features of the selected slums, Surat

Aspect	*Krishna-Nagar*	*Dindayal Nagar*	*Jada Bawa No Tekro*	*Bombay Colony-1*	*Bombay Colony-2*	*Gulab-chand Ni Chali*	*Tas ni Vadi*	*Rawaliya Faliya*	*Average*
Total Households	472	764	123	54	250	68	130	128	1,989
Sex ratio	689	874	593	872	571	852	713	991	792
Household size	4.9	4.9	4.3	5.2	4.2	5.7	4.8	5.8	5.0
Literacy rate - Male	59.6	49.7	55.6	61.7	64.9	65.7	69.0	62.0	61.0
Literacy rate - Female	42.9	39.7	31.3	48.8	38.6	47.8	41.9	52.3	42.9
Just read + primary education only–Males*	61.8	74.0	62.2	51.7	66.0	50.7	85.0	74.7	65.7
Just read + primary education only–Females*	54.4	82.3	66.7	42.5	88.3	66.0	92.3	75.0	70.9
LFPR (age 15-59)–Male	65.8	67.0	69.1	74.5	79.2	78.7	77.0	67.6	70.6
LFPR (age 15-59)–Female	66.9	53.3	66.7	70.7	68.2	75.0	72.6	68.2	64.6

* Proportion of those who are literate

Note: LFPR = Labour Force Participation Rate

Source: Primary Survey, 2010.

recession can also be seen in the area and it has resulted into change in occupation of many people. People who were engaged in diamond and textile industry are now either vegetable/fruit vendors or working as waiters in the small eateries near the railway station. A great shift from formal to informal sector can be seen in this particular settlement.

The primary survey was of 375 sample households, comprising 1,868 individuals. The overall sex ratio in these selected slums is 792 (Table 3.7), which is surprisingly higher than that of Surat city (764). But, across the slums there is a significant variation in the sex ratio, ranging from 571 in Bombay Colony-2 to 991 in Rawaliya Faliya. The average household size of the sample is 5.0 but is 4.2 in Bombay Colony-2 where even the sex ratio is the lowest, indicating presence of large number of single-male migrants here. Conversely, slums with highest sex ratio are the ones with highest household size as well.

The literacy rate represents persons who can read and write. The level of education of these slum dwellers is even more disappointing. The literacy rate in all the slums is very low for both males and females. The average literacy rate is 51.9 per cent; 61.0 per cent for males and 42.9 per cent for females (Table 3.7), while that of Surat city is 89.0 per cent as per census 2011. Interestingly, Rawaliya Faliya, which had the highest sex ratio also, had the highest female literacy of 52.3 per cent. In males around 65 per cent and in females around 70 per cent could only read or have studied up to the primary standards (7th grade). The level of education in females is significantly low. The secondary and higher secondary schools are some distance from these settlements plus quality of education is not up to the mark. Most of the boys drop-out in 10th grade when there is a common examination for the entire state. They drop-out either without appearing in the examination or after they fail in the first trial. It was reported that in case they fail the 10th grade examinations, they invariably find some odd jobs or get involved in diamond units or power-looms rather than reappearing for the examination. The parents are not ready to send the girl child very far for secondary education. The schools where these children are enrolled are not well-equipped. Many a times there is no toilet facility in the school. It is very difficult for a girl child to sit in the school for the entire day (11 a.m. to 5 p.m.) without such facility.

The Labour Force Participation Rates (LFPR), the per cent of working population in the age group 15-59, is also low given that in the low-income households, everyone is required to work to keep the family out of poverty. The LFPR was only 70.6 per cent for the males and 64.6 per cent for the females for all the settlements together (Table 3.7), when the figures should have been above 80 per cent. It is likely that the low LFPRs are an outcome of the economic recession of 2008.

Overall Status of Slums

The living conditions of people and the physical conditions of all the slums are more or less similar except Gulabchand Ni Chali where a court case is going on regarding the ownership of the slum land. The housing condition in Gulabchand Ni Chali is pitiable. The dwellings can collapse any time. During monsoon the condition is even worse. Residents say it very confidently that once the legal case is in their favour, they would build *pucca* houses without any delay. They reported that they would also construct individual toilets and bath space after the land conflict was resolved. The settlement is highly crowded and residents with family extensions want to add extra rooms after the settling of the land issue. While in Krishnanagar, Dindayalnagar and Bombay Colony-2 the housing conditions are much better, they still have some *katcha* houses. In Krishnanagar and Dindayalnagar, residents earn monthly rent from their additional floors and extended rooms. People in Bombay Colony-2 are ready for further rehabilitation if they are given bigger houses while residents of other settlements are wary of eviction from their current locations. However, the "occupancy card" received from SMC is a source of legitimacy for the slum dwellers. In these three slums, households have even taken loans to invest in their houses and business which is missing in the rest of the settlements; except in Rawaliya Faliya where people have upgraded their houses over the years. Property tax bill is also one of the important documents legitimising the occupancy of the slum dwellers. Almost all houses in all the slums receive property tax bills except Tas Ni Vadi.

Individual water supply and sewerage are made available to every slum by the SMC, but all households do not have individual toilets. MHT has helped in getting individual toilets to some of the households wherever it has intervened. There are slums with no space at all for individual toilets like Bombay Colony-1 and Gulabchand Ni Chali. In these slums, common toilets are available. The condition of these toilets is dreadful and unhygienic. The slums with common toilets have reported common cases of diseases like malaria and chikengunia. This study establishes a noticeable link between secured tenure and quality of life. A decent house is a right of every citizen.

Individual Case Studies

In absence of a large systematic survey to understand the shelter related dynamics in Surat, we have documented cases of individual settlements, households and one category of urban residents, the migrants, to illustrate how the city-level dynamics affect individual households. We first present the case of two individuals, whose shelter related issues represent the situation in the city, followed by the living conditions of migrant workers and finally, the history of an informal settlement.

Rehabilitation—A Mere Promise

The difference among the slums which have tenure security provided by state intervention and the slums without such security is quite evident. Those rehabilitated are fortunate to get a serviced plot in the same ward, have not been affected in their livelihood security, while the rehabilitation package also improved their living conditions. However, not all evictees have been given rehabilitation. In that case, their situation deteriorates and creates more miseries.

The case of Divaliben and Vitthalbhai illustrates this process and also raises doubts about the SMC claim of covering every displaced household under the rehabilitation package. Near one end of Nehru Bridge on river Tapi, is a bus depot. To protect this bus depot from inundation, an embankment was constructed recently, which resulted in the eviction of the residents of a slum named Subhashnagar on the river bank. Estimated 3,000 hutments were located on the land, which belonged to the Irrigation Department of the State Government. The residents claim that the slum existed for about five decades (which could be an exaggeration by the slum dwellers to prove their legitimacy). On February 16, 2009, all the hutments were demolished by the SMC. They were promised that those affected would be rehabilitated in two-room with one kitchen house, but, not all were covered under the rehabilitation scheme and resultant adjustments by the slum dwellers was pitiful. When the research team visited the site, it saw a spectre of two children lying on one step of the embankment; on the step above the elder siblings were lying and on one more step above that their mother was cooking on a wood stove below a plastic sheet roof supported on four bamboo sticks. Compared to such a shelter, any poor man's mud house would look like a luxurious dwelling!

There are still some families living on the embankment, in spite of the SMC's claims of having rehabilitated all. One would see number of such temporary shelters erected on the embankment. In other words, some of the households evicted from Subhashnagar, have either not been rehabilitated or if rehabilitated, they were neither given an appropriately located house or there has been some mismanagement in the entire process such that the evictee could not get thc allotted house. Whatever may be the case, the rehabilitation process was not proper.

Divaliben, aged 60, is one such woman, whose house number 2158 was on the site on which she has now erected a temporary shelter. Her full name is Divaliben Tulsibhai Devipujak, who became a widow at the age of 40. She bore three sons, two of whom died of illness and the surviving third son is neither willing to keep her with him nor support her. Amidst such a personal tragedy, her hut was bulldozed by the SMC. At the age of 60 (the average LEB in India is about 65 years), she has been thrown on the footpath. She comes from Radhanpur Taluka of Banaskantha, a permanent drought prone region of Gujarat. Because of water shortage, she and her husband migrated to Surat 40 years ago. Her husband spent his life repairing and making tin boxes and their covers. Saving from their hard labour, they constructed a temporary shelter for themselves on the bank of river Tapi. But, her husband died at a very young age due to epilepsy. In her short married life, she gave birth to three sons. She thought that when her sons would grow up, her life condition would improve. The third surviving son did not study and he too, like his father, got into the business of repairing old tin boxes. He constructed a temporary hut for his family while she lived in the hut constructed by her husband.

Divalibhen sells mud toys, balloons, wooden swords, etc. to children as an itinerant vendor, carrying load in a cane basket on her head. At her age, in the hot summer, she feels dizzy and even faints sometimes. There is no old age security or pension for her. In such a situation, her son is the only social security, but has abandoned her. Her vision is poor; she feels tired, her back and her knees pain after walking long hours with the cane basket on her head, but, she has no option but to go out and earn. She earns about Rs. 10-15 per day, which gets consumed for food expenses. The day she is unwell and cannot go out to sell, she has to depend on the neighbours for food. In the 2006 floods, she lost her *katcha* house, all her utensils, bedding and above all her identity proofs like all other slum dwellers. They survived on the government supply of food packets from the helicopter. When the flood receded after four days, all the huts were destroyed. Everywhere one looked, one would find mud and muck. No one had a single paisa in the pocket and no roof over the head. She said: "I was not sure whether my son and his wife would keep me in their hut." Amidst the crisis, government gave a compensation of Rs. 2,500 from which she constructed a tent like structure of tarpaulin. As if all these problems were not enough, this temporary shelter too was demolished by the SMC after about 7-8 months of the flood. All other huts were also demolished and the whole slum was evicted. She now has neither shelter security nor food security, because in the process she has lost her ration card.

They were all promised a *pucca* house against their hut. But, the SMC did not fulfil this promise even after about eight months of demolition. Before demolition, she and her son had one hut each. Her house number was 2,158 while her son's was 2,157. But, then the SMC said that she and her son would not get individual house each. They have allotted one house between both of them. As of now, she is living on the embankment in a tent. This tent has been demolished by the anti-encroachment squad twice. In the last demolition, the dwellers were caned and she too was hit with a baton about three-four times, in spite of her age. During the survey, all were given the last warning of removing their tents and shifting out from there.

Her son Vithalbhai does not like the idea of sharing a single dwelling unit between his family and his mother. His family is large; four daughters and three sons, besides himself and his wife. He works for nearly 12 hours a day, buying waste, fixing and selling tin boxes and earns about Rs. 40-50 per day. His income is too meagre to feed his large family two square meals a day. He does not have ability to feed his mother. Two years ago, he lost his hut, and government gave compensation of only Rs. 2,500, evidently not enough to even buy plastic sheets to erect a temporary shelter, for which, he then borrowed Rs. 20,000 at an interest rate of 3 per cent per month from a money lender. This shelter too was demolished by the SMC while he was still paying off his debt. So, instead of incurring debt again, he decided to erect a temporary structure of bamboo, make a roof of tarpaulin and make walls from metal sheets prepared from hammering the steel boxes collected from households. Vithalbhai said: "one can accept to stay hungry but cannot stay without a roof over one's head. We are somehow managing to pass days in such a temporary and weak house, which can fall down even if someone kicks. Sometimes, we go to bed hungry. Government could not accept that we were living in such a bad condition and they came and destroyed our house eight months ago. Since then, all nine of us are living on this embankment in the open. I am unable to repay the loan. I cannot sleep in the night because of this tension. There is, of course, constant uncertainty about my income. We have to bear seeing our children go hungry. We have no money to rent a house. My eldest son is studying in school and is 12 years of age. But, I think, I will have to take him out of the school and put him to labour so that we all can eat. On top of it, we have to spend Rs. 2 per person to use the public latrine nearby. How can we afford to pay Rs. 18 per day to defecate once a day from our income of Rs. 40 per day? It has become increasingly difficult to live even one day now."

Shantaben of Tadkeshwar

An enterprising woman in an incrementally developed settlement, is Shantaben, living in Tadkeshwar, Part-1 slum on Bhatar Road. The slum has 310 dwelling units. This was a relocation site of people who were shifted out from Majura gate (a central location) in 1986 because the Civil Hospital road was to be widened. They were provided tents to stay initially when they were shifted to this area. When they were shifted to Tadkeshwar site, it was an undeveloped land, close to a creek. The area was low lying, which would get flooded in monsoon. The residents, who settled there, partly filled it up and partly over time with the development coming in, the area was filled up. Now, that it has become livable, only 155 houses are going to be retained and the rest are going to be demolished and the residents are to be rehabilitated in the newly constructed JNNURM units. The slum is on the SMC land. It has water supply line provided by the SMC. But, there is no drainage. There is stone paving on the internal roads. Because there is no drainage, some people who have individual toilets have constructed septic tanks. The streets lights are provided by the SMC. In the year 1992, the houses were valued and started getting property tax bills. An individual toilet scheme was introduced in 1993. Prior to that, the SMC had provided them common toilets.

The settlement has a *balwadi* (kindergarten) in a room constructed by a NGO named Navsarjan. The NGO runs a private tuition class in the room in the morning for giving extra coaching to the slum students so that they could improve their school performance. The tutor is paid by Navsarjan. The coaching by Navsarjan is *in lieu* of the parents' efforts. In all these, it is presumed that children are not going to learn much in attending the regular schools, whether private or public. Every child pays Rs. 700 per year for this tuition class and is given one bag and three notebooks. The tuition class is for one year, at the end of which each child receives a certificate. Students of class 1-7 attend the tuition class and all of them study together. After 12.00 noon, this same space becomes a *balwadi*. The room is also used as a community hall. It is also used for holding meetings of the *mahila mandal* (women's association), named Nari Shakti Mahila Mandal. The same space is used for sewing classes as well, once the *balwadi* finishes. When there was a *yuvak mandal* (youth association) in the slum, the space was also used by them. Now, the *yuvak mandal* is not functional. The school is called Navsarjan Mahila Mandal School.

Shantaben Tukeram Chauhan is the vice-president of Nari Shakti Mahila Mandal, set up by the Navsarjan Trust. Her interview was conducted in her *pucca* house. The house had a high plinth because of past experience of water logging. She has an individual toilet and also water supply. Her house consists of three *pucca* rooms and a kitchen, out of which two rooms have been rented out. The living conditions are quite good. They have electricity. She said that when they came to live here 22 years ago, they had to walk through knee-high muck.

Shantaben is an employee of Navsarjan. Her income was Rs. 3,000 per month during our survey. She has a sewing machine and earns Rs. 2,000 from sewing per month. Her husband earned Rs. 7,000 per month from painting buildings. She has rented out two rooms and getting Rs. 700 as rent and Rs. 300 as electricity charges and property tax from each tenant. The family income would be about Rs. 14,000 per month on the whole. Her son is studying in 10th grade and daughter goes to a local college. She purchased the sewing machine by taking a loan of Rs. 4,500 from Lok Vikas Nidhi (LVN), a micro-finance institution, whose head office is in Ahmedabad.

Shantaben's financial arrangements every month were as follows:

1. Rs. 100 contribution to the savings groups. Each savings group has 25 members. Tadkeshwar has 11 savings groups. Shantaben leads three such groups. A member could not contribute more than Rs. 100 in the savings group then, a standard norm across Surat irrespective of the microfinance institution. The total collected amount of Rs. 2,500 per month was deposited in the Central Bank, which is a nationalized bank. Each savings group operates its own account, with the signature of three women members.
2. Rs. 3,000 per month was contributed by her to the *vishi* (Chit

fund). There are 24 members of *vishi*. So, every month Rs. 72,000 gets collected. Then one person's name is selected through lottery who takes the entire collected fund. The person does not have to return the money. Thus each person gets a chance to avail the fund money after 24 months that is once in two years.

3. She was repaying a housing loan of Rs. 50,000 taken from LVN. LVN has been extended credit by Axis Bank. Since it is an unsecured loan, the loan amount could not exceed Rs. 50,000. Unsecured loans are given in case of house without legal land tenure. Rate of interest was 1.5 per cent per month, i.e. 18 per cent per year. For them this was cheaper, as the local money lender gave them loan at 24 per cent interest. The loan was to be repaid in 30 months. She is paying Rs. 2,045 as monthly installment for the housing loan.
4. She had also borrowed Rs. 20,000 from Sahara India, an informal finance institution and did not divulge the installment paid for this loan repayment.
5. In all, she was paying Rs. 5,145 (Rs. 100 + Rs. 3000 + Rs. 2045) per month to various microfinance institutions. All her income was being spent on repaying various loans she had taken. Even then, the family has Rs. 9000 income to run the household and save.
6. She had invested total of Rs. 1,70,000 on extending her house. She had met this cost through Rs. 50,000 LVN loan + Rs. 72,000 from *vishi* + Rs. 20,000 loan from Sahara India (Total Rs. 1,42,000) and the rest are from her own savings.

Shantaben's case indicates the micro-level entrepreneurship in the slums in Surat and support of the microfinance institutions for the same. However, this is not an atypical case, although worth mentioning here, on account of the innovative nature of the case.

Rental Housing for Single Male Migrants

Rental housing is vital option for the low-income households. Among them, those who come to the cities as seasonal migrants, rental housing is the only option. A section of migrants in the cities do not have intention of settling down in the city, and rental housing remains the major option for them. A major segment of the seasonal and also long-term migrants are the single-male migrants, who do not want to invest even in informal ownership housing. They stay as tenants in the existing informal housing, sharing or hiring a room in the existing houses. Such hired rooms are used in rotation through the day or through the year. Some migrants tend to use the same space shared with the other migrants at different times of the day. Some migrants use the same room for certain months in a year and when he leaves another one takes his place. There is rarely an incidence of single female migrants renting rooms. No such cases came across during the studies carried out which are presented in this book.

One such settlement, offering rental housing to the migrants working in the diamond industry and power-loom workers is Nikhalasnagar in Katargam area. According to the residents and the officials of the SMC, the living conditions in Nikhalasnagar were very bad some years ago. Nikhalasnagar is surrounded by the power-loom units and the first thing one can experience is the constant loud noise of machinery from these units. The units work in day and night shifts and so the noise virtually does not stop. By all standards, the living conditions in this area were dreadful. The SMC decided to tar the wide roads and lay stone paving on the narrow lanes of the settlement. The internal lanes are so narrow that only two people can pass (Exhibit 3.10). But, the stone paving and the tarred roads have changed the appearance and micro environment of the settlement. In fact, the residents use the semi-open spaces such as verandahs to sleep. When the decision to pave the roads was conveyed to the residents, they were very happy, anticipating the possibility of sleeping outside in the summer months. We saw a

Photo Credit: CUE.

Exhibit 3.10: Living conditions, Nikhalasnagar

10 square feet room that was shared by 14 men; seven of them using the room in the night time and seven others used it in the day time as they were night shift workers. We were informed that this was a common situation. There was no toilet or bath space or kitchen. There was a common kitchen from where all these single-male migrants bought their food. Rarely, some rooms housed families. Now, the settlement has common toilets outside the settlement as sewerage lines could not be extended within the slum. But, on the whole, the living conditions have improved on account of the SMC's initiative.

From Plastic Sheets and Mud Huts to Low Income Housing Societies

This case is about a settlement in the south-west zone of Surat city, which has concentration of industries and hence high slum population as compared to other zones of the city. The two main wards here with large slum population are Pandesara and Bamroli. Some of the slums in these areas are now treated as SEWS colonies. Apekshanagar and Jai Jawan-Jai Kisannagar for example are such low-income societies situated in Bamroli ward of the city. The tenure and living condition of these two settlements are more or less similar. Living conditions in Apekshanagar can be seen in Exhibit 3.11.

The total area of Apekshanagar is 47,763 square metres with a broad road and streets in good condition covering 11,464 square metres of the settlement area. The population of Apekshanagar is 4,500 with 726 households. Apekshanagar falls in the survey numbers 154/2, 155/2 and 156 of SMC (Exhibit 3.12). Originally farmlands, these plots were put under the reservation of the first SUDA Development Plan of 1980[10], for the EWS housing. This meant that the Gujarat Slum Clearance Board (GSCB) could have developed housing here. But, because the GSCB has been inactive for long time and in general, the farms were sold to an agent for plotting and informal housing construction.

In 1980, the land received the NA permission for residential purpose (*See* Box 3.1 for the contents). Apekshanagar came within the jurisdiction of the SMC in the year 1984. Plot number 155 belonged to a person named Chhimkabhai and later ownership transferred to his six sons and two daughters. The land ownership document contains names of all the eight heirs of Chhimkabhai as owners. The plot was subsequently sold to Kanjibhai and his sons, who obtained the power of attorney over the plot and hence his name was also mentioned in the ownership document. The adjoining plot, numbered 156, is in the name of Dayalbhai, Jamubhai and Chandubhai, but we assume it was sold to Kanjibhai, though there are no documents to support it. Lastly, a nearby plot number 154/2 in 1980, belonged to three persons; Balubhai Kanjibhai Patel, Paniben Valabhai Patel and Ravliben Durlabhbhai Patel. All the three were from the same family. They had the power of attorney[11] of this land. Kanjibhai gained control of all these land parcels and plotted 726 sub-plots of 12′× 35′ i.e. 42.6 sq.mt. size each in an orderly way to develop Apekshanagar (Exhibit 3.12). These plots were then sold to the migrants from Maharashtra, Uttar Pradesh, Madhya Pradesh and Bihar. The sub-plotting and sale started from about 1985 and all the plots were sold-off on stamp papers of Rs. 20 initially and later at Rs. 500. Therefore, the residents do not have legal ownership of the plots. Each plot has been given a number. We saw documents of plot no. 35. This plot was sold to Sadhuram Hardev Mistri, who holds a stamp-paper document. This person also gets a property tax bill from the SMC with the name of land owner, which is Balubhai Kanjibhai Patel, mentioned along with his own name.

Photo Credit: CUE.

Exhibit 3.11: Living conditions, Apekshanagar

Most of the houses in Apekshanagar are *pucca*. All the houses have been given individual numbers by the SMC for the purposes of levying property tax (Exhibit 3.13). Initially, people constructed dwellings using plastic sheets, wooden sheet, mud, broken

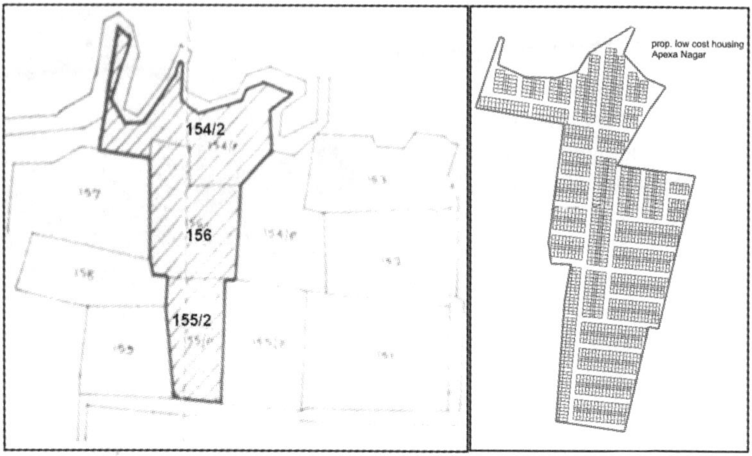

Source: CUE.
Exhibit 3.12: Apekshanagar Layout, Surat

bricks and stones. Gradually, they have invested in the houses and constructed *pucca* brick walls and cement-concrete roofs. Some dwelling units have become ground plus one or even ground plus two storeys.

The settlement got electricity connection in 1992. Drainage line was laid in 2003 and water supply came the next year in 2004. A municipal councillor named Dhansukhabhai contributed Rs. 5,000 from his development fund[12] for the drainage and water supply line. Every household was charged Rs. 1,500 for the drainage connection and Rs. 1,700 for water supply connection. However, water supply is only for two hours a day, from 6 a.m. to 8 a.m. Internal tarred roads and pavements have been constructed in 2005 which are fairly wide. The entire infrastructure in Apekshanagar has been provided by the SMC under 63/2 section of the BPMC Act. The local leader of the settlement, Lakshmanbhai Patil belonging to the Congress Party, wanted to ensure that land ownership is transferred to the current occupants. However, given that this is a private land, it has not been possible.

The slum dwellers have invested in the houses gradually. From this settlement, 210 households have one family member saving with the SEWA Bank and are associated with the MHT. These members have taken loans for construction and repair of the houses. Many houses have more than two rooms but the owners stay in one or two rooms and give the other room on rent. If the rented rooms are semi-*pucca* they get rent of Rs. 600 and if it is *pucca* the rent is Rs. 900 per month in the year of our

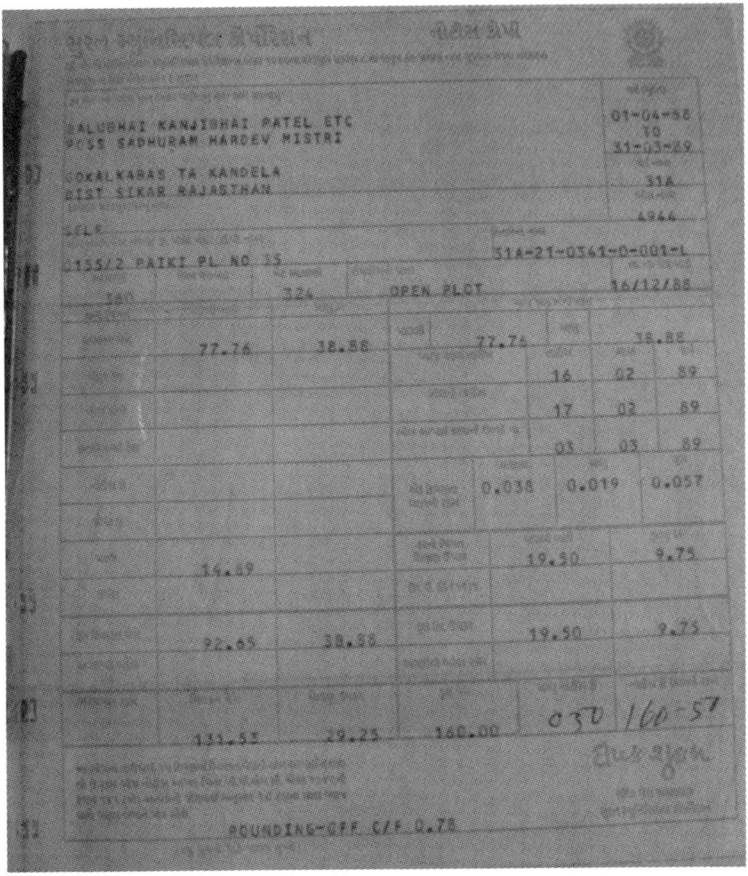

BALUBHAI KANJIBHAI PATEL ETC
POSS SADHURAM HARDEV MISTRI
GOKALKARAS TA KANDELA
DIST SIKAR RAJASTHAN
SELF
0155/2 PAIKI PL NO 35
01-04-88 TO 31-03-89
51A
51A-21-0341-0-001-L
380 324 OPEN PLOT 16/12/88
77.76 38.88 77.76 38.88
16 02 89
17 02 89
03 03 89
0.038 0.019 0.057
14.89 19.50 9.75
92.65 38.88 19.50 9.75
131.53 29.25 160.00
ROUNDING-OFF C/F 0.78

Source: Primary Survey.
Exhibit 3.13: Property tax bill, Apekshanagar

survey. Electricity bill is excluded from this rent. Many have taken loans for starting or expanding their businesses as well.

Ashaben Patil, 36 years old, has been staying in Apekshanagar over last 10 years. She cuts the threads of the *saris* and gets 50 paise per *sari*. She can complete 30 *saris* on an average in a day. So, she hardly earns Rs. 15 to Rs. 20 a day. Her husband also does some odd jobs. Somehow they manage to save Rs.20 a day and invest regularly in the SEWA Bank. They took loan twice for their house. From the first loan of Rs. 5,000 they constructed a toilet and a bathroom and from the second loan of Rs. 10,000, they did the flooring in the house. She feels that she is very fortunate that they selected Apekshanagar to stay when they came to Surat. Here the SMC does not come to evict unlike other slums where her relatives are staying. "My husband and I thought first we would do the house and then we arrange money for children's education as they are still studying in primary school."

Godawariben Ramprakash is staying in Apekshanagar over the last 18 years with her husband and three children. Originally, they are from Bihar. She also cuts threads of the *saris* and her husband does odd

Box 3.1: The Non-Agricultural (NA) Permission for Land Plots in Apekshanagar

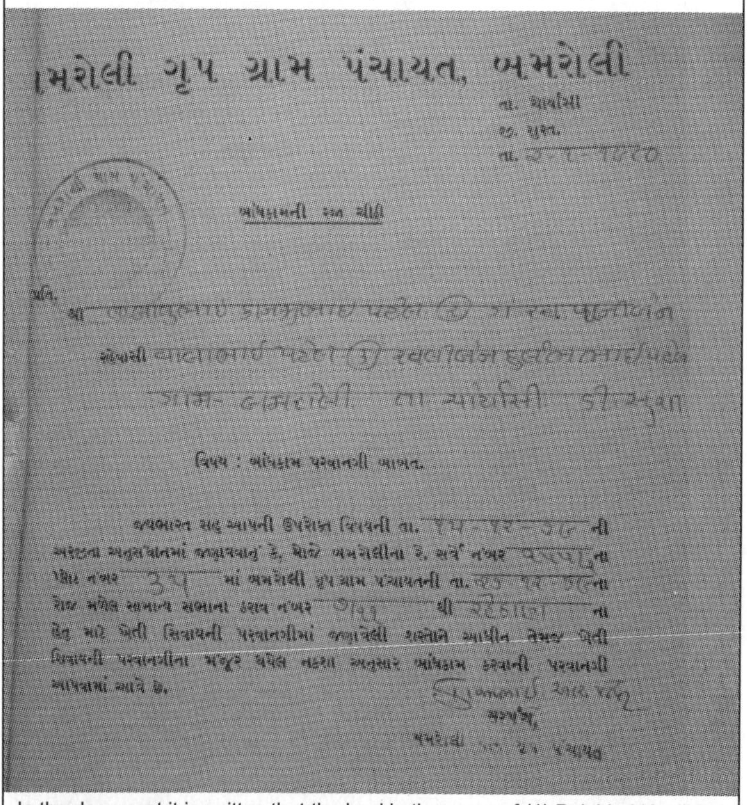
અમરેલી ગ્રુપ ગ્રામ પંચાયત, અમરેલી

In the document it is written that the land in the name of (1) Balubhai Kanjibhai Patel (2) Paniben Valabhai Patel and (3) Ravliben Durlabhbhai Patel is given permission to construct a residential structure.

Source: Primary Survey.

jobs like painting houses during Diwali time and otherwise works in textile mills. She also saves with the SEWA Bank and took a loan of Rs. 10,000 and constructed two semi-*pucca* rooms in the space behind her house. She charges Rs. 600 rent for each room in which the electricity bill is not included. She said initially she was not convinced with the idea of saving because their income was not enough but it was good that she saved and now she has generated a source of income from that.

Geetaben Mithileshbhai Pande came to Surat with her husband in 1997 and has been living in Apekshanagar since 2005. Before coming to Apekshanagar, they were living at Udhana Darwaja, in a rental house. Geetaben's brother-in-law and his wife also stay with them. She has two boys, one 13 years old and another six years old, staying in their native place, Nalanda, Bihar with her parents-in-law. They had to come to Surat because their income from farming was not enough. They selected Surat because they had some contacts from the village, with the help of whom they settled in Surat. Her husband got assistance from their village men to find a job and also find a room on rent. This rented room was near Udhana Darwaja, in the centre of the city. When they were staying at Udhana Darwaja, Geetaben was engaged as domestic help in nearby high income colonies. Now she does not work and stays home because she does not want to face the criticism of her community people, emanating from the fact that she has left her sons back home. The community taunts her that she is living a cosy life in Surat city while her children are at native village. Her husband works in dyeing and painting unit in textile mills. His income is Rs. 2,500 per month and hence they cannot afford to keep their children with them in the house here. Here, in Apekshanagar, they have their own house. They had purchased the house for Rs. 10,000 five years ago. They had borrowed money from the village contacts at an interest (she did not clarify) for purchasing this unit. This was only one room unit. They have chosen Apekshanagar because there is a large *Bihari* community here. They stick to their own community for social interactions. On shifting to Apekshanagar, she became a member of MHT and started saving in the *bachat mandal* (saving association). Then she took two loans, one of Rs. 10,000 and then of Rs. 15,000. With these amounts they constructed two additional rooms, which they have rented now. She deposits Rs. 100 per month in the savings account. Rent from each room is Rs. 700 and she charges Rs. 200 for electricity bill every two months. She says that they are using rental income for repayment of the loan taken from the village contacts. It seems that they are also using this amount for MHT loan repayment. On asking about the legal documents they possess, she said she does not have a ration card and that is her complaint against the authority but while cross-checking with her, the research team came to know that she does not want to forgo her existing ration card of the home village and wants to have another one in Surat city, which obviously is not possible.

There are thus, many cases in this settlement of incremental housing mobility from being a tenant in some earlier settlement but then coming to Apekshanagar and purchasing a house or a plot of land, whatever was available at the time of their purchase. They could incrementally invest in house upgrading as the settlement was on a private land and hence were not prone to demolition by the local government. This is also a planned informal settlement with well laid out plots and roads. There is also an informal sector developer. This can be called an informal commercial plotting of lands for low-income housing. Not just in Surat, but in many other cities of India, there are such informal planned urban peripheries, which cater to the housing demand of the low-income households.

NOTES

1. Research is funded under the research project titled "Inclusive Urbanisation—Social Protection for the Slum and Pavement Dwellers in India", a CEPT University—Mahila Housing SEWA Trust (MHT) project, under the programme 'Social Protection in Asia', managed by Institute of Development Studies (IDS), Sussex and Institute of Human Development (IHD), New Delhi and funded by Ford Foundation and IDRC. Authors acknowledge the contribution of Chintan Shah in fieldwork for this research. This research would not have been feasible without the support of the team of Mahila Housing Trust's office in Surat. We are extremely grateful to Bijal Bhatt, Co-ordinator, MHT and her colleagues in Surat for very generous support for this research work in Surat.
2. Annual pilgrimage to Mecca paid by the Muslim community.
3. The Brocade art was introduced by the Parsi community, which came from Iran and settled in Surat. They introduced their art of brocade canvas in Surat. Women in nearby villages developed this business as a cottage industry.
4. This para is sourced from *SMC's City Development Plan* (CDP), 2006-2012, p. 10.
5. Surat Municipal Corporation website - www.suratmunicipal.gov.in accessed on November 1, 2008.
6. Zonewise slum population for the year 2011 is not available when this

paper was finalized and so the latest data (2005-06) available with the SMC has been used.

7. The BPMC Act has now become Gujarat Municipal Corporation Act.
8. Copy right of all the photographs in the chapter is of the Centre for Urban Equity (CUE), CEPT University.
9. A Gujarati caste. The main occupation of *Bharwads* is cattle grazing.
10. Source: http://www.suratmunicipal.org/content/townplanning/main.shtml (accessed on January 25, 2011).
11. Power of Attorney is the legal right to develop and sale the land obtained by the holder from the land owner.
12. All elected representative are given a certain amount of funds for carrying out local development funds. Thus, the councillors of a city, Members of the state legislative assembly and the Members of Parliament have funds allocated for such works.

4

From Basic Services Delivery to Policy Advocacy

The Case of Pravinnagar-Guptanagar, Ahmedabad[1]

Rajendra Joshi, Pooja Shah and *Keren Nazareth*

Community Mobilisation

Community mobilisation is an important process of democratisation in any society. This is all the more important in developing economies where low income communities must be mobilised for participation in the agenda of development. In the tripod of urban governance—the state, civil society and market, civil society as an agency of change has been more proactive in poverty alleviation and empowering the urban poor communities than the state, as far as Indian experience is concerned. The state of Gujarat has been at the forefront in implementing the neo-liberal policy agenda of economic growth and has registered high rate of overall economic growth as well as per capita income over the last decade (Hirway *et al.*, 2014). Gujarat state's approach to poverty reduction has been through a trickle down method and the idea of democracy remains narrowly confined to elections. However, the state has a long history of volunteerism whose roots can be traced to Gandhian philosophy and movement[2] for national independence as well as the philanthropic roots that can be traced to early capitalism. In particular, Ahmedabad City has a tradition of both, volunteerism as well as philanthropy, both resulting in widespread activities of Non-governmental Organisations (NGOs).

This chapter illustrates the process of mobilisation of slum dwellers around the question of their access to basic services, through the intervention of an external agency of change, a NGO named Saath based in Ahmedabad. The intervention did not, however, remain confined to organising the community for service delivery, but moved on to organising the community for policy advocacy and participatory local governance. In the normal course of development of cities in developing countries, low income residents continue to live without basic services for long periods of time, although the city governments have mandatory responsibility to provide basic services, in particular, water supply, sanitation, roads and street lights to all city residents. Such a situation arises because of number of factors: lack of finances, lack of technical and managerial capability to provide basic services, lack of ability to implement city development plans, location of the low income settlement in inaccessible sites or peripheral sites making extension of basic facilities technically infeasible[3], and above all lack of political will to provide services to 'illegal' residents of the city—slum-dwellers living without legal land tenure. An intermediating organisation, thus, in such circumstances has a very important role to play, as this case study illustrates.

A low income settlement, henceforth referred to as slum, is considered legal if it has been notified as a regular settlement by the local government. A slum resident is considered legal if she/he has a legal address, obtained through valid documents given to him/her by the various tiers of government, such as an Identity Card issued by the local government, a ration card (for the purchase of commodities from the public distribution system) issued by the state government and an election voter card issued by the Central Government. The resident may have individually accessed electricity, given that in the wake of economic reforms, Ahmedabad Electricity Company (AEC) has been privatised and individuals willing to pay have become clients of the electricity company. In short, the process of accessing basic services is a process of accretion. Over time, the settlement can be conferred with a legal land title, or a property right. The settlement under discussion in this chapter, Pravinnagar-Guptanagar, yet does not have a property right, but, has a *de facto* tenure security on account of community mobilisation as well as public policy of extending basic services to the slum.

This chapter narrates the process of community development in Pravinnagar-Guptanagar with the assistance of an external agency, gradual improvement of its physical environment, improvement in awareness and empowerment of the community in general but of the women of the community in particular, experience of women acting as agents of change and in the process empowering themselves to negotiate not just in the public domain but also in the private domain, and role of specific individuals in triggering this local change. The backdrop of this change is the introduction of a participatory slum development programme named Integrated Slum Development Programme (ISDP) by Saath, in conjunction with the Slum Networking Project (SNP) of the local government, thc Ahmedabad Municipal Corporation (AMC).

Housing, in other words, shelter, is synonymous with the dignity and security of a family. This chapter is also a documentation of Saath's experience of upgrading Pravinnagar-Guptanagar, a community of migrants from different parts of Gujarat and Rajasthan, the difficulties faced by the community and Saath in the entire process, the outcomes in terms of physical improvement and then moving beyond it for encouraging and empowering the community to participate in larger city level development processes.

What is Community Mobilisation?

The concept of community mobilisation is strongly linked to the development paradigm. For example, some community mobilisation efforts lay emphasis on material improvement or income enhancement considering the latter as the enabling condition for improving other conditions of life. Then, the objective of community mobilisation becomes economic empowerment. Some community mobilisation is for the objective of empowerment of the vulnerable population through education, whereas some have the objective of deepening democracy through laying emphasis on cooperative efforts of the people for development purposes. In the last two types of efforts, economic development is a by-product of the community mobilisation process whereas in the first one, the goal is economic development. Often, communities organise to cope with adverse situations in the absence of the State.

Whatever may be the approach, there are some core elements in the community mobilisation process: these lay emphasis on self-help efforts of the people, planning on the basis of felt needs of the people, concern with integrated and balanced development of the entire community, training and development of local leadership (Kavoori, 1974). The aim of community mobilisation should be all sided development of the community including social, political, economic, cultural and moral development, making the community self-sufficient and self-reliant (Mehta, 1974).

Community mobilisation is in no way a new idea. It is often said that community mobilisation is old wine in a new bottle. Local welfare mechanisms have been in existence for long and there is a long history of local organising actions for local improvement, mainly on voluntary basis. Community development as an idea has emerged from such local initiatives and has acquired special importance in recent times, particularly in the context of the State's failure in delivering welfare to the populace.

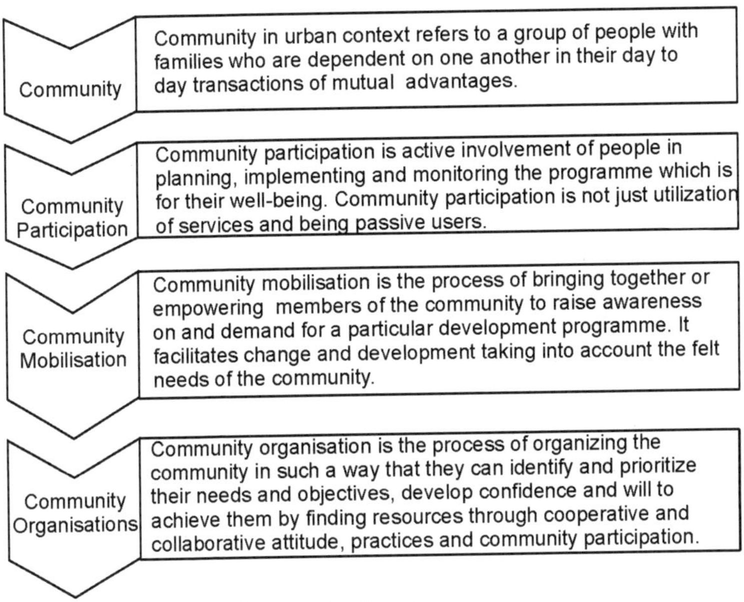

Fig. 4.1: Community to Community Organisation.

Community mobilisation is a part of a process that starts from a community and ends in community organisation. Part of the process includes mobilising necessary resources, disseminating information, generating support, and fostering cooperation across public and private sectors in the community.

What one person calls a community may not match another person's definition of it. From a sociological perspective, the notion of community refers to a group of people united by at least one common characteristic, such as belief and values, religion, language, territory, culture, occupation etc. Community therefore is a flexible concept. Communities may be viewed as systems composed of individual members and sectors that have a variety of distinct characteristics and interrelationships (Thompson *et al.*,

1990). Where there is a mechanism of local self-governance, important decisions are usually made at the community or settlement level by the community members themselves. This is called community participation. Proper management of resources is the best possible way for the development of the community and when people plan and do things, it is called community mobilisation. Where there is community mobilisation, people take charge of their local reality and transform their and their community's lives.

It is not easy to define community mobilisation, although everyone knows what the term means in practice. Community mobilisation can be defined as a process designed to promote better living, if possible with the initiative of the community itself, but if not so, then by the use of techniques for motivating the community in order to secure positive, active and enthusiastic response towards a movement for change. It is a process where, generally, there is an external agent of change who motivates and organises community for a desired goal. In most cases, the desired goal is improvement in the standard of living.

There are nearly as many definitions of community mobilisation today, as there are communities and organisations using it as a strategy. But here community mobilisation can be defined as, "a capacity building process through which community members, group or organisation plan, carry out and evaluate activities on a participatory and sustained basis to improve their access to basic amenities, education, health services and their overall standard of living either on their own initiative or stimulated by others" (Grabman and Snetro, 2003). Thus, community mobilisation is a process by which, a community recognises its needs, prioritises them, develops confidence and will to work among the people, locates resources—internal as well external—and in doing so develops co-operative and collaborative attitudes within the community.

Participation is the essential element of any community mobilisation. As community participation increases, community ownership and capacity increases, resulting in community action and continuous improvement in quality of community life in a sustainable manner. It brings together policy makers and opinion leaders, local, state, and central governments, professional groups, religious groups, and individual community members. Community mobilisation empowers individuals and groups to take some kind of action to facilitate change. A community mobilises when people become aware of a common need and decide together to take action to create shared benefits. Those concerned about the issue must create the momentum for mobilisation or else it cannot be sustained over time. Once it is decided to mobilise the community to conduct or expand activities, a community coalition is required to be built. Further, a democracy can only flourish when it has deep roots in a self-reliant community with a sense of social responsibility. Community mobilisation makes it feasible and practicable to provide people a chance of practicing self governance and understanding its difficulties (Dayal, 1960). In the spirit of Abraham Lincoln; community mobilisation may be defined as development of the community, by the community and for the community.

The process of community mobilisation in urban areas is more difficult than in rural areas, since the urban communities are characterised by occupational relations in contrast to the caste and kinship relations found in rural areas. But in India, the situation is not so critical, as even in the cities, migrants assemble according to their castes, kinships and localities. The pattern is prevalent in almost all the slum areas. Many a times it is a challenge for the agency mobilising the community, to integrate it with other castes and religion people.

The genesis of any community mobilisation is a deep felt urge from the hearts of the deprived people for development and improvement. In cities, the slum dwellers see around themselves other people from the same city, enjoying a much better quality of life than themselves—residing in better houses, using all the basic amenities, paved streets, good roads, better medical facilities, quality education for their children and all what is considered indispensable for better living. Most of the time, the urban poor are not aware of the Government programmes and policies or they are not willing to pay for it. In such a situation, an external agency may present the community with handy solutions to their problems and show a possibility of change. The local community has to accept the idea and own the solution themselves. Any imposition from external agency, even for best solutions for the community would not work. Imposition could take a meaning of self-interest of the intervening agency and this may not work. A good metaphor to represent the process of community mobilisation is "You can bring horse to water but you cannot make it drink". Hence, an important dimension of the process of change through community mobilisation is to constantly motivate and educate the community towards options and methods of change.

Ahmedabad and the Slum Networking Programme (SNP)

Ahmedabad is the seventh largest metropolis in India, with a population of 6.5 million in 2011[4] and an area of 466 square kilometres[5] with her expansion in February 2006 from 198 square kilometres and population of 3.5 million. The city has 600 years of history, but, is known in contemporary history for its role in the national freedom struggle. Here, Father of the Nation, Mahatma Gandhi, established an *ashram* on his return from South Africa and started his active engagement with the Indian freedom movement. His ideas of volunteerism, trusteeship and simple living found their roots in the ethos of the city, leading to large number of NGOs establishing roots in the city. This case study of community mobilisation is, therefore, in a sense, an outcome of the voluntary ethos of the city, linked to the Gandhian ideology that has dominated the public discourse in Ahmedabad City.

Ahmedabad, otherwise, is a prosperous city. Since, city level per capita incomes are not available, we have to look for proxy indicators of economic wealth. Ahmedabad is recognised as one of the few financial hubs in India. In the recent years, the city's real estate market has registered about 250 per cent to 300 per cent increase and the western periphery of the city is dotted with many high income 'gated communities'. The speculative land market has also penetrated the eastern periphery of the city. It needs to be mentioned that the city is bifurcated into two distinct parts, the western globalising part and the eastern industrial part under decline due to decline of large-scale industries and high level of informalisation of the work and economy (Mahadevia, 2002a, 2002b).

Ahmedabad entered a phase of severe economic crises from late 1980s to late 1990s during which her main economic base, cotton textile mills closed down and a large section of labour force was displaced from organised to unorganised sector (Mahadevia, 2002a). The retrenched labour shifted to the power loom industries at almost half the salaries and to self-employment—37 per cent of males and 65 per cent of females were self-employed in 1999-2000 (Mahadevia, 2008) without any social security. Regularly employed (a large section among them have some social security) workers among the males decreased from about 45 per cent in 1987 to 33 per cent in 1999, over a 12 year period and that among the females also decreased from 30 per cent to 20 per cent (Mahadevia, 2008). A survey of 1,000 households in 1998-99 in Ahmedabad estimated that around 75.3 per cent of the total workers were in informal employment, which included 70.2 per cent employed in the informal sector and 5.1 per cent employed in the registered industrial units but having no social or employment security (Unni, 1999).

A study conducted by Unni and Uma Rani (2002), on the income and employment in the city of Ahmedabad points out rapid growth of employment in informal sector than in the formal sector. The share of employment in informal sector was 77 per cent and it generated 47 per cent of the total city income. In short, the poor contribute to the globalising economy of Ahmedabad as much as the non-poor. But the poor do so without receiving the due economic or other civic amenities or services at par with the well to do people.

An estimate of population living in slums in Ahmedabad puts this figure at 41 per cent living in the slums and *chawls* in 1990 (ASAG, 1992). A more recent figure says that 25.77 per cent are living in slums[6], while the population census gives an estimate of 13.46 per cent living in slums in the city (Office of the Registrar General and Census Commissioner, India 2005: 22). A primary survey of all the slums carried out by Mahila Housing SEWA Trust (MHT) on behalf of the AMC in early 2000 states that there are around 710 slums in the city housing around 0.9 million population[7]. The physical environment, in terms of housing conditions and availability of basic services determines the productivity and consequently the quality of life in these slums which require significant improvement.

Among the many firsts, the city has an innovative slum development programme, initiated by the AMC in 1996-97 with the participation and partnership of the NGOs of the city. This is the Slum Networking Programme (SNP) (*See* Acharya and Parikh, 2002; Joshi, 2002; Dutta 2002). This programme was for improving physical infrastructure in the slums and also social infrastructure wherever the NGOs were present. The idea of SNP was to integrate the slum dwellers into the mainstream of society. It was felt that the fragmented efforts made to provide infrastructure facility to the slums during the last few decades did not have desired results and therefore, could not change the character of the poverty in the city nor did it help in improving education, health and sanitary conditions in the slums. This partnership-based slum development programme had community at its core, partnering with the social institutions, industry organization (private sector), local government (here the AMC), and the NGO that acted as a facilitator, for extending physical and social infrastructure in the slums. The SNP aimed at giving dignity to the community and treated the slum dwellers as partners rather than beneficiaries in the project. So the project was treated as a participatory planning and implementation programme rather than simply a charity programme.

The Slum Networking Project had mainly two components:

(i) *Improvements in Physical Environment:* This component contained the following seven facilities—(i) water supply to individual households, (ii) sewerage to individual households, (iii) individual toilets, (iv) roads and paving, (v) storm water drainage, (vi) street lighting, and (vii) tree plantation.

(ii) *Community Development and Social Infrastructure:* This component consisted of formation of neighbourhood groups, women's groups (*mahila mandal*) and youth groups (*yuvak mandal*) with the active involvement of NGO(s). Through this, the slum residents were encouraged and convinced to share the costs of the project, participate in the decision making and then post-project maintenance of the assets created. NGOs also took up the work of extending education and health facilities like non-formal education programmes, maternal and child health. They also engaged themselves in providing vocational training. The cost for community development component was around Rs. 1,000 per dwelling unit, out of which, NGOs shared 30 per cent of the cost. The cost of additional activities was also borne by the NGOs. The slum dwellers were extended the facility of micro-finance at their doorstep by the SEWA Bank. The community was expected to pay Rs. 2,100 as their contribution to the project and they need to pay this amount upfront. Those who could not pay were extended the credit by the SEWA Bank.

Under this project, slums selected for upgradation were given an assurance that they would not be displaced by the AMC for at least 10 years. In other words, the slum dwellers were been assured a *de facto* slum tenure for duration of 10 years. This has been done through a resolution by the AMC. This 'no demolition' policy has acted as a major incentive for the slum dwellers to participate in the project.

Introducing Pravinnagar-Guptanagar, Vasna

In essence, the story of Devuben (Box 4.1) is the story of empowerment of the women in Pravinnagar-Guptanagar and consequently, development of this settlement. The slum is located in Vasna ward, in the west zone of Ahmedabad municipal area (see Exhibit 4.1). When the slum developed, it was on the south-west periphery, but with the expansion of city limits in 2006, it has been engulfed by the city. On one side is of the ward is Ashram Road, a major thoroughfare of the city, running parallel to the river, and eventually joining the Ahmedabad-Rajkot highway in the south and National Highway (NH) number eight going to Delhi, in the north. The southern part of the slum abets one of the ring roads of the city. The Ashram Road section is a very busy road, with the city's public transport buses as well as inter-city buses operating on it. There are large commercial establishments on this road. This main road, therefore, is always very crowded. There is a large city bus terminal and also a public health centre of the AMC nearby. In terms of access to public facilities, this slum is very well located.

The population of Pravinnagar-Guptanagar is 7,416 persons in 1,314 households and in the area of approximately 80,000 sq.mt. The sex ratio of the settlement is 996 with an average household size of 6, indicating long-settled households. The literacy rate is 75.5 per cent in which male literacy rate is high at 85.0 per cent and female literacy rate is 66.2 per cent which is lower than average male and female literacy of Ahmedabad of 87.8 per cent and 71.1 per cent respectively.

The land of Pravinnagar-Guptanagar and surrounding settlements was a grazing land of Vasna village, now merged within the AMC. It is one of the four slums in a cluster of about 5,000 slum households. This cluster was formed after the flooding in the River Sabarmati in 1973 and the slum dwellers on the riverbank, who lost their houses shifted to Pravinnagar-Guptanagar and nearby areas, forming slums. Some of the flood affected households were shifted to Sankalitnagar, a new settlement designed and facilitated by the NGO, Ahmedabad Study Action Group (ASAG). The first occupants of the Pravinnagar-Guptanagar were 250 to 300 households of the *Bhils*, a tribal community. Their settlement is now a *chawl* (a section of a settlement) of the Pravinnagar-Guptanagar and is called *"Ranavas"*. Subsequently, people of *Kathiyawadi* community (from Kathiawar, now called Saurashtra region of Gujarat state) came to live in the settlement. They formerly lived in Ambawadi area of

Table 4.1: Community-wise household distribution

Community	*No. of Households*
Harijan/Bhil/Vaghri	290
Vanjhara/Marwari	307
Bharvad	200
Kathiyawadi	517
Total	1314

Source: Primary Survey.

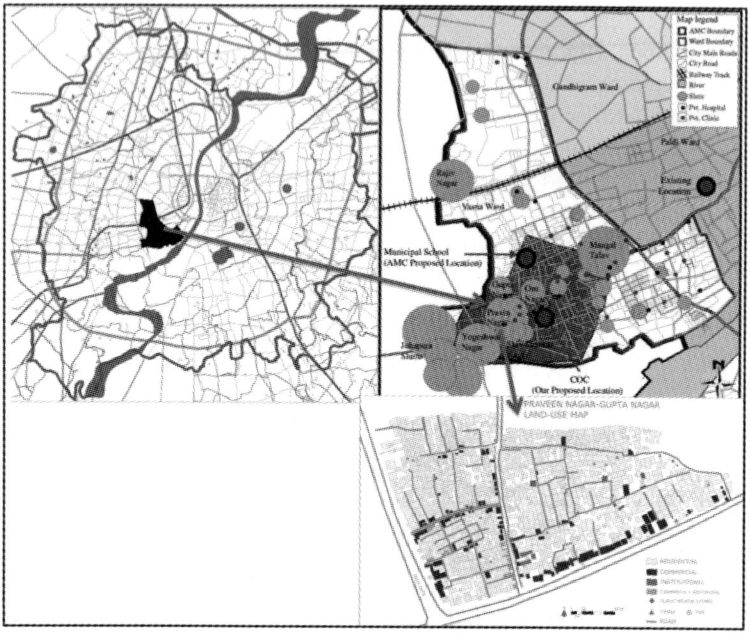

Source: (i) Vasna ward map http://www.emeraldinsight.com/fig/3240010204005.png
(ii) Pravinnagar-Guptanagar Land use by CUE.

Exhibit 4.1: Vasna Ward in Ahmedabad, Pravinnagar-Guptanagar in Vasna Ward and Land use of Pravinnagar-Guptanagar

Ahmedabad. These *Kathiyawadi* people called their relatives from within and outside of Ahmedabad city thereby enlarging the community. As of now, this community has the largest number of households compared to other communities; 517 out of 1,314 total households in Pravinnagar-Guptanagar (Table 4.1).

This site developed as a slum because of its proximity to central Ahmedabad, availability of a public transport hub at Vasna and affordable land prices. Further, there was no legal owner of the land present at the time of encroachment on this land. The land belongs to a category called "*Inamdar Zameen*[8]", which was given as a gift by the former feudal lord under the Moghul rule. But, over time, some of these giftees died and the lands remained without formal land owner. The land parcel was assessed for property tax, but, no one came forward to pay tax. Incidentally, in 1976, a person named Hirabhai Govindbhai Patel paid due tax for the

Box 4.1: Devuben: My Story of Debt to Development

Devuben's story combines two different dimensions of the human spirit, on one hand the desire to live a fulfilling life and on the other hand a facilitative role played by a Civil Society Organisation (CSO) seeking to empower the community. Her determination to survive, to surmount poverty, and to progress goes hand in hand with empowerment of the community.

"I belong to a small village called Sapar near Rajkot city. In 1988, my husband lost Rs. 70,000 in his electronics business and we had no means to repay the debt. One of our relatives made my husband an offer to start an electrical business in Ahmedabad, which brought us to this city. For the first 15 days, we stayed with a relative in a slum near the railway tracks. Then we moved out to a rental place in a hutment colony named Rajivnagar, where the living conditions were deplorable with huge rats running around, which made me stay awake the whole night. The next day, I forced my husband to shift out of this settlement and we shifted to Pravinnagar-Guptanagar to a rental hut. This settlement was also filthy; the roads were *katcha*, there was no sanitation or drainage, residents defecated in open, sullying the roads and garbage was strewn around everywhere. To add to these woes, there was no water supply and we queued up everyday from 4 a.m. to 10 a.m. just to fetch two pots of water. There were quarrels. Women got so tired every day due to fetching water and doing morning household chores that they could neither supervise their children's education nor take up employment to earn additional income for the household.

We had to survive in the city. Thus, my husband and I took additional loan of Rs. 50,000 from a local money lender. To repay that loan, we sold all the family jewellery, mine as well as my mother-in-law's. Around that time, I learned about the enterprise of *papad*[9] and *khakhra*[10] making and joined the endeavour to earn Rs. 200[11] per month, working from 9 a.m. to 6 p.m. In addition, I joined a sewing class, where, because I could not afford the fee of Rs. 25, I offered to sweep and clean the office instead. I was there for six months and when I found out that I was pregnant, I quit the *khakhra* making and asked my father to buy me a sewing machine. I worked out of home from then on.

One day, Sonalben[12], from Saath visited our neighbourhood enquiring about status of vaccinations in the slum and informing us about a camp to be held the next day. I took my new born daughter to the camp and then asked Saath members if there was any work opportunity for me. They told me that they were about to start a *balghar* (pre-school/nursery) in the slum. I told them that I had studied up to 9th grade and also enjoyed working with children and would, therefore, like to try working in it. They hired two women for the *balghar*, one was Kailashben from my area and other was me. We were first trained in various methods, techniques and also the theoretical aspects of childcare and development. I think my dedication and hard work made me popular among the children. Gradually parents began trusting me as well. After discussions on the Slum Networking Project (SNP) had begun in our area (in mid-1990s), I along with the rest of the Saath team began going to each house discussing the programme with them and also held community meetings. It was a new experience for me; I was interacting with people from different communities, regardless of caste, class or religion. People started recognising me in the community and I knew everyone by their first names. It was a very fulfilling experience.

Meanwhile in 1995 we bought our own house for Rs. 35,000. It was a hut. Today we have built a *pucca* house on that same piece of land. I have two children, one daughter studying in 11th standard and a son who is in 9th standard. I want to educate them. I have told them that they can study, as much as they want.

I was appointed as the manager of Sakhi Mahila Mandal (SMM), when it was set up in 1996. After the 2001 earthquake, I remember collecting materials for the affected people in Kutch. We then went to Kutch and that was when Saath expanded its work in rural areas. During the communal violence of 2002, Saath initially collected relief materials from the households and when Rajendrabhai (the head) asked who among the Saath team was willing to work in relief camps, I volunteered along with others. All of us knew that there was no compulsion whatsoever, but most of us joined in. I did not tell my husband, because I knew he would never allow me to go. So I told him that we were going for fieldwork. A van would come to the settlement to pick us up and then drop us. After a few days, my husband suspected what I was doing and I had to tell him. I then shared my experience of the camps with him; of how the victims were suffering, how the children felt threatened and so on. I also told him that it was safe to go there.

Working in the relief camps changed my life, it opened my eyes. I too had gone in with some fear and prejudice, but all that changed the moment I stepped into the camp. The stories of horror that I heard shook me. We started activities with the children and women. Not many people in my community and locality understood why I was doing it, and it was a struggle having to explain myself all the time. But, I did, I shared my experience of the horror of those camps. I feel that many people started understanding the gravity of what had occurred. Over a period of time Saath set up an office in Juhapura (2002 riot-affected Muslim area) and today we have all our organisation's programmes running in Juhapura. In the year 2007, I was appointed as a co-ordinator of the Urban Resource Centre (URC) for the whole Vasna area.

Today, I feel proud of myself and my work and I know my husband and children are proud of me too. I know that I am looked up to within my community, as a leader. I am not afraid to try new things and from working in the *balghar* to coordinating the URC at Vasna—I know I have come a long way."

—Devuben Parmar, Co-ordinator, URC, Vasna

entire land and received informal rights on the land. He sold plots of the land, on the Rs. 10 stamp papers to people who wanted to stay here. There was an intermediary in the process, a slum lord, who then begun collecting Rs. 20 per month from every household, as protection money. While such land transactions were going on, the AMC, in its Development Plan of 1976, reserved part of the land of the settlement as a Green belt, and froze any legal land development on the plot. But, the informal transactions continued. Thus, the land tenure is locked between reservation in the city's Development Plan and informal landowner.

After the SNP implementation started, the residents had begun receiving property tax bills from the AMC. Once that begun, they questioned the slum lord about validity of his rent (protection money) collection. The residents also demanded rent receipt from him. He could neither answer their questions nor give them the rent receipt. Gradually, the residents stopped paying the protection money. After all, the settlement was semi-legalised by the local government and the people needed no protection. In the city's Development Plan, part of Pravinnagar-Guptanagar is on the land reserved as Green belt. Although, the Green Belt reservation has been lifted, the settlement's status has not been legalised.

The settlement started expanding because of influx of the relatives of the residents of Pravinnagar-Guptanagar and of surrounding settlements. Unlike in the other areas of Ahmedabad, different communities settled here. There are different *chawls* (*vas*) for different communities, so in one slum people stay in their respective community *chawl* or lane like in a village. There were approximately 100 houses of Muslims also who shifted to Juhapura, across the road from Pravinnagar-Guptanagar, after the 2002 communal violence in Ahmedabad. The settlement received new residents from Juhapura, the Hindus who shifted to Pravinnagar-Guptanagar after the same event.

Chronology of Interventions

The Entry Level Intervention (1991-1993)

Saath started its activities in Ahmedabad from Behrampura area. Saath's initial activity was to mobilise the youth through an action research course. This led to the formation of a youth group called Ekta Yuvak Mandal (EYM). The EYM prioritised the needs of the area as sanitation, tuberculosis control and affordable credit. EYM acted as a facilitator in the AMC's 90:10 toilet construction scheme as well, where 90 per cent of the cost was borne by the AMC and 10 per cent by the beneficiary. This was followed by TB elimination programme and later a credit co-operative society was established. Saath worked for one year in Behrampura on TB elimination activities and a credit programme, along with extending basic services.

After this initial start up, Saath sought suggestions from the residents of Behrampura on another location where it could start its activities. One of the predominant communities in Behrampura being *Marwari*, they suggested another location which had concentration of *Marwaris* and that was Pravinnagar-Guptanagar, where Behrampura residents had relatives. Thus, in 1992, Saath visited Pravinnagar-Guptanagar for the first time. The process through which Saath came to the settlement was, therefore, quite accidental.

The first activity of Saath in the settlement was to just have a talk with the leaders of the various communities living in the settlement as everyone's involvement was required for the development of Pravinnagar-Guptanagar. Saath members would visit the settlement everyday and discuss with people how they could assist them in bringing a positive change in their lives. The task was stupendous on two counts. Saath was new to the area and did not have any record of interaction with the people. The question was why people would trust some external agency that talked about change and change through participation when the political parties always talked about free welfare for the poor! The second difficulty was getting all the residents together for a discussion about the settlement. To address the latter, Saath decided to conduct a household survey to understand the immediate needs of the residents of Pravinnagar-Guptanagar. In April 1992, four women of the settlement, on behalf of Saath, carried out a survey of 100 households in Pravinnagar-Guptanagar, charging only Rs. 1 per questionnaire.

The results of this survey suggested that Saath should start health and education programmes in the settlement. Thus, Saath started a health centre in the settlement in 1992. Not having any infrastructure in the settlement, Saath started the vaccination programme under a tree while the organisation was searching for a place in Pravinnagar-Guptanagar to start a health centre. Saath employed three women of the settlement to help out in health programmes. Simultaneously the NGO also started education programme. Initially Devuben (Box 4.1) and Kailashben worked in the education programme. The settlement residents did not trust the health initiative and because of superstitions did not want their children to be vaccinated. Hence, the task of convincing the residents to take benefit of Saath's health programme was difficult. They also did not trust the education initiative because Devuben and Kailashben were from the settlement itself and the residents suspected their ability to teach their children. But, Saath persisted and made every effort to win the trust of the residents; some members of the organisation would visit the settlement everyday, discuss with the residents about their concerns, noted their requirements and in the process also convinced them to participate in their programmes.

Box 4.2: Snapshot of Saath

Saath is a NGO registered as a Public Charitable Trust (E-7257) with the Charity Commissioner, Ahmedabad in February 1989. In Gujarati the word Saath means, 'Together, Co-operation, a Collective or Support'.

Saath conceptualised an Integrated Development Programme aimed to address all developmental aspects of a slum by converging state, NGO and private sector resources with community needs for the slums of Ahmedabad in 1989. Saath is present in two states—Gujarat and Rajasthan; 17 towns and cities, 160 villages, and two districts in Gujarat; and in six districts in Rajasthan.

Right from the beginning, Saath has envisaged development as a participatory process and defined its role as that of facilitating these processes towards improvement in the quality of life of the urban and rural poor. Saath runs programmes for women, children, men and youth in areas of livelihoods, capacity building, health and education, physical infrastructure improvement, URCs, slum development and natural resource management. It also has a documentation and research cell and provides development support to other organisations or agencies.

Coverage of Saath's activities at the time of the study in 2011 was[13]:

- 4 URCs reaching out to 100,000 population in slums. This number could increase to 200 URCs across Gujarat in 7 Municipalities.
- 48 Ummeed centres in Gujarat and 8 in Rajasthan.
- 7 Pre-school Education centres in Ahmedabad.
- 1 Community Video Unit reaching approximately 100 people everyday, through day and night screenings.
- 5 Microfinance branches with more than 10,000 members.
- 200 Urmila Home Managers and 200 clients.
- 155 Self-help Groups (SHGs) in rural areas with artisans.
- 5 Youth groups with 148 members.
- 3 Education Centres for child labour in Ahmedabad and actively participating in 'Curb Child Labour Campaign' in Viramgam and Dholka talukas of Gujarat state.

In 1993, Saath rented a dwelling in Valmiki *vas* and started a health centre there, addressing the health concerns of women and children. Deliveries were done at home attended by untrained *dais* (midwives). All types of superstitions related to pregnancy and childcare were prevailing among the people. There was an immediate need to bring scientific approach to health care, particularly of women. There was also need to convince people to vaccinate their children. The health centre, besides carrying out its regular work of conducting two health camps every month, holding health check-ups of pregnant women and regular consultation on gynaecological problems, also engaged in educating women about maternal and child health care. Arrangement was made for a lady doctor to monitor pregnant women and conduct sonography.

Complications related pregnancies, if any, were attended to. Pregnant and lactating mothers were given nutrition supplements twice a month, which consisted of 2 bananas, half litre milk, 100 grams dates, dry coconut and 1½ kilograms sprouts. Initially, women would sell-off the free nutritional supplements given to them by the centre to a nearby shop for small amounts of money. Saath's fieldworkers made great effort to make these women understand the importance of nutritional food for them and their unborn child.

These were not the only hurdles. The health centre was also working on TB and in this case too, they had to overcome the false notions of the residents regarding the disease. Thus, health care programme included not just vaccination of pregnant mother and infants, nutritional supplements to pregnant and lactating mothers and treatment of diseases such as TB, but also substantial health education to inculcate scientific view about health.

Simultaneously a crèche was started in Bharwad *vas*. Five women—Devuben, Madhuben, Ramilaben, Kailashben and Ramilaben joined the school as teachers. As discussed earlier the slum dwellers were sceptical about the ability of these women in imparting education to their children. Residents were of the opinion, "How could these women, who were living among them, impart professional education?" These five women succeeded as they were given an intense training of fifteen days on how to deal with the children, what should be the atmosphere of the class, language skills, how to teach math, curriculum development, how to tell stories, and overall development of the children based on an approach of seven steps of child's development. These women were trained by one child psychologist, who emphasised Montessori Method of teaching, which had tools of teaching such as storytelling, drama, etc. A conscious decision was made by Saath to hire more people and it hired Pravinbhai, who then was the only man working at the community level along with above mentioned five women.

It was not easy to get the children to school. They had to visit every house in the settlement to enrol children. But, with great patience and hard work, they managed to enrol 32 children, which constituted their first batch of students. The team conducted three home visits daily, meetings with the parents, exposure visits—taking children on bus rides, visits to the zoo and a steady stream of dialogue with the parents to build the confidence of the families. Subsequently, the enrolments increased.

Improvement in their children's ability made the parents believe in the teachers and Saath's efforts in education area. And hence, from 1993 onwards, the education programme became more intense than before. After one year of starting the education programme, parents asked Saath to introduce meals as well, thinking that if the children got some food in between then they could attend the school for longer hours, say for three to four hours a day. In order to sustain the *balghars* a fee of Rs. 10 was introduced to cover the food costs, which the parents willingly accepted to pay. Eventually, parents started paying the monthly fees for pre-school, supplementary and special classes and also the conveyance cost for picnics to gardens, zoo, post office, bus station etc. Teachers began holding regular meetings with the parents. Parents were regularly informed of their child's progress; everyday, one teacher would go to the house of three students to meet the mothers and tell them about their child's behaviour in the class, progress in various subjects and interests. At the time of the study, the parents paid Rs. 75 per month.

From Children to Women (1993-1996)

Saath also felt that there was an urgent requirement of the residents in Pravinnagar-Guptanagar to acquire skills that would increase their incomes. Three types of courses to impart such skills were started in 1993; tailoring and embroidery, electric gadget repairing and scooter repairing. The tailoring and embroidery course has continued since then. The participants in this course have been women and adolescent girls, who use these skills at home or for taking up earning from home. The course has also provided an important forum to the adolescent girls to also talk about their concerns relating to various aspects of marriage. Like other programmes, for this programme also, participants pay fees and bear the material costs making the effort financially self-sustainable.

All these activities by Saath in the settlement brought recognition for the organisation and also trust of the residents. To bring about a sense of community, local workers, mostly women, were chosen from almost all the six different communities. This approach went a long way in reducing traditional myths and hostilities amongst different communities leading to an understanding that concerns the communities faced were common to all communities, especially for women. Through this process, for the first time, residents from different communities started to communicate with each other.

Seeing the progress of the active women members of Saath from the settlement and their increased respect in the family as well as the settlement, other women of the settlement showed their willingness to join the development programme. In 1995, general consensus had veered around setting up a *mahila mandal* in the settlement. The main objective was to bring women from the community together and give them a platform to tackle their own concerns and have their voice heard in the community. Saath adopted a strategy to take men of the community into confidence before setting up the *mahila mandal* so as to avoid conflict. As most traditional communities, Pravinnagar-Guptanagar was and still is largely a male dominated community. The women as individuals and as a collective were not strong at that point to counter or stand up to the opposition within their homes or the community. Saath arranged a meeting with the men to inform them that they were setting up a *mahila mandal.* This worked well, there was no opposition and the *mandal* began its work smoothly. Some might call that process as seeking permission from men like in any patriarchal society, but, it indeed worked. It is hard to take an ideological position in this matter.

On May 8, 1996, Sakhi[14] Mahila Mandal (SMM) was formed. SMM, a women's organisation is the Community Based Organisation (CBO), which sustains the slum development programmes. When it was started, the men thought this organisation would be anti-men and hence did not permit their wives to join the SMM. When they realised that the women were working for the welfare of the slum, the men begun to co-operate. The core group of SMM is formed with the workers of the various programmes like, health workers, teachers etc. During the course of implementing various integrated slum development programmes, the women acquired technical and managerial skills essential for sustaining the CBO and very importantly, have earned trustworthiness as leaders. The governing committee is regularly elected and the accounts are regularly audited. Members pay an entrance fee and annual subscription.

Starting the SNP (1996-2001)

While working on health in the community, Saath realised that all health problems evidently emanated from the complete lack of basic services, water supply and sanitation, in the area. This is when the idea of SNP struck roots in 1996. Lack of water supply resulted in people not taking a bath regularly, there was no sanitation and hence there was open defecation and garbage was not lifted. Devubhen's story narrates the condition of when they had moved into the settlement. Saath identified a pressing need for basic services like water supply, sewerage, storm water drainage, individual toilets and bath space. However, the resources required were extensive and exorbitant for the slum dwellers and the organisation. Discussions with the residents about installing a drainage system showed that residents were ready to pay for these facilities. In fact, around 300 houses had already installed their private, illegal drainage system and a few houses had unapproved water connection.

Saath initiated talks with Mr. Himanshu Parikh, the man behind the Indore SNP. There was a general misconception that it was technically impossible to get infrastructure into slums as they had limited open space, which was cleared on knowing more details about the Indore project. Meanwhile, Saath, by then, had already participated in the first SNP in a slum called Sanjaynagar, Naroda ward, in Ahmedabad in June 1995 and realised that this was a feasible approach for Pravinnagar-Guptanagar as well.

The 1996-2002 period has been a major turning point in the lives of the residents of Pravinnagar-Guptanagar. Discussions for getting the basic services were going on with the residents of the settlement. After intense discussions it was decided that SNP should be initiated in the settlement. Saath negotiated with the AMC and Arvind Mills (the private sector participant in the first SNP in Ahmedabad) to include Pravinnagar-Guptanagar in the pilot project because it felt that the strategy of the project, which is cost sharing and payment by residents, provision of basic services at a household-level and the lead by the urban local body (ULB) were really sound and sustainable.

The AMC provided an estimate of Rs. 14,000 as per household, which included Rs. 2,000 as the household contribution and Rs. 100 in addition (to Rs. 14,000) as one time maintenance charges. As discussed above, some households had already spent to get unapproved water connection while some had paid Rs. 500 to the community leaders to get the connections. These households, therefore, were not ready to pay more towards the water and sewerage connections. The fieldworkers of Saath convinced them that what they would get through SNP would be legal and then no municipal officials would come to demolish the facility. There was initially resistance from the residents to chip in their share of the SNP. This is common; some or the other households are duped by the local politician or a local strongman through a promise of some or the other infrastructure, which is reneged on. In Pravinnagar-Guptanagar also, some households had paid Rs. 500 to some persons who had promised a pipeline, but had vanished after collecting the money. But, by then, Saath had worked in the settlement for five years and the residents had begun trusting the organisation. Gradually, all households paid up their share of

Rs. 2,100 for the SNP and Rs. 3 lakh were collected by July 1997 for the purpose.

However, the first crisis occurred when Arvind Mills pulled out of the project due to differences with the AMC during the implementation of the pilot in Sanjaynagar, Naroda. This caused the project to almost come to a standstill. In order to continue the project, it was nccessary to secure the remaining Rs. 6,000 (of the total Rs. 14,000 on each dwelling), which was originally meant to have been Arvind Mill's contribution. The AMC bailed out the impasse by accepting to take responsibility of even the private sector's share, so that the project could go on. Then, the AMC officials visited the area to start the project.

To ensure the residents that their share of money would not be taken away by Saath, a way out was found; women were asked to open an account with the SEWA Bank, where the households would deposit their contribution to the project. The SEWA Bank was invited to set up a kiosk in the settlement thrice a week to mobilise the community contribution. Over a year, all contributions had been collected. The money was given to the AMC only when the work was completed to the satisfaction of the slum residents. In spite the collection of money, the AMC had not begun work. This caused an uproar in the community and Saath had to step in and strongly follow-up with the AMC. Work commenced in 1998 and slowly people saw the infrastructure come up. The community members were so deeply involved in the process that they went to the extent of checking the materials used. There were instances when the work was stopped because the materials used were of poor quality.

The work was completed in 2000 and the water was sourced through a bore well. Total of 1,227 households benefited in Pravinnagar-Guptanagar from SNP. In 2001, a function was organised by the AMC to hand over the services to the people. Finally, the project had received large publicity as a novel project and the settlement received lot of attention and hence visitors.

Post-project maintenance of infrastructure is always a main problem and for that purpose, Saath and SMM helped the residents form five housing associations—Ekta, Navsarjan, Valmiki, Jaybhim and Rishi, within the settlement with the objective of keeping a check on upkeep and maintenance of the infrastructure.

There is an interesting history to the Pravinnagar-Guptanagar dwellers obtaining legal electricity connections. To do so, the one-time case was Rs. 10,000 in late 1990s, which was unaffordable and the dwellers obtained the electricity illegally through paying the middlemen who pilfered the same from the public connections. These connections did not have any earthing and were unsafe and had already caused death of a child and injuries to livestock from electrocution. In 2003-04 Saath put forth a proposal to the United States Agency for International Development (USAID) to get support for slum electrification. The USAID did support and extended assistance of Rs. 8,000 on the condition that the household contributed Rs. 2,000. This is how each household obtained legal meters.

Initially, the AEC resisted this attempt to extend individual metered connections to the slum dwellers. Saath and MHT together intervened and took the matter to court. Judgement was in favour of the slum dwellers and the AEC had to extend metered connections to the slum households. The USAID had contributed towards meeting a major part of the expenses for an individual metered connection. After this initial success of the programme, Saath pushed for a reduction in the cost of the connection. Realising the potential of a large market at the bottom, the AEC, which is now a private company (Torrent Power), reduced the initial one time connection cost to just Rs. 2,500 from Rs. 10,000 earlier and any slum dweller could approach the company directly to get an individual connection. At the time of our survey, over 80 per cent of the slums in Ahmedabad had legal connections.

The SNP had a spill-over effect. Saath was formerly engaged in training the women and youth for income generation, of which the women's training achieved success and women were getting work at home. Thereafter, a collective income generation programme was started in the Pravinnagar-Guptanagar in June 1998. Organising for the SNP helped in organising for income generation activities. It was decided to concentrate on the services sector of the economy, which is the fastest growing sector in urban India and not on the traditional home manufacturing of *bidis, papads, khakhra* and *agarbattis*, as was the practice in many NGO-led income generation activities. It was decided to introduce tailoring, market research support, vegetable sorting and home managers (domestic help) programme for income generation. These programmes subsequently took new and more organised forms than before. This is discussed in the next sub-section.

A micro-credit programme was fallout of the SNP. It was started in July 1998 by the SMM. It is known that a micro-credit programme meets the regular needs of finance for various purposes for low-income households. In Pravinnagar-Guptanagar, the SMM initiated a one-year savings activity. The membership target for the savings group was set at 95, this target was overshot and 100 women joined the savings programme.

The SMM opened an account with the SEWA Bank in which the savings were credited bi-monthly. Each member had their own SMM passbooks, which were regularly updated based on their deposits or withdrawals. The *mahila mandal* decided to start a loan committee and offered loans in the

Box 4.3: Benefits of Microfinance

Case 1: Ranjanben (33) lives with her husband Babubhai (35), a plumber and a daily wage earner making about Rs. 2,000 per month. Ranjanben does tailoring (stitching computer covers) earned around Rs. 2,000 per month. They live with their three sons—Prakash, who is a plumber and earned Rs. 2,000 per month and Mukesh who does light fittings and earned Rs. 1,500 per month. Their youngest son Ketan is studying in a public school and was then living in a hostel.

Ranjanben opened a savings account in the SMM in the year 1997 with an amount of Rs. 25. She first took a loan from the SMM for the small sum of Rs. 800 for the construction of her house, the remaining required amount she borrowed against her jewellery. Within two months, she was able to return the SMM loan and then took another loan of Rs. 15,000 from them against her house documents. This loan was taken by her to get back the jewellery she had mortgaged with a jeweller at the monthly interest rate of 5 per cent. She returned this loan to the SMM within two years after which she took a loan of Rs. 5,000 for renovating her house, which she returned in seven months. At the time of survey, she was repaying a loan of Rs. 15,000 taken for *pucca*-roof construction of which only Rs. 7,000 remained to be repaid.

***Case 2*:** Khaniben Atmaram Solanki opened a savings account with Sakhi Bachat Mandal in 2002. She began with a saving of around Rs. 100. She has three children, the eldest (Kokila) is married, the middle daughter (Charul) is 22 years old and has completed her Bachelors in Art and has a diploma in aviation from the Frankfinn Institute. Her youngest daughter, Deepika is 18 and has been suffering from severe mental stress. Her husband works in BSNL as an accountant and earned just Rs. 5,000 per month.

When Charul decided to take the course at Frankfinn, they found out that it would cost them Rs. 1,00,000. Charul being a bright student, after the due process was selected and had to pay Rs. 13,000 at the beginning and then at an Equal Monthly Instalment (EMI) of Rs. 8,000 thereafter. The family took a loan from Sakhi Bachat Mandal of Rs. 15,000 at the rate of 18 per cent per annum against a security of a savings instrument named Kisan Vikas Patra (KVP)[15] valued Rs. 10,000, without much of paper work. Charul has completed her aviation studies and obtained her first job with the Singapore Airlines as their ground hostess, earning a salary of Rs. 5,000 per month. After Charul's job, their lives have changed. She is the first girl in their community to have become an air hostess in a well reputed international airline. This has made a big difference in their social standing within their community. It has also opened newer opportunities for Charul. She has become a different person as she has gained in self-confidence. The next loan that they took was of Rs. 15,000 in order to take back the jewellery that they had pawned at the jeweller's, taken earlier.

range of Rs. 2,000 to Rs. 5,000 at the monthly interest rate of 1.5 per cent in 1999. Even loans were made available for the residents' contribution for the SNP. Norms for credit were also decided in consultation with the savings group members and a committee was set up to oversee the programme. The committee is elected annually. This programme dovetailed well into the SNP programme and both together led to housing upgradation.

In fact, a housing upgradation programme supported by a microfinance programme works very well for the low-income communities and without microfinance the success of the house upgrading is limited. A few households also took loans from the SMM for paying off other loans. But such cases were few and most loans from the SMM were taken for setting up a business, education of children, home improvements such as adding a storey, strengthening the walls, terraces, etc., and to get legal electricity connections. In short, the micro-finance programme supplemented the housing programme and together led to significant improvement in the living conditions of the dwellers of Pravinnagar-Guptanagar.

Consolidation (2002-2004)

The year 2002 was a critical turning point in Gujarat's history because of the communal violence, wherein approximately 2,000 people died in the state and Ahmedabad too had witnessed large scale violence. The communal tempers were high and there was a deep polarisation within the communities. Large-scale violence was concentrated in the Muslim localities, which also witnessed large influx of population that came seeking refuge. Hence, relief camps were started in many Muslim localities and one such relief camp was set up across the road from Pravinnagar-Guptanagar in Juhapura area, which Devuben helped in running (Box 4.1).

Pravinnagar-Guptanagar itself also felt the direct impact of this severe disturbance. Approximately 100 Muslim families moved out of the settlement to Juhapura area or elsewhere for personal security reasons. Similarly, the last few non-Muslim families living in Sankalitnagar (Juhapura) moved to Pravinnagar-Guptanagar. Thus, this microcosm of Ahmedabad was also homogenised on the basis of religion due to large scale political circumstances. The Muslim neighbourhood of Juhapura, which housed approximately 2.5 lakh population (Mahadevia, 2007), is just across the road from Pravinnagar-Guptanagar. In the volatile period of February-end 2002 to June 2002, this road had become a boundary between the two communities; some called it a border. The residents of

Pravinnagar-Guptanagar had seen violence, heard gunshots and spent sleepless nights during the peak of violence and so was the case on the Juhapura side. But, once the violence had stopped, a community meeting was held in Pravinnagar-Guptanagar to discuss whether the community members had participated in violence or not. It was concluded that the perpetrators of violence in the neighbouring Juhapura area were outsiders and not members of their community.

Meanwhile, in response to the need of the hour, Saath begun relief activities in the camp in Juhapura, where the Muslims affected by communal violence had congregated. The atmosphere was very tense as it was known that the violence had some sort of State's ruling party's support, if not engineered by the ruling party. To work in the relief camps to support the Muslim population could be seen as a 'pro-Muslim' act, not any humanitarian act, and likely to bring wrath of the ruling party or if not that at least censure of the ruling party.

Once the violence had subsided and the new state government was in place by the end of the year of 2002, Saath decided to carry forward its development experience to Sankalitnagar in Juhapura. It decided to work for long-term rehabilitation and with that purpose set up its office in Sankalitnagar. Thereafter, it formed local-area committees and started negotiations with the AUDA to bring in trunk services in Sankalitnagar. The residents were willing to bear rest of the costs of services. But, narrating this experience would be digressing from the community mobilisation story of Pravinnagar-Guptanagar. But, this engagement with Sankalitnagar had another deep impact on the community activities in Pravinnagar-Guptanagar itself.

One of the larger challenges for Saath at this point was to create a secular team, which could work in both areas—Pravinnagar-Guptanagar and Juhapura. Saath fell back on its time tested strategy of mixed teams formed of members belonging to different communities. Saath had done this earlier, when the residents' committees for maintaining the SNP assets were set up, and it did the same now. However, the challenge this time was tougher. Post-2002 violence, every *Ahmedabadi* (resident of Ahmedabad) viewed himself or herself as a Hindu or a Muslim. To bring communities together in times of such heightened inter-community tensions and mistrust was going to be a difficult task. This hurdle was overcome successfully. Local area development teams were formed for the purpose. While doing so, even gender balance and caste balance was taken into consideration. This helped build rapport at the professional level and eventually at the community level as well. In other words, associational network was put together for a common purpose of local development and negotiations with the local government. People, who did not interact with each other earlier, began sharing more informal relationships than before after working together as a team for a common purpose.

Besides resolution on the communal harmony issue, other consolidations could be observed in the settlement. In this phase, SMM's role increased greatly to the extent of becoming facilitators for local development activities and Saath began consciously moving towards supporting and facilitating larger programmes. The change was visible because as compared to the hands-on work in 1992, Saath took a step back and more of the programmes were being implemented by the SMM. The SNP was the beginning, where the SMM took an active role in mobilising the community, carrying out meetings and through this their confidence had increased. Simultaneously, the residents of the communities observed the permanent changes through SNP and this cemented their trust in the work that SMM members were doing.

Another visible change seen in the Pravinnagar-Guptanagar during this phase was increased investments in the home improvement. This was an outcome of the SNP that provided community level infrastructure and *de facto* tenure security for 10 years. Individual household's access to water and toilets at the house level brought down the incidence of diseases and reduced health expenditure. The SNP intervention and community associations led to general increase in awareness leading to increase in number of families sending their children to schools—both private and government and most importantly an increase in enrolment of girls in school. Also, women's time being freed because of water supply coming to the homes also led to women paying more attention to their children's education. On the whole, the SNP intervention through community processes led to remarkable change in the physical and social development of the residents of the settlement (*See* Joshi, 2002 for more details on these aspects).

With basic services being taken care of, people were able to focus on important needs such as employment, education, improvement of their houses. The SNP in Ahmedabad and elsewhere has shown that when water, sanitation and infrastructure are provided to people, there is an independent change in the status of education, employment and health. What had started out as a health intervention for women and then as livelihood project for women and young girls had expanded to building of women's capacity, housing conditions improvement and eventually community mobilisation for managing their settlement locally.

In this consolidation phase, a new programme was initiated and which was training women working as housemaids to become professional home managers. Urmila Home Managers trains women from slums in how to be more efficient home managers. The programme also ensured job security for these women through formal, legal contracts with clients. At the time of our study, it had created steady income of Rs. 3,000 (average) for 200 women in Ahmedabad.

Saath had also begun to work with youth, as mentioned earlier. A large number of young people in slums either dropped out of school at an early age or quit studying after the tenth standard. This led them to join the casual labour force with very little bargaining power and no chance at improving their skills. The vocational training programmes at the time focused on skill enhancement, but with no linkage to the market or component of enabling youth to identify potential job options. What this meant was that the circle of poverty continued to the next generation. Saath's intervention with youth aimed at breaking this hapless cycle.

The *Ummeed* (meaning hope) programme[16] was designed and implemented as a market based product. It was started out as Ek Mouka Udaan with its first centre in Behrampura and had a batch of 120 in 1995. Since then, the programme has expanded to over 60 centres across Gujarat and Rajasthan, with multiple funding partners and reaching to over 25,000 youth since its inception. *Ummeed*'s innovation was in its strategy to approach the issue from both demand and supply side. Each *Ummeed* centre undertook market research on available employment options and then assessed the employment need of the youth and accordingly designed the courses and their curriculum. The relevant trainers were hired and programme was marked among the slum dwellers. The course was for a period of three months and targeted the youth (both men and women) in the age of 18-35 years. Each centre is physically set up within the slums, which makes it accessible to the slum youth. The programme goes a step beyond traditional and other vocational courses, by providing the assurance of placement at the end of the training. The Vasna centre was set up in 2007 and had enrolled 1,009, trained 770, and placed 410 youth at the time of the study.

Linking Phase—From Settlement to Community-based Urban Governance Structure (2005-2009)

This phase of work in Pravinnagar-Guptanagar is similar to the Linking-up and Self-Evaluation phases described by Oakley (1991). The linking phase focuses on networking, building outside contacts, building alliances, articulation with outside support. Self-evaluation is about adjusting strategies, its replication and expansion. The organisation, post-SNP, moved from a programmatic mode into a sectoral one. Livelihoods, microfinance, information dissemination, health, and education were identified for programmatic intervention. For example, in livelihood sector, the programmes worked with women, youth and men to build their capacities and further help link them with employment. The SMM over a period of time had evolved from a platform for women in the area, into a decision-making body and also a recognised authority on different concerns within the Pravinnagar-Guptanagar. It has been recognised also as an organisation engaging with the government on slums and urban poverty concerns.

The work was then expanded to setting up local structures that could assist in local governance. These were called the URCs, set up by Saath in 2007 creating a link between the state government, local government (the AMC) and the people. They were to play a dual role, that of bringing information, services and schemes to the people and allowing the service providers (government, corporate, private) to understand specific needs of various target groups. The National Government, under the JNNURM programme, mainstreamed the idea of the URC, which were expected to develop and nurture the human and knowledge resource base to support capacity building for improved city governance on a continuing basis, with an emphasis on increasing access of the urban poor to basic services and create space for their participation in the developmental process.[17]

The CBOs set up in this development journey by Saath have, over the time, become programme partners of the latter, who has now become a facilitator, focusing on networking with external agencies, fund raising, expanding the programmes, advocacy at local, state and national level and partnering with local and national level organisations for various joint programmes. The CBOs manage their own programmes.

Learnings

This case study presents a case of improvement in living conditions through women's empowerment on one hand and also increase in aspirations and vertical mobility of those at the bottom of the urban hierarchy through an agency. The settlement has remarkably changed and so have the lives of its residents. For transformative change, women's agency is extremely important. The case of Pravinnagar-Guptanagar clearly shows the transformation in individual women's lives as well as transformation in the settlement in terms of physical and social development.

Ahmedabad is a city with an ethos of volunteerism, rooted in the Gandhian value system. This ethos has led to establishment of voluntary agency that would channelize people's own energies and initiatives into constructive direction. Many agencies have followed a path of 'struggle and constructivc engagement' whereas some others have followed the path of 'constructive engagement'. This case study is engagement of a NGO, Saath, for constructive engagement with the community. This case study also shows that a process of change through an external agency mobilisation is gradual and incremental and not instantaneous, as some of the government programmes require. Also, it indicates that the process has to be internal to the community. In the end, however, the results can be a significant transformation of a settlement in physical terms as well as in terms of social development. Today, some individuals in the community have been able to forge links with the globalising society.

Incidentally, the local government had a programme for slum development through extending short-term tenure security and seeking community participation, which assisted the community mobilisation. The residents could be mobilised for a common goal of slum upgradation, which then expanded to involve the community in general, in particular the women of this community, in urban governance programme. Thus, a civil society organisation alone, can also not deliver welfare unless the state comes forward with proactive policy and supporting financial resources. The SNP is a scheme that represents this development of governance that rests on the tripod of the local government, the community and the facilitating NGO as three main actors. Such mutual agreements and beneficiary partnerships are needed and they work. The key learning is that the state is a predominant actor in a development process and it cannot pass on its responsibility to anyone else.

A community cannot progress without having an integrated approach to increase welfare of the urban poor. Micro finance alone, or education alone would not be sustainable. The mobilising actor could enter a community to mobilise on a particular development aspect, determined through the felt need of the community, and then build synergy around it through other interventions. This has been crucial to the success of intervention in Pravinnagar-Guptanagar. A shelter intervention, particularly when there is tenure security element attached to it, along with community mobilisation, has a great transformative potential. In the interim stages, it also has potential to reduce vulnerabilities and hence also has promotional potential. A community-based functioning along with micro finance also has a protection element to it. The experience of Pravinnagar-Guptanagar development is a strong case representing all these elements of Social Protection.

Table 4.2: A Chronology of Integrated Development

Year	*Activities, Project and Programmes*	*Issue/Sector*
1991	• Social animator course for youth, EYM Registered	Youth Health Local institution building
1992	• Via referrals of the *Marwari* community focus on Pravinnagar-Guptanagar—out of corporation limits, needy area. • Survey conducted	Community development
1993	• Based on survey activities started in Pravinnagar-Guptanagar—Community health centre a crèche started	Health Education
1994	• Health services • Education—Supplementary classes • Livelihood intervention—sewing classes, electric, automobile repair	Health Education Livelihood
1995	• Process of forming CBOs initiated. • Discussions about SNP were underway	Health Education Livelihood Local institution building Physical infrastructure Services
1996	• Introduction to Sanjaynagar as a pilot-study • Savings were initiated • Registration of SMM, as a CBO	Health Education Livelihood Local institution building Physical infrastructure Services Savings
1997	• Initiation of SNP • Health, Education programmes were started in Pravinnagar-Guptanagar • Process of starting Urmila and livelihood programmes initiated • Savings and loans	Health Education Livelihood Local institution building Physical infrastructure Services Savings and loans

(*Contd.*)

Table 4.2: (*Contd.*)

Year	Activities, Project and Programmes	Issue/Sector
2000	• Slum Electrification Project • SNP	Health Education Livelihood Local institution building Physical infrastructure Services Savings and loans
2002	• Communal riots in Gujarat—relief, rehabilitation • Registration of Co-operative, CBO • Human Rights Education Programme	Communal harmony Disaster management Local institution building
2003	• Working in riot affected areas—developmental activities	
2004	• Jeevandan, RCH, ICDS merged with crèche	Health Education
2005	• Ek Mouka Udaan	Youth employment
2006	• URC Process Initiated • Saath Livelihood Services (Regd.)	Internal Governance Livelihood
2008	• Handing back ICDS centres to government • Increase in services at URC • Initiation of discussion for URC expansion • Construction worker registrations • Child Labour initiative—urban • Youth group formation	Disability Services Creation of business plans Internal systems

Source: Compiled by CUE.

NOTES

1. Research is funded under the research project titled "Inclusive Urbanisation–Social Protection for the Slum and Pavement Dwellers in India', a CEPT University—Mahila Housing SEWA Trust (MHT) project, under the programme 'Social Protection in Asia', managed by Institute of Development Studies (IDS), Sussex and Institute of Human Development (IHD), New Delhi and funded by Ford Foundation and IDRC. We will like to acknowledge the support of Saath community workers for sparing time to discuss with us the whole process.
2. Mahatma Gandhi, the Father of the Nation, and the pre-eminent political and spiritual leader of India's independence movement, started his activities from Ahmedabad after he returned from South Africa. He was the pioneer of *satyagraha*—peaceful resistance to tyranny through mass civil

disobedience, firmly founded upon *ahimsa* or total non-violence—which led India to independence and inspired movements for civil rights and freedom across the world. Gandhi is commonly known around the world as ***Mahatma* (Great Soul) Gandhi.** His philosophy has left deep imprints in Ahmedabad City, its ethos, and its institutional development. The voluntary organisation movement in Gujarat has its antecedents in Gandhian philosophy.

3. Many low-income settlements are on the river banks, banks of encroached lakes, low-lying areas that get inundated in monsoon, and on other lands unsuitable for human habitation.
4. As per population Census of 2011.
5. From the AMC budget of 2009-10, see http://www.egovamc.com/amc_budget/Budget_2009-2010.pdf, accessed on March 16, 2009.
6. 1998 slum estimate is from Swarna Jayanti Shehri Rojgar Yojana (SJSRY) survey and 2001 estimate is from the AMC as given in Ahmedabad's CDP (http://jnnurm.nic.in/missioncities.htm).
7. The number of households residing in a slum was found out through a survey conducted by SEWA and SAATH. The total slum population has been calculated considering a family size of 5. As per Census figures of 2001, a population of 439,843 resided in slums. This figure has not been considered as it includes only those slums which have clusters of more than 60 houses.
8. *Inamdar Zameen* = Land given as gift, in the times of kingdoms, the ministers were sometimes given the land by the Kings as a gift for their deeds. Now some of these lands do not have a legal owner and encroached by a person or group of people.
9. A food item, made from lentil dough, rolled into thin round flat six to ten inch round pieces, which are dried and then packed for marketing. *Papad* is fried or roasted before serving as food.
10. *Khakhara* is also food item. It is dry *chappati*, prepared in such a way that it can be stored for long periods at room temperature.
11. Wages in 1988-89.
12. Community mobiliser from Saath.
13. Some of these activities will be described at length in due place.
14. *Sakhi* means a female friend.
15. An investment scheme of the Government of India.
16. This programme has discontinued due to the lack of interest from the AMC and the State government.
17. Source: Toolkit for Financial support for Comprehensive Capacity Building for Improved Urban Governance and Poverty Alleviation of JNNURM, 2009.

5
Mobilising Women for Change
The Case of Sanjaynagar, Ahmedabad[1]

Pooja Shah and *Bijal Bhatt*

This chapter illustrates the process of mobilisation of women of a slum around the question of their access to basic services, through the intervention of an external agency, a non-governmental organization (NGO), the Mahila Housing SEWA Trust (MHT) based in Ahmedabad. It narrates the process of community development in a slum called Sanjaynagar, gradual improvement of its physical environment, and empowerment of the community in general. It also narrates the stories of the women of the community in particular, with the experiences of their acting as agents of change, in the process empowering themselves to negotiate not just in the public domain but also in the private domain, and role of specific individuals in triggering this local change. The backdrop of this change is introduction of a participatory slum development programme named the Slum Networking Programme (SNP) by the local government, the Ahmedabad Municipal Corporation (AMC)[2].

Housing, in other words, shelter security, is very essential for women's dignity and women themselves consider house as the most important of all needs for their well-being and security. It is commonly heard from the SEWA members and activists: "Secure house is the first and most important demand coming from women." This chapter is also a documentation of MHT's experience of upgrading Sanjaynagar (a community of migrants from north India), the difficulties faced by them and the MHT in the entire process and finally, the outcomes in terms of physical improvement as well as the women's agency moving to participate in the larger city level development processes.

The Mobiliser and the Community

Gujarat Mahila Housing SEWA Trust

The Self Employed Women Association (SEWA) is trade union of poor, self-employed women workers based in Ahmedabad and registered in 1972. SEWA's main goals are to organise women workers for full employment and self-reliance. In 1992, SEWA's Executive Committee decided to consolidate all housing related activities of SEWA and affiliate organisations such as the SEWA Bank on account of increasing demand for housing and infrastructure services from their members. A new organisation, named Mahila Housing SEWA Trust (MHT) was formed and registered in 1994 with the overall objectives of improving housing and infrastructure conditions of poor women in the informal sectors, to influence housing and infrastructure related urban and rural development policies and programmes, and bring the benefits of these policies within the reach of the poor women. The MHT has been envisaged as women's own institution to take care of their housing needs. The main activities of MHT at the time of this research were earthquake reconstruction, housing upgradation in both urban and rural areas, infrastructure upgradation, technical support linked to housing and financing of housing and infrastructure needs of the urban poor in general. One of the slum settlements where the MHT has intervened and mobilised the community for infrastructure extension is Sanjaynagar.

Involvement of the MHT with housing upgradation began as a NGO, mobilising the slum residents to partner with the local government for slum upgradation. But, then, upon insistence of the beneficiaries as well as the Community-based Organisations (CBOs), MHT also entered into constructing infrastructure within the slums for the slum communities. This contractor-role of the MHT, which is very important given that no regular contractor is willing to undertake infrastructure works in slums, has been up scaled through formation of a company named Awass SEWA Private Limited, a social enterprise for construction activities. This company trains women masons and construction workers and employs them on the infrastructure projects in the slums. Coming back to the slum upgradation task, as of September 2009, the MHT had undertaken and completed infrastructure work in 45 slums of Ahmedabad under the SNP and had reached out to 3,386 households[3]. In addition, the MHT has begun to participate in the Slum Redevelopment Schemes (SRS) under the state government's housing policy and assist in forming

Resident Welfare Associations (RWAs) at the rehabilitation sites of those rehoused in new BSUP housing after their displacement due to various city-level development projects.

The MHT has also been active in facilitating the slum households to avail of water supply and sanitation under the existing schemes of the AMC. One such scheme was the '500 NOC Scheme', which aimed to help the slum residents acquire 'No Objection Certificate' (NOC) on payment of Rs. 500, that is necessary for getting legal, individual household level water and sewage connection. In slums where this scheme is applicable, a community mobilised by the MHT provides information to the slum dwellers and motivates them to access benefits of this scheme. The MHT also facilitates micro finance access to slum residents through its sister organisation, the SEWA Bank, encourages formation of CBOs and trains the residents to monitor the scheme implementation efficiently. The MHT has also built the capacity of the CBOs, so that they can interface with the urban local bodies (ULBs), and procure and maintain improved infrastructure services.

Sanjaynagar

Sanjaynagar is located in Amraiwadi ward in the east zone of Ahmedabad city with an approximate area of 3,131 square metres. There were 117 households with population of 600 persons in the slum. At the time of our survey, the sex ratio was 953 and the literacy rate was 61.3 per cent; with male literacy rate of 63.4 per cent and female literacy rate of 59 per cent, both lower than the average rates at the city level which was 93.8 per cent of males and 84.2 per cent of females in 2011. Majority of the male members were engaged in casual labour in the nearby small-scale industries while some were occupied in retail vegetable vending. Almost all the families in Sanjaynagar are originally from the states of Uttar Pradesh and Rajasthan, settled here around 35 years ago. Women, particularly migrants from Uttar Pradesh, do not go out of the house for work and hence they are constantly in search of home-based work. During our survey, the women were into home-based work of making incense sticks (*agarbattis*).

The Process of Change

The Question of Land Tenure

The general notion is that, it is easier to upgrade a slum located on the

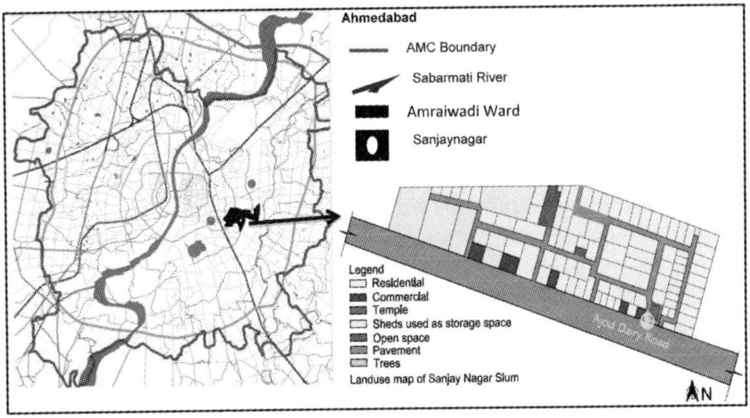

Source: Prepared by CUE.

Exhibit 5.1: Amraiwadi ward in the Ahmedabad municipal boundary and land use map of Sanjaynagar

local government land, in this case, the AMC land. However, if the municipal land has some reservation under the city's development plan, then granting of land tenure and upgradation process gets complex. The local government may not want to give away the land to the slum community, if it has other planned use for the land. In that case, the local government may not issue a NOC for that piece of land and the NGO cannot proceed with bringing water supply and sewerage to the slum. In case the slum land is not reserved for any purpose, then NOC has to be obtained for proceeding with slum upgradation. For slums on partly municipal and partly private land, obtaining an NOC is complicated.

Sanjaynagar is situated on a private land, belonging to a person named Jiva Gopal, whose name appears on the property tax bills received by this slum's residents. The residents have *de facto* tenure security and hence do not fear eviction. But, they do not have land ownership documents to offer as guarantee in case they would like to take a loan for house improvement.

Pre-SNP Stage

The first SNP was implemented in Naroda ward in a slum also named Sanjaynagar and by 2001, ten slums were covered under the SNP. The MHT had decided to go ahead with implementing SNP in other slums in

Ahmedabad, considering it to be a very useful programme that would bring public-community partnership into slum development. Somehow, the MHT had to put in great efforts through several representations to convince the AMC officials for faster NOC procedures. This persuasion by the MHT was also to bring in pro-poor projects such as slum infrastructure in priority of the AMC besides city beautification.

While holding discussions with the deputy municipal commissioner, the MHT realised that there was no database on the slums in the city to assist in slum selection for various projects. To this, the AMC decided to carry out a slum census of 1,700 slums and *chawls* of Ahmedabad City. The AMC, the MHT and the Saath came together for this purpose and conducted a comprehensive survey of slums and *chawls* in the city. The AMC provided the required funds to facilitate the survey.

The survey was so designed as to assist the AMC in prioritising the slums for SNP. This required not just information on infrastructure in the slum but also on possibility of future development in relation to the city's development plan and the availability of the off-site infrastructure. Thus, the survey included canvassing of three questionnaires. The first questionnaire collected data on existing level and quality of infrastructure; for example, mapping of dilapidated pipelines within the slum if any, availability of water supply, whether this was as stand-post or individual connection, availability and type of toilet, availability and type of sewerage, etc. These data were necessary for the councillors interested in using their discretionary funds to provide these facilities in a slum. There is no system of updating the AMC's database about availability and level of services in each slum unless the AMC itself provides these services. This questionnaire was meant to identify the slums most deficient in the three basic services, viz. toilets, sewerage and water supply, which could then be selected for the SNP.

Questionnaire 2 dealt with the issue of land reservation and other land related facts such as land ownership, land survey number, area of the plot, Town Planning Scheme[4] number, road lines adjoining the plot, ongoing litigation on land, if any etc. This was important because the AMC had to issue a 'no eviction' certificate for which legal status of the land was essential. The third questionnaire focused on the type and level of services outside the slums. It contained details on the existing network of pipes, their diameters, sewage pumping stations available in the vicinity etc. This information was required to link the slum level infrastructure (to be provided) with the main city networks.

This survey brought clarity on the issues of land ownership, need to obtain permission of the land owner in case if the slum was on private land, how to address the question if there was absentee land owner, status of existing services and hence decision on whether to provide new infrastructure or improve the existing one, etc. For example, the survey was able to establish whether zonal level intervention, such as augmenting the water pressure or increasing the pipe diameter to improve water supply in a slum was necessary or a slum level intervention was sufficient enough for improving water availability in the slum. It also identified needs of the slum dwellers. The survey could identify slums where land ownership clearance was not a problem. With the help of this survey, a list of settlements was drawn where SNP could be started immediately. In this list, one of the slums—Sanjaynagar in Amraiwadi was given to the MHT for implementation of SNP. Was this the right process? Could not the AMC have asked the MHT to select a slum from the listed slums for intervention, which the MHT could have chosen based on its links with the community? Was the AMC treating the NGO just as a contractor to implement some of the difficult development activity that it should have done on its own? These questions, however, would remain in the hypothetical realm now given that the MHT has already implemented the SNP in Sanjaynagar, Amraiwadi.

Before Community Mobilisation

To initiate the implementation of SNP in Sanjaynagar, the MHT first obtained NOC for the slum. The next stage was to mobilise the community for the purpose. This has a small history. Earlier, the MHT went ahead with SNP on a verbal NOC from the AMC. A NOC also means 'no eviction' guarantee. But, as discussed before, NOC process is not straightforward and all slums may not get a NOC. Also, the process is time consuming, which tries the patience of the slum dwellers. The slum residents may lose interest in the project or may even lose trust on the NGO. In such a milieu, when the slum is not given a NOC and the NGO collects contributions from the people, an awkward situation arises and allegations of fraud could be made against the NGO. MHT, with its experiences decided to obtain a written NOC from the AMC before proceeding with community mobilisation and accepting residents' contribution for this project.

There is certain level of cynicism among the slum dwellers when people from outside visit their settlement for either a survey or with an idea to intervene in the slum. MHT had no prior contact with Sanjaynagar and hence did not know anyone in the settlement through whom it could start the SNP implementation. According to the process set up by the AMC for the SNP, there has to be an NOC obtained from the AMC for the slum, a clearance on the land ownership from the town planning department, followed by an approval from the land owner in case the slum is on a private land and then consent of the slum residents to participate in the programme. Subsequently, the residents had to pay Rs. 2,100 for joining the SNP. However, it was not as easy as it sounds.

Notwithstanding the fact that the MHT had no contact in the slum allotted, the MHT team visited the slum for the first time on December 17, 2002, introduced themselves as well as the organisation and then stated the purpose of their visit to the slum. In the beginning, the MHT members, talked to a few people they came across randomly which confused people. Then they realised their mistake and decided to first contact any community leader in the settlement. People guided them to meet Mr. Phulansinh Kanojiya, who was active in organizing social functions such as *Navratri* (a folk dance festival of Gujarat spread over nine days) in the settlement. The MHT team explained Mr. Kanojiya the purpose of their visit, concept of SNP and role of MHT in getting basic services to the slum settlements.

In this interaction with Mr. Kanojia, an interesting fact emerged. The area councillor Mr. Gangaram had promised provision of water supply, toilets, sewerage connection, street lights and pavements in the slum. The councillor had promised a contribution of Rs. 1,100 per household while the individual households were required to contribute Rs. 500. Mr. Kanojiya had already collected contribution from the dwellers and given it to the councillor. But, then, the councillor did not meet the obligation and people were left high and dry. Hence, they had become sceptical of any such initiatives, where they were required to contribute for services. No wonder, the people expected the local government to extend these services free of cost! The residents had also filed a court case in this matter, which was subjudice when the MHT members visited the slum. Thus, residents of Sanjaynagar would not contribute Rs. 2,100 for the SNP programme, opined Mr. Kanojia. The MHT members explained again that they had not come to collect any contribution at that point and only wanted consent of the slum residents. To this also, there was no response and Mr. Kanojiya stuck to his position of no co-operation by the slum dwellers. He also sarcastically said that they were listening to the MHT members because they were women and if they were men they would not have allowed them to even stand in the slum. Some people displayed abrasive attitude towards the MHT members.

With its long experience of working with slum communities, the MHT decided to interact with the women of the community. They, therefore, inquired about female leader(s) in the settlement who took interest in organising social functions. Mr. Kanojiya gave the names of Naginaben, Puniben and Naniben, engaged in organising various events in Sanjaynagar. MHT members met these three women, explained them the SNP project and engaged them in a dialogue on the SNP in the slum. These three women were also sceptical and not of the opinion to implement the SNP in their slum. They were predetermined that residents would not sign the consent letter. Even those three women were not convinced to sign the consent letter without their husbands' permission. On asking the way out, Naginaben suggested that the MHT team organise a slum-level meeting with the women, to explain the programme and then persuade them to sign the SNP application letter.

The difficulty was to find an appropriate time for the meeting as mornings and evenings the women were occupied with the household work and in the day, these women were engaged with *agarbatti* making. There was a vacant plot in the settlement, which belonged to a person called Rajubhai where all these women gathered to make *agarbattis*. MHT decided to conduct a meeting with the women while they were working on making *agarbattis* on this plot. MHT members introduced the SNP in detail to all the women present and informed them how the city government wanted to help them with water supply, sanitation, streetlights and pavements. To this the women replied that they did not have any say in these decisions and if MHT wanted to do anything in Sanjaynagar, they would have to talk to the male residents. Unless their husbands permitted them, they could not sign any document. And, hence, the MHT was back to square one.

The MHT members, therefore, decided to meet the male members of the settlement. A majority of male members in Sanjaynagar worked in surrounding textile mills so they were not available in daytime. MHT members were asked to come at night, at about 8 p.m., to hold meeting with all the households. This simple task also presented a challenge as Sanjaynagar and the neighbouring settlements are known for illicit activities like illegal liquor sale and consumption in late evening, followed by incidents of eve-teasing. Being females, all MHT members were hesitant to go to the settlement at night. However, they did go to hold the meeting. In a settlement of 117 households, only 15 male members came for the meeting. MHT again explained the advantages of SNP and informed them that it was a government scheme under which they could get entire basic infrastructure and they do not have to pay immediately with an additional advantage of a *de facto* tenure of 10 years. MHT also showed them the list of slums to be covered under the SNP prepared by the AMC. However, at the end of the meeting no household was convinced to sign.

MHT members gave application forms to Naginaben and requested her to convince people to enrol. After a week, when the MHT members went to Sanjaynagar, Naginaben returned blank application papers. She said no one was ready to take initiative. The MHT members realised the problem of proceeding with the activity when women were not independent in taking decisions and that they would rather trust the councillor, notwithstanding his fraud, than the MHT, whom they did not know at all. MHT members insisted the women to give them in writing (which MHT can forward to AMC) that they do not want SNP to take place in Sanjaynagar and asked Naginaben to return the application forms.

Breaking the Ice

When MHT asked to give the refusal in writing and that they would never come back to Sanjaynagar, Naginaben said "I will keep the forms with me for few days and I will think about it and let you know." When next time MHT went to Sanjaynagar, all women were making *agarbattis* in Rajubhai's plot. That time too no one had signed the application form. When asked why, MHT got these replies, "Why should I sign first?" "My husband has asked me not to sign first; if someone else signs then I will sign." MHT asked Naginaben to sign first. It was little difficult to convince her to take the initiative but at the end she signed the application form. Thereafter, 14 more women, who were present there, signed the application form. Taking those 15 signatures, MHT went to all other households and at the end of the day got around 55 households to sign on the application form. The ice was broken; a beginning of trust between the slum residents and the NGO had begun (*See* Box 5.1 depicting individual story).

With a consent letter from the community, property tax bills and 7/12 document[5] (land ownership document) of the land on which Sanjaynagar is situated, the MHT approached the AMC for starting the process of SNP in the slum. The going was not easy and the MHT had to follow up with the AMC officials every 10-15 days on the progress with

Box 5.1: In Punibhen's Words

"My family is living in Sanjaynagar for many years. I came to stay here after my marriage. At that time, there was no individual water supply in the households. There was a stand post outside the settlement and all the households would fetch water from there. All the women would rise at 5 a.m. to fetch water and there would be fights amongst us. No household had a toilet because of absence of sewer line. The slum across—Patravali Chali had common toilets, we used their toilets although we were not allowed and there were constant fights. There was also open defecation in the slum. Sanjaynagar is situated on the main road so we used to go after 9 p.m. for this purpose. I used to feel ashamed but there was no other way. There used to be great difficulty in monsoon because of slush and poisonous insects around. Further, it was not possible to invite any guest to stay overnight."

"Tired with all these, some of us purchased illegal connection of water supply and sewer line. The main line was passing from the main road. We connected that to our houses. We paid Rs. 500 for sewer line and Rs. 1,500 for illegal water supply per household. This was in 1988. It was illegal and not properly constructed, not very deep from the road surface. It used to break very often if heavy vehicles passed on it. Many times the housing societies near Sanjaynagar complained about us as they would not get enough water and so AMC officials would come and cut our illegal lines. Our men would manage to get the connection again, for which we again had to pay. Phulansinh said that he would manage to get us these services for legal connection of water and sewer as he had connections to a political party. So we paid Rs. 500 per household to Phulansinh, which he said he had given to Gangaram—the councillor of our area. But then nothing happened. Whenever we enquired about the use of the money and when we were likely to get the facilities, he would give a standard answer that the process was going on and we would get the facilities soon. After waiting for some time, they (male members of the community) have filed a court case on the matter."

"When this case was going on, the MHT members came to our area. Initially we did not trust them. We thought if the people of our own settlement and our own councillor cannot bring us facilities, how these strangers would do it. The MHT members started coming to Sanjaynagar two-three times a week and showed us all the documents of AMC and explained the *Parivartan* (transformation—the name for SNP) scheme in detail. We are poor and cannot afford to pay for water and sanitation again and again. When MHT members said that we do not have to pay immediately we just had to sign on the letter, we thought there would be no harm in just signing a paper."

SNP sanction. The AMC had a policy of commencing implementation work only when at least 80 per cent households had consented for SNP. In Sanjaynagar, only 55 of the 117 households (47%) had given their consent for SNP. The MHT, with its long-standing reputation and trust convinced the AMC officials for starting at least the primary survey work in the slum. It was important to start the SNP implementation in order to take the slum dwellers into confidence otherwise households who had given their consent would also regret their decision. According to MHT members, they had to mobilise not just the slum dwellers but also the AMC for the SNP in Sanjaynagar.

Inception Studies for Identifying Package and Beneficiaries

After about a month of submitting the documents, the MHT members went to Sanjaynagar with the AMC officials, namely the estate officer, the ward officer, the surveyor and the zonal officer for investigating the slum. There was a detailed survey of the slum for number of households, existing infrastructure, road details, hindrances in extending household level infrastructure, etc. The process required that firstly, the ward officer demarcated the area for SNP implementation. The town development officer, who is in-charge of preparing a Town Planning Scheme, assessed any need to remove houses or part of the houses to bring in infrastructure. Sometimes, if space is not enough in the settlement for physical infrastructure then demolition of some houses is required. In such cases, the town development officer suggests and the ward officer marks on the map the house that has to be removed. However, in Sanjaynagar, there was no need to demolish any house. At this stage, the ward officer also marked the land use of the slum. In Sanjaynagar, out of 123 structures; there were 23 commercial structures (shops and store houses) and two temples. After two visits of the AMC for assessing the demand for water and sanitation facilities, it was decided that ten houses had decided to share the facilities between two houses and three houses wanted to share a common facility.

Seeing the AMC officials with maps and measuring the houses and investigation of the settlement, people again felt threatened that AMC had deceitfully made them sign and this could be followed by eviction. The MHT members had a tough time explaining that there would not be any eviction for at least next ten years after the implementation of the SNP. The survey was followed by allotting a number to each house. These numbers were written with a chalk. The residents misunderstood this as numbers given for demolition of the houses and hence they erased the number given. The following day, the MHT members explained them the purpose of numbering, which meant formalising their residential status as in legal residential complexes. Such mistrust of the state is a common response pattern among the low-income citizens.

Further, with the help of its sister organisation, the SEWA Bank, microfinance activities were extended to women in each household. These women opened accounts with the SEWA Bank. Meanwhile, MHT continued to persuade the remaining households to participate in the SNP. Among the unwilling households were those who lived in the slum as tenants, who were subsequently convinced to join the scheme. Everyone eventually joined the project. Those who had existing individual toilets (but with a soak pit given that there was no trunk sewerage line in the slum) were asked to contribute Rs. 300 less than the general contribution of Rs. 2,100. And to be able to do so, there was another round of surveys to map the exact level of existing services. Thus, the problem of free-ridership was resolved in the SNP slums in general and also in this particular slum.

Cultivating Financial Literacy

Right at onset, a need for microfinance was envisaged so that the community could pay up its own contribution. The AMC had already approached mainstream banks for the purpose but it did not work out. Then, the SEWA Bank, through the MHT, approached the slum dwellers with a microfinance scheme suitable to them, under which, the participating households had to open an account with SEWA Bank and deposit Rs. 50 in their accounts, to avail a loan of Rs. 1,600. With its previous experiences, the MHT was convinced that payments by the people were directly related to the initiation process and progress of the work and people would require to save, so as to be able to pay their own contribution for the programme. The SNP implementation would take over two-year period and people might have to contribute gradually over time and for which savings were needed. Slum dwellers were in a need of a loan because they had to contribute 80 per cent of their share in the project at the onset of the project. This was the condition put in by the AMC. For getting the SEWA Bank loan, they have to open an account in the bank with Rs. 50, which the slum dwellers were hesitant to do. Slum dwellers wanted the work to be commenced first and the AMC according its policy, demanded that the former should give their share first. There was a deadlock. But, the deadlock was broken by Naginaben; she opened the bank account with Rs. 50. Some other women followed her.

The issues were not resolved yet. The SEWA Bank is a sister concern of SEWA and is working for women. Only women can open an account in SEWA Bank and for which they require a ration card and a passport size photograph. In most households, woman's name was just not there in the ration card. MHT assisted the residents to get renewed ration cards so that the woman's name could be entered in the card with a postal address of Sanjaynagar. This process took about three months. Since residents were not willing to get passport size photographs taken due to cost factor, the MHT brought in a photographer to take pictures of the slum dwellers that MHT paid directly.

The problems in opening the bank account did not stop there. Every time the SEWA Bank employees went to the settlement to start the process of opening the account, only two or three would come forward. For the SEWA Bank employees too, it was difficult to go such a long way for just a few accounts. The routine was: MHT staff would go to the slum and inform them about the SEWA Bank employees' visit the next day and request them to be present at a particular time at certain place. The next day they would accompany the bank employee to the slum; while the member of the SEWA Bank would wait in someone's house and MHT staff would go from house to house to call women, and women would give excuses such as "today I don't have money, tomorrow my husband will get his salary so I will open my account tomorrow," "I thought you people will not come today so I just paid money to the *baniya* (grocer) an hour ago," "I have money but I am not in good terms with her (the woman at whose house bank employee is waiting) so I will not come to her house for my account," "my husband has asked me to open up an account only in front of him," "why should I open an account in my name and not in my husband's name," etc. There was no progress in spite of the fact that MHT staff explained them that both, the MHT and the SEWA Bank, were organisations run by women and would only deal with women and not men. Women did not understand this.

The MHT was persistent. They went to the slum in late evening, in spite of the problem in the slum of finding some male members in inebriated state, to convince them that it was important for women to open bank accounts in their own names. Sometimes, some male members in a drunken state would abuse MHT women. With great efforts, the MHT succeeded in opening up the accounts of every resident with SEWA Bank. The Bank gave passbooks (Annexure 5.1) and receipts to all account holders. This was followed by a survey of households to know whether all had opened an account or not. MHT prepared a list of all households, name of the account holder with account number.

A small difficulty was encountered and this could happen in any other slums as well if the financial institution was to work with women alone. In cities, there are many single male migrants. In fact, in Ahmedabad, males from certain states come alone, leaving their spouses and family behind in the native home. There were two such houses where there were only single male migrants who were not eligible to get a loan from the SEWA Bank. On issuance of a letter from the MHT that the residents of these two houses were participating in SNP and would contribute towards the project, they were permitted to open an account in the SEWA Bank, but, with the limited purpose of crediting their contribution towards SNP.

Having accomplished the task of opening the bank accounts, the process moved on to another issue. After opening the accounts, people were irregular in depositing money for SNP. The contribution decided was Rs. 10 per household per week. MHT had to go door-to-door to collect this amount. The progress of work depended on the amount contributed. The project implementation lost its pace. The challenge in any infrastructure development scheme is that if the pace is slow, cost escalates on one hand and it is extremely costly for a bank to provide collection services at the doorstep. Being sister organisations, the MHT and the SEWA Bank worked together to find solutions for day-to-day problems of managing the savings accounts (*See* Box 5.2 for how these problems were addressed).

Box 5.2: Practical Solutions to Practical Problems in Account Management

Problem: Essentially a savings account facility should allow people to withdraw but then the necessary contribution would never get accumulated if people would withdraw.

Solution: SEWA Bank would allow withdrawals only if MHT officially intimated them in individual cases.

Problem: The problems with the proof of residence were deterring the process of account opening and the implementation of the programme.

Solution: In such cases, MHT would give a certificate on its own letter head stating that the organisation was working in this slum for a certain time period and knew that the woman was a resident of the slum. The Bank accepted that certificate.

Problem: As the programme took long, MHT had to undertake continuous visits to the slums to maintain the trust of the people. Also, the contribution came in small amounts of Rs. 10 to Rs. 20 and that too sparingly, and since size of the settlements were very small the operations were very costly for the Bank.

Solution: MHT collected the money on behalf of the bank. This was difficult, because MHT cannot technically issue a receipt in the name of the SEWA Bank. It was then decided that MHT would collect the money and issue its own receipt. Next day, it would give the original receipt from the Bank, after the collection is deposited with SEWA Bank. The organisers would then take back the receipt issued by MHT.

The MHT developed a Management Information System (MIS) to monitor the required payments by the slum residents. For the purpose of monitoring payments, payment ranges were devised which were, up to Rs. 500, Rs. 501 to Rs. 1,000, Rs. 1,001 to Rs. 1,500, Rs. 1,501 to Rs. 2,000. Then each household was put in a particular payment bracket (Annexure 5.2). Once a household cleared one payment bracket it would be extended the pre-ordained category of service. On clearance of the first category of payment, a household would get an individual toilet constructed. On clearing the next category, the household would be provided individual water supply, and so on. Thus, the services would be extended as and when the households paid their dues. MHT constantly motivated the households to pay for emphasising that it was not a charity and community itself has to pay infrastructure.

Initiation of Mandal (Association)

MHT members decided that an association of the women in the slum should be created so that they would themselves manage their accounts and deal with all issues of the settlement. Indirectly, making an association would also encourage women to come out of their houses, a very important behavioural change for the community where women never took decisions on their own. The idea was also to make women self-reliant not even dependent on MHT. A decision to form a CBO in Sanjaynagar was taken to keep a check on all the works done under the SNP. MHT members held a meeting with all women in Sanjaynagar and asked them to take leadership for their own settlement. MHT asked them to select a leader among them to follow up the SNP work. MHT also informed that their *mandal* when formed would prepare inventory of materials that would come from the AMC for SNP and then would take care of the same. They also said that the *mandal* leaders would have to come to the MHT office for all the meetings as part of training requirements. The women were informed that the *mandal* will be responsible for speedy implementation of the SNP and *mandal* can also register a complaint and follow it through the AMC in case of delay in work.

Similar to all other processes in the settlement, CBO formation too went through some rough path. Women of Sanjaynagar were not at all interested in taking any leadership. They responded "we are paying money and we are taking responsibility of our own house to pay for SNP but we will not take responsibility of any other households." MHT staff took some women from Sanjaynagar for exposure visit to other settlements where SNP had been implemented and where women had organised into a *mandal* that took the full responsibility of seeing the project successfully through. Even after three meetings with the women of the slum, MHT was unable to convince them for forming a CBO. The second excuse given by the women was their illiteracy and hence their inability to handle the legal issues and also collect money. "We are illiterate, how can we handle the work with city government? How can we go for collection of money and attend meetings in MHT leaving our work (*agarbatti* making), husbands and children aside? Our husbands will not allow us to go out on our own." Ironically, the same men who were earlier abusing MHT staff and not allowing the MHT to enter the settlement, wanted to form their own *mandal* and some of them also expressed their willingness to become leader of the *mandal* to which MHT refused arguing that they only worked with women.

MHT expressed their concern that without a CBO and a leader SNP would be difficult. At the same time, MHT also motivated them by promising full support for all works that the *mandal* would do and that their deed was a public action for attaining basic facilities. Women selected Naginaben as their leader. Naginaben was hesitant to this because her husband Pavanbhai would not allow her as in their caste it was not appropriate for women to go out for work. The MHT took him to its office and gave him an insight of the work done by MHT and also made him understand that Naginaben was not to go to MHT office everyday but required in the office only to attend occasional meetings. He hesitantly accepted. Naginaben became the first president of the *mandal* formed of 11 women of Sanjaynagar. A lady named Malaben was appointed as a treasurer to handle the finances and Naniben was appointed as vice president. Finally, the *mandal* was formed in March 2002, approximately 8 months after the MHT's first visit to Sanjaynagar.

Educating the Mandal

The ultimate aim of the SNP and the aspiration of the MHT was to make the slum dwellers aware of their own needs. Again when MHT asked the women to come to the MHT office for training, MHT staff had to put in great efforts to bring them to their office. Everyday, two MHT staff would go to Sanjaynagar and would move from door-to-door and ask women to join them for training. But, the women would once again give excuses: "I am still not done with my cooking; My children have not come from school yet; I will not come today because my mother-in-law is not well;

I have to wash clothes; yesterday we came back very late and my husband scolded me so I will not come now." Everyday almost two hours were spent in gathering women to take them to the MHT office by auto. The men instructed the MHT staff to ensure return of their spouse back home by 4 p.m. MHT workers would themselves come and drop the women of the settlement back everyday after the training at MHT office completed. The training was held in the afternoon, so that women could complete their housework and then reached home in time to finish their evening domestic chores.

The training, consisting of various aspects such as introduction to the SEWA and all departments, about the city and its various development programmes and then hands-on training for 20 days. In the first two days, they were introduced to the SEWA and given motivating information on the SEWA movements and individual stories of women whose lives had changed and importance of women's role in domestic financial management. Examples of women's leadership qualities were also demonstrated. In other words, they were exposed to the idea of their self-worth. The next two days were spent in making them understand the need of a CBO and explaining them how to form it. This training module trained women to work as a group in common interest and they were also explained the importance of their responsibilities as members of such an organisation. In the following two days, they were given information of Ahmedabad city, the AMC and how the latter provided them basic services. For this, women were taken on an exposure visit to the ward and zone offices of their area. They were taught to register complaints in a particular department as well as how to fill application form to avail the AMC facilities. The seventh and eighth days were allotted to problem solving in a given situation in a way to enhance their participation in any development project. They were also given introduction to the materials used for construction under the SNP, such as bricks, stones, pipes for water supply and sanitation etc. Then for two days, they were taught how to check the quality of materials used during the entire project implementation, how to use them, maintain them and keep them safe. They were also informed about the cost of materials how to manage the inventory of these materials, maintain records of the stock and the register of the inventory. The next four days were spent on explaining the basic services and its maintenance. On the seventeenth and eighteenth day, these women were introduced to the door-to-door scheme of solid waste management of the AMC. They were educated about how to dispose the solid waste, importance of disposal of solid waste, health aspects of it, and the CBO's effort in maintaining the settlement clean. At this stage, they were also taken to exposure visit to the health department of the zone office. At the end of the training they were taught how to maintain the accounts of the *mandal* during the implementation of SNP and after the completion of work. They were also taken to another slum where SNP had already been implemented.

Involvement of Local Politicians

The *mandal* put an application for registration on October 11, 2003 and received the approval on January 19, 2004. This registration was done in the office of Bombay Non Trading Sales Tax department and the *mandal* received a Non Trading Corporation Certificate along with a registration number. Women contributed the necessary fees of Rs. 20 required for registration. On registration, they prepared a letterhead in the name of Sanjaynagar Mahila Housing SEWA Mandal (*See* Annexure 5.3). For any application to the AMC, the *mandal* uses this letterhead then onwards (Annexure 5.4).

After the newly formed *mandal* became well versed with all the aspects of SNP and started functioning, Phulansinh came into the picture and objected that "we are going to get everything for free from the councillor then why are we forced to pay Rs. 2,100?" Even the councillors thought that their power had reduced because such slums were his vote banks.

The ward had three councillors then. One of them, Maniben, paved the streets in the slum overnight. MHT explained to her, that the paving would be damaged when the sewer line would be laid. But, she did not heed. The AMC had introduced an amendment in the SNP scheme, which allowed a councillor to contribute up to a maximum of Rs. 1,100 per household in the settlement as contribution towards the households' own contribution. This amendment was brought in to solicit the councillors' support for the scheme. Since Phulansingh, the local level leader, had good relations with the councillor named Gangaram, he was instrumental in bringing Gangaram on board by using councillor's funds for the SNP. Gangaram also showed interest so as to enable him a strong hold on the settlement again. The MHT also was keen that local councillor supported the scheme and so they went to meet him and explained him the SNP. Since the councillor has a strong connection and hold over the local slum communities, he was also asked to convince the remaining sceptics in the settlement to join SNP. Councillor Gangaram called a meeting in

Sanjaynagar and asked people to trust MHT, contribute towards the scheme and announced his own contribution of Rs. 90,000 from the councillor's fund. This was a turning point for SNP in Sanjaynagar. However, out of Rs. 90,000, only Rs. 50,000 were pledged by Gangaram for SNP in Sanjaynagar, which came to Rs. 600 per household (Annexure 5.5). After this, households in Sanjaynagar were supposed to pay Rs. 1,500 per household instead of Rs. 2,100. However, later Gangaram let down the people and did not contribute his promised share of Rs. 50,000. MHT paid that share to the AMC.

Roadblock in Implementation

Even though the local politician let down the community and did not contribute his committed share, due to pursuance of the MHT, the project was approved. Finally, in September 2005, the AMC issued work order, almost two years after the registration of the *mandal*. Soon, the *Khat Muhrat* (ceremony to lay foundation stone) was done by Gangaram and the project implementation started.

Firstly, the drainage line was laid, which took nearly eight months to complete and after that water line was constructed in the middle of 2006. Simultaneously, construction of individual toilets also started which took nearly six months. Once, the main water supply and drainage lines were laid in the slum, individual households were connected to the network depending on the amount paid by the household. If household had paid only Rs. 500 so far, then, that particular household would not be given individual connection. Seeing the other households using the individual toilets and individual water tap, everyone promptly began paying their due instalments.

The case of implementing SNP in Sanjaynagar illustrates how local vested interest attempt to stall change at the local level if their personal

Box 5.3: Threats from a Local Muscleman

"Once Raju came to my house at 10 O'clock in the night, in totally drunken state. My husband was not at home. My mother-in-law was there with me. He banged my door and started shouting in abusive language. He was shouting that if SNP implementation would be done he would push me out of the settlement, harass my family and he would make our lives miserable. My mother-in-law was very frightened. She and my husband ordered me strictly to stop my leadership for improvement of the settlement. But I was firm. I did not stop."

—Naginaben

interests were hurt. A person named Rajubhai, a local hooligan who operated illegal liquor business, did not want the project to be implemented fearing that if the AMC entered the slum he would not be allowed to operate his business. He also feared this project's success would empower the women and that would loosen his hold over the slum as a local *goonda* (a strong man). Hence, he created many obstructions; once, while the sewer work was going on, he came with four musclemen and began beating the construction workers and the engineers. MHT's staff member Purnimabhen was also present on the site. While the construction workers and the engineers ran away from the site, Purnimabhen could not and the women of the settlement had to hide her in one of the houses for three hours before she was escorted to board an auto rickshaw and leave.

Rajubhai was not willing to participate in the SNP and was not ready to pay his share of the SNP. All the women of *mandal* went to his house and requested him to co-operate for the project. He owned four houses in Sanjaynagar and wanted facilities in all the four houses without paying anything. After deciding among themselves, the women paid for one of his four houses. The women of the *mandal* took a middle way and made the other women of the settlement understand and convinced them to pay Rs. 20 if they wanted the sewer line and water supply soon. They knew it was not the right way but at that time it was the only way. Their husbands were not told about it otherwise the men would not have allowed their wives to pay for that *goonda*—Raju. They wanted the facilities as soon as possible and they knew that Rajubhai would not let that happen. They went to all the houses of Sanjaynagar and collected Rs. 20 per household and paid on behalf of Rajubhai. When the work started, Rajubhai was behind the bars in a case of murder and so rest of the work completed without his interruption.

The width of the street was hardly 2 feet. It has been both MHT's and AMC's experience that a minimum of 4 feet distance is required between the sewer line and the water line to ensure that if a leakage happened there would be no pollution of water. It was necessary to cut the houses by about 2 feet. People were obviously not ready for it. They argued that it was not possible for large families to live in small houses. Some critiques alleged that the MHT had finally been instrumental in cutting their houses. They were made to understand that widened streets would facilitate vehicles to come in, which was necessary at least when someone died or when someone had to be carried to the hospital. Once again, Naginaben took the lead and cut her house then everyone in the settlement agreed to cut their houses.

The streets were still narrow to take a 20 metre long pipe inside the settlement from the main road. MHT convinced one household to allow the pipe to pass through its dwelling by cutting hole. Needless to say that this was not easy. Lastly, the stone paving was done in Sanjaynagar and the construction work was finished in August 2006. After completion of infrastructure work, a household survey was done to find out how many had received the facility and how much of payment was due. The MHT conducted seven surveys during the whole process of SNP implementation.

Post-Project Activities

Once the physical infrastructure was laid, it was time to pay the AMC the pre-fixed beneficiary contribution. It was not possible for MHT to withdraw money from the individual accounts in the SEWA Bank and so the entire contribution (which was originally Rs. 2,100 per household) was transferred to account of Sanjaynagar Mahila Mandal, already opened in the SEWA Bank. This account was authorised to be operated by two signatories of the four office holders, the president, the vice president, the finance head and the monitor of the *mandal*. The four women who held these positions respectively were Naginaben, Naniben, Malaben and Puniben. These women were active and had shown initiative at different stages when no one from the community was willing to come forward to participate in the project.

It was decided to take Rs. 100 per household as maintenance charges. It was also decided that from the amount collected in the *mahila mandal* account, a maintenance amount was to be retained in the account and the rest was to be given to the AMC as the settlement's contribution. Since Rs. 600 was to come as contribution from the municipal councillor, each household had to contribute Rs. 1,500, of which Rs. 1,400 were to be given to the AMC and Rs. 100 kept aside for maintenance purposes. But, as discussed earlier, the councillor did not keep his promise and the remaining amount of Rs. 40,000 was contributed by the MHT. A cheque of Rs. 1,21,500 was given to the AMC from Sanjaynagar Mahila Mandal account with the signature of president, vice president, monitor and the finance head. The work was completed and payments to the AMC were settled in September 2006 (*See* Annexure 5.6).

It was then the time to maintain the new created assets. This is a bigger challenge for Indian cities in general and the slums in particular than constructing the assets. Learning from many upgradation programmes implemented in the past has been that once the implementing public authority moves out the assets created begin to degrade. If maintenance mechanism is not put in place, the slum can slip back to pre-project situation. While the project implementation was going on, in March 2005, MHT had organised a meeting with the slum dwellers, in particular the women, to discuss the post-project maintenance in the settlement. It was agreed that a person would be employed for door-to-door garbage collection and sweeping the streets. For both these tasks, the *mandal* would collect Rs. 10 per household, out of which, Rs. 7 were towards paying the sweeper for door-to-door garbage collection and sweeping the streets and Rs. 3 were to be saved in the account of the *mandal*. MHT had suggested any woman from the slum could do this work. Since no one in the slum belonged to the *Harijan* caste (traditionally engaged in such a work), no one came forward. Then, a woman from a nearby settlement was employed. The problem of solid waste management had been thought of before-hand and once the infrastructure was laid, the new system of waste management was introduced.

According to AMC regulations on solid waste management, one sweeper appointed should cover minimum of 200 dwellings. But, Sanjaynagar had only 117 households. And so, it was decided that the person appointed would also cover the neighbouring slum called Patrawali Chali. The *mandal* took the contract for even cleaning this neighbouring slum and then applied to the AMC to carry out solid waste management in Sanjaynagar and Patrawali Chali. The Sanjaynagar Mahila Mandal obtained the work order for solid waste management in 2005 after necessary inspection. MHT provided a guarantee on behalf of the *mandal*. On sanctioning the work order, the AMC provides cycle rickshaw to collect the waste. Since, a woman was to do this work, and it is difficult for her to cycle down wearing a *sari,* MHT requested the AMC to provide a pushcart instead of a cycle rickshaw. AMC had no objection as the former was worth Rs. 3,700 against Rs. 4,200 of the latter at that time.

This arrangement continued smoothly for two years till 2007, when, AMC changed its solid waste management policy and decided to award ward-wise contracts. To invite contractors, a tender was invited, with the condition of non-refundable tender-fees payment of Rs. 1,000 and an advance (but refundable) amount of Rs. 5,000 to be deposited with the AMC. Sanjaynagar Mahila Mandal decided to bid for the contract and applied for the same. The residents of the slum bore this expenditure and applied for the tender. Because, there is very high income from waste, many were interested and the tender notice realised into many bids. At the time of opening the tender bids, there was a very large and unmanageable crowd at the AMC office. Not expecting such massive interest and crowd, it became difficult for the AMC to manage the event well and the tender notice was cancelled. The AMC decided to continue with the same system for the time-being. The *mandal* lost Rs. 1,000 as the tender fees were not returned by the AMC.

Sanjaynagar Mahila Mandal has taken up the solid waste management activity as one of their regular income-generation activities. With the saving of Rs. 3 per household per month, they erected a board with name of the settlement "Sanjaynagar" inscribed on it at the entrance of the settlement which costed them Rs. 480. The leader, Naginaben supervises the activity of garbage collection and she goes to the AMC office for this purpose every month. The *mandal* was paying her Rs. 300 per month for supervision. Interestingly, the *mandal* has paid back MHT an amount of Rs. 25,000 from the Rs. 40,000 that the latter paid to the AMC to tide over the crisis created on account of the councillor not meeting his promise. The slum dwellers did not grumble, as the *mandal* was earning some money through solid waste management. This was big evolution for a community that was hesitant to pay Rs. 50 for opening an account to one paying for their own facilities.

The *mandal* has also made a fixed deposit in the SEWA Bank, once again through the income generated from solid waste management. Households in Sanjaynagar have also started paying the property tax bill as they realised that the property tax bill was an important tenure status document. Households begun saving regularly with the SEWA Bank and some also took loans from the Bank for various purposes including repairing and upgrading their houses. Some households also took life insurance and health insurance policies from *Vimo*—SEWA (SEWA Insurance—another sister organisation of SEWA).

The property prices have increased in the settlement after the SNP intervention. The rentals increased to Rs. 1,000 per month after the project from Rs. 400 earlier. Price of an average house increased to Rs. 80,000 from Rs. 15,000. But, no one had yet sold their house and gone elsewhere. A sense of ownership of the settlement has arisen after the SNP from complete apathy and lack of interest in improving the settlement before the SNP.

Becoming Part of City Level Network—Vikasini

The Sanjaynagar Mahila Mandal then became a part of city-level federation of *mandals*. At the settlement level, it was realised that the successful mobilisation at the local level should be taken up one step and that women should be exposed and linked to city-level issues. The MHT had also decided that once they had formed about 100 such *mandals*, they would make a federation of these *mandals*. MHT organised a workshop with all *mandals* they had been instrumental in setting up and as an outcome of it, decided to form a *Mahamandal*—a bigger federation including some of the members of all the *mandals*. This federation was given the name *Vikasini* meaning 'woman as a developer'. Sanjaynagar Mahila Mandal also joined this bigger platform.

The structure of *Vikasini* is that leader of one *mandal* regularly monitors other two *mandals*. From Sanjaynagar Mahila Mandal, Naginaben is in charge of monitoring other *mandals* in Ahmedabad city. She has been given the responsibility of Bavaji na Chhapra and Bhikhadeva No Vado in Amraiwadi ward, located near Sanjaynagar so that it would be easier for her to monitor these settlements regularly. The leaders of all the *mandals* are given information of various government schemes and they, taking help from the NGOs, educate the slum dwellers about the benefits of these schemes and then motivate them to participate in these schemes.

All the leaders meet once a month in the MHT office, when they give report of their activities, people's responses and reactions and their experiences. The following month's activities are planned; some are given new tasks whereas others are asked to continue with the ongoing tasks. Thus, there is a continuous collective review of the work carried by the leaders. This process also provides a possibility of a collective continuously updating its work in response to new challenges emerging. The MHT has also ensured that there is continuous education and capacity building of the leaders. Thus, the members of the *Mahamandal* were taken on an exposure visit to Kutch, the driest district of Gujarat state, to introduce them to different methods of water harvesting, bio gas plant and benefits of both the technologies. While this chapter was being written, the scheme of constructing *pucca* (permanent) ceiling of the houses by the MHT was underway in the city. Women members of *Vikasini* were carrying out a survey in the areas allotted to them. The survey was to estimate number of households willing to incur cost of *pucca* ceiling to replace their tin-roofs and take a loan from the SEWA Bank and then assess if they could service the loan on monthly basis.

At the time of writing this case, the residents of Sanjaynagar were interested in taking a loan from the SEWA Bank to construct a *pucca* ceiling on their houses and also wanted to invest in their houses. They also wanted to add another floor to their existing single storey house. Their aspirations have increased. There is a remarkable change in their aspirations, from total ignorance towards the settlement, to raising their voice as a community and collectively demanding better standards of living.

Conclusions

This case presents that the lives of the urban poor improve through their own efforts. But when these efforts are supported by the state policy, the results could be faster. When a state is dysfunctional in terms of human development and women's empowerment, an external agency has to take over the responsibility. This case study shows that the agency of voluntary organisation, now termed as NGO, has intervened to facilitate improvement in quality of life of the slum dwellers and enable them to obtain their entitlements.

This case represents a situation when the AMC approached a NGO to mobilise a community to participate in a slum development programme, financed by the AMC to the tune of 80 per cent of the cost. The NGO is external to the settlement and has no history of contact with the dwellers, which proved to be extremely difficult in mobilising the community. Persuasiveness of the NGO, the MHT, finally helped and through the women's agency, physical improvement of the slum was successfully completed.

The community mobilisation has remained restricted to immediate surroundings' improvement, although a few individual women have gained experience of public work and have become active and confident in dealing with income generation and community work. Culture plays a very critical role in the impacts felt at household and individual level in situations where external agency intervenes. Residents of Sanjaynagar are predominantly from Rajasthan or Uttar Pradesh of north India. In the latter, women are not allowed to go out of the house for earning extra income. After all the efforts made by the MHT, women continued to be engaged in home-based work of making *agarbattis*. Despite the fact that their time is saved from filling water for household purposes and they have time to take up income-generating activities, post-project, this change has not been observed in Sanjaynagar. Women, continue to play the traditional role of a homemaker, with a few exceptions of women whose names have been mentioned in this chapter.

Though one can observe a drastic change in the physical condition of the settlement, the upliftment of the community is not up to full level. Not much change has been observed in education levels which should have been the by-product of women's empowerment. Though women of Sanjaynagar are heading towards becoming a part of a city-level network through *Vikasini*, they still have no role in decision making in family matters. They still find it difficult to participate in taking decisions about the settlement and their husbands and other men in the settlement are still in dominating position. These women do not have any role about the future of their children which still is under control of the man of the house. Though the women of Sanjaynagar have come a long way and brought a visual change to the settlement, they have a long journey to reach independent and equal status in the society.

Lastly, the AMC's intention of extending the services to the slums is part of the *de facto* slum development policy. However, it is located within the neo-liberal paradigm of asking the poor communities to share part of the cost, however, small that amount may be. The poor communities willingly in other cases, and in this case through persuasion of the MHT, agree to share the costs of services extension only because they do not see any other way of accessing these services on their own.

Table 5.1: Time Line of Sanjaynagar's Development

Year	*Event*	*Actors*	*Activities*
2001	Survey of 700 slums of Ahmedabad city	AMC, MHT, SAATH	Prioritisation of slums for SNP
2002	First visit to Sanjaynagar	MHT	Explaining to slum leaders who were not co-operative
2002	Second visit	MHT	Explanation of the scheme without much success
	Third visit	MHT	Unsuccessful in convincing the residents for SNP
	Another visit	MHT	Asked the residents to give in written that they do not want SNP
	Visit to collect the consent letter	MHT	15 women signed on the consent letter
July 17, 2002	Started opening accounts in SEWA Bank	MHT, SEWA Bank	Women opened accounts in SEWA Bank by paying Rs.50
November, 2002	Creation of *mandal*	MHT, Women of Sanjaynagar	Initially resistant and opposed by husbands women setup a *mandal*
December, 2002	Training of *mandal*	MHT, Members of *mandal*	*Mandal* took extensive training of 20 days.

(*Contd.*)

Table 5.1: (*Contd.*)

Year	*Event*	*Actors*	*Activities*
October 11, 2003	Application for registration of *mandal*	MHT, *mandal*	Applied for Bombay Non Trading association certificate
23rd April 2004	First survey	MHT	MHT did the first survey in Sanjaynagar to get the estimate of number of households and basic facilities already available.
January 19, 2004	Registration of *mandal*	Women of Sanjaynagar	Received registration certificate and *mandal* prepared their own letter head
April 1, 2005	Door to door scheme	Residents	MHT motivated the residents for cleanliness and the scheme started.
May 2, 2005	Grant from councillor sanctioned	Chairman, standing committee, AMC	A grant of Rs. 40,000 from councillor's budget sanctioned.
September 1, 2005	Received the work order from AMC	MHT and *mandal*	Work order to start the construction work was received from AMC
September 2, 2005	Levelling surface in Sanjaynagar	AMC, Engineers from MHT	Engineers and contractors went to Sanjaynagar for exact measurements and levelling the surface of the soil.
September 6, 2005	*Khat mahurat*	Residents, Councillor, MHT	Ceremony of starting a new construction was done by the councillor—Gangaram.
September 25, 2005	Work for drainage started	AMC, MHT	The houses were cut for widening the streets
November 14, 2005	Construction of individual toilets started	AMC, MHT	
May 10, 2006	Work of drainage was completed	AMC, MHT	
May 15, 2006	Individual toilet construction completed	AMC, MHT	
May 20, 2006	Work of water connection started	AMC, MHT	Regular deposits of contribution towards SNP by people. Money put in SEWA Bank.
June 30, 2006	All the individual water connections were provided	AMC, MHT	
July 1 to Dec. 7, 2006	Stone paving in the settlement	AMC, MHT	
September 19, 2007	Payment to AMC	Mandal	A cheque of Rs. 1,21,500 was sent to AMC for SNP by the leaders of the Sanjaynagar Mahila Mandal
Nov. 21, 2008	Formation of *Vikasini*	MHT, *mandals*	A federation was formed which helps in capacity building
June 2009	Audit of account		After this the account and transactions of the *mandal* are being audited.

Annexure 5.1

A Sample of Saving Account's Passbook, SEWA Bank

This contains photograph, saving account number, name of the account holder, residential address and occupation of the account holder.

ફોન ૬૫૮૨૫૯૭, ૬૫૮૧૬૫૨ ૧૦,૦૦૦-૧૧-૨૦૦

શ્રી મહિલા સેવા સહકારી બેંક લિ.

૧૦૯, સાકાર-૨, ટાઉન હોલ સામે,
એલિસબ્રીજ,
અમદાવાદ-૬.

સેવિંગ્સ ખાતાની પાસ બુક

બચત ખાતા નં.

નામ શ્રી

સરનામું

ધંધો

Annexure 5.2

Management Information System

Mahila Housing Trust - SanjayNagr-Amraiwadi6(May6)4-51

A/C NO	NAME	A1	A2	Last Date	Deposit	With draw	Balance	Last Month	This Month	Total +/-
	↓ 0 to 500 ↓									
5761	MAMATABEN MANGALBHAI NAI	SANJAYNAGAR	B/H UTTAM DERY	3/8/2006	57.00	0.00	57.00	8	8	0
6056	KAMLABEN KAMALKISHOR AGRAWAL	SANJAYNAGAR,	B/H UTTAM DARY	3/8/2006	57.00	0.00	57.00			
6201	PREMBEN BATILAL JOGI	SANJAYNAGAR	B/H UTTAM DARY	3/8/2006	114.00	0.00	114.00			
6974	MANGILAL SUNDAJI KHATIK	SANJAYNAGAR		3/8/2006	172.00	0.00	172.00			
6283	JYOTIBEN SITARAM KHATIK	SANJAYNAGAR	B/H UTTAM DERY	3/8/2006	206.00	0.00	206.00			
7864	SHANTABEN MANEKLAL KHATIK	SANJAYNAGAR	B/H UTTAM DARY	3/8/2006	258.00	0.00	258.00			
5928	SANTABEN SUGANAJI KHATIK	SANJAYNAGAR	B/H UTTAM DAIRY	3/8/2006	339.00	0.00	339.00			
5849	YASHOGHARABEN TRAMBBHAI GODBOLE	SANJAYNAGAR	B/H UTTAM DAIRY	3/8/2006	359.00	300.00	59.00			
	↓ 501 to 1000 ↓									
8286	SAVITRIBEN RAJENDRAKUMAR SHARMA	SANJAYNAGAR	B/H UTTAM DERY	3/8/2006	705.00	650.00	55.00	1	1	0
	↓ 1001 to 1500 ↓									
8034	GITABEN JANARDAN PRAJAPATI	SANJAYNAGAR	B/H UTTAM DAIRY	3/8/2006	1017.00	950.00	67.00	21	21	0
6345	BHARATSING MOTISING RAJPUT	SANJAYNAGAR	B/H UTTAM DARY	4/15/2006	1047.00	790.00	257.00			
6052	PUSHPABEN HARIPRASHAD NAI	SANJAYNAGAR	B/H UTTAM DARY	4/4/2006	1082.00	870.00	212.00			
6202	KELABEN BHURABHAI YOGI	SANJAYNAGAR	B/H UTTAM DARY	3/8/2006	1107.00	1050.00	57.00			
7895	SUSHILABEN PRAKASHBHAI BHATIA	SANJAYNAGAR	B/H UTTAM DAIRY	3/8/2006	1111.00	1050.00	61.00			
7200	SHOBHADEVI BECHANPRASHAD KANOJIA	SANJYNAGAR	B/H UTTAM DARY	3/8/2006	1119.00	1050.00	69.00			
8591	REVIBEN MASRUBHAI CHAUHAN	SANJAYNAGAR		3/8/2006	1151.00	1050.00	101.00			
8609	SHYAMLAL BENIMADHAV GUPTA	SANJAYNAGAR	B/H UTTAM DERY	3/2/2006	1200.00	900.00	300.00			
8287	LAXMIBEN VINODKUMAR PARAGHI	SANJAYNAGAR	B/H UTTAM DERY	3/25/2006	1202.00	800.00	402.00			
6054	RAJENDRABHAI SHREEDAYARAM KORI	SANJAYNAGAR,	B/H UTTAM DARY	3/8/2006	1207.00	1100.00	107.00			
6067	SHUBHADRABEN SHESHRAV DHARMIK	SANJAYNAGAR	B/H UTTAM DARY	3/8/2006	1209.00	1100.00	109.00			
8319	GUDIBEN KARMASHANKAR VISHVAKARM	SANJAYNAGAR	B/H UTTAM DARY	3/25/2006	1209.00	700.00	509.00			
6060	DURGABEN GAYARAM PRAJAPATI	SANJAYNAGAR,	B/H UTTAM DARY	3/8/2006	1210.00	1100.00	110.00			
6204	JASHODABEN BHAGAVATPRASAD GUPTA	SANJAYNAGAR	B/H UTTAM DARY	3/25/2006	1423.00	950.00	473.00			
5859	MEVATIBEN RAMDIN NAI	SANJAYNAGAR	B/H UTTAM DAIRY	4/4/2006	1425.00	1250.00	175.00			
6059	LILABEN RAJKUMAR VISHVAKARMA	SANJAYNAGAR,	B/H UTTAM DARY	3/8/2006	1427.00	1270.00	157.00			
8748	JAYPRAKASH RAMAJI KANOJIA	SANJAYNAGAR	B/H UTTAM DERY	2/25/2006	1500.00	1400.00	100.00			
8810	RAMPRATAP GANGABASIN YADAV	SANJAYNAGAR	B/H UTTAM DERY	2/25/2006	1500.00	1400.00	100.00			
8823	LILABEN MOHANBHAI VAGHELA	SANJAYNAGAR	B/H UTTAM DERY	3/6/2006	1500.00	1200.00	300.00			
8824	LAXMIBEN CHEHARABHAI VAGHELA	SANJAYNAGAR	B/H UTTAM DERY	2/25/2006	1500.00	1400.00	100.00			
8827	RAMGOPAL SHIVBALAK MORYA	SANJAYNAGAR	B/H UTTAM DERY	4/15/2006	1500.00	800.00	700.00			
	↓ 1501 to 2099 ↓									
7359	RAJKISHOR SHIVDATT YADAV	SANJAYNAGAR	B/H UTTAM DARY	3/8/2006	1501.00	1400.00	101.00	54	54	0
8536	HARISH ASHOK KHOBARAGADE	SANJAYNAGAR	B/H UTTAM DERY	3/8/2006	1501.00	1400.00	101.00			
8537	MANOJ KAILAS NAI	SANJAYNAGAR	B/H UTTAM DERY	3/8/2006	1501.00	1000.00	501.00			
8606	FULCHANDBHAI RAMPYARE KANOJIYA	67 SANJAYNAGAR	AMRAIWADI	3/8/2006	1501.00	1000.00	501.00			
5860	SANGHMITRABEN ISHWARBHAI PATIL	SANJAYNAGAR	B/H UTTAM DAIRY	3/8/2006	1502.00	1400.00	102.00			
8544	KAMLA KAILAS NAI	SANJAYNAGAR	B/H UTTAM DERY	3/10/2006	1502.00	500.00	1002.00			
8545	CHHOTELAL MULANATH YOGI	SANJAYNAGAR	B/H UTTAM DERY	3/29/2006	1502.00	1100.00	402.00			
8693	KAMLABEN HARISHANKAR RAJPUT	SANJAYNAGAR	B/H UTTAM DARY	3/8/2006	1502.00	900.00	602.00			
8694	SANGITABEN RAKESHBHAI KHUSHVAH	SANJAYNAGAR	B/H UTTAM DARY	3/8/2006	1502.00	1400.00	102.00			
8284	FULVATIBEN ASHOKBHAI SHARMA	SANJAYNAGAR	B/H UTTAM DERY	4/20/2006	1503.00	550.00	953.00			
8285	SHOBHABEN PRAMODBHAI KANOJIA	SANJAYNAGAR	B/H UTTAM DERY	4/15/2006	1503.00	1000.00	503.00			
8607	SUNITABEN LAKHANSIHN RAJPUT	SANJAYANAGAR	AMRAIWADI	3/8/2006	1503.00	950.00	553.00			
7952	LILABEN MAHESHBHAI RATHOD	SANJAYNAGAR	B/H UTTAM DARY	3/8/2006	1504.00	1400.00	104.00			

Annexure 5.3

Registration Certificate of the Mandal

SCHEDULE-III
(See Section-16)

Non Trading Corporation Certificate.

N T C. G/12965

Office of the Registrar of
Non-TradingCorporation
C/4 Sales Tax Bhavan
Ashram Road,
Ahmedabad 380009
Date:-19/01/ 2004

CERTIFICATE OF INCORPORATION

I here by certify that SANJAY NAGAR MAHILA HOUSING SEVA MANDAL is this day incorporated under the Bombay Non-Trading Corporation Act-1959 (Bombay-XXVI of 1959) and that the Corporation is limited by Shares.

Given under my hand at Ahmedabad this day 19th January Two Thousand Four

THE REGISTRAR OF NON-TRADING CORPORATION G.S. AHMEDABAD

Place :- Ahmedabad.
Date :- 19/01/2004

Registrar,
Non-Trading Corporation,
Gujarat State, Ahmedabad.

Annexure 5.4

Letterhead of Sanjaynagar Mahila Mandal

Sanjaynagar Mahila Housing SEWA Mandal
In front of Ashima Building, Opposite A.E.C, Amraiwadi, Ahmedabad – 38008
Date of Registration : 19-01-2004
Number : NTC-/ G/12965

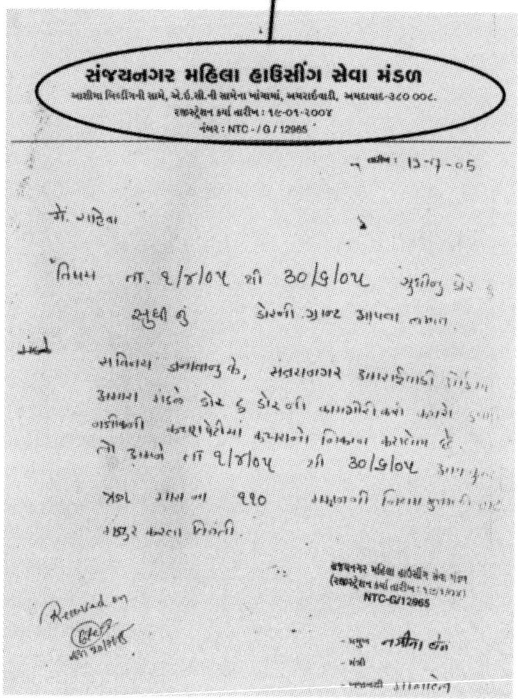

સંજયનગર મહિલા હાઉસીંગ સેવા મંડળ
નંબર : NTC - / G / 12965

NTC-G/12965

Annexure 5.5

Councillor Gangaram's Written Promise for Donation of Rs. 50,000

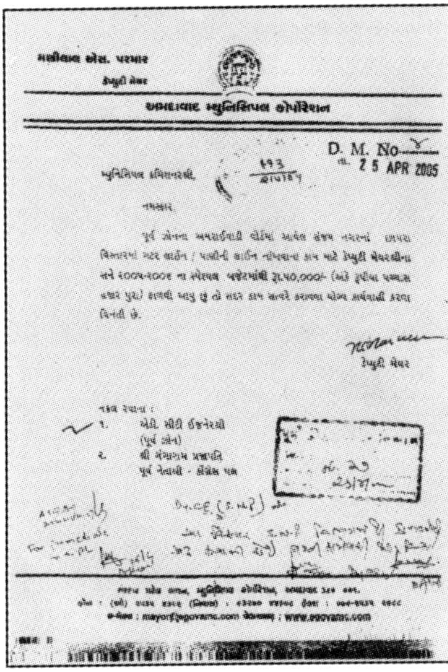
D. M. No.
25 APR 2005

This letter is to the Municipal Commissioner of Ahmedabad city from the Deputy Mayor Mr. Manilal Parmar dated April 25, 2005. It mentions that Sanjaynagar slum of Amraiwadi ward of East zone has been awarded Rs. 50,000 for water and sewerage line from Deputy Mayor's special budget. A copy has been sent to Additional City Engineer of East zone and Councillor Mr. Gangaram Prajapati.

Annexure 5.6

Receipt from AMC on payment of Rs. 1,21,500 made by Sanjaynagar Mahila Mandal on September 22, 2006

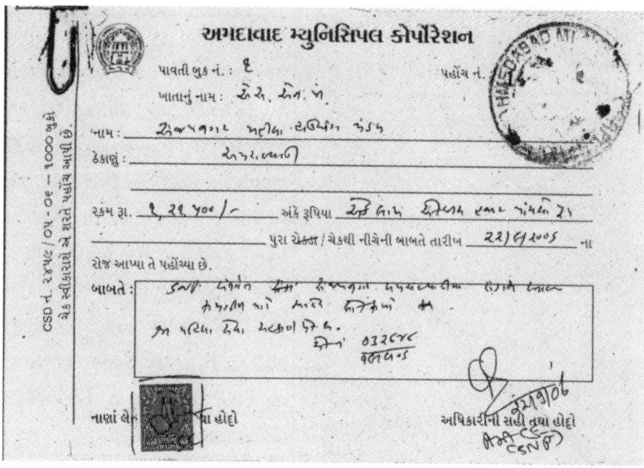

અમદાવાદ મ્યુનિસિપલ કોર્પોરેશન

પાવતી બુક નં.:   પહોંચ નં.

ખાતાનું નામ:

નામ:

ઠેકાણું:

રકમ રૂા.   અંકે રૂપિયા

પુરા રોકડા / ચેકથી નીચેની બાબતે તારીખ

રોજ આપ્યા તે પહોંચ્યા છે.

બાબતે:

નાણાં લેનારની સહી તથા હોદ્દો   અધિકારીની સહી તથા હોદ્દો

NOTES

1. Research is funded under the research project titled "Inclusive Urbanisation —Social Protection for the Slum and Pavement Dwellers in India', a CEPT University—Mahila Housing SEWA Trust (MHT) project, under the programme 'Social Protection in Asia', managed by Institute of Development Studies (IDS), Sussex and Institute of Human Development (IHD), New Delhi and funded by Ford Foundation and IDRC. We would like to acknowledge the fieldwork assistance from the community workers of MHT.
2. See chapter 4 for the introduction to Ahmedabad city and the SNP.
3. All statistics in this paragraph and then subsequent paragraphs on MHT are from: http://www.sewahousing.org/index.php?p=Urban&c=t&gallery=UrbanActivities (accessed on April 6, 2010).
4. Town Planning Scheme has been explained in the earlier chapters.
5. 7/12 *Utara* = In Indian constitution, village is considered as a fundamental unit of administration from the British rule in India. There are 18 village forms according to the constitution. The combination of 7th (Diary of Mutations) and 12th (Record of Crops and Tenancies) village form is called 7/12 *Utara*.

6
Leaving Poor to their Own Devices
The Case of Amraiwadi, Ahmedabad[1]

Darshini Mahadevia, Pooja Shah and
Pavan Kumar Ankinapalli

Introduction: Slums in Amraiwadi

A survey conducted in 2001 by the Ahmedabad Municipal Corporation (AMC), Mahila Housing SEWA Trust (MHT) and Saath to identify slums for the Slum Networking Programme (SNP), stated that of the total 1,666 slums and *chawls*, 458 (or 27%) were located in the east zone of the city (Annexure 6.1). Ahmedabad city is divided into six zones in which the new west zone has been included in the municipal limits in the year 2006. Amraiwadi is among the ten wards in the east zone and has the largest number of slums and *chawls* among the wards in this zone (Annexure 6.2). Visually too, the ward appears to be consisting of largely slums and *chawls*. Some of the adjoining wards such as Bapunagar has many large public housing units. This was one reason for selecting this ward besides the presence of the MHT in the ward for the SNP projects.

Amraiwadi has historically developed as an industrial area. Since the beginning of the 20th century the cotton textile mills were located here and later the new industrial estates housing small-scale industries came up around. While the cotton textile mills were typical Fordian welfare units, with organized and well paid labour-force housed in employee housing, the small-scale industrial units were typically unorganised manufacturing employing unprotected labour. The textile mill housing was referred to as *chawls,* which are single room dwelling units laid in a row and provided with common water and sanitation facilities. East Ahmedabad is marked by such low-income housing settlements. Subsequently, all the informal housing that came up to house unorganised sector workers, were on the model of the mill *chawls* and were also called *chawls*. Most of these new *chawls* came up on informally subdivided private lands that were declared as reserved in the city's Development Plan (DP) or for acquisition under the Urban Land Ceiling and Regulation Act (ULCRA), 1976.

Another significant phenomenon occurred during late 1980s and early 1990s. The cotton textile mills went into decline and closed. But, their *chawls* continued to house the former cotton textile mill workers. The parent unit, the textile mill having shut and the residents of these *chawls* no longer being the employees of the mills, the mill owners were not interested in maintaining such dwellings. Since these *chawls* were under rent control legislation, the owners could not increase the rent. The owners, therefore, did not renovate the *chawls* which then deteriorated into slum type of housing. To get rid of the burden, a few *chawl* owners offered the occupants to purchase their dwelling units. Such transactions indeed took place in many *chawls*. We found in our field study several instances of *chawls* where partial sale of the dwelling units had occurred. In some *chawls,* the owners had stopped collecting rents and the occupiers became the *de facto* owners. In some of the closed mills, parts of the lands were encroached by the poor and recent migrants by the side of the former *chawl*. On the whole, even the industrial *chawls* have deteriorated into slums.

The owners of the lands under the informal settlements themselves subdivided their lands and sold the plots. In some cases, where the owners deployed middleman to sell the plots or even subdivide land into plots for sale, the middlemen were working like an informal sector developer. A middleman operates through Power of Attorney (PoA) obtained from the owner. The plots are sold to the buyers through recording the transaction on a piece of paper on which a revenue stamp is affixed or more generally on a stamp-paper of some denomination[2]. In the local language it is called a *parchi* (meaning a document). While this is not a land ownership document, the buyers consider such documents as valid and are content with them as establishing their right to use the land transacted thus. These new settlements through the informal subdivisions of land are also called *chawls* as already mentioned. Generally, the land plots or subsequent plot with a house is purchased by the occupants. However, in some instances such *chawls* have been developed only for purpose of renting.

Agriculture lands on the urban periphery also enter into the informal housing market. When such lands realise the potential of development the owners subdivide them and sale themselves or through a developer in the informal sector at prevailing market rate (which are generally lower than the formal market's rates). They do not bother to obtain Non-agricultural (NA) conversion permission, either because of the time and cost attached to the procedure or because they do not feel the need. Hence, there is no formal sale-deed. The land ownership document, called 7/12 document, continues in the name of the real owner(s). In such transactions too, the process of development of *chawl* is the same as described in the previous paragraph. In the survey in this ward, the team found that the sale-agreements were made on a stamp paper of Rs.10. The four slums in the survey and then many others in the vicinity that had been visited had developed in this manner.

When a *chawl*/slum comes up on the land notified for acquisition under the ULCRA, the original farmer's name is on the land ownership document and it is marked as land to be acquired in the official land records. Since the land has not been acquired, it remains locked as marked for acquisition and no further permission for development is allowed on such lands. In essence, the land transactions on such lands marked for acquisitions freeze. But, such a state offers high degree of tenure security to the dwellers, except that they are unable to obtain legal title to the land and hence are unable to offer the land as mortgage in case they would like to take a housing loan.

In some of the slums, there have been either NGO or government intervention. SNP has been done in Sanjaynagar through a strong intervention of the MHT. Under SNP, this slum has been given *de facto* tenure for 10 years by the AMC (*See* chapter 5 for the case study). In Gopalnagar, there is intervention of two NGOs, the MHT and World Vision while in Patravali Chali, MHT has intervened and tried to extend basic services. In both these settlements, the residents receive the property tax bills. Surabhagat Ni Chali is settled on private land but the councillor of that area has provided community toilets and pavements in the settlement. Even in this slum, residents receive property tax bills.

Slums/*chawls* have also developed on the industrial lands, in particular on the lands of old mills. This has been discussed earlier. While some *chawls* had common basic facilities and some had none at all. Over time, some *chawl* residents managed to get illegal water supply and constructed soak pits. The units changed hands many times even if they were under rent control. When the owners stopped collecting rents, the tenants became *de facto* owners but not legal owners: they could neither transact the property in the legal market nor offer the property as a mortgage for loan. Even when the textile mills closed down and the workers were retrenched, *chawl* residents did not become homeless; they continued to live in these *chawls* in spite of their *chawl's* deterioration. The rents collected were as low as Rs. 5 or Rs. 7 that the workers did not feel the pinch of retrenchment. Even the price of a cup of tea at the roadside stall would cost about Rs. 4 in 2009. Satyamnagar is one such settlement. Because of this situation, it was also not selected for SNP. Some of the residents of this settlement have themselves managed to get individual water taps, individual toilets and bath space. While the tenure situation of this land is not very clear, evidently it is more secure than the slums on municipal land.

One slum selected in this study is on the AMC land and is an interesting case. It is located on a pond, which was gradually filled and encroached upon as the slum expanded. However, only a part of the slum is on former pond whereas remaining part is on the AMC land. *Talavadi* in Gujarati means a small lake or a pond and *chhapra* in a local language means huts hence this slum is called Talavadi Na Chhapra, which means huts on the pond or pond-side. This pond is the property of the AMC. This slum has expanded through accretion and at the time of the survey, there were 1,200 dwelling units in this slum. Households on the part of the slum on the demarcated pond area had received notice of eviction as the city has begun reviving all such encroached upon former water bodies to increase ground water recharge in the city. Water tables in Ahmedabad are very low and the city has been forced to purchase water from external sources incurring heavy expenditure. In general, slums on the bank of river, lake side, near open drain lines, railway lines etc., are highly insecure as they could face eviction anytime. With the environmental agendas as well as city infrastructure projects coming up in many cities, such slums have been marked for demolition.

The AMC had divided the land of Talavadi Na Chhapra into three plots. One of these was approved by the AMC for implementing the SNP, wherein a non-profit organisation called World Vision had mobilised the residents and the MHT had implemented the SNP. The remaining two plots were considered as encroachment and their dwellers, who had already experienced evictions twice, received new eviction notices at the time of our study. Since the SNP has been implemented only on one segment of the slum, we did not find much improvement in the living conditions in the whole slum, like we found in another SNP slum nearby named

Sanjaynagar (case presented in chapter 5), which had higher tenure security as compared to Talavadi Na Chhapra because of its location on private land. The evicted households from Talavadi Na Chhapra come back and squat again on the same land after every eviction.

Four slums in the sample, namely Sanjaynagar, Gopalnagar, Surabhagat Ni Chali and Patravali Chali, are on private land since the AMC does not have any direct control over such lands, it cannot evict the dwellers without any legal process.

Methodology and Sample Profile

The study was carried out in three steps. The first step was to select a ward for the study in the eastern zone of the city. After selecting the ward Amraiwadi, a few slums were shortlisted with the help of city-level slum survey data (2001 Survey for SNP). The second step was to visit these shortlisted slums and verify the available data and get a general idea of tenure situation in them. Six slums were selected from the shortlisted slums to carry out a detailed study. Both qualitative and quantitative investigation were carried out in the study area with the help of Focus Group Discussions (FGDs) and a structured questionnaire survey which was the third step of the study. The tenure arrangements have been analysed based on the data of ownership of the land, documents available with the households, coveragc of slum under any development scheme by the government or non-government organisations, land reserved in the city's DP or the Town Planning Scheme, slum size, receipt of property tax bill and age of the slum. Many of the details were obtained through the FGDs with the slum dwellers as well as from various city government departments. The six slums selected for the survey are: Sanjaynagar, Patravali Chali, Talavadi Na Chhapra, Gopalnagar, Satyamnagar and

Table 6.1: Sample size and profile, Amraiwadi, Ahmedabad

Name of the slum	*Total households*	*Sample households*	*Sample (%)*
Sanjaynagar	117	16	13.7
Patravali chali	400	35	8.8
Gopalnagar	350	33	9.4
Surabhagat Ni Chali	150	19	12.6
Satyamnagar	2,000	199	10.0
Talavadi Na Chhapra	1,200	135	11.3
Total	4,217	437	10.6

Source: Primary Survey.

Surabhagat Ni Chali. Sample was 10 per cent households which was 437 households (Table 6.1) covering 2,189 persons. All the selected six slums showed a mix community living unlike Pravinnagar-Guptanagar presented in chapter 4.

For the purpose of analysis, the slums have been categorised into three groups, those on private land have been put as slums in catcgory 1, those on other lands such as mill lands, trust lands, etc. as category 2 and those on public lands as category 3. Since all dwellers have been living in the slum for more than 20 years, there was not much variation in their years of stay and therefore, an analysis by year of stay was not been considered. The further analysis in the chapter is by the three categories of land ownership. The overall sex ratio in the sample is 899, which is higher than the city and the state average. The sex ratio in the sample households on private lands was 935 (Table 6.2), which is the highest among the three categories of slums defined by their land ownership status.

Table 6.2: Sample profile, Amraiwadi, Ahmedabad

Land ownership	*Total households*	*Sample households*	*Sample population*	*Sex ratio*
Private	1,017	103	474	935
Mill land	2,000	199	1,006	863
Public	1,200	135	709	927
Total	4,217	437	2,189	899

Source: Primary Survey.

Tenure Status

As mentioned above, the tenure status is determined at the settlement level depending on the ownership and earmarked use of the land. Since the local government does not have jurisdiction of slums on private lands, they have the least threat of eviction. Thus slums on private lands have the highest security of tenure but without legal land title. Same is the case with the slums on the textile mill lands. The most insecure slums are those on the public lands. This would be also established through statistical analysis towards the end of the chapter. At the same time, tenure security is also defined at individual household level depending on the documents that each household holds. The documents such as sale document on a stamp-paper (a quasi-legal document of financial transaction), property tax payment receipt or even property tax bill, electricity bill, voter's ID card, and a ration card, give *de facto* tenure status to the household. Hence, in a settlement with *de facto* tenure status, residents could have differential level of security.

Chart 6.1: Summary of slums selected for study, Amraiwadi ward

Particulars	*Settlement Name*					
	Sanjaynagar	*Patravali Chali*	*Gopalnagar*	*Surabhagat Ni Chali*	*Satyamnagar*	*Talavadi Na Chhapra*
No. of Households	117	400	350	150	2000	1200
Land Ownership	Private	Private	Private	Private	Mill land	Municipal
Documents with Household	10 years *de facto* tenure, property tax bills, stamp papers document, electricity bill	property tax bills, stamp paper document, electricity bill	property tax bills, stamp paper document, electricity bill	property tax bills, stamp paper document, electricity bill	Electricity bill	Electricity bill
Tenure Status	Strong *de facto*	Weak *de facto* tenure	Weak *de facto* tenure	Weak *de facto* tenure	Insecure tenure	Insecure Tenure
Housing condition	Semi-*pucca*	*Pucca*/ semi-*pucca*	*Pucca* semi-*pucca*	Semi-*pucca*	*Pucca*/semi-*pucca*	*Katcha*
SNP	Yes	No	No	No	No	Yes (in part of the settlement)
Individual water tap	Yes	Yes	Yes	Yes	Yes	Yes
Individual Toilets	Yes	Yes	Yes	Community/ personal	Yes	Yes
Who provided toilets	SNP	Self	Self	Self /AMC	Self	NGO
Individual Bathing space	Yes	Some of the HH	Some of the HH	Some of the HH	Some of the HH	Some of the HH
Sewer line	Yes	Yes	Yes	Yes	Yes	Yes
Rain water Drain	Yes	Yes	Yes	Yes	Yes	Yes
Garbage collection	Yes	Yes	Yes	Yes	Yes	Yes
Paved Roads	Yes	Yes	Yes	No	Yes	No
Street lights	Yes	Yes	Yes	Yes	Yes	Yes

Source: Primary Survey.

There are four slums on private lands in the sample, of which one, Sanjaynagar has strong *de facto* tenure (Chart 6.1) and the other three, Patravali Chali, Gopalnagar and Surabhagat Ni Chali have weak *de facto* status. The slum on the mill land, Satyamnagar as well as Talavadi Na Chhapra on municipal land have insecure tenure. Nonetheless, they receive electricity bills. Sanjaynagar was with 10 years of *de facto* tenure under the SNP at the time of our study. The households in this slum were receiving property tax and electricity bills and had carried out property transactions *via* stamp-paper document. Households in the other three slums on private lands also have similar documents as in Sanjaynagar but do not have 10 year *de facto* tenure from the AMC. The households located on the mill lands in Satyamnagar are tenants and hence do not have right over the property. They would not be evicted but do not also have any documents to support their residency in the city. Hence, they have been classified as insecure tenure. But, the most insecure of them all are the households living in Talavadi Na Chhapra on municipal land.

Eighty per cent households living on public land claim that they own their current house (Table 6.3), although, in fact the occupants have encroached upon the land and also have low tenure security and no document of property transaction except 10 per cent of them. There is also rental market in the slums, however, only about 4 per cent households living as tenants when on the whole 10.5 per cent and in the slum on the mill land, 16 per cent were living as tenants. In spite of illegal status of the slum on public land, around 17 per cent of them were receiving property tax bills. Two-thirds of households in slum on the mill lands also owned a house, indicating they had purchased it from the original owner and 57 of the total households were also receiving property tax bills. In all the slums on private lands, only half of them (51.5%) have some document of property transaction (Table 6.3), often a document of sale on stamp-paper as mentioned above. Three-fourths of them are now getting property tax bills. Even in these slums, two in every three

Table 6.3: Tenure Status (%), Amraiwadi, Ahmedabad

Land ownership	*Owning house*	*Having any document of property transaction*	*Paying rent*	*Receives property tax bills*
Private	66.0	51.5	8.7	74.8
Mill land	66.8	69.9	16.1	56.8
Public	80.0	10.2	3.7	17.0
Average	70.7	45.0	10.5	48.7

Source: Primary Survey.

households have constructed their own house. This indicates that they had purchased the plot from the land owner or a developer who had subdivided the land and sold the plots and then constructed their own dwelling unit. Although, with varying degree of tenure security, 90 per cent or more households in all the slums stated that they were living there for more than 20 years.

Physical Conditions in Slums

Housing Conditions

It has been argued repeatedly by researchers as well as policy advocates that a shift from insecure to perceived tenure security would result in residents making significant investments in their housing. Further, it has also been found that the investment is incremental and hence improvement is also incremental. Any action by the government to increase perceived security of tenure also gives the slum residents a legal address and thereby urban citizenship. With insecure status, people are not willing to invest and they continue to live in the shabby dwelling for a lifetime. This can be observed in this survey as well, wherein, in slum on public land 78.5 per cent households were living in *katcha* houses[3] and just 1.5 per cent in *pucca* houses (Table 6.4). This slum is Talavadi Na Chhapra, where *pucca* and semi-*pucca* houses are only in the part where SNP has been implemented.

Table 6.4: Housing conditions, Amraiwadi, Ahmedabad

Land Ownership	*Percentage of Households*							
	Living in house that is			*With no. of rooms*				*Living in house with separate kitchen*
	Katcha	*Pucca*	*Semi-pucca*	1	2	3	*More than 3*	
Private	43.7	4.9	51.5	69.9	27.2	1.9	1.0	24.3
Mill land	4.5	24.1	71.4	64.8	33.7	1.0	0.5	15.6
Public	78.5	1.5	20.0	65.2	33.3	1.5	0.0	11.1
Average	36.6	12.6	50.8	66.6	31.4	1.5	0.5	16.2

Source: Primary Survey.

Nearly a quarter of the houses in the slum on the mill land are *pucca*, double the average proportion of the surveyed households (Table 6.4), probably because these were constructed by erstwhile mill owners. But, the mill *chawls* were largely semi-*pucca* houses and hence 71 per cent of the households lived in such housing in trust owned and industry owned land. Even in slums on private lands, more than half (51.5%) are living in semi-*pucca* houses. But, in this category, 44 per cent are living in *katcha* houses. While talking to some of the women of Sanjaynagar and Patravali Chali, it was found that the residents were waiting for some scheme from the AMC or the SEWA Bank to finance construction of ceilings. Households are ready to take loan to do so and may approach SEWA Bank for their individual product loan. On the whole only 12.6 per cent households are living in *pucca* house and nearly half the surveyed households in this ward are living in semi-*pucca* houses.

Two-thirds of houses have single room and there is very little variation across the land ownership category as regard the size of the house. This is a reflection of lack of affordability for large houses in this industrial ward of the city. Lastly, a quarter of the households in the private slums have a separate kitchen area whereas this proportion in the slum on public land is only 11 per cent. Thus, conditions of housing of those living on private lands is far better than those living on public lands and the former are willing to take loans to improve their housing conditions whereas the latter are not willing to do so.

Basic Services Availability

In spite of insecure status in the slum on public land, 96 per cent of the households had individual water connection and none depended on hand pump (Table 6.5). In fact, dependency on hand pump was noticed only in the slum on the mill land (4%). Further, 13 per cent households in the slum on mill land depended on common public water tap and hence just 81 per cent had individual water connection. Given these minor differences

Table 6.5: Source of domestic water supply (%), Amraiwadi, Ahmedabad

Land ownership	*Main source of water*				
	Individual connection	*Public tap*	*Private water supplier*	*Hand pump*	*Neighbour's connection*
Private	94.2	2.9	1.9	0.0	1.0
Mill land	80.9	12.6	1.5	4.0	1.0
Public	95.6	2.2	0.7	0.0	1.5
Average	88.6	7.1	1.4	1.8	1.1

Source: Primary Survey.

in water source, nearly 89 per cent of the surveyed households had individual household level water connection and another 7 per cent depended on public taps, indicating that the water supply situation was not too bad in the slums surveyed in this industrial ward. It also shows that the water supply availability is not linked to either land ownership or tenure status and that the AMC was supplying water to all the slum settlements in the ward.

Table 6.6: Details of obtaining individual water supply (%), Amraiwadi, Ahmedabad

Land ownership	*Period since individual connection available (years)*				*Agency responsible for individual water connection*		
	0 to 5	*5 to 10*	*10 to 15*	*More than 15*	*AMC*	*NGO*	*Self*
Private	36.1	24.7	10.3	28.9	62.9	13.4	23.7
Mill land	64.0	16.1	6.2	13.7	89.4	0.6	9.9
Public	90.7	9.3	0.0	0.0	69.0	27.1	3.9
Average	65.9	16.0	5.2	12.9	73.8	13.7	12.5

Source: Primary Survey.

About 66 per cent of the households have received individual water connection (if they have) in the last five years and another 16 per cent in last five to ten years (Table 6.6). In the slums on private lands 60 per cent, in the slum on the mill land 80 per cent and in the slum on public land all of them had obtained individual water connection in the last 10 years. In short, individual water supply connection has come to the households in the last decade only and for three-fourths of them, the AMC has supplied this connection. The NGO has played a role in extending individual water supply connection in one slum on the private land (which is the Sanjaynagar). In slum on the public land also, 27 per cent of households have obtained individual water connection through the NGO named MHT, who has facilitated extension of basic services in two slums in the sample. In Sanjaynagar, MHT facilitated SNP implementation and the basic services were provided by the AMC. But, because the MHT had mobilised the households for the purpose, they presume that the MHT had provided them individual water connection. Nearly a quarter of the households living on private land stated that they had obtained individual water connection on their own, indicating that they might have obtained it without the AMC knowledge, most probably obtained an 'illegal' connection through some local unofficial actors. But, the water supply was only once a day and all households had to store water in either a tank constructed for the purpose (41%) or in buckets or pots.

As high as 90 per cent of the households stated that they had adequate water supply. On further probing, average water consumption per household in these six selected slums was 52.8 litres per day or 10.5 litres per capita per day (LPCD), which was quite low. According to the Bureau of Indian Standards (BIS), IS: 1172-1993[4], minimum water supply of 200 LPCD should be provided for domestic consumption in cities with full flushing systems. The IS: 1172-1993 standards also mentions that the amount of water supply may be reduced to 135 LPCD for the Low Income Groups (LIG) and the Economically Weaker Sections (EWS). The Ninth Five Year Plan (1997-2002) of the Government of India (GoI) had advocated the requirements of water in urban areas as 125 LPCD in cities with the planned sewerage systems; 70 LPCD in cities without planned sewerage system; and 40 LPCD for those collecting water from public stand-posts (Government of India 1997-2002).

The World Health Organization (WHO) classifies the supply and access to water in four service categories— (1) no access (water available below 5 LPCD), (2) basic access (average approximately 20 LPCD), (3) intermediate access (average approximately 50 LPCD), and (4) optimal access (average of 100-200 LPCD) (Howard and Bartram 2003). Thus, all households in this study fall into the second category, those with basic access, however, closer to the category of no access rather than the category of intermediate access. Just about 12 per cent households in all the slums stated that the water was of average or bad quality whereas 88 per cent of them stated that the water quality was good or very good.

Research has shown that security of tenure in particular improves sanitation access and households construct individual toilets. As soon as tenure situation improves, the households attempt to save money and construct an individual toilet for themselves because the common toilets are not maintained properly. Also, the external agency, such as local government or a NGO could assist the households in constructing an individual toilet. However, there has to be enough space available outside the dwelling unit to do so. Households do not choose to have a toilet inside the house. In slums where it is technically not feasible to get a sewerage line up to the house or construct a toilet due to space constraint, common toilets have to be constructed. Thus, in Surabhagat Ni Chali, the councillor of the area has provided common toilets, as the slum has weak *de facto* status and the households were not willing to invest in toilets. In Talavadi Na Chhapra where houses do not have space to build individual toilets and also do not have any tenure security, households have opted for common or shared toilets wherever possible with the help of MHT.

Table 6.7: Access to toilets (%), Amraiwadi, Ahmedabad

Land ownership	*Toilet type*					*If shared then no. households sharing*
	Individual	*Shared*	*Settlement*	*Pay and use*	*Open defecation*	
Private	83.5	9.7	3.9	1.9	1.0	11
Mill land	80.4	11.1	3.0	5.0	0.5	10
Public	91.9	1.5	0.0	0.7	5.9	18
Average	84.7	7.8	2.3	3.0	2.3	13

Source: Primary Survey.

The data, however, show no relationship between the tenure security and availability of toilets. For example, the most vulnerable of all the settlements is the Talavadi Na Chhapra on the municipal land, where as high as 92 per cent households had individual toilets. Even then 6 per cent of the households defecated in the open (Table 6.7). The largest extent of sharing was observed in the slum on the mill land where 14 per cent shared a toilet either at the settlement level or among few households and another 5 per cent used pay and use toilet. Situation of toilet access in the private slums was not much different than the slum on mill lands. But, in Sanjaynagar, nearly all households had access to individual toilet on account of implementation of the SNP.

Similarly, sewerage connection is also not related to tenure security or land ownership of the slum as almost all the households claim that their dwelling units have sewerage connection and that too, all underground. The fact is that except the slums where SNP has taken place, the sewer connections are not legal. The slum dwellers have linked their household drains to the main sewer lines on the road. These sewerage lines choke from time to time and create problems such as spread of filth and its odour in the settlement. At such times, health and hygiene of the dwellers, in particular of the children suffers. Nearly 30 per cent households stated that their sewer lines choke intermittently.

About 70 per cent households had obtained household level sewerage connection in the last five years only and another in the last 5-10 years

Table 6.8: Period of getting individual sewerage connection, Amraiwadi, Ahmedabad

Land ownership	*Period since individual connection available (years)*			
	0 to 5	*5 to 10*	*10 to 15*	*More than 15*
Private	37.5	40.6	9.4	12.5
Mill land	58.9	11.1	4.4	25.6
Public	94.9	5.1	0.0	0.0
Average	69.5	15.4	3.7	11.4

Source: Primary Survey.

indicating that the improvement in the sewerage situation has taken place only in the last one decade (Table 6.7). In the slum on the public lands, this has improved only in the last five years. A quarter of the households in the mill land slum had obtained individual sewerage connection 15 years back.

Piles of garbage and waste of all kinds littered everywhere has become a common sight in the urban life in India. Many cities generate more solid waste than they can collect or dispose. Even when municipal budgets are adequate for collection, safe disposal of collected waste often remains a problem. Dumping and unmanaged landfills are sometimes the main disposal methods in many Indian cities. Sanitary landfills are the norm in only a handful of cities. Inadequate collection and unmanaged disposal of solid waste presents a number of problems for human health and productivity. Slum dwellers in particular are more vulnerable to the un-collected waste generated by them than any other waste. The waste management begins with the availability of dustbins at the household level. On the whole, 72 per cent households in the studied slums stated that they had a dust bin in their house, from which 60 per cent deposited their household waste in the settlement level dustbin. The variation across different categories of slums in this regard is low, hence we have not reported them separately. Around 25 per cent households in all the slums give the garbage directly to the sweepers who came to the slum daily, whereas 3 per cent disposed the waste in the open. More than 90 per cent of the surveyed households mentioned that the AMC was providing slum cleaning services and 85 per cent stated that their slum was cleaned daily. Only 5 per cent households reported that the residents of the settlement themselves clean up the settlement.

The AMC carries out the following solid waste management activities: door to door waste collection, street sweeping, cleaning of public toilets and latrines, cleaning of open defecation and spraying of insecticides, transportation of collected waste from above sites to the specified waste storage container sites through containerised handcart and transportation of dead bodies of small animals, like dogs, cats, pigs etc., to the specified site. In slums on private lands, 2.9 per cent households responded that the Community-based Organisation (CBO) keeps the settlement clean. In fact during SNP implementation in Sanjaynagar, a CBO of women was formed to check on materials and construction. The same CBO is now managing the door-to-door solid waste collection in Sanjaynagar and the surrounding slums (*See* chapter 5). While the AMC paid salaries to these sweepers, the CBO only supervised the work.

Table 6.9: Electricity connection (%), Amraiwadi, Ahmedabad

Land ownership	*Having electricity in house*	*Having electricity meters*
Private	96.1	93.2
Mill land	95.5	91.0
Public	87.4	84.4
Average	93.1	89.5

Source: Primary Survey.

Though slum electrification programme has provided a large number of slum dwellings with electricity in Ahmedabad City, around 12 per cent of the households do not have electricity in the slum on public land (Table 6.9). In the slums on private lands, just 4 per cent households did not have any electricity connection. While 90 per cent households (among those having a connection) had legal electricity connection, 10 per cent had taken illegal connection, which is moderately low. The Ahmedabad Electricity Company (AEC), now owned by a private sector company named Torrent Power, had introduced a scheme in the slums to give the households a legal connection at a very low one time connection charges and also minimum monthly rent slab (*See* chapter 4). Thus, extent of illegality of electricity connections in the slums in the city is very low. Interestingly, while the land is illegal, households have legal electricity connection, indicating that if the supplier intends to give legal connections in the slums, the households living in such settlements would get a form of legal identity.

Education Levels

The study shows a positive relationship between the land ownership and education status. Both, male and female literacy rates are the highest among the slums on the private lands, the literacy rates being 73.9 per cent and 62.0 per cent respectively (Table 6.10). The literacy rates are the lowest in Talavadi Na Chhapra, the slum on public land; the male and female rates are 57.3 per cent and 41.1 per cent respectively. The slum on the mill land falls in between. As discussed earlier, the slums on private lands have higher tenure security than those on the public land and we can conclude that higher level of tenure security results in higher literacy levels. From the FGDs, it was found that the households are presently interested in sending their children, including girl children, to school and hence we expect that the literacy rates in these slums will improve.

Table 6.10: Literacy rate (%), Amraiwadi, Ahmedabad

Land ownership	*Literacy rate*	
	Male	*Female*
Private	73.9	62.0
Mill land	69.4	58.6
Public	57.3	41.1
Average	66.5	53.6

Source: Primary Survey.

Poor endowments are a significant reason for households to continue in poverty. One of the important endowments that can pull out the households from the poverty is education. And lack of this endowment would increase their vulnerability to labour market and other risks. But only literacy (person who can read and write) is not a sufficient tool to measure educational endowment. The level of education is more important for a productive labour force.

Out of 57.3 per cent literate males in Talavadi Na Chhapra, around 29 per cent can only read and 41 per cent have only primary education. About 70 per cent males can just read or write or have studied up to class 7, which is not very useful for getting high employment opportunities. Just 3.8 per cent males have studied up to class 12 and only 2.8 per cent males, i.e. 6 persons are graduates while there are no post-graduate males in this slum (Table 6.11). In contrast, in the slums on private lands, 30 per cent of literate males have secondary education and around 10 per

Table 6.11: Education levels, Amraiwadi, Ahmedabad

Land ownership	*Male*						
	Just read	*Up to 7*	*Up to 10*	*Up to 12*	*Graduate*	*Post-graduate*	*Others courses*
Private	14.9	21.0	29.3	9.9	7.2	1.7	16.0
Mill land	25.9	33.1	18.7	7.7	2.9	1.1	10.7
Public	28.9	41.2	15.2	3.8	2.8	0.0	8.1
Average	24.1	32.5	20.2	7.2	3.9	0.9	11.2
	Female						
Private	19.0	26.1	26.8	5.6	3.5	0.0	19.0
Mill land	32.2	34.1	19.4	3.3	2.6	0.0	8.4
Public	33.6	38.6	17.9	2.1	2.9	0.7	4.3
Average	29.2	33.2	20.9	3.6	2.9	0.2	10.1

Source: Primary Survey.

cent literate males have studied upto higher secondary. Further, 7.2 per cent males are graduates, which is significantly higher than the proportion for the other two categories of slums.

Unfortunate part of Indian education system is educated unemployment. Many people prefer to take a job-oriented diploma or certificate course in computers, accounting, graphic designing, mechanical training, electrical training, plumbing etc. Even that proportion is higher in the private land category. In contrast, in the slum on the public land, just 8 per cent of the males have undergone any vocational training course and hence here, most males would be employed as unskilled labour.

Similar situation can be observed with regard to the education level among the women. First, the percentage of those just able to read (29%) also those who have studied up to class 7 (33%) is higher among women as compared to the males. Thus, 62 per cent females are just able to read or with low level of education. As among males, even among the females, the educational achievements are worst in the slum on the public land (Talavadi Na Chhapra) as compared to the slums on private lands. Out of 41 per cent females who are literate, around 72 per cent in Talavadi Na Chhapra (public land) have only primary education. But this proportion is low (45%) in the four slums on privately owned lands. Further, 5.6 per cent females in slums on private land have studied up to class 12 (this percentage for the slums on public land is 2.1) and 3.5 per cent have become college graduates in the former while this proportion is 2.9 per cent in the latter.

A small number of women in the slums have studied after school. In a traditional Indian society, it is uncommon for a woman to continue studies after marriage. It is still more important for a girl child to learn cooking and home management rather than attain formal education in many of the communities. Women are not allowed to go out to earn extra income even in many of the slum communities. Another reason is, of course, the threat of sexual harassment. The women in Amraiwadi slums were therefore always in search of home-based work. One striking fact is that in the slums where tenure security is high, 19 per cent women have done other courses which are not similar to the courses done by males. Women generally go for courses like sewing, knitting, embroidery, handicrafts, *mehendi*[5] etc., with which they get some petty jobs to be done at home. During the FGDs, it was found that some of the girls have also joined courses like nursing and computers which have proved quite productive for them. Though dropout rate has not been measured here, one can observe that a large number of students have dropped out from schools after the age of 14 which is 7th grade. In all, even among females, like in case of males, the slum households on private lands, which have consolidated in the urban system on account of high perceived security of tenure, have achieved higher education level as well as higher literacy rate than the slum households on public land.

Employment, Income and Assets

On the whole, the Work Force Participation Rates (WFPRs) are very low in the surveyed slums. On an average, the male WFPR was 32 per cent and the female WPR was 17 per cent (Table 6.12), which was far lower than the city's average WPR in 2001. There is a vicious cycle of poverty— low skills, low work availability and low income, resulting in low skills and low work availability. Further to low work availability, the quality of work available is also very poor. Two-thirds of the employed males and about four-fifths of the employed females are engaged as casual labour in the sample. Casual labour has the highest incidence of poverty (Dubey *et al.,* 2001; Dubey and Mahadevia, 2001). Hence, in general, one would expect high incidence of poverty in the slums in Amraiwadi. However, across the three categories of slums, there is some diversity.

To begin with, there is male female differential in the WFPRs as well as in type of work they are engaged in. After casual labour, the next two important employment categories are industrial labour (7.6%) and private jobs (7.3%) for males and personal services (6.3%) and industrial labour (5.7%) for females. Women are not working in transport and business sectors and also not working as shop-keepers and vendors whereas men are not engaged in home-based work. As mentioned already, women from many communities in this ward stated that they would not go out to work; either because of social non-acceptance or fear of security or both. Hence 2.3 per cent of the female workers worked from home.

The male WFPRs were highest in the slums on the private lands (35.9%) and lowest in the slum on the public land (27.4%). Female WFPR is the highest in the last category of slum (on public land) at 22 per cent followed by the slums on the private lands (16.6%) followed by slum on the mill land (13.5%). It appears that the slum on mill land, Satyamnagar is more traditional with women not going out to work. One can observe low female WFPR in the slum on the mill land not because of high income

Table 6.12: Work force participation rates and employment sectors*, Amraiwadi, Ahmedabad

Type of work	*Land ownership*			
	Private	*Mill land*	*Public*	*Average*
		Male		
Work force participation rate	35.9	33.3	27.4	32.0
Casual labour	58.0	71.1	67.3	66.9
Industrial labour	5.7	12.2	1.0	7.6
Government service	0.0	0.0	1.0	0.3
Private job	10.2	7.8	4.0	7.3
Shop keeper	0.0	0.0	3.0	0.8
Construction	4.5	0.6	2.0	1.9
Transport	3.4	1.7	3.0	2.4
Vendor	0.0	1.7	4.0	1.9
Petty business	5.7	0.6	10.9	4.6
Personal service	12.5	4.4	4.0	6.2
		Female		
Work force participation rate	16.6	13.5	22.0	17.0
Casual labour	81.6	65.1	88.0	78.4
Industrial labour	0.0	15.9	0.0	5.7
Home based work	7.9	1.6	0.0	2.3
Government service	0.0	1.6	0.0	0.6
Private job	5.3	4.8	0.0	2.8
Construction	0.0	3.2	6.7	4.0
Personal service	5.3	7.9	5.3	6.3

* These categories have been generated by observing the data and have not been matched with Census or NSSO categories.

Source: Primary Survey.

of males; in here the male WFPR is just 33.3 per cent and 71 per cent of them are casual labour. Low male WFPR in Talavadi Na Chhapra, the slum on public land indicates that women have to come out to work and hence the female WFPR is 22 per cent, the highest among the three categories of slums.

Highest proportion of males employed in private job among the three categories of slums is in those on private land (10.2%), while in Talavadi Na Chhapra, just 4 per cent and in Satyamnagar, the slum on the mill land this proportion was just 7.8 per cent. Among the females also, private sector jobs have been accessed by women in the slums on private lands (5.3%) and the women living in Satyamnagar (4.8%). A job in private sector also means that the worker has to have some skills and some level of education, which is quite low in Talavadi Na Chhapra.

Further, in Talavadi Na Chhapra, while the male WFPR is very low, two thirds of the employed males were working as casual labour. This is an indication of higher incidence of poverty amongst the dwellers here. The impact has been relatively high female WFPR. But, women too are predominantly engaged as casual labour. They do not even work out of home. Probably, insecure tenure means that women do not invest in home-based work. Further, besides casual work, 6.7 per cent women were working in the construction sector and another 5.3 per cent in personal services. There was very little diversity of work opportunities available for women in this slum. A surprise element is that 10.9 per cent of men in this slum have their own petty businesses, which were in metal waste collection and brewing and sale of cheap liquor. In short, this slum with insecure tenure has relatively higher incidence of poverty as compared to other surveyed slums.

Satyamnagar, a slum on the mill land, has low female WFPR, as already discussed above, but also has the highest proportion employed as industrial workers among the three categories of slums. On the whole, 7.6 per cent employed males were in industries, but in Satyamnagar this figure was 12 per cent. Female employment in the industries was observed only in this slum.

Personal service category includes teachers, plumbers, electricians, mechanics etc. In slums on private lands where 19 per cent males have taken certificate courses or diploma, 12.5 per cent males are engaged in professions related to such courses. Among women, the personal services meant working as teachers and household help. In the slum on the private land, women are engaged in making *aggarbattis* at home as well as in a small unit operating out of the slum. Thus, in slums on private land, 7.9

per cent of the working women worked from home. Also, higher order of tenure security means that home-based work is possible as there is no fear of eviction. Lastly, there is miniscule proportion of workers employed in government services, primarily on account of low literacy and very low educational levels.

The employment available to the urban poor is of very piteous quality in general which is true for the study area as well. They either work as casual labour or are self-employed where the income is irregular. On the whole, only one in six workers had any regular income, the rest were either daily wagers, self-employed or had irregular work (which meant that they do not have work for part of the year). A quarter of the employed males had regular income in the slums on the private lands. Similarly, because a significant proportion of males in the slum on mill land were working in industries, one in every five employed males in this slum also had regular income. This proportion in the slum on public land was only 4 per cent. Most of the self-employed males were vegetable vendors, auto or bus driver or seasonal workers. The women largely had irregular work. Nearly 98 per cent of those employed in Talavadi Na Chhapra, and 80 per cent in the slums on private lands had irregular work, which was largely as self-employed. Only in the slum on the mill land, where women were working in industries, about a quarter of them had regular income.

Discussions with the residents revealed that the self-employed did not get same type of work/trade round the year. They might be engaged in different odd jobs as per different seasons of the year. For example, those engaged in petty trade might be selling vegetables for large part of the year but might also be selling kites during the kite festival, make and sell idols before the festival of *Navratri*[6], or fire crackers before *Diwali*. Those finding casual labour shifted locations and worked largely in the construction sector doing manual labour like filtering sand and lifting bricks and buckets of cement on their heads. In other words, the self-employment and irregular work included diverse type of activities and trades that varied depending upon the market requirements. These workers, therefore, were always vulnerable to ever changing technology and economic growth fluctuations.

The type of employment in the slums covered in the study indicates a situation of poverty as casual labour employment is very strongly related to poverty (Dubey *et al.,* 2001; Dubey and Mahadevia, 2001). The incomes from such activities are not enough to invest in housing. Also, irregularity of income would mean inability to get a housing loan or plan for long-term investments in productive assets. Imparting of skills along with assistance in job placement on one hand and shelter security on the other so that the households could consolidate and move on, is necessary to pull these households out of poverty.

Table 6.13: Household and per capita income, Amraiwadi, Ahmedabad (current prices)

Land Ownership	*Average monthly income (Rs.)*	
	Household	*Per capita*
Private	3,654	794
Mill land	3,031	594
Public	3,058	577
Average	3,248	650

Source: Primary Survey.

The average monthly income of all the slums in this ward was very low, Rs. 3,248 for a household and Rs. 650 per capita (Table 6.13) at current prices in 2009. The average income of the households was lower than the poverty line per capita expenditure of Rs. 951.4 for 2009-10 for Gujarat (Planning Commission, 2012). However, the situation across all the slums is not so bad. The average per capita income in the slums on private lands was higher, although below the official poverty line, at Rs. 794, whereas in the slum on the mill land and slum on public land the per capita incomes were much below the poverty line, at Rs. 594 and Rs. 577 respectively. Thus, only in slums on private lands, where a quarter of the working males have regular income and jobs are available in the private sector, households had possibility of coming out of poverty, if the macroeconomic conditions permit. The slums on private lands have improved their life and income because they have been left to themselves; they have not faced demolitions and hence have high perceived security of tenure. Their life improvement is incremental and the state policy should assist such processes, something which we have not seen in the recent years.

Expenditure patterns vary by slum category. In Talavadi Na Chhapra, the slum on the public land, low household income has meant that 48 per cent of their expenditure was on food items and another 6 per cent on cooking fuel (Table 6.14). Poor basic services in the slum seem to have influenced health status and the households were spending about 11.5 per cent of their total expenditure on health, which left very little to spend for education and hence only 0.2 per cent was allocated for education.

Table 6.14: Distribution of expenditure, Amraiwadi, Ahmedabad (%)

Expenditure item	*Private*	*Mill*	*Public*
Food	32.6	21.8	47.7
Cooking fuel	6.2	7.0	5.7
Clothes	2.3	2.7	1.6
Consumer durables	1.7	5.4	2.5
Education	1.4	2.4	0.2
Health	5.6	12.5	11.5
Recreation and entertainment	0.8	0.0	0.5
Communications	3.1	6.8	4.8
Housing	16.2	15.4	1.7
Basic Service charges	2.1	0.7	0.0
Electricity	7.7	7.4	7.7
Transport	4.3	8.6	3.9
Debt repayment	0.0	4.4	8.7
Insurance premium	15.5	4.2	3.1
Taxes	0.6	0.6	0.4
Total	100.0	100.0	100.0

Note: Expenditure on some items was reported for one year, which has been converted into per month for the table.

Source: Primary Survey.

They were spending 8.7 per cent of the total expenditure on debt repayment, possibly on borrowings from the money lenders. However, many women in this slum were also members of the SEWA Bank and were paying instalments to the Bank for some of the borrowings for consumption expenditure. These households were not paying anything for basic services in the settlement firstly because these services were being provided by the AMC. Also, being squatters, their expenditure on housing was also low, just 1.7 per cent of their total expenditure. Even though their incomes were below the poverty line, the households expended about 4 per cent of their total expenditure on transport, mainly for work purpose. The private electricity company, Torrent Power, has extended individual connections to most slums in Ahmedabad irrespective of its legal status and hence in Talavadi Na Chhapra, households were expending 7.7 per cent of their total expenditure on electricity. There is a case for formalizing tenure so that the households start investing in housing and improve their living conditions which would result in reducing their health expenditure.

Slums on the private lands allotted about one-third of their total expenditure on food and another 6.2 per cent on cooking fuel. Their expenditure on housing was the highest among all the three categories of slums, 16.2 per cent as compared 15.4 per cent in the slum on the mill land and 1.7 per cent in the slum on public land. In the mill land slum, housing expenditure was on rent whereas in the private land slums, housing expenditure was on instalment for housing loan repayment,

The households on private lands had also taken insurance and were spending about 15.5 per cent of their total expenditure towards payment of premium. They were also spending 2.1 per cent, highest among all the three categories, on basic services as various charges for different services, which the slums in the other two categories were not paying as much or not at all. An outcome of relatively better basic service levels and housing conditions was that their health expenditure was the lowest in terms of proportion of the three categories of slums.

A fact to note is that all the slum households were paying some amount as taxes to the local government. In essence, the tax is property tax and the proportion of the total expenditure on this item was 0.6 per cent for the slums on private land and mill land and 0.4 per cent for the slum on public land.

Table 6.15: Asset ownership, Amraiwadi, Ahmedabad (%)

Land ownership	Households having following assets										
	TV	Fridge	Radio	CD Player	Mobile phone	Landline phone	Cycle	Scooter	Cooking gas	Fan	Light
Private	72.8	1.9	10.7	13.6	42.7	1.0	61.2	15.5	48.5	96.1	96.1
Mill land	68.8	1.5	3.5	6.0	40.2	0.5	60.3	7.0	33.2	95.5	96.0
Public	55.6	3.0	7.4	9.6	30.4	0.7	35.6	4.4	8.9	80.0	87.4
Average	65.7	2.1	6.4	8.9	37.8	0.7	52.9	8.2	29.3	90.8	93.4

Source: Primary Survey.

Improvement in perceived security of tenure means increased investment in assets. Almost all households had some assets (Table 6.15). However, the households living on the private lands had more assets than the households in other two categories of slums. For example, while 72.8 per cent households on private lands had a television (TV), only 55.6 per cent of households on public land owned this asset. Twenty per cent households did not have a fan and 13 per cent households did not have a light fixture in the slum on public land; this proportion in the other two categories of slums was just 4 per cent. About half the households on the private lands had a cooking gas while this proportion in the slum on public land was only 9 per cent. This indicates that the women living in the latter slum use *chulha* (hearth) for the purpose of cooking which is harmful to health and environment.

Urban Citizenship

The poor are generally unaware of the amenities/schemes/policies available to them from the government and sometimes even if they know, the process of getting access to various facilities is very tedious and time consuming on account of the paper work required. Getting facilities or their entitlements such as a ration card, either a general card or a Below Poverty Line (BPL) card may also mean paying bribes to the local government officials. Only 14 per cent households in the study area reported that they had a ration card (Tale 6.16). The possibility of holding a ration card increases with secure tenure and higher income, as we see with regards to households on private lands where 17 per cent households held a ration card. Although, as discussed above, the households living on mill land and public land had incomes lower than the official poverty line income, only 1.5 per cent households in these two categories of settlements had access to BPL Card. Thus, the real poor households were excluded from accessing subsidised government schemes, as BPL card is mandatory for the same. The study, therefore, calls for universalisation of basic entitlements such as food, education and health.

Table 6.16: Possession of documents of entitlements (%), Amraiwadi, Ahmedabad

Land ownership	*Having ration card*	*Having BPL card*	*Having election card*
Private	17.09	0.84	18.57
Mill land	13.42	1.29	16.50
Public	11.28	1.27	15.80
Average	13.93	1.14	16.95

Source: Primary Survey.

One expected that all the households would at least have an election card against which, just 17 per cent households stated that they held. When some widows were asked whether they received the widow pension or not, they replied that they did not know whether they were eligible and even if they were eligible, it was not possible for them to go to municipal office on account of the distance and required paper work. The slums where NGOs were active, there was obviously more awareness about the policies for the urban poor and the slum dwellers took their help to access such facilities.

Planning Needs

Many a times, the policy makers completely miss the link between livelihoods of the urban poor and transport. Access to affordable transport is one of the most important factors in determining livelihoods for the urban poor. Further, the poor often prefer to stay in the congested dwellings without any security so that they can walk to their workplace rather than move to distant locations for secure housing. In Amraiwadi, 70 per cent of the head of the households walked or cycled to work (Table 6.17). Hence, for 73 per cent of them, their work place was within 4 km distance from their residence.

Table 6.17: Travel distance and mode for main household earner, Amraiwadi, Ahmedabad

Land ownership	*Distance to work (km)*			*Mode used*						
	0 to 4	*4 to 8*	*More than 8*	*Walk*	*Bicycle*	*Bus*	*Scooter*	*Auto-rickshaw*	*Shuttle auto*	*Other*
Private	50.0	42.1	7.9	14.5	47.0	21.7	8.4	3.6	1.2	3.6
Mill land	80.6	11.9	7.5	22.5	56.7	4.2	8.3	0.8	0.8	6.7
Public	87.8	12.2	0.0	40.4	29.8	5.3	1.8	8.8	0.0	14.0
Average	72.8	22.1	5.1	25.8	44.5	10.4	6.2	4.4	0.7	8.1

Source: Primary Survey.

There was, however, some variation in the travel pattern among three types of slums. The main earners of the slums on private land travelled longer distance than the main earners of other two categories of slums; only half of them worked within 4 km distance and 42 per cent travelled 4 to 8 km for work (Table 6.17). This meant that they could not walk to work; 47 per cent of them bicycled and 22 per cent used the public bus. Only 8.4 per cent used personal motorised transport in this category of slums. So, even though households in this category of slums were relatively better-off, 62 per cent of them use non-motorised transport (NMT).

In contrast, 40 per cent of the main earners in slum on public land, Talavadi Na Chhapra, walked to work and another 30 per cent bicycled. Thus, 70 per cent of the main earners in this settlement used the NMT.

Due to low income and hence low affordability, only 5.3 per cent took bus. But, as high as 14 per cent took other transport means, which are called *chhagda* (a six-seater), which is a para-transit mode, meant to seat six people but in fact more people are crammed in. They charge the same rate as the public bus. This six-seater para-transit is a very unsafe mode to travel and has reported many accidents but the poor do not have choice because of limited routing and poor timings of public buses. About 80 per cent of the main earners in the mill land slum walked or bicycled to work and 8.3 per cent used their private motorised transport mode to work. For these workers, dependence on other mode of transport was also high (6.7%) and dependence on public bus was low (4.2%). Lastly, in the second and third category of slums, work location of 80 per cent of the main earners was within 4 km distance, hence they walked to work.

The second earner of the household is generally from among the women. Their location of work as well as travel modes was not very different from that of the main earners, who were generally men. They reported that they walked to work or took shuttle (shared) auto-rickshaw or the six-seater. Sometimes they had to take an auto-rickshaw to reach on time. A similar pattern could be seen except in the slum on the public land. About 44 per cent of them even bicycled (Table 6.18). The only difference can be seen in the slums on private lands where 62 per cent of the second earner worked within 4 km distance while this figure for the main earner was 50 per cent. During our FGDs, the women were complaining that after walking or cycling for average 6 to 8 kilometres a day in the heat and so much of physical labour at the work, it was very difficult for them to do the household work. Adding to that fatigue, malnourishment also adversely affected their health.

Table 6.18: Travel distance and mode for second household earner, Amraiwadi, Ahmedabad (%)

Land ownership	*Distance to work (km)*			*Mode used*						
	0 to 4	*4 to 8*	*More than 8*	*Walk*	*Bicycle*	*Bus*	*Scooter*	*Auto-rickshaw*	*Shuttle auto*	*Other*
Private	61.5	38.5	0.0	46.2	30.8	23.1	0.0	0.0	0.0	0.0
Mill land	81.3	12.5	6.3	30.0	60.0	5.0	0.0	0.0	5.0	0.0
Public	71.4	28.6	0.0	20.0	40.0	10.0	0.0	10.0	10.0	10.0
Average	71.4	26.5	2.1	32.1	43.6	12.7	0.0	3.3	5.0	3.3

Source: Primary Survey.

Table 6.19: Travel distance and mode for school children, Amraiwadi, Ahmedabad (%)

Land ownership	Distance to school (km)			Mode used						
	0 to 2	2 to 4	More than 4	Walk	Bicycle	Bus	Scooter	Auto-rickshaw	Shuttle auto	Other
Private	63.6	27.3	9.1	65.4	7.7	3.8	3.8	15.4	0.0	3.8
Mill land	62.5	37.5	0.0	100.0	0.0	0.0	0.0	0.0	0.0	0.0
Public	28.6	71.4	0.0	100.0	0.0	0.0	0.0	0.0	0.0	0.0
Average	51.6	45.4	3.0	88.5	2.6	1.3	1.3	5.1	0.0	1.3

Source: Primary Survey.

Most of the children go to school which is at a distance of 2 kilometres except in the third category of slum (Talavadi Na Chhapra), where secondary school is not available nearby, and 71 per cent children travelled 2 to 4 km for school (Table 6.19). In category 1 slums, households who could afford a little more in fees than what the municipal schools charged, sent their children to private schools which were at a distance of more than 4 km and hence in these slums 8 per cent children bicycled and about 15 per cent of them travelled by auto-rickshaw, which functions like a school-bus in absence of a school bus for most schools in Ahmedabad. Otherwise, 88 per cent children walked to school on an average and in the slums in category 2 and 3, that is slum on mill land and slum on public land, all children walked to school.

Urban planning in general should be conscious of this work-home as well as school-home relationship and should also be planning transport systems to pass by the residential areas of the urban poor. Work place can be near to the homes if the residential areas of the poor in the city are well spread across the city and are interspersed with high-income neighbourhoods. Land markets do not allow that and in the neo-liberal policy regime times even planners appear to have abandoned the idea of interventions in land markets.

An alarming area for planning to improve is shelter security across the urban India. When the households were asked about their preferences with regard to housing, more than 80 per cent of the household reported that they preferred tenure regularisation in their current slum (Table 6.20). They wanted the land title on their name or their slums's name or long-term lease rights. They did not prefer to move anywhere else. Only 14 per cent stated that they wanted to move to another location. In fact, they mentioned that they wanted to shift to a better location, but, in the same ward or nearby wards of Khokhara and Rakhial as they did not want to move far from their current work locations. About 5 per cent stated that they want to redevelop the slum on the same site. This could also be redevelopment into apartment type buildings. There was not much variation in aspiration with regards to housing across the slums.

Table 6.20: Housing preferences, Amraiwadi, Ahmedabad (%)

Land Ownership	*Housing option preferred*		
	Redevelop this settlement and stay here	*Move to a new better place*	*Want land tenure regularisation*
Private	8.0	12.9	79.1
Mill land	3.8	14.9	81.3
Public	4.0	14.0	82.1
Average	5.3	13.9	80.8

Source: Primary Survey.

Impact of Tenure on Well-being

The research hypothesis is: shelter security, determined through land tenure security leads to improvement in physical living conditions (in other words reduces deprivations in physical quality of life), improvement in capabilities firstly on account of improvement in literacy rates, then educational levels, and then empowerment to negotiate in the administrative and political space with improvement in employment and incomes. It is not the other way round; incomes lead to improvement in education and then shelter security. It can be argued that education improvement could lead to empowerment and increase in incomes and consequently improvement in living conditions and shelter security. Here, the argument is that all other interventions of development such as improvement in access to education and health would amount to nil if there were no shelter security.

The variables that construct tenure security have been taken as independent variables and the social protection outcome variables have been selected as dependent variables. There are 12 dependent variables defined for the logistic regression analysis. The independent variables are land ownership, house document (even the quasi-legal), payment of property tax and indicators of urban citizenship such as ration card, BPL card and election card. The definition of variables is given below.

Independent Variables

Land ownership: Three categories of land ownership, namely private land, public land and mill land have been observed in the study area. Two dummy values were created: 1 for public lands and 0 for private and mill lands which are non-public lands.

Property tax: This variable has been created using the question "*whether the household is paying property tax?*" If the household was paying property tax dummy value of 1 was assigned and dummy value of 0 was assigned for non-paying households.

Years of stay: For the analysis, duration of stay, which was a continuous variable, has been converted to a dichotomous variable. This variable is created by taking dummy value of 1 for years of stay more than 20 and dummy value of 0 for less than 20 years. We also tried this analysis for other cut-off points for duration of stay. But this data set has very little variation and around 90 per cent of the households have been living in the slum for more than 20 years.

House document: This variable was been framed using "*do you possess any quasi-legal document for the house*?" Dummy value of 1 was assigned if the households have a house document (even the quasi legal) and 0 for otherwise. The types of documents that a household possesses have been discussed earlier in the chapter.

Ration Card, BPL Card and Election Card: These are three variables. Households were asked to state whether they possessed these cards.

Chart 6.2: Independent variables, Amraiwadi, Ahmedabad

Variable	*Value*
Years of stay—20	1 for more than 20 years 0 for less than or equal to 20 years
Land ownership	1 for public 0 for private and others
Property tax	1 for paying property tax 0 for otherwise
House document	1 for Yes 0 for No
BPL card	1 for yes 0 for no
Election card	1 for yes 0 for no
Ration card	1 for yes 0 for no

Dummy value of 1 was assigned if the households possessed the card and 0 for otherwise. Possession of Ration card, BPL card and Election card are often independent of legal residential status as all these are extended to the households before election irrespective of the household's tenure status. But these documents then create entitlements. Hence, we have included these three as independent variables as well in our analysis.

Dependent Variables

Type of housing: This variable has been created from responses on housing type, where the response categories are: (i) *pucca;* (ii) semi-*pucca*; and (iii) *katcha*. Since there are three categories, for analysis, housing type was recorded into a dummy variable: 1 for *pucca* and semi-*pucca* and 0 for *katcha*. We also tried out assigning a value of 1 for *pucca* and 0 for *semi-pucca* and *katcha*. However, the results were stronger in the former than the latter categorization.

Number of rooms: Households were asked to state the number of rooms they have. A dummy value of 1 was assigned to the households having more than 1 room and 0 for otherwise.

Number of assets: Households were asked about owning of the different consumer durables/assets at their home. Sixteen types of consumer assets were found in the households. To convert the continuous variable (which ranges between 0-16), dummy value of 1 was assigned if the households have more than 4 assets and 0 for less than or equal to 4 assets. We also tried with other cut-off points such as more than 6 assets, but could not get robust results.

Agency supplying water: This variable has been created by asking "*which agency supplies water*?" A dummy value of 1 was assigned if the water was supplied by the local government[7] and 0 for other agencies.

Sewer line: Households were asked to state whether they had sewerage connection to their settlement. A dummy value of 1 was assigned if the households had sewer line connection and 0 for otherwise.

Storm water drains: This variable has been created by asking "*do you have separate storm water drainage in your system*?" Dummy value of 1 was assigned if the settlement had the facility and 0 for otherwise.

Toilet facility: Households were asked to state whether they had toilet facility available to them or not. Dummy value of 1 was assigned if the households had the facility and 0 for otherwise.

Bath space: This variable was recorded as dummy variable by asking availability of the bath space at household level. Value of 1 was assigned if the households had the facility and 0 for otherwise.

Employment 1: This variable was for the household head and there were number of options for this variable. Among these, we used a dummy value of 1 if the household head's employment was regular and 0 for otherwise.

Employment 2: This variable was for the household head and there were number of options for this variable. Among these, we used a dummy value of 1 if the household head's employment was non-casual and 0 for casual.

Employment 3: This variable was a composite variable of the number of people working in a household and the type of employment taken up by the household members. A dummy value of 1 was assigned if at least one of the employed members in the household was a casual labour and value of 0 assigned if all of the household employed members were non-causal labour.

Number of people working in a family: The number of people working in a household variable was collected from household information data. This was collected as a continuous variable and recorded using dummy values: 1 if more than 1 person was employed in a household and 0 for otherwise.

Income: This variable was collected as a continuous variable and recorded in the analysis using dummy values: 1 for monthly income of more than Rs. 2000[8] per household and 0 for otherwise. We tried with other income cut-offs but could not find any reliable result.

The Relationships

Factor analysis is used to know whether some underlying pattern of relationship exists among variables; discovering a new set of factors; or confirming existing factor(s) as being the true factor(s). Essentially, the factors defining shelter security have been derived using proxies as we do not have any straightforward or single indicator of tenure status. Because the variables constructing shelter security are many, the factors were subjected to oblique rotation to ensure that all variables are ascribed to a factor, and none is allocated to two or more factors (Okoro, 2000).

Table 6.21 shows the results of the component factor extraction among the households in the sample. The table also shows the respective Eigen values and percentage of variance for the factors. The rule of thumb here is that, only factors with Eigen values more than 1.0 should be used

Chart 6.3: Independent variables, Amraiwadi, Ahmedabad

Variable	*Value*
Type of housing	1 for *pucca* and semi-*pucca* 0 for *katcha*
No. of rooms	1 for 2 or more than 2 rooms 0 for one or less rooms
Assets	1 for more than 4 0 for 4 and less than 4
Agency water supply	1 for public 0 for others
Sewer line	1 for yes 0 for no
Storm water drainage	1 for yes 0 for no
Latrine facility	1 for Yes 0 for No
Bath space	1 for yes 0 for No
Employment-1	1 for non-casual labour 0 for casual labour
Employment-2	1 for regular employment 0 non regular employment
Employment -3	1 for at least 1 casual labour in household 0 for no casual labour
No. of people working in a family	1 for more than 1 0 for 1or less than 1
Income	0 for less than or equal to 2000 1 for more than 2000

in further analysis. This criterion of identifying factors that explained the variance in the data was chosen because of the relatively large number of variables. It shows that only two variables had Eigen values greater than 1.0 and together were explaining 60 per cent of the variance in the data set. Further, one single factor, public land ownership explained 34.56 per cent of the variance, suggesting that this was the single most important factor determining shelter security as well as the well-being variables. Property tax payment was another variable explaining the data set variance of 25.7 per cent. Both these are independent variables in our hypothesis. Thus, the variables of tenure are indeed defining achievements with regard to other variables.

Table 6.21: Factors explaining data variance among variables, Amraiwadi, Ahmedabad

Sl. No.		*Eigen Values*[9]	*% of Variance*	*Cumulative %*
1.	Public land ownership	1.382	34.560	34.560
2.	Property tax	1.029	25.727	60.287

Public land ownership is explaining the highest factor loading (with a value of –0.468) (Table 6.22), explaining that if the land is owned by a public agency then the shelter security is low and achievements with regard to social protection are low. The other important variable—property tax payment, explaining 25.7 per cent of the variance, has the factor loading of 0.881 explaining that there is higher security of tenure in the case of settlements paying property tax and this is so with regard to the households in settlements on private lands.

Table 6.22: Oblique rotated factor component correlations (factor loadings), Amraiwadi, Ahmedabad[10]

Sl. No.		*Service related factors*	*Land related factors*
1.	Public land ownership	–.262	–.468
2.	Property tax	.881	–.008

Logistic Regression[11]

Logistic regression analysis uses techniques of multiple regression analysis to research situations in which the variables are categorical. Since many of the variables in the data set are dichotomous, bivariate analysis has been carried out to observe and measure the impacts of tenure and other independent variables (which have been explained above).

The regression results presented in Table 6.23 shows impact of public land ownership on the dependent variables. Public land ownership has negative impact on the quality of housing. The possibility of having *pucca* housing decreases by 59 per cent in slums on public lands, showing that households living on public lands face eviction threat and hence do not invest on housing improvement. Most of the households staying on public lands do not possess any documents to support their residency in that place and hence are more vulnerable to eviction threat. This probability of eviction threat has a significant impact on the aspects of physical quality of life and overall well-being. The availably of bath space decreases by 29 per cent, possibility of having more than four assets decreases by 69 per cent if the household is living in a slum on public land. Regularity of employment of the household head decreases by 71 per cent among households indicating that looming eviction threat affects employment. Also, the possibility of holding a ration card decreases by 36 per cent as these are not recognised as citizens of a city. The local government officials do not like to legitimise the residents squatting on public lands, fearing that they would stake claims on the land encroached upon. Lastly, the likelihood of income being more than Rs. 2,000 per month decreases by 91 per cent in case of households on public lands.

Table 6.23: Impact of public land ownership, Amraiwadi, Ahmedabad

Dependent variable	*B*	*Wald*	*df*	*Sig.*	*Exp (B)*
Pucca housing	–.879**	2.212	1	.137	.415
Assets more than 4	–1.152*	4.117	1	.042	.316
Availability of bath space	–.342	.394	1	.530	.710
People working in family more than 1	.125	.048	1	.827	1.133
Income more than Rs. 2,000	–2.363*	5.976	1	.014	.094
Household head as regular employed	–1.230**	1.959	1	.162	.292
Household head as non-casual labour	.151	.064	1	.800	1.164
At least one casual labour	.108	.053	1	.818	1.114
BPL card	–.061	.009	1	.926	.941
Ration card	–.438**	2.329	1	.127	.645

Note: *p <0.10; ** p < 0.20.

The impact of property tax on *pucca* housing, number of assets and non-casual labour employment of the household head has been positive. The possibility of *pucca* house increases by 131 per cent if the household is paying property tax (Table 6.24). The results are significant at 49 per cent. Payment of property tax has been higher in the case of private lands (*See* Table 6.3) and hence the probability of investing in house quality is higher in the settlements on the private lands. Further, possibility of owning more than four assets increases by 212 per cent if the households are paying property tax at 73 per cent significance level. Lastly, the possibility of household head being non-casual labourer increases by 503 per cent in the households paying property tax. This relationship is significant at 77 per cent.

Table 6.24: Impact of property tax, Amraiwadi, Ahmedabad

Dependent variable	*B*	*Wald*	*df*	*Sig.*	*Exp(B)*
Pucca housing	.836	.440	1	.507	2.306
Assets more than 4	1.138	.793	1	.373	3.120
Availability of bath space	–2.590*	3.213	1	.073	.075
Persons working in family more than 1	–.772	.377	1	.539	.462
Income more than Rs. 2,000	22.936	.000	1	.999	9.145E9
Regular employment	–2.121	1.139	1	.286	.120
Non casual labour	1.797	1.434	1	.231	6.029

Note: * p<0.10; ** p<0.20

Conclusions

It is evident from the investigation, that public land ownership has negative impact on the quality of housing. Most of the households staying on public lands do not possess any documents to support their residency in that place and hence are more vulnerable to threat of eviction. The possibility of having *pucca* housing decreases by significant proportion in slums on public lands, indicating that they face eviction threat and hence do not invest on housing improvement. This probability of eviction threat has a significant impact on the other aspects of physical quality of life and well-being indicators such as having individual toilets, bath space and various household assets. The education levels of these various categories of land ownership directly relates to the security of tenure. Logically, the slums on the public lands should receive the facilities and tenure faster as it is in the purview of the government. However, the study presents a different picture of absolute apathy of the authorities towards the slum dwellers who are part of the city for long period of time now. It is rather easier for the slum dwellers on the private lands to get into the main stream and generate documents of their identity as a resident of the city and get the basic services from the authorities. The question posed by this chapter is that would the slum dwellers be able to upgrade their standard of life when they are left to their own devises without even shelter security. Insecurity of tenure is very well linked to the exclusion from the urban citizenship, overcrowding in already degraded area, inadequate infrastructure, very low standards of education endowments and livelihood opportunities.

Annexure 6.1

Zone-wise Slums and Chawls, Ahmedabad

*Zone**	*No. of Slums*	*No. of Chawls*
East	52	406
West	163	82
North	129	303
South	209	81
Central	155	86
Total	708	958

* The New West Zone has been recently included in the municipal limit. Data is not available on slums of this zone.

Annexure 6.2

Ward-wise Slums and Chawls in East Zone, Ahmedabad

Wards in East zone	*No. of Slums*	*No. of Chawls*
Amraiwadi	11	76
Bapunagar	0	16
Bhaipura	0	73
Gomtipur	2	40
Khokhara	8	19
Nikol	3	40
Odhav	14	27
Rajpur	0	50
Rakhial	14	65
Total	52	406

NOTES

1. Research is funded under the research project titled "Inclusive Urbanisation – Social Protection for the Slum and Pavement Dwellers in India', a CEPT University – Mahila Housing SEWA Trust (MHT) project, under the programme 'Social Protection in Asia', managed by Institute of Development Studies (IDS), Sussex and Institute of Human Development (IHD), New Delhi and funded by Ford Foundation and IDRC. Authors acknowledge the contribution of Chintan Shah in fieldwork for this research.

2. We have found that in the early years the document of sale was done on Rs. 20/- stamp-paper and which increase to Rs. 50 subsequently. Some documents are also on higher value of stamp-paper.
3. A *katcha* house is made of temporary wall materials and temporary roof materials. *Pucca* housing is when the wall and roof materials are all of permanent type. Semi-*pucca* houses are in-between, when the walls are of permanent materials and roof of temporary materials.
4. Bureau of Indian Standards (BIS) website - http://www.bis.org.in/ accessed on December 1, 2012.
5. The traditional art of painting hand and feet with application of paste of a shrub called *Mehendi* or *Henna.*
6. Festival of folk dance of Gujarat state.
7. Provision of basic services (water supply, sewerage and public health) has been one of the key responsibilities of the ULBs in India.
8. The average monthly income of the household in Amraiwadi is Rs. 3,248. The regression analysis carried out using this as cut of point hasn't produced significant results.
9. Only variables with Eigen values more than 1 are presented.
10. The factor loadings for variables are taken using Kaiser's rule of thumb which says that variables with coefficients of 0.3 and above may be used to name a factor.
11. The logistic regression assumes that the outcome variable, Y is categorical, but logistic regression doesn't model this outcome variable directly. For simplicity we assume that Y is dichotomous, taking on values of 1 for positive outcome and 0 for negative outcome. In theory, the hypothetical, population proportion of cases for which Y = 1 is defined as p = P(Y =1). Then, the theoretical proportion of cases for which Y = 0 is $1 - p = P(Y = 0)$. In the absence of other information, we would estimate p by the sample proportion of cases for which Y = 1.

    Let:

    $P_i = Pr(Y=1/X= x_i)$

    Then we can write the model:

    $\text{Log}\,(P_i/1\text{-}P_i) = \log it\,(P_i) = \beta_0 + \beta_1 x_1$

    The parameter β_0 gives the log odds of an independent variable. In the table 1, for example, β_0 gives the log odds of the households stayed in the slum for 20 or less than 20 years and β_1 shows how these odds differ for the household stayed more than 20 years in the slum.

    If we rewrite the model in terms of odds as:

    $(P_i/1\text{-}P_i) = \exp\,(\beta_0 + \beta_1 x_1)$

    Or in terms of the probability of the outcome occurring as:

    $Pi = \exp\,(\beta_0+\beta_1 x_i)/\,(1 + \exp\,(\beta_0+\beta_1 x_i))$

    Conversely the probability of the outcome not occurring is

    $1 - Pi = 1/\,(1 + \exp\,(\beta_0+\beta_1 x_i))$

7

Tenure Security through External Agency Intervention

The Case of Vasna, Ahmedabad[1]

Darshini Mahadevia, Pooja Shah, Rutool Sharma and *Pavan Kumar Ankinapalli*

Introduction

Vasna ward is located in south-western part of Ahmedabad, on the western bank of river Sabarmati. The area falls within the jurisdiction of Ahmedabad Municipal Corporation (AMC). Based on survey conducted by Mahila Housing SEWA Trust (MHT) in the year 2002, there were 24 slums in Vasna Ward housing 7,406 households (Annexure 7.1). Then, around 33 per cent of the total houses of the ward were slum dwellings. Out of the total number of slums, 20 slums were on private land, three on AMC lands and one on state government land. Slum Networking Project (SNP) had been carried out in two slums in Vasna ward.

The study was undertaken with two questions: (i) what was the relationship between level of security and involvement of external agencies and (ii) whether the quality of life of the residents in slums with intervention of external agency was better than the residents of slums without external agency intervention. The hypothesis was that presence of an external agency increases tenure security of slum households and also leads to improvement in the quality of life of the slum residents. Here the word tenure security has been used in a broad term. There are different levels of tenure security prevailing in the slums of Ahmedabad which is explained in the latter sections.

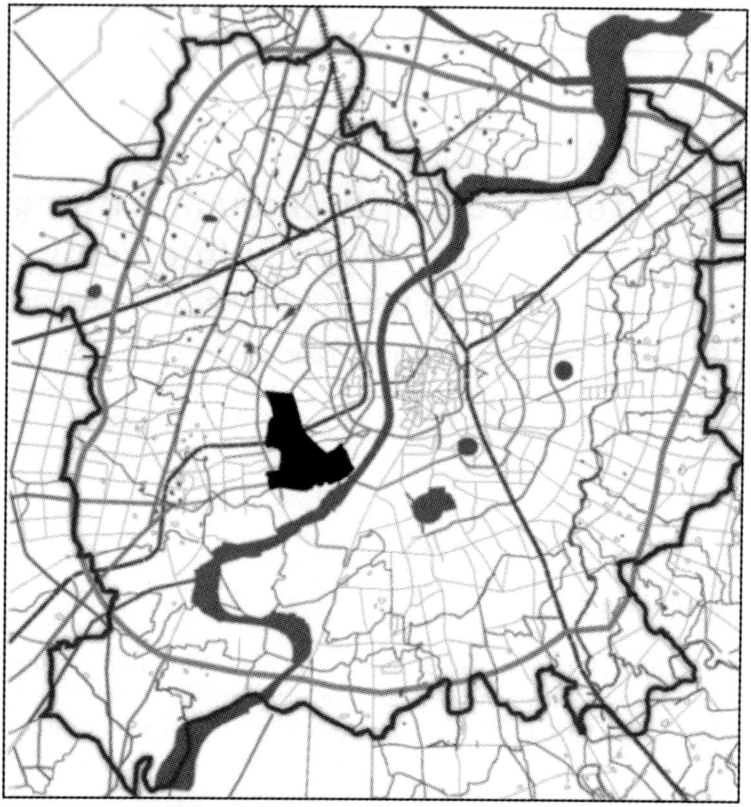

Source: Map prepared by CUE.
Exhibit 7.1: Vasna Ward in Ahmedabad

The study was undertaken in four stages. The first step was to create detailed ward-level database of the slums with respect to land ownership, number of households, population, presence of services like water supply, sewerage, storm water drainage and electricity, presence or absence of an external agency and extent of involvement of this agency in slum development. Second step was to shortlist slums for survey based on the data. For this study, six slums were shortlisted, viz. Pravinnagar-Guptanagar, Sorainagar, Mangal Talav Na Chhapra, Yogeshwarnagar, Jadibanagar and Shri Omnagar for detailed investigation. Among these six, three slums already had some extent of an NGO intervention in assisting the dwellers access basic services. SNP was implemented by the Saath in Pravinnagar-Guptanagar and by the Mahila Housing SEWA

Trust (MHT) in Jadibanagar. Further, MHT had intervened in Sorainagar for water supply. Saath had commenced work on micro finance in Mangal Talav Na Chhapra. In the remaining two slums, Yogeshwarnagar and Shri Omnagar, there had not been any NGO intervention.

The third step was carrying out Focussed Group Discussions (FGDs) in each of the six slums. In slum named Pravinnagar-Guptanagar, separate FGDs with men, women, young men and young women were carried out. The fourth stage was carrying out structured questionnaire survey. Our research team, in collaboration with Uday Urban Resource Centre (URC), a Community-based Organisation (CBO) established by Saath, undertook primary surveys in these slums. The total sample selected was 529, through stratified sampling based on community groups (Table 7.1). Identification of communities was easy as the households of same community resided

Table 7.1: Slum-wise community grouping, Vasna, Ahmedabad

Sl. No.	*Name of the slum*	*Population*	*HH size*	*Community*	*No. of HH*	*Sample size*
1.	Pravinnagar-Guptanagar	6,750	5.14	*Harijan/Bhil/Vaghri*	290	31
				Vanjhara/Marwadi	307	33
				Bharwad	200	21
				Kathiavadi	517	55
				Total	**1,314**	**140**
2.	Jadibanagar	550	6.11	*Patni/Bhaiyaji/Darbar*	90	29
				Total	**90**	**29**
3.	Sorainagar	3,875	5.00	*Dantani/Harijan*	410	45
				Marwadi	150	17
				Kathiavadi	150	17
				Total	**710**	**79**
4.	Yogeshwarnagar	4,000	4.44	Mixed Community	900	148
5.	Mangal Talav Na Chhapra	2,275	5.00	*Dantani*	300	40
				Vanjhara	200	30
				Vankar (kathiayadi)	250	30
				Total	**750**	**52**
6.	Shri Omnagar	3,250	5.00	*Harijan*	150	30
				Marwadi	500	50
				Total	**650**	**80**
TOTAL		**20,700**			**3514**	**529**

Source: Primary Survey.

together in a cluster. This was observed in all the slums except Yogeshwarnagar, where the sample was not stratified.

All participants were ensured of freely airing their views in the FGDs. The key points of discussion and debate in FGDs included issues of land ownership, land or house transaction documents, availability and adequacy of basic services, socio-economic and cultural background of the slum dwellers, their present standard of living and future prospects, details regarding involvement of NGOs as well as government agencies in slum development, housing preferences, their perception about development of the slum etc. Through these discussions, different types of documents held by the slums dwellers and factors providing a sense of tenure security could be understood. For example, it was found that slum dwellers in this ward held an agreement of land plot sale on a stamp-paper (of value ranging from Rs. 20 to Rs. 200), which indicated transaction and the sale value of the plot. But, this was not the land ownership document. The land ownership document is named 7/12 record, which has the name of current as well as past owners and also names of all others who have some stake in the plot of land (mainly the tenant cultivators who were given occupancy rights). The name of the land owner is mentioned in property tax bill also. If the slum was on the municipal land, no transaction documents were available with the residents. Copies of land ownership documents, land transaction documents, property tax bills, receipts and electricity bills were collected during the FGDs. The FGDs assisted the research team in developing understanding of the dynamics and nature of tenure security prevailing in all these slums.

Table 7.2: Conceptualizing levels of tenure security

Factors constructing tenure	*High* de facto	*Weak* de facto	*Insecure*
External agency intervention	Yes		
Land document	Yes	Yes	
Land reservation in master plan			Yes
Administrative instruments	Yes	Yes	
Entitlement extension	Yes	Yes	Yes
Extension of basic services	Yes	Yes	Yes
Duration of stay	Yes	Yes	Yes

Source: Mahadevia (2010, 2011).

The six slums were divided into three categories of tenure security: (i) high *de facto* tenure security, where SNP was implemented, a NGO was present, the slum dwellers possessed any land related document, including informal one such as a stamp-paper agreement, a large proportion of slum dwellers paid property tax, majority of slum dwellers had a Voter ID card, had long duration of stay and had access to basic services provided by the AMC. (ii) Weak *de facto* tenure where there was no NGO present, but had similar conditions as in previous category. (iii) Insecure tenure where slum was on land reserved for other purposes in a Master Plan, did not have any informal land occupancy document and the majority of households did not pay property tax. In essence, the slums located on reserved lands, which were generally public lands, were the slums most vulnerable to the threat of eviction.

Profile of the Slums

1. Pravinnagar-Guptanagar

The settlement of Pravinnagar-Guptanagar is located along two major roads, 132 feet Ring Road that circles around the city and Paldi-Vasna road that connects to National Highway No. 8C. The land of Pravinnagar-Guptanagar and surrounding settlements earlier was a grazing land of Vasna village. Pravinnagar-Guptanagar was one of the four slums in a cluster of about 5,000 slum households. This cluster was formed after the flooding in the Sabarmati river in 1973 in which the slum dwellers on the river bank lost their homes and were then shifted to Pravinnagar-Guptanagar and Sankalitnagar. Residents were ready to pay if the land was sold to them. In all the four FGDs with men, women, youth and young girls, a common response was that the basic services were all good and they all were happy post SNP. The only problem in the settlement was lack of an open plot or community hall for recreation and community interactions. At the time of the survey, which was in early 2009, almost all the construction workers of the settlement had been adversely affected by the global economic meltdown.

Sorainagar

Sorainagar slum is on private land. The owner or his agent had subdivided it into small land parcels and sold it to the residents. This transaction was carried on Rs.20 stamp paper. The original owner of the plot was unknown and hence it was now difficult to locate the exact history of this transaction. Other than the stamp paper document, the residents did not have any other legal or quasi-legal document. The residents, however, have been receiving an annual property tax bill from the AMC since three years prior to the survey. Looking at all this, it was clear that the slum did not have high level of tenure security. The households did not have individual water supply and the AMC had installed a public stand-post in the settlement. Because the slum was located near Sabarmati river, the water table was comparatively high and hence a few households had also installed personal hand pumps, but the water quality was not suitable for drinking. All the internal roads of the slum were *katcha*. Sewerage and storm water lines although had been installed, poor design led to choking, overflow and even back flow in monsoon. Monsoons created water-logging followed by slush on the roads. Thus, in all, the slum residents did not have good physical living conditions. AMC had provided very small size individual toilet in each household by collecting Rs. 500 from them, but, without proper sewerage lines, the toilets were not used. Many households did not have bath space. There was electricity with individual electric meters. The biggest problem for the residents was transportation on account of its location at a distance of 1.5 km from the main road and the connecting road was narrow and *katcha*, hence it was difficult for even an auto-rickshaw to enter inside the settlement. Residents faced great difficulties in emergencies. People were willing to cut their houses for widening and paving the street but there was no guidance whatsoever to help them do so. Street lights provided were not properly functioning, therefore, it was not safe for women to go out after sunset. Many girls reported incidences of sexual harassment. There was limited open space within but plenty of vacant lands were located outside the settlement. Majority of house structures were semi-*pucca* while the *katcha* structures were at the rear of the settlement.

Yogeshwarnagar

Yogeshwarnagar had the worst living conditions amongst all the six selected slums. There were no basic services like water supply or sanitation system. This was because there was no NGO intervention in the slum. Majority of houses were *katcha* or semi-*pucca*. There was a high threat of eviction and hence the residents did not want to invest in housing. They were ready to pay for the basic services but no agency had come forth for the purpose.

Jadibanagar

According to the residents of this settlement, Jadibanagar was formed 25 years ago on an agricultural land which was then subdivided into plots by its owner named Phulabhai. The plots were sold to the people on Rs. 20 stamp paper. The settlement availed of water supply and sanitation through SNP implemented by the MHT and the AMC. Prior to implementation of SNP, the residents purchased water from a few individual households with illegal water lines or a hand pump by paying Rs. 100 per month. Thereafter, the AMC provided a common tap outside the settlement. The SNP was five years old at the time of our survey and each household, therefore, had its own individual connection. People said "water quality was very good if water was supplied." Ironically, the settlement had a well-functioning sewerage line much before the SNP but it was damaged during the SNP implementation and the new one was of poor quality that often choked. After the SNP, the settlement remained clean and hence had fewer epidemic cases than before. The houses were semi-*pucca* with *pucca* walls and *katcha* ceiling. Sense of tenure security had increased after the SNP. The households were receiving property tax bills. They could avail loan from the SEWA Bank for house repairs.

Shri Omnagar

Shri Omnagar was on a private land. The residents did not know much about its origin. Unlike other settlements, houses in the front were *pucca* and in better condition while houses inside the settlement were in very poor condition. There were commercial establishments on the main road. These were mainly recycling units where old wooden doors, windows and furniture were sold. Very few houses had individual water supply while the rest had a hand pump. Some households had neither of the two and depended on a public tap outside the settlement. The water pressure in the individual taps was very low as the secondary lines had been taken from the main water supply line on the main road. Very few houses had individual toilets. Only a few streets had been paved by the residents themselves over time. The level of paved streets had become higher than the houses and hence during the monsoon water entered the houses. A few houses received property tax bills and the residents felt insecure as they had no documents to support their claim of stay in the settlement. However, since it was a private land, they had not experienced any eviction so far.

Mangal Talav Na Chhapra

Mangal Talav Na Chhapra, as the name suggests, was on land of a pond and hence government land. There was a crematorium and a lake on this land which was encroached upon by slum dwellers. The residents said that this slum existed since 1954, which is doubtful. The AMC had provided water supply and sanitation facilities and also paved the entire slum. Most of the people were either domestic workers or rag pickers. There was a serious problem of flies and mosquitoes. There was no garbage collection by the AMC. There were no street light in the settlement

Table 7.3: Status of all selected slums, Vasna, Ahmedabad

Parameters	*Pravinnagar Guptanagar*	*Jadibanagar*	*Shri Omnagar*	*Sorainagar*	*Yogeshwar nagar*	*Mangal Talav Na Chhapra*
General details						
Land Ownership	Private	Private	Private	Private	Private, green belt	Municipal
Age of slum (years)	40	35	45	35	40	55
Demography						
No. of Households	1314	90	650	775	900	455
Population	6750	550	3250	3875	4000	2275
Housing						
Housing condition	Pucca	Semi-pucca	Semi-pucca	Semi-pucca	Semi-pucca	Katcha
SNP	Yes	Yes	No	No	No	No
Infrastructure						
Individual tap	Yes	Yes	Yes	Yes	No	Yes
Individual toilets	Yes	Yes	Yes	Yes	Yes	50% H/H
Toilets provided by	SAATH	MHT	Individually	AMC	AMC	Individually/ World Vision
Individual bath	Yes	Yes	Yes	No	No	No
Sewer line	Yes	Yes	Yes	Yes	No	Yes
Rain water drain	Yes	No	No	No	No	No
Garbage collection	Yes	No	Yes	No	No	No
Paved roads	Yes	Yes	Partial	No	No	Yes
Street lights	Yes	Yes	Yes	Yes	No	No
Electricity	Yes	Yes	Yes	Yes	Yes	Yes
Amenities						
Anganwadi	Yes	No	No	Yes	No	No
Health centre in settlement	Yes	No	No	No	No	No

Source: Primary Survey.

and the residents faced great difficulty in entering the settlement in the late evening and night. The settlement also has local liquor brewing dens, which is an illegal activity in Ahmedabad as there is alcohol prohibition in the state of Gujarat. Poverty was quite visible here. Saath had begun to organise women of this slum into savings groups.

Tenure Security Level

With this study methodology, selected slums were classified into three tenure categories based on the documents available with the households, land ownership status and actors and institutions present in the slum (*See* Table 7.2). The tenure status of each slum is presented in Table 7.4. Pravinnagar-Guptanagar and Jadibanagar have high *de facto* tenure security. In these settlements, SNP has been implemented and hence even though the residents do not have the 7/12 documents of land ownership they have high *de facto* tenure. Sorainagar and Shri Omnagar have weak *de facto* tenure security. The residents of Omnagar said that the owners of woodwork factories located on the periphery of this slum have political connections. In Sorainagar, though SNP has not been carried out the SEWA has intervened. They have collected money from households for provision

Table 7.4: Slum-wise level of tenure security and related parameters, Vasna, Ahmedabad

S. No.	*Name of slum*	*Land ownership*	*Documents with dwellers*	*SNP*	*Experience of demolition*	*Tenure status*
1.	Pravinnagar-Guptanagar	Private	Stamp paper, Property tax bill, Electricity Bill	Yes	No	High *de facto*
2.	Jadibanagar	Private	Stamp paper, Property tax bill, Electricity Bill	Yes	No	High *de facto*
3.	Sorainagar	Private	Stamp paper, Electricity bill	No	Yes	Weak *de facto*
4.	Yogeshwarnagar	Private, green belt	Stamp paper	No	Yes	Insecure
5.	Mangal Talav Na Chapra	Municipal	Electricity Bill	No	Yes	Insecure
6.	Shri Omnagar	Private	Stamp paper, Electricity bill	No	No	Weak *de facto*

Source: Primary Survey.

of basic facilities like water supply connection, toilet and connection to sewerage lines. Mangal Talav and Yogeshwarnagar have insecure tenure. The residents of these slums neither received property tax bills, nor did they have any supporting documents to prove ownership. Since Yogeshwarnagar was located on the green belt reservation and Mangal Talav Na Chhapra was on municipal land, therefore, there were less chances of these getting secured tenure. Both these settlements have experienced incidence of eviction in the past.

Table 7.5: Sample in each tenure status, Vasna, Ahmedabad

Tenure category	*Total households*	*Sample households*	*Sample population*	*Sex ratio*	*Household size*
High *de facto*	1,404	175	1,068	993	6.1
Weak *de facto*	1,360	221	1,300	937	5.9
Insecure	1,350	133	733	1,042	5.5
Total	4,114	529	3,101	980	5.9

Source: Primary Survey.

As mentioned in the earlier section, a total of 529 households were taken as samples with a total population of 3,101. Surprisingly, the sex ratio was favourable and the household size was lower in slums with insecure tenure.

Physical Conditions in Slums

Housing Conditions

In the surveyed households, 42.4 per cent of those with high *de facto* tenure had *pucca* (permanent) houses whereas among those with insecure tenure and vulnerable to eviction, only 24.4 per cent had *pucca* houses (Table 7.6). Also, in the latter category, overwhelming 54.4 per cent had *katcha* (temporary) shelter whereas in high *de facto* tenure only 31.8 per cent households had *katcha* house. The sample survey did indicate that the quality of house structure improves with the improvement in tenure status.

Does improvement in tenure status lead to expansion of house? It does; the sample showed that with improvement in tenure status from insecure to weak *de facto* tenure, households added an additional room (Table 7.6). In insecure tenure category, 58.7 per cent or three in every

Table 7.6: Housing quality, Vasna, Ahmedabad

Tenure Status	*Quality of housing (%)*			*No. of rooms (% H/H)*			
	Katcha	*Semi-pucca*	*Pucca*	*1*	*2*	*3*	*> 3*
High *de facto*	31.8	25.9	42.4	42.2	46.2	9.8	1.7
Weak *de facto*	38.9	22.3	38.9	31.8	52.2	14.6	1.3
Insecure	54.4	21.2	24.4	58.7	30.2	9.0	2.1
Average	42.2	23.1	34.7	45.1	42.2	11.0	1.7

Note: *Katcha* house is one where the building materials are of temporary nature; *pucca* house is one where the building materials are of permanent nature; semi-*pucca* is a category in between the above two.

Source: Primary survey.

five households lived in single room house and only 30.2 per cent lived in a two-room house. But, with improvement in tenure status to weak *de facto* category, households living in single room reduced to 31.8 per cent and those living in two-room house to 52.2 per cent. In high *de facto* tenure category, the number of rooms did not change much and contrary to expectation, the single room dwelling households increased. This could be primarily explained by one settlement (Jadibanagar) with high *de facto* tenure had about 59 per cent households living in single room house due to space constraint. Pravinnagar-Guptanagar, high *de facto* tenure, had only 39 per cent households living in single room house. Residents of Jadibanagar were looking forward to finance from the SEWA Bank to increase a floor in their houses.

Basic Services

Vasna was a peripheral ward lacking basic municipal services such as water supply networks, sewerage and drainage networks, and waste management system as found by a survey in 2005 (Mahadevia and Brar 2008) till the SNP was implemented in some slums of the ward. The situation has improved significantly since then and trunk infrastructure has been laid in the ward, in particular after the extension of the AMC limits in 2006.

Access to basic services increases significantly with improvement in tenure security. Thus, nearly 90 per cent of the households in high *de facto* tenure category had individual (household-level) water supply connection whereas among those in insecure tenure category, only 19 per cent had an individual water supply connection (Table 7.7). However, in some settlements the AMC decided to provide water supply through public taps. In the slums with insecure tenure status, 52 per cent households used public taps for accessing water for domestic use. It was possible that the local government may not extend water supply at all within a settlement then the households make their own arrangements such as sourcing water through a hand-pump, as in the case of settlements in weak *de facto* tenure category wherein 49 per cent households and in insecure tenure category 22 per cent households used hand-pump.

Given the fact that this ward has been on the periphery where the AMC had not expanded its water supply network, NGO facilitation through the SNP had brought individual water supply connection. In such slums, 91 per cent households had obtained individual water supply connection through NGO facilitation. Also, in high *de facto* tenure category, more than 95 per cent of households with individual water connections had given credit for getting water supply to either SNP or NGO. In contrast, majority of households (86%) in insecure tenure category having individual connections had approached the AMC on their own to get connection, where only 18 per cent of the total households had individual water supply connections. Thus, access to water supply was high in slums when an external agency was involved in negotiations with local government. Also when an external agency was involved as an intermediary between the slum dwellers and local government, more households agreed to get legal water supply connections, even though it required payments.

The respondents of primary survey of slums with high *de facto* tenure were quite satisfied with the quantity and quality of the water. Seventy per cent households replied that the amount of water was adequate and 68.8 per cent people were satisfied with the quality of water; 77 per cent of the respondents in weak *de facto* tenure status slums also said that the quantity of water supplied was adequate. A large number of households were dependent on hand pumps for water and did not have individual connections. In the insecure tenure category, water supply was inadequate and around 52 per cent households relied on public taps. More than 70 per cent of the respondents said that the quality of water available at public post was of good quality.

During FGD in Yogeshwarnagar (insecure tenure category) it was found that there were only two public taps shared by 900 households. Thus, the number of people dependent on these stand posts was very high and water quantity available was inadequate. Also these public taps were located outside the settlement across the main road. Every morning

Table 7.7: Status of basic services by tenure, Vasna, Ahmedabad

Indicators of basic services	*High de facto*	*Weak de facto*	*Insecure*	*Average*
Water Supply Source (%)*				
— Individual connection from municipal supply	89.5	28.5	18.7	44.9
— Public tap	4.1	17.7	51.8	25.8
— Privately arranged	4.7	3.8	6.7	5.2
— Hand pump	1.2	48.7	22.3	23.3
Agency assisting in accessing individual water supply (%)*				
AMC	9.1	48.9	86.1	48.0
SNP/NGO	96.1	24.4	11.1	43.9
Households with access to toilets (%)	100.0	94.9	97.9	97.7
Type of toilet of those with access (%)				
—Personal	93.6	86.1	68.9	82.3
—Sharing	5.8	8.2	10.4	8.2
—Community	0.6	0.6	17.6	6.9
—Pay and Use	0.0	0.0	1.0	0.4
Agency assisting in accessing individual toilet (%)				
—AMC	3.5	36.7	45.8	28.7
—NGO/SNP	94.4	44.4	25.0	54.6
—Self	2.1	18.9	29.2	16.7
Households having sewerage connection (%)	98.3	94.4	73.2	87.9
Type of sewerage (%)*				
—Underground	100.0	98.0	84.0	94.0
—Open	0.0	2.0	14.2	5.4
% households reporting drainage choking	58.0	76.2	44.4	59.5
Households reporting storm water drainage (%)	64.6	69.4	43.3	58.2
Type of storm water drain (%)				
—Underground	100	90.8	67.6	85.4
—Open drain	0	1.7	20.6	8
—Other	0	7.6	11.8	6.6
% Households reporting water logging	31.1	42.6	54.3	43.2
% Households reporting electricity meters	97.1	96.9	85.4	92.7

* The totals do not add to 100 per cent as all the options are not represented in the Table.

Source: Primary Survey.

at 5 a.m., women of the settlement queued up for filling water and all of them had experienced quarrels arising due to frustration over inadequate water quantity. Instances have been recorded of children, following their mother and crossing the road, getting hit by passing vehicle. A few household in Yogeshwarnagar had hand pumps, but the water quality was very bad and not suitable for drinking purposes.

Mangal Talav Na Chhapra (insecure tenure category) was a low income settlement and the residents were employed in marginal jobs. The local Member of Legislative Assembly (MLA) had managed to get individual water connections to some houses located on the main road. Further, some households located along the lake-side in the same settlement had faced demolitions four times and did not have any water connection. In Sorainagar (weak *de facto* tenure) SEWA had collected contributions from households to install basic services in the slum. Water lines were laid in the entire slum, but were not in working condition due to several design problems. Hence, people still had to depend upon hand pumps. Due to improper provisions of water supply in the slums, there was no reliability of quality and quantity of water supply and the respondents purchased water from private suppliers at very high costs.

Very small proportion of households was without any toilet access and hence defecating in the open was restricted to just 2.3 per cent households in the entire sample (Table 7.7). In case of slums with high *de facto* tenure, all households had access to toilet and 93.6 per cent households had access to personal (individual household-level) toilet. In fact, the construction of individual toilet was very important component of the SNP. Thus, availability of personal toilet improves with tenure status. In the weak *de facto* category of tenure, those who did not have a personal toilet shared it with other households and their proportion was 8.2 per cent. In the slums with no security of tenure, 28 per cent shared a toilet, which included 17.6 per cent households using community toilet and 10.4 per cent households sharing a toilet with another neighbouring household.

With this service as well, an external agency presence had helped the slum dwellers to get individual toilets. Almost 55 per cent of the slum dwellers in all the three categories had recognised the efforts of either NGO or SNP for provision of individual toilets within their slum (Table 7.7). As per tenure category, approximately 95 per cent households of slums in high *de facto* tenure category, 45 per cent households in weak *de facto* tenure category and 25 per cent households in insecure tenure category have given credit to an external agency for helping them to avail facility of individual toilet. Thus the slums where external agencies were involved, the level and provision of services was significantly high. Wherever the external agency was not present, then the households depended on themselves, as were the 29 per cent households in insecure tenure category in accessing individual toilet. Also the level of peoples' participation was high when an external agency was involved as an intermediary between the slum dwellers and the urban local body. People were also willing to pay partly for having individual toilets in their households.

The households of the slums falling under high *de facto* category got individual toilets due to implementation of SNP. Few households did not participate in SNP due to financial constraints, distrust on the external agency or due to eviction threat (and thereby not wanting to spend money on additions in the house). However, due to the SNP when the slum obtained *de facto* tenure, the households that had not participated in the SNP also constructed their own toilets themselves as they were assured of no eviction guarantee for 10 years. In order to facilitate and encourage slum dwellers to construct individual toilets, the AMC launched a scheme in Yogeshwarnagar and Sorainagar to provide a water closet, a door, two bags of cement, tiles and other material to each household at rate of Rs. 500 only. Many households in these two slums took advantage of this scheme. However, as the tenure status of Mangal Talav Na Chhapra was not clear, neither the AMC nor any external agency had extended help to this slum to construct individual toilets. Hence, large number of households here were dependent on public toilet or open defecation in this slum. Some road-side houses were provided individual toilets by a local MLA.

Vasna ward had full coverage of drainage line when we undertook this survey. Even then, 12 per cent households in the surveyed slums did not have sewerage connection (Table 7.7) on account of 27 per cent households in insecure tenure category not having any sewerage connection. The AMC has not connected slums without tenure security, i.e. slums which may be displaced in future. Further, 14.2 per cent households in the third tenure category had open sewerage, which indicates that the households themselves may have constructed some open drain for waste water disposal.

In all the three categories, 60 per cent of the total households have reported choking of sewerage lines. According to the respondents of high *de facto* tenure, the reason behind choking of drains was lack of proper maintenance of drains at regular intervals. They said that after laying the infrastructure, the services need to be maintained properly by the AMC, especially before monsoons, which was not happening. Also, the drains were laid without considering core engineering and technical principles like slope of drainage lines, depth of drainage lines from ground level, joints, diameter of pipes etc., that led to backflow of waste and rain water during monsoons. Besides, the faulty drainage line design, the pipes broke whenever there was any vehicular movement.

Availability of storm water drain within the settlement increased with the improvement in tenure status; 65 per cent households reported existence of storm water drain in high *de facto* tenure category and just 43.3 per cent stated so in insecure tenure category (Table 7.7). Also, in the former, if the storm water drain existed then it was underground whereas in the latter, just 67.6 per cent stated that was the case. Thus, as in case of waste water disposal, in case of rain water draining, the residents may have made a temporary arrangement in the slums with insecure tenure status. Also, there was better maintenance of drainage and sewerage system if the tenure security was high as compared to insecure tenure. Only 31.1 per cent households reported water-logging in the former category whereas 54.3 per cent households reported the same in the latter category. Since presence of a NGO was one of the indicators of high *de facto* tenure, these slums also had better maintenance of assets created on account of presence of an institution.

Electricity access has become universal after the private sector came in as they considered slums as clients and provided electricity connection. The connection charges per household were reduced from Rs. 10,000 in 2004 to Rs. 2,500 presently so that the slum households could afford the initial high costs. Thereafter, the monthly bills were charged at the minimum rate making the operational costs of electricity also bearable. In return, the households obtained an address, as the bills mention the address of the customer. Electricity bills, therefore, gave an identity to the slum dweller, which was essential for him/her for entitlement claims. In the survey, 94.4 per cent households had electricity in the house and 92.7 per cent had an electricity meter (Table 7.17). The incidence of both was slightly higher in slums with high tenure security as compared to those with insecure tenure.

Employment

Workforce participation rate (WFPR) decreases amongst males as well as females when the degree of tenure security reduces from high *de facto* to weak *de facto* status. But, a shift from weak *de facto* tenure to insecure tenure, the WFPR increases. An interesting trend observed was that among the females living in settlements with insecure tenure, the WFPR was even higher than for the females living in settlements with high *de facto* tenure. The male WFPR for high *de facto*, weak *de facto* and insecure tenure categories were 53.7 per cent, 49.9 per cent and 52.0 per cent respectively and the female WFPRs were 26.6 per cent, 19.3 per cent and 33.0 per cent respectively (Table 7.8). High female WFPR is generally indicative of poverty and thus women come out to work in effort to prevent households from falling into poverty. This data, therefore, indicates that there was a likelihood of high incidence of poverty among the households living in settlements in insecure tenure. The type of work women in the most insecure category do also points to poverty in their households. Most of the women in Mangal Talav Na Chhapra were rag pickers, who stated during the FGD that they took up this work as they were not qualified for any other work and that their income was not adequate to cover their children's education expenditure.

More than half of the employed males living in the studied slums were engaged as casual labour (Table 7.8). Among the females, overwhelming employment was in personal services such as domestic help (47.0%), whereas only 38.6 per cent of the females were employed as casual labour (Table 7.8). The proportion of personal service in females was even more in the high *de facto* tenure category, the reason being Saath's initiative of Urmila Home Managers, which trained women from the slums to be efficient home managers and then assured their placement along with formal contracts.

Interestingly, the proportion of the employed working as casual labour increases with the decline in tenure security, indicating that employment seemed to become more and more stable with the improvement in tenure security. As much as 82.1 per cent employed males in insecure tenure slums were casually employed, while this proportion for high *de facto* tenure category was 50.5 per cent. Similarly, these figures for females were 41.0 per cent and 33.8 per cent respectively. In high *de facto* tenure slums, some new employment opportunities seemed to have emerged among the males; for example, employment in private sector (33.6%), employment in financial services (0.4%), shop owners (1.4%) and employment in government services (1.1%). Also, in these slums, employment in personal services was lower than in the slums with weak *de facto* tenure status.

Males in the insecure tenure slums were not into any small-scale entrepreneurial activities or in any high or medium skilled employment,

Table 7.8: Work force participation rates and employment sectors, Vasna, Ahmedabad

Employment categories	*Tenure Status*			
	High de facto	*Weak de facto*	*Insecure*	*Average*
Work force participation Rate (%)				
Male	53.7	49.9	52.0	52.0
Female	26.6	19.3	33.0	26.6
Persons	40.2	34.6	42.7	39.4
Male				
Casual labour	50.5	58.4	82.1	64.3
Own business	1.8	2.7	0.3	1.5
Social services	0.4	0.0	0.0	0.1
Financial services	0.4	0.0	0.0	0.1
Government service	1.1	0.9	0.0	0.6
Home-based work	0.0	0.0	0.0	0.0
Diamond + other industries	0.0	0.4	0.0	0.1
Personal services	2.1	3.5	1.4	2.2
Private service	33.6	18.1	16.2	22.9
Shop owner	1.4	0.0	0.0	0.5
Skilled construction labour	5.3	11.5	0.0	5.1
Vendors	2.8	4.4	0.0	2.2
All others	0.7	0.0	0.0	0.2
Total	100.0	100.0	100.0	100.0
Female				
Casual labour	33.8	41.2	41.0	38.6
Government service	0.7	1.2	0.0	0.5
Home-based work	0.0	2.4	0.0	0.5
Diamond + other industries	0.0	1.2	0.0	0.2
Personal services	53.2	34.1	48.3	47.0
Private service	11.5	11.8	10.1	10.9
Vendors	0.7	8.2	0.6	2.2
All others	0.0	0.0	0.0	0.0
Total	100.0	100.0	100.0	100.0

Source: Primary Survey.

as we see zeros in most of the better paying employment categories like the home-based work for example garage, mechanical work, tailoring and embroidery, handicraft items, spare parts repairing etc. In slums with weak *de facto* tenure, there was more diversification of employment compared to slums with insecure tenure. A house can be a good start for a small-scale entrepreneurial activity. A house is a workplace for many and this fact is not only restricted to slums. However, when the house is not secure one would certainly hesitate to invest in the same place as a livelihood earning base. Further, there was lack of any small enterprise because location of some slums, such as Sorainagar, was away from the roads and there was lack of market for their products.

There were some employment categories where females were absent. These were own business, social service, financial service, government service, shop owner and skilled construction labour. Hence, these entries have been removed from Table 7.8. Females in the insecure tenure category were either in casual labour, in personal services or in private services.

Income, Expenditure and Savings

While the average household income per month of the surveyed households was Rs. 4,965, that in the households with high *de facto* tenure was Rs. 5,537 (Table 7.9), which was 1.12 times of the average and 1.3 times of the average income (of Rs. 4,238) of households with insecure tenure. There was a very strong relationship between tenure security and household income, the latter increasing with the improvement in the former. The same relationship between tenure and monthly per capita income can be seen. Average monthly per capita income in high *de facto* tenure slums was Rs. 907 while that of weak *de facto* and insecure categories was Rs. 895 and Rs. 743 respectively although the family size in the high *de facto* tenure slums are higher than the rest of the slum (refer to Table 7.1). An interesting observation was that even if the overall WFPR was higher for households living in insecure tenure category than the rest of the tenure categories, the former's average monthly income and monthly per capita income were lower than the households in the two other tenure categories. The reason was that the insecure slums had

Table 7.9: Average monthly household and per capita income, Vasna, Ahmedabad

Tenure Status	*Average monthly household income (Rs.)*	*Average monthly per capita income (Rs.)*
High *de facto*	5,537	907.7
Weak *de facto*	5,191	895.0
Insecure	4,238	743.5
Average	4,965	841.5

Source: Primary Survey.

very high proportion of workers employed as casual labour. In addition, women who were engaged in domestic help in the slums with high *de facto* tenure were associated with Urmila Home Managers and so they obtained their remuneration regularly. While in other two categories, majority of women who were engaged in domestic help generally found jobs by themselves and so their income was neither regular nor fixed.

The expenditure pattern demonstrates a strong relationship with the tenure security. On food, slum dwellers having comparatively high tenure security, spent 22.9 per cent of their total expenditure whereas in low tenure security this proportion was 30.6 per cent and in no security slum, it was 40 per cent (Table 7.10), indicating that the larger share of total expenditure was devoted to food as the level of tenure security declines. Lower the income, higher is the share of food in total expenditure, indicates that incomes were lower for those living in insecure tenure category. This corroborates with the income data of the sample. In terms of cooking fuel expense, a converse pattern can be seen; in high *de facto* tenure slums it was the highest and lowest in insecure tenure category slums. This was because most of the households with high *de facto* tenure used Liquefied Petroleum Gas (LPG) as cooking fuel. In other two categories, households were using hearth with biomass as energy. Many of the

Table 7.10: Distribution of expenditure, Vasna, Ahmedabad

Expenditure Item	*Tenure status*		
	High de facto	*Weak de facto*	*Insecure*
Food	22.9	30.6	39.7
Cooking fuel	3.6	1.8	1.1
Clothes	2.6	4.1	3.8
Communication	2.5	3.5	3.9
Education	6.8	3.4	4.1
Health	5.4	3.7	4.4
Housing	12.9	9.5	7.9
Electricity	6.8	10.1	4.6
Basic services charges	2.8	2.0	4.8
Consumer durables	13.1	2.9	7.7
Transport	6.8	5.7	4.4
Debt repayment	6.8	14.8	7.9
Insurance premium	2.9	6.6	4.6
Recreation and entertainment	4.2	1.3	1.1
Total	100.0	100.0	100.0

Note: Expenditure on some items was reported for one year, which has been converted into per month for the table.

Source: Primary Survey.

households did not have a separate kitchen and so they cooked outside their dwellings on the street.

Households in high *de facto* tenure status devoted 6.8 per cent of their total expenditure on their children's education while households in weak *de facto* and insecure status devoted lesser proportion of their expenditure on the same at 3.4 per cent and 4.1 per cent respectively on this. In third category, the proportion was higher than that of category 2 because Yogeshwarnagar had two *anganwadis* inside as well as a *gyanshala* (primary school) and the households sent even their girl children to these schools.

Expenditure on housing can be directly linked to the tenure status of the slums. Households in slums with high *de facto* tenure spend 12.9 per cent of their total expenditure on housing, which was the highest in terms of expenditure share among the three tenure categories. There were two reasons for this; increase in spending on housing on account of no threat of eviction and also increase in expenditure to maintain the created assets. The households living in slums with insecure tenure spend only 7.9 per cent of their total expenditure on housing, which was the least in terms of proportion among the three categories (Table 7.10). Households in the insecure category devoted relatively higher proportion of their expenditure on basic services, which was very obvious as they did not have access to subsidised services of the AMC.

Expenditure on some luxury items like consumer durables and entertainment was much more in high *de facto* tenure status slums than in the other two categories; 4.2 per cent expenditure was incurred on recreation and entertainment by the slums households in this category, while the proportion was far lower on this item in the other two categories of slums; 1.3 per cent and 1.1 per cent respectively. Slums with high *de facto* tenure expended the least on proportion of total expenditure on debt repayment among the three and the most towards transport among the three categories of slums.

Table 7.11: Incidence and amount of savings, Vasna, Amraiwadi

Tenure Status	*% HH having saving*	*Average savings per month (Rs.)*
High *de facto*	32.6	231
Weak *de facto*	16.9	196
Insecure	23.2	122
Average	24.4	198

Source: Primary Survey.

Savings incidence as well as average amount saved also had strong relation with the tenure status. 32.6 per cent of the households living in slums with high *de facto* tenure saved and the average savings of those who saved was Rs. 231 per month (Table 7.11). In weak *de facto* tenure slums, only 17 per cent households saved and their average monthly savings was Rs. 196, both lower than the former. Proportion of households saving in insecure category was 23 per cent, which was higher than in weak *de facto* status slums, but the average amount saved was the least among the three categories and was only Rs. 122 per month. In both SNP slums, which were under high *de facto* tenure category, the women's savings groups started before the SNP implementation, an institutional intervention that continued post-project. For SNP process in Pravinnagar-Guptanagar, *see* chapter 4. In Mangal Talav Na Chhapra (insecure tenure), the NGO—Saath had begun to organise women's savings groups. At Jadibanagar too, the SEWA Bank first came for micro-credit programme for the women, and then based on the formation of local women's groups, the MHT, a sister organisation of SEWA Bank, stepped in to implement the SNP. Savings can be introduced in the slum households, even when they do not have a legal address, if a local institution intervenes to organise. We have observed this in all the slums in our sample.

Education

The total literacy rate from the primary survey for male and female together came as 68 per cent (Table 7.12), which was lower than the literacy rate of 89.62 per cent for Ahmedabad city in 2011. However, it was interesting to note that the total literacy rate in all the three tenure types was almost equal (69.5 per cent in high *de facto* tenure category, 71.2 per cent in weak *de facto* tenure category and 63.8 per cent in insecure tenure category). The male and female literacy rates in slums with weak *de facto* tenure were 83.7 per cent and 58.7 per cent respectively when in high *de facto* tenure were 80.6 per cent and 58.7 per cent respectively. Evidently, the literacy rates were low in the slums in insecure tenure category, 71.8 per cent for males and 55.1 per cent for the females.

This ward has location advantage as it is well-connected with rest of the city. This improved the slum dwellers' access to education facilities. This ward has a large proportion of its population belonging to middle and higher income groups. Hence, the ward has many private schools, which were also accessed by the slum dwellers. Being close to the location of educational facilities, there was high awareness among dwellers about education and hence many had put their children in private schools. Thus, the literacy level in all the three tenure categories did not vary much with the changing tenure.

Table 7.12: Literacy rate and education levels, Vasna, Ahmedabad

	High de facto	*Weak de facto*	*Insecure*	*Average*
Literacy Rate (%)				
Male	80.6	83.7	71.8	78.3
Female	58.2	58.7	55.1	57.3
Persons	69.5	71.2	63.8	68.0
Level of education of literates who have completed their education—males (%)				
Just read	19.9	19.5	28.3	22.4
Up to secondary	34.6	30.3	39.3	34.7
Up to higher secondary	36.3	43.2	27.9	35.8
Graduate	5.8	4.1	1.6	4.0
Post-graduate	1.0	0.8	0.8	0.9
Other courses	2.4	2.1	2.0	2.2
Level of education of literates who have completed their education—females (%)				
Just read	30.2	31.9	30.5	30.7
Up to secondary	33.7	39.6	34.0	35.4
Up to higher secondary	28.6	20.1	28.9	26.5
Graduate	3.5	3.5	3.6	3.5
Post-graduate	0.5	1.4	0.5	0.7
Other courses	3.5	3.5	2.5	3.1

Source: Primary Survey.

Level of education is an important parameter that helps in understanding the type and quality of available workforce. A trend similar to literacy rate was observed in level of education among male and female. The level of education was higher in slums with high and weak *de facto* tenure category as compared to the slums in insecure tenure category. The education level of male literates was higher than female literates in all the three tenure categories, indicating families' preference towards male child's education. Although the literacy rates did not directly correspond to tenure status as expected, the male educational achievements did. While about 20 per cent of the educated males stated that they could just read and write in the slums in high and weak *de facto* tenure category, in the last tenure category, 28.3 per cent stated so

(Table 7.12). Thus, even though 71.8 per cent males in last tenure category stated they were literate, one in every three of them could only read and by that could not be considered fully literate. In the high *de facto* tenure category, 36.3 per cent males reached higher secondary school and another 5.8 per cent had reached graduate level. These figures for insecure tenure category were 27.9 per cent and 1.6 per cent respectively. In slums in weak *de facto* tenure category, a large proportion of males, 43.2 per cent had reached higher secondary school level, much higher than in the slums in high *de facto* tenure category, but just 4.1 per cent of the educated males had reached graduate level. Once again, there were certain households in the slums in the middle tenure category, which were doing well with literacy and we will have to look for explanations beyond the definition of tenure. With regard to educational achievements of females, there was less variation across the three tenure categories and also an unclear pattern as far as the link with the tenure status was concerned. Nonetheless, 31 per cent of the literate females reported that they were able to just read in all the slums studied.

During discussions, it was found that the slums where all the basic services were available, the women did not have to engage themselves in fetching water could spend more time with her children. She then took interest and devoted her time for children's education. She also went out to earn as the extra income was useful for children's education. Although the slum residents stated that they did not differentiate between male and female children with regard to education, in practice, the preference was given to the male child. For example, male children were sent to private schools for high school education, while female children were not. Generally, the female child was educated only up to secondary level, after that they were not sent to school.

There were several reasons for not encouraging higher education of female child. One of the major reasons was the conservative belief that a girl had to learn household tasks so as to perform household duties well after marriage. In one of the FGD with teenage girls, it was reported that many girls wanted to continue studies but their mothers were asking them to leave the studies and help them out in the house. In lower income households where both the parents had to go out to work to earn money, the older female child looked after the house, cooked and took care of her siblings. Another main reason was not finding adequate number of properly educated grooms for the educated girls. In some of the cases girls were convinced that education was going to be a waste and only their skills in cooking, sewing and house-keeping would help them in future. Some girls also reported cases of sexual harassment as one of the reasons for being afraid to go to school, as the schools for higher education were far and lack of public transport facility meant they had to walk and be possible targets for sexual harassment. However, some girls did continue their higher education or joined vocational courses after constant persuasion by the NGOs working in the slums. It was also informed that the youth of slums also joined various vocational courses related to computers, spoken English, salesmanship, marketing etc. This was due to constant efforts by NGOs like Saath. They pursued the youth to join livelihood programme *Ummeed* (meaning hope) that was initiated by Saath and also appreciated by the Government of Gujarat. This programme aimed at giving livelihood skills and vocational training to the youth. This programme was discontinued at the time of going to press.

Entitlements

In India, poor are identified through issuance of a BPL Card by the state government either through a survey or on the recommendation of a local elected representative. A BPL card holder is entitled to certain amount of subsidised food grains from a Public Distribution System (PDS) shop, a health insurance scheme named Rashtriya Swasthya Bima Yojana (RSBY), free or low cost treatment in government hospitals, education tuition waiver or scholarship, etc. Like other studies, this study also found that the poor were not able to get a BPL Card and hence their access to various public schemes and subsidised facilities was very limited. Large number of the surveyed households had an Above Poverty Line (APL) Card, which provided them residential identity but not access to subsidised schemes. In our surveyed slums, about 18 per cent households did not have a ration card and only 19.3 per cent a BPL Card (Table 7.13). While, incidence of having a ration card was higher among the households in high and weak *de facto* tenure categories, 27 per cent households living in insecure tenure category did not have a ration card. So if the tenure security was low, the possibility of getting a ration card reduced. Further, while per household income was the highest in the households with high *de facto* tenure security; these also have the highest proportion of households holding a BPL Card (29.4%). Inappropriately targeted subsidised schemes and facilities can be seen even in the survey. Thus, organising for SNP had also had other collateral benefits and one of that was procuring a ration card and that too, a BPL Card. Further, nearly 92 per cent households had their voting-age population holding an election card. With regard to this card, not much of difference could be found across the tenure categories except that in the last one 12 per cent did not have a voting card.

Table 7.13: Access to different ID cards (%), Vasna, Ahmedabad

Tenure Status	*Having ration card*	*Having BPL card*	*Having election card*
High *de facto*	85.3	29.4	94.7
Weak *de facto*	88.2	10.6	95.3
Insecure	72.9	19.6	87.7
Average	81.5	19.3	92.3

Source: Primary Survey.

Transport

Around 78.2 per cent of the main earners of families in all the slums travelled up to 5 km everyday, another 13.5 per cent travelled between 5 to 10 km and only 8.3 per cent travelled more than 10 km for employment (Table 7.14). Nonetheless, in the slums with high *de facto* tenure, 17 per cent of the main earners travelled for more than 10 km for work, indicating that they might be involved in better categories of work to travel so long and also have higher mobility. The reason for the same was use of scooter (motorised two wheelers) and bus for commuting by those in high *de facto* slums. A very large proportion of those living in slums in insecure tenure category (86%) worked within 5 km distance and used mainly shuttle (shared) auto-rickshaw for commuting to work.

The distance and mode used for work travel by the second earner of the household was little different than the first earner. On the whole, only 4 per cent of them went beyond 10 km for work but this distance was traversed by only the second earners in slums in high *de facto* tenure category where 11 per cent of them did so (Table 7.14). The reason of not traversing long distances for work was that the second earners of the households were mainly women, who did not go long distances for work. Given that lesser distances were travelled by the second earner for work, 32.6 per cent of them walked to work and 18.8 per cent cycled. As many as 23.2 per cent use shared auto or six-seater auto. In both the above tables, public transport (bus) should have more people travelling by it but it was not the case. During the FGDs, people had complained about inadequacy of public bus and fatigue caused due to long distances of walking.

Table 7.14: Travel distance and mode, Vasna, Ahmedabad

Tenure Status	*Distance to work (km)*			*Mode used*						
	0 to 5	*5 to 10*	*> 10*	*Walk*	*Bicycle*	*Bus*	*Scooter*	*Auto*	*Shuttle auto*	*Others*
Main earner										
High *de facto*	64.7	18.1	17.2	26.3	26.3	15.8	15.8	4.6	8.6	2.6
Weak *de facto*	84.3	10.2	5.5	14.8	40.1	14.8	14.8	2.1	11.3	2.1
Insecure	85.7	12.0	2.3	24.1	18.2	7.1	5.9	10.6	33.5	0.6
Average	78.2	13.5	8.3	21.7	28.2	12.5	12.2	5.8	17.8	1.8
Secondary earner										
High *de facto*	67.7	21.0	11.3	31.1	25.7	16.2	4.1	6.8	13.5	2.7
Weak *de facto*	89.8	10.2	0.0	31.9	26.1	11.6	7.2	4.3	18.8	0.0
Insecure	93.7	6.3	0.0	34.9	4.7	3.5	3.5	16.3	37.2	0.0
Average	83.7	12.5	3.8	32.6	18.8	10.4	4.9	9.1	23.2	0.9

Source: Primary Survey.

As expected, children were enrolled in schools within 5 km distance of their home (94% of children did so) and as transport expenditure is unaffordable and children tend to walk to school. The study found that 84 per cent of them did so (Table 7.15). However, in slums with high *de facto* tenure, 17.6 per cent children travelled more than 5 km for going to school and hence 12 per cent of them went by auto rickshaw and another 4.7 per cent went by shared auto rickshaw. These families were able to afford sending their children to relatively better schools than the ones available in the locality. There was no practice of slum children going to

Table 7.15: Travel distance and mode for school children, Vasna, Ahmedabad

Tenure Status	*Distance to work (km)*			*Mode used*					
	0 to 5	*5 to 10*	*>10*	*Walk*	*cycle*	*Bus*	*Scooter*	*Auto*	*Shuttle auto*
High *de facto*	82.4	14.7	2.9	72.1	9.3	2.3	0.0	11.6	4.7
Weak *de facto*	98.7	1.3	0.0	84.8	7.6	2.5	1.3	3.8	0.0
Insecure	100.0	0.0	0.0	94.2	3.8	0.0	0.0	1.9	0.0
Average	93.7	5.3	1.0	83.7	6.9	1.6	0.4	5.8	1.6

Source: Primary Survey.

school by bus as neither did the municipal nor private schools where they were enrolled have any school bus service. Nearly 94 per cent children in slums with insecure tenure walked to school and another 4 per cent bicycled.

Measuring Impacts of Tenure Security

The Variables

The research hypothesis was: shelter security, determined through land tenure security leads to improvement in physical living conditions (reduces deprivations in physical quality of life), improvement in capabilities on account of firstly improvement in literacy rates, then educational levels and then empowerment to negotiate the administrative and political space and improvement in employment and incomes. It was not the other way round; incomes lead to improvement in education and then shelter security. It can be argued that education improvement could lead to empowerment and increase in incomes and consequently improvement in living conditions and shelter security. Our argument that all other interventions of development such as improvement in access to education and health would be nil, were there no shelter security.

The variables that construct tenure security have been taken as independent variables and the quality of life outcome variables have been selected as independent variables. There were 12 dependent variables defined for the logistic regression analysis. The independent variables were land ownership, house document (even the quasi-legal), payment of property tax and indicators of urban citizenship such as ration card, BPL card and election card. The definition of variables is given below.

Independent Variables

NGO intervention in slum development: Households were asked to state whether there was an intervention of NGO in slum. A value of 1 was assigned if there was an intervention by NGO and 0 for otherwise.

NGO intervention in mobilising savings: This variable was created using the question "*where do you save?*" if the households were saving with a NGO a dummy value of 1 was assigned and 0 for otherwise.

Land ownership: Two categories of land ownership, namely private land and public land have been observed in the study area. Two dummy values have been created: 1 for public lands and 0 for private lands.

Chart 7.1: Independent variables

Variable	*Value*
NGO intervention in slum development	1 for Yes 0 for No
NGO intervention in mobilising savings	1 for Yes 0 for No
Years of stay-20	1 for more than 20 years 0 for less than or equal to 20 years
Land Ownership	1 for Public 0 for private and others
Property tax	1 for paying property tax 0 for otherwise
House document	1 for Yes 0 for No
BPL card	1 for yes 0 for no
Election card	1 for yes 0 for no
Ration card	1 for yes 0 for no

Property tax: This variable has been created using the question "*whether the household pays property tax?*" If the household pays property tax, dummy value of 1 was assigned and dummy value of 0 was assigned for non-paying households.

Years of stay: For the analysis, duration of stay, which was a continuous variable, was converted to a dichotomous variable. This variable was created by taking dummy value of 1 for years of stay more than 20 years and dummy value of 0 for less than 20 years. We also tried this analysis for other cut-off points for duration of stay. But this data set has very little variation and around 90 per cent of the households have been living in the slum for more than 20 years.

House document: This variable has been framed using question "*do you possess any quasi-legal document of the house*?" Dummy value of 1 was assigned if the households have a house document (even the quasi-legal) and 0 for otherwise.

Ration Card, BPL Card and Election Card: These are three variables. Households were asked to state whether they possessed these cards. Dummy value of 1 was assigned if the households possessed the card and 0 for otherwise. Possession of Ration card, BPL card and Election card are often independent of legal residential status as all these are extended to the households before election irrespective of the household's tenure status. But these documents then create entitlements. Hence, we have included these three as independent variables in our analysis.

Dependent Variables

Type of housing: This variable was created from responses on housing type, where the response categories were: (i) *pucca,* (ii) semi-*pucca*, and (iii) *katcha*. Since there were three categories for analysis, housing type was recorded into a dummy variable: 1 for *pucca* and semi-*pucca* and 0 for *katcha*. Assigning a value of 1 for *pucca* and 0 for semi-*pucca* and *katcha* was also tried but the results were weaker than the previous categorisation of this variable.

Number of rooms: Households were asked to state the number of rooms they had. A dummy value of 1 was assigned to the households having more than 1 room and 0 for otherwise.

Number of assets: Households were asked about owning of the different consumer durables/assets. Sixteen types of consumer assets were found in the households. To convert the continuous variable (which ranges between 0-16), dummy value of 1 was assigned if the households had more than 4 assets and 0 for less than or equal to 4 assets. Other cut-off points such as more than 6 assets were also tried but without getting robust results.

Agency supplying water: This variable was created by asking "*which agency supplies water*?" A dummy value of 1 was assigned if the agency supplying water was local government[2] and 0 for other agencies.

Sewer line: Households were asked to state whether they had sewerage connection to their settlement. A dummy value of 1 was assigned if the households had sewer line connection and 0 for otherwise.

Storm water drains: This variable was created by asking "*do you have separate storm water drainage in your system*?" Dummy value of 1 was assigned if the settlement had the facility and 0 for otherwise.

Toilet facility: Households were asked to state whether they had toilet facility available to them or not. Dummy value of 1 was assigned if the households had the facility 0 and for otherwise.

Bath space: This variable was recorded as dummy variable by asking the availability of the bath space to the households. Value of 1 was assigned if the households had the facility and 0 for otherwise.

Employment-1: This variable was for the household head and there were number of options for this variable. Among these, a dummy value

Chart 7.2: Independent variables

Variable	*Value*
Type of housing	1 for *pucca* and semi-*pucca* 0 for *katcha*
No. of rooms	1 for 2 or more than 2 rooms 0 for one or less rooms
Assets	1 for more than 4 0 for 4 and less than 4
Agency of water supply	1 for Public 0 for others
Sewer line	1 for yes 0 for no
Storm water drainage	1 for yes 0 for no
Latrine facility	1 for Yes 0 for No
Bath space	1 for yes 0 for No
Literacy rate of household	1 for more than 65 per cent 0 for less than or equal to 65 per cent
Employment-1	1 for non-casual labour 0 for casual labour
Employment-2	1 for regular employment 0 non-regular employment
Employment-3	1 for at least 1 casual labour in household 0 for no casual labour
No. of people working in a family	1 for more than 1 0 for 1or less than 1
Income	0 for less than or equal to Rs. 2,000 1 for more than Rs. 2,000
Food expenditure as per cent of income	1 for less than or equal 50 per cent 0 for more than 50 per cent
Food expenditure as per cent of income	1 for less than or equal 40 per cent 0 for more than 40 per cent
Food expenditure as per cent of income	1 for less than or equal 60 per cent 0 for more than 60 per cent

of 1 was used if the household head's employment was regular and 0 for otherwise.

Employment-2: This variable was for the household head and there were number of options for this variable. Among these, a dummy value of 1 was used if the household head's employment was non-casual and 0 for casual.

Employment-3: This variable was a composite variable of the number of people working in a household and the type employment taken up by the household members. A dummy value of 1 was assigned if at least one of the employed members in the household was casual labour and value of 0 was assigned if all of the household employed members were non-causal labour.

Number of people working in a family: This variable was collected as a continuous variable and recorded in the analysis using dummy values: 1 if more than 1 person was employed in a household and 0 for otherwise.

Income: This variable was collected as a continuous variable and recorded in the analysis using dummy values: 1 for monthly income more than Rs. 2000[3] per household and 0 for otherwise. Other income cut-offs were also tried but without good result.

Relationships among the Variables

Factor analysis was used to know whether some underlying pattern of relationship exist among variables; discovering a new set of factors; or confirming existing factor(s) as being the true factor(s). Essentially, the factors defining shelter security have been derived using proxies as we do not have any straight forward or single indicator of tenure status. Because, the variables constructing shelter security were many, the factors were subjected to oblique rotation to ensure that all variables were ascribed to a factor, and none was allocated to two or more factors.

Table 7.16 shows the results of the component factor extraction among the households in the sample, in Vasna. The table also gives the respective Eigen values and percentage of variance for the factors. The rule of thumb here is that only factors with Eigen values more than 1.0 should be used in further analysis. This criterion of identifying factors that explain the variance in the data was chosen because of the relatively large number of variables. It shows that six variables had Eigen values greater than 1.0 and together were explaining 61 per cent of the variance in the data set. These are all independent variables and it indicates that the independent variables were correctly selected. NGO related factors together explained 30.5 per cent of the variance, suggesting these two were most important factors determining tenure security as well as the outcome variables related to living conditions, education, economic status and access to entitlements. Years of stay, land ownership, payment of property tax and possession of informal document of house or land transaction, were other important variables explaining the data set variance of about 8 per cent to 6.5 per cent each. It has to be noted that these variables were the independent variables in the hypothesis.

Table 7.16: Factors explaining data variance among variables, Vasna, Ahmedabad

Sl. No.	*Variables*	*Initial Eigen values*		
		Total	*% of Variance*	*Cumulative %*
1.	NGO intervention in slum development	3.183	18.722	18.722
2.	NGO intervention in mobilising savings	1.997	11.747	30.469
3.	Years of stay more than 20 years	1.426	8.388	38.857
4.	Public land ownership	1.358	7.991	46.848
5.	Payment of property tax	1.265	7.439	54.287
6.	Informal house document	1.098	6.459	60.746

Logistic Regression[4]

Logistic regression analysis uses the techniques of multiple regression analysis to research situations in which the variables are categorical. Since many of the variables in the data set are dichotomous, bivariate analysis[5] has been carried out to observe and measure the impacts of tenure and variables constructing tenure on the outcome indicators. The results for Vasna ward are presented in Table 7.18, which are bivariate logit regressions of independent variables with the dependent variables. The independent variables are of tenure security and dependent variables are outcome variables of living conditions, human development, economic status and access to entitlements. All the dependent variables can be called outcome variables of tenure security. The findings of the bivariate logit regression for slums in Vasna ward are presented below:

(i) The NGO intervention in slum development had significant and positive relationship with variables of living conditions, namely size of dwelling unit (number of rooms), water supply by public agency, toilet facility, sewer line connection and availability of independent bath space. All these results were significant at more than 80 per cent level. If a household was living in a settlement which has NGO intervention, likelihood of having more than one room in the dwelling unit increased by 109 per cent; likelihood of getting water from public agency increased by 252 per cent; the likelihood of it having toilet facility increased by 375 per cent; likelihood of having sewer connection and independent bath space increased by 385 and 141 per cent respectively.

(ii) The NGO intervention in slum development also improved the economic status and had positive and significant relationship with number of persons employed in a household; household head having non-casual employment, household income to be more than Rs. 2,000 per month and per capita income to be more than Rs. 650 per month; and food expenditure as a proportion of expenditure to be less than 50 per cent, with the likelihood of improvement in these variables are 102 per cent, 65 per cent, 47 per cent, 49 per cent and 54 per cent respectively. These relations were significant at between 90 per cent and 60 per cent.

(iii) The NGO intervention in slum development did not have any significant impact on the literacy rate.

(iv) NGO intervention in slum for the purpose of micro finance had positive relationship with house quality, which improved by 310 per cent; owning more than one room house improved by 107 per cent; access to sewerage connection improved by 189 per cent and also access to independent bath, which improved by 54 per cent.

(v) The likelihood of household head being non-casual labour improved by 102 per cent, likelihood of having at least one casual labour in the household reduced by 48 per cent, likelihood of income being more than Rs. 2,000 increased by 136 per cent and likelihood of per capita income more than Rs. 650 increased by 46 per cent in case there was a NGO intervention for microfinance related activities.

(vi) Undoubtedly, the likelihood of household saving increased by 520 per cent in case there was NGO intervention in savings. This could result in increase in household assets, which indeed had increased by 408 per cent in case there was micro-finance NGO in the slum.

(vii) The probability of holding a BPL card went up if there was an NGO working on microfinance issues in the slum. These relationships, however, were not significant. Any NGO intervention could assist the slum dwellers in accessing BPL card. But, that did not seem to be happening as the relationship was inverse and significant.

(viii) The duration of stay of more than 20 years also had strong positive relationship with variables of living conditions, namely having *pucca* or semi-*pucca* house quality (improving by 102%), having more than one room in dwelling unit (improving by 33%) and water supply by public agency (improving by 117%), with

Table 7.18: Bivariate logit regressions, Vasna, Amraiwadi

Dependent variables	*Independent variables*											
	NGO intervention in development		*NGO intervention for microfinance*		*Duration of stay more than 20 years*		*Public land ownership*		*Property tax bill/receipt*		*Any document of house/land*	
	% change	*Sig.*	*% change*	*Sig.*	*% change*	*Sig.*	*% change*	*Sig.*	*% change*	*Sig.*	*% change*	*Sig.*
House quality was *pucca* or semi-*pucca*	5.1	0.907	309.8	0.002*	102.4	0.188*	–73.6	0.241*	47.6	0.433	931.7	0.000*
More than one room in dwelling unit	108.9	0.057*	106.8	0.057*	33.3	0.195*	-48.6	0.512	113.7	0.068*	9.4	0.820
Public agency supplying water	252.0	0.001*	11.9	0.783	117.0	0.148*	–	–	16.3	0.730	89.2	0.162*
Availability of toilet	375.1	0.204*	14.8	0.908	79.2	0.649	715.5	0.999	323.8	0.279*	–	–
Sewer line present	385.0	0.035*	189.2	0.123*	–24.2	0.772	-99.2	0.002*	45.0	0.587	1412.6	0.012*
Independent bath space	141.5	0.051*	53.9	0.356*	40.8	0.916	-89.9	0.066*	90.8	0.170*	431.5	0.000*
Literacy above 65 per cent	11.2	0.775	9.5	0.809	4.4	0.924	–	–	25.2	0.575	24.4	0.562
More than one person working in a family	102.2	0.073*	21.2	0.630	17.4	0.740	–60.6	0.353*	33.5	0.499	32.0	0.490
Household head as non-casual labour	65.0	0.239*	101.5	0.108*	9.6	0.862	–56.6	0.424	21.1	0.688	195.7	0.015*
Household head as regular employed	27.8	0.552	32.1	0.513	154.2	0.081*	–100.0	0.999	10.8	0.823	360.4	0.000*
At least one casual labour in the household	–9.1	0.803	–48.2	0.087*	–39.9	0.259*	24.3	0.999	1.3	0.975	–46.5	0.114*
Household income of more than Rs. 2000	46.8	0.375*	135.9	0.054*	425.2	0.020*	–85.3	0.115*	57.0	0.336*	165.4	0.030*
Per capita income of more than Rs. 650	48.8	0.313*	46.3	0.352*	133.8	0.068*	–60.2	0.358	58.7	0.302*	7.8	0.849
Savings	–11.6	0.802	519.8	0.000*	23.5	0.199*	–15.3	0.879	140.8	0.093*	245.6	0.017*
More than 4 assets	51.2	0.491	408.4	0.009*	991.6	0.035*	–88.2	0.070*	73.7	0.399	443.7	0.014*
Food expenditure as % of expenditure less than 50	54.0	0.395*	21.7	0.711	39.9	0.602	–84.4	0.107*	52.5	0.472	4.3	0.933
Having BPL card	–63.4	0.056*	77.5	0.249*	–66.6	0.060*	168.4	0.471	8.5	0.883	–17.1	0.707
Having voter card	39.3	0.617	–49.8	0.313*	–82.3	0.269*	31.4	0.999	35.0	0.662	245.4	0.099*
Having ration card	–42.6	0.302*	19.4	0.757	–17.5	0.766	607.0	0.999	380.3	0.004	119.2	0.166*

Note: * Are significant relations.

significance levels up to 80 per cent. The duration of stay was not related to (or does not have any impact on) availability of water from the urban local body; availability of a toilet at household level and presence of sewer line in the settlement. This means that these outcomes are influenced by other factors that construct tenure security. level.

(ix) With regard to economic status, duration of stay was positively and significantly related to regular employment of the household head (by 154%), household income more than Rs. 2,000 (by 425%), per capita income more than Rs. 650 (by 134%), households saving (by 24%), and having more than four assets (by 992%). The relationships were significant up to 70 per cent level. Duration of stay had significant (at 75% level) negative relationship with at least one member of the household employed as casual labour, the incidence increasing by - 40 per cent.

(x) Duration of stay had negative and significant impact on holding of a BPL card (at 94%) and voter ID cards (at 74% significance level). The last result was contrary to our understanding and therefore, could be freak. The first observation was self-explanatory as income increases with duration of residence in a settlement. Thus, while duration of stay was an important component of tenure security, it explained only certain outcomes.

(xi) The relationship of public land ownership with the outcome indicators were all negative, indicating that the slums on public lands did not experience any improvement in living conditions or economic status and had insignificant relationship with access to entitlements. For example, if a slum was on public land then possibility of having a *pucca* or semi-*pucca* unit decreased by 74 per cent, of a sewer line connection by 99 per cent, independent bath by 90 per cent, more than one person working in a family by 61 per cent, household income more than Rs. 2,000 per month by 85 per cent, of having more than four assets by 88 per cent and food expenditure less than 50 per cent of the total expenditure by 84 per cent.

(xii) This indicates that the households living on public lands faced eviction threat. They did not possess any documents to support their residency in that place and hence were more vulnerable to eviction threat. This observation was a contradiction to general understanding in literature that the slums on public lands have higher level of tenure security than the slums on private lands (Durrand-Lasserve and Selod, 2007).

(xiii) The impact of property tax was positive and significant on number of rooms in dwelling unit (by 114%), availability of toilet (by 324%), independent bath space (by 91%), household income more than Rs. 2,000 per month (by 57%), per capita income more than Rs. 650 per month (by 59%), households saving (by 141%) and households possessing more than 4 assets (by 74%). The surprise result here was possibility of increase in at least one casual worker in the family by 57 per cent when the household received a property tax bill, indicating this to be a freak relation. Lastly, access to a ration card increased by 380 per cent if the household had received a property tax bill or had its payment receipt.

(xiv) Holding any document of house or land, even of a quasi-legal status such as a stamp paper agreement of sale of land or house extended some tenure security to the households, leading to improvement in availability of toilet by 89 per cent. This variable had positive relation with many of the variables of economic status. The possibility of household head not being casual labour improved by 196 per cent, household income above Rs. 2,000 per month improved by 165 per cent, and possibility of saving improved by 246 per cent and household possessing more than four assets improved by 444 per cent. Even, the possibility of holding a voter card and a ration card improved by 245 per cent and 119 per cent respectively if the household holds any document related to house.

(xv) None of the tenure variables were related to the education status variables.

Conclusions

The study of slums in Vasna ward indicates that *de facto* tenure security helped in enhancing living conditions, human development, economic status and access to entitlements and there was no need to aim for legal tenure security in the first instance. Tenure security was constructed firstly through presence of an external agency in the slum, followed by duration of stay and then availability of some quasi-legal document of house ownership. Further, even property tax bills sent to the households led to increase in perceived tenure security. In this chapter, the term *de facto* tenure security has been used to denote this. Thus, tenure security was a fluid concept and many actions of the civil society and of the local government could create *de facto* security of tenure. Even having electricity meter extends some sense of perceived security. In the specific case of Ahmedabad, peculiarly, since the electric supply was by a private agency and in its desire to extend clientele base, it gave electric connections to the slums where the dwellers were willing to pay initial connection charges. This flexibility may not have been feasible, if the electricity company was a public one, as was the case before privatisation. But, this does not mean that privatisation of other basic facilities would extend customer status to the slum dwellers and by that extend some security of tenure and by that logic privatise the basic services.

There were different levels of *de facto* tenure security. In this study, two levels have been categorised; high *de facto* tenure and weak *de facto* tenure. The former one was where there was either a guarantee of no eviction for a specific period of time or presence of an external agency that could be banked upon for support in times of eviction threat. The third tenure status was insecure status, where there was eviction threat. Unlike in literature, where there was stylisation of levels of tenure security, in this study only two levels of *de facto* tenure status have been clearly established.

Generally, it is assumed that employment would lead to income and then to secure tenure. This chapter argues this trickle down does not always work. Tenure or supply side dynamics or policies play a very important role in the welfare of the poor; it reduces the time period of consolidation of an urban household. In hostile policy environment, as in case of urban India where the neo-liberal state is becoming increasingly hostile to the poor, and there is elite capture of urban land and resources, supply side policy interventions are extremely important. Thus, if tenure comes first, it can have positive impacts on the lives of the urban poor.

Lastly, do we have to wait till the urban poor can be extended legal land titles or property rights as Hernando De Soto has been arguing? This study indicates that we do not need to wait for these drastic changes to occur. Small steps taken at appropriate time, such as extending even basic services and levying taxes as well as support of NGOs or even organising the poor by themselves for their tenure security would help in improving the living conditions in the slum settlements. These would have beneficial impacts on also employment and human development indicators. Hence, instead of thinking of the best options, it was better to begin with what was feasible and then gradually move towards the best.

Annexure 7.1

List of Slums, Vasna

Sl. No.	*Name of slum*	*Sl. No.*	*Name of slum*
1.	Bhikabhai Juvabhai Na Chhapra	13.	Pravin Nagar Na Chhapra
2.	Chandranagar Na Chhapra	14.	Rabari Vado
3.	Das Ordi Na Chhapra	15.	Rajiv Nagar
4.	Desai Vas	16.	Rampura Gam's Chhapra
5.	Gupta Nagar Na Chhapra	17.	Sorainagar Na Chhapra
6.	Indira Nagar	18.	Someshwar Nagar Na Chhapra
7.	Jadiba Nagar Na Chhapra	19.	Sompura Na Chhapra
8.	Kachiya Vas	20.	Sreyas Na Chhapra
9.	Malav Talav Chamunda Nagar	21.	Tajbibi Badshah Khan Na Chhapra
10.	Mangal Talav Na Chhapra	22.	Vallabh Nagar Na Chhapra
11.	Narayan Nagar	23.	Velabhai Ni Chali
12.	Shri Om Nagar Na Chhapra	24.	Yogeshwar Na Chhapra

Source: Data collected from the files of AMC.

NOTES

1. Research is funded under the research project titled "Inclusive Urbanisation—Social Protection for the Slum and Pavement Dwellers in India", a CEPT University—Mahila Housing SEWA Trust (MHT) project, under the programme 'Social Protection in Asia', managed by Institute of Development Studies (IDS), Sussex and Institute of Human Development (IHD), New Delhi and funded by Ford Foundation and IDRC. Authors acknowledge the contribution of Chintan Shah and Uday Resource Centre in fieldwork for this research. Would also like to acknowledge the support of Niraj Jani for the fieldwork.
2. Provision of basic services (water supply, sewerage and public health) has been one of the key responsibilities of the urban local bodies in India.
3. The average monthly income of the household in Vasna was Rs. 3,350. The regression analysis carried out using this as cut of point hasn't produced significant results.
4. The logistic regression assumes that the outcome variable, Y was categorical, but logistic regression doesn't model this outcome variable directly. For simplicity we assume that Y was dichotomous, taking on values of 1 for positive outcome and 0 for negative outcome. In theory, the hypothetical, population proportion of cases for which $Y = 1$ was defined as $p = P(Y = 1)$. Then, the theoretical proportion of cases for which $Y = 0$ was $1 - p = P(Y$

= 0). In the absence of other information, we would estimate p by the sample proportion of cases for which Y = 1.

Let:

$$P_i = \Pr(Y=1/X = x_i)$$

Then we can write the model:

$$\text{Log } (P_i/1\text{-}P_i) = \log it\ (P_i) = \beta_0 + \beta_1 x_1$$

The parameter β_0 gives the log odds of an independent variable. In Table 1, for example, β_0 gives the log odds of the households stayed in the slum for 20 or less than 20 years and β_1 shows how these odds differ for the household stayed more than 20 years in the slum.

If we rewrite the model in terms of odds as:

$$(P_i/1-P_i) = \exp\ (\beta_0 + \beta_1 x_1)$$

Or in terms of the probability of the outcome occurring as:

$$P_i = \exp\ (\beta_0 + \beta_1 x_i)/[1 + \exp\ (\beta_0 + \beta_1 x_i)]$$

Conversely the probability of the outcome not occurring was

$$1- P_i = 1/\ [1 + \exp\ (\beta_0 + \beta_1 xi)]$$

5. The logistic regression assumes that the outcome variable, Y was categorical, but logistic regression doesn't model this outcome variable directly. For simplicity we assume that Y was dichotomous, taking on values of 1 for positive outcome and 0 for negative outcome. In theory, the hypothetical, population proportion of cases for which Y = 1 was defined as p = P(Y = 1). Then, the theoretical proportion of cases for which Y = 0 was $1 - p$ = P(Y = 0). In the absence of other information, we would estimate p by the sample proportion of cases for which Y = 1.

   Let:

$$P_i = \Pr(Y = 1/X = x_i)$$

   Then we can write the model:

$$\text{Log } (P_i/1 - P_i) = \log it\ (P_i) = \beta_0 + \beta_1 x_1$$

   The parameter β_0 gives the log odds of an independent variable. In Table 1, for example, β_0 gives the log odds of the households stayed in the slum for 20 or less than 20 years and β_1 shows how these odds differ for the household stayed more than 20 years in the slum.

   If we rewrite the model in terms of odds as:

$$(P_i/1 - P_i) = \exp\ (\beta_0 + \beta_1 x_1)$$

   Or in terms of the probability of the outcome occurring as:

$$Pi = \exp\ (\beta_0 + \beta_1 x_i)/\ (1 + \exp\ (\beta_0 + \beta_1 x_i))$$

   Conversely the probability of the outcome not occurring was

$$1- Pi = 1/\ (1 + \exp\ (\beta_0 + \beta_1 x_i))$$

8

Informality and State-led Intervention for Slum Improvement in a Mid-sized City

The Case of Nanded[1]

Renu Desai

Introduction

Urban poor and low-income inhabitants of Indian cities rely on informal access to land and housing to meet their shelter needs, leading to the cities comprising large areas of informal settlements. Initially, these settlements are characterised by poor housing quality, lack of basic services and low tenure security. Over time, their residents try to incrementally upgrade their housing, basic services and infrastructure, and living conditions as well as enhance their tenure security. These incremental improvements take place through a range of processes such as individual and collective self-help, political mobilisation and patronage, and government policies, legislations and programmes. Incremental improvements do not always take place though, and many informal settlements are subject to demolitions and evictions, often without adequate alternatives, giving rise to new informal settlements elsewhere in the city. In fact, the emergence of informal settlements is often tied to cycles of state-led demolitions and evictions that have been integral to the processes of urbanization and development. Moreover, over the past two decades, government authorities have increasingly reduced their support to processes of incremental improvements in informal settlements, turning more and more to a policy of eviction, one that is often tied into projects of urban renewal and capital accumulation (*see*, for example Bhan and Shivanand, 2013; Coelho and Raman, 2010; Desai, 2014). Where residents have been resettled, they have been shifted from their low-rise, high-density informal settlements to flats, far from their earlier locations. Even under Central Government programmes like the Basic Services for the Urban Poor (BSUP), a sub-mission of the Jawaharlal Nehru National Urban Renewal Mission (JNNURM) (2005-2014), the approach taken in most cities was to demolish informal settlements and relocate residents to new formal housing built on the urban periphery.

This chapter is located in this context of widespread urban informality in Indian cities, the dynamics of incremental upgrading of informal housing, the broader shift towards eviction and relocation over the past two decades, and a possible re-emphasis on upgrading in future programmes. It is also located in a context where research largely has tended to focus mostly on metropolitan cities to the neglect of understanding smaller cities and the informal processes that shape them and the spaces of shelter for their urban poor.

This chapter examines urban informality in Nanded, a city of 5.5 lakh population (2011 Census), located on the banks of Godavari river in Marathwada region of Maharashtra state. It examines the different types of informal settlements found in the city and the processes that have led to their emergence, improvement and further development. Central to these processes in recent years has been the approach taken by the local municipal government, the Nanded Waghala City Municipal Corporation (NWCMC), under BSUP of *in-situ* redevelopment of slums although the NWCMC also did carry out some evictions and demolition accompanied by resettlement housing built under BSUP. Under this approach, the NWCMC converted a large number of *katcha* houses (i.e. houses built out of temporary materials) on State Government and municipal lands as well as on *gunthewari* or unauthorised layouts to *pucca* houses (i.e. houses built out of permanent materials like brick and concrete). Basic services and infrastructure were also supposed to be upgraded in these settlements. As part of this approach, the NWCMC also attempted to accommodate many of the concerns, demands and desires of residents which emerged during the BSUP implementation process. This approach, while having a number of limitations, has facilitated an incremental upgrading process in many of Nanded's informal settlements. The paper discusses the implications of this approach for improvement of informal housing.

The second section first provides an overview of informal settlements in Nanded and then discusses the two main types, squatter settlements and *gunthewari* layouts, found in the city. It discusses their characteristics and outlines some of the processes that have led to their emergence, improvement and development. The following section describes the BSUP sub-mission, outlines the approach through which NWCMC has implemented it in Nanded, and analyses this experience. In conclusion, the chapter discusses what Nanded tells us about informal housing in urban India as well as how the Nanded BSUP approach can aid our learning on processes and challenges around housing interventions for the urban poor, particularly around *in-situ* redevelopment and upgradation of informal housing. This chapter is based on research carried out in early 2013, and involved collection of secondary data on slums and slum policies from the NWCMC, city-level interviews on BSUP and case-studies of settlements where BSUP was implemented[2].

Informal Settlements in Nanded

The housing supply in Nanded has been predominantly constituted by the private sector, with limited public initiatives (NWCMC, 2006). The only large housing supply initiative by the public sector was by the City and Industrial Development Corporation (CIDCO), a state-level agency, in the 1980s, when they developed a township in south Nanded (south of the river) which comprised about 11,000 Low-Income Group houses and plots. Prior to that, the Maharashtra Housing and Area Development Authority (MHADA) had constructed about 1,000 dwelling units for different income categories between 1972 and 1982. Under Valmiki Ambedkar Awas Yojana (VAMBAY), 600 houses were built in the early/mid-2000s (NWCMC n.d). Since the urban poor and the low-income groups are priced out of the formal-sector private housing market, and there have been limited attempts by the state to provide affordable housing for them, the majority have turned to informal housing.

There are varying figures for the slum population of Nanded. According to the 2011 census, there is a population of 126,326 living in slums within the city's municipal boundaries. NWCMC's 2006 City Development Plan refers to 58 slum settlements with a population of 154,020, with a population of 107,365 living in 25 notified slums and 46,655 in the 33 proposed-to-be-notified slums (NWCMC, 2006). This means that between 23 to 28 per cent of the city's population lived in slums.

The official definitions for a slum in India use criteria of dilapidated housing and inadequate level of services for defining them. Since these conditions are mostly found in squatter settlements, that is, encroachments on public or private lands, not just slums but even informal housing, which is a much broader category, often get equated with squatter settlements. However, informal housing is often more varied. Moreover, as research is increasingly revealing, not all informal housing is of the urban poor and low-income groups and certain types of middle-class and elite housing developments may be a mix of the formal and informal, and while certain kinds of informal housing are bestowed with greater legitimacy by the state, others are not [*see* Bhan (2013) for a discussion on the categories of legal/illegal, formal/informal, and legitimate/illegitimate]. What is of interest to us here is that in Nanded, NWCMC expanded the definition of slums by passing a resolution that any settlement with more than 25 houses and having inadequate infrastructure was a slum for the purpose of BSUP.[3] This led NWCMC to include both squatter settlements and many *gunthewari* or unauthorised layouts as slums. Below I outline the characteristics of these two types of informal settlements and the processes through which they have emerged, improved and further developed.

Squatter Settlements

Squatter settlements in Nanded are on different types of landownership: municipal, State Government and Central Government lands. Today, 25-30 settlements are on municipal lands and 10-12 on State Government and Central Government lands. Some settlements are also on land owned by the *gurudwara*[4], but which was leased by the Nanded Textile Mill (NTM) and which are inhabited by workers of NTM. Under the Slum Upgradation Programme, basic amenities like open drains, pathways, water supply lines and street lights were provided in few slums (NWCMC n.d.). While this was much before the NWCMC had expanded its slum definition to include many *gunthewari* layouts, it is possible that some of the 58 notified or proposed-to-be-notified slums are *gunthewari* layouts. As already mentioned, according to NWCMC, the total population of these 58 settlements is 154,020, with 107,365 in the notified slums and 46,655 in the proposed-to-be-notified slums. It is not clear what criteria were followed for selecting settlements for slum notification, but from research on slum notification elsewhere in Maharashtra it is safe to speculate that landownership, land use of the said land in the Development Plan, and political patronage towards the settlement and local-State political relations (since the State Government notifies slums) played a significant role in this (*see*, for example Desai and Jajoo 2013). In terms of level of services, the NWCMC data tells us that about 90 per cent population in the notified slums is covered by water supply (through public stand-posts) and sanitation services (through public toilets). In case of the proposed-to-be-notified slums, the water supply coverage ranges from 25 to 60 per cent in different slums, while the sanitation coverage is nil in about 17 settlements and ranges from 25 to 60 per cent in the rest. For roads and street lighting, about 37 per cent of the total road length is surfaced and about 63 per cent have street lights (NWCMC 2006: 78).

Generally, squatter settlements seem to have enjoyed high tenure security in Nanded. However, there is evidence of evictions from as far back as the 1970s and 1980s, after which the evictees were relocated on municipal or State Government land without formal tenure, thus creating new informal squatter settlements. For instance, in the mid-1970s, squatters were evicted from the Godavari floodplain. They were allotted 10×15 ft. plots on a State Government land by Shankar Rao Chavan, Maharashtra's Chief Minister at the time. This was, however, without any formal tenure. At the time, this land was on the city's periphery and amidst an undeveloped area, therefore, not many of the original families stayed on. The *Dalit* community that came to inhabit the settlement, which came to be called Jai Bhim Nagar, also faced an eviction. However, their mobilisation by the Dalit Panthers led to permission to return to the settlement with the eviction threat receding over subsequent years. The municipal government began to collect tax from them at some point and thus *de facto* tenure security increased. Thus, a combination of political patronage, community mobilisation and the local state's welfare practices towards some slums (extending some services like water and collecting tax in return) led to some improvement and enhanced tenure security in Jai Bhim Nagar.

Another instance of an informal settlement that emerged through eviction and relocation without formal tenure is Lumbini Nagar. Road-widening in the Itwari area, that is, the city's historic core, in the early 1980s had led to evictions, with the evictees being shifted out of the core to this plot of municipal land on the city's edge. As explained later, BSUP, a state intervention for improvement of slums, was implemented in many of Nanded's slums, including Jai Bhim Nagar and Lumbini Nagar, through an approach of *in-situ* redevelopment. This enhanced tenure security further although the implications for improvement of infrastructure and services have been more mixed.

In recent years, some of the city's squatter settlements have been demolished for development projects (road-widening, bridge construction, airport extension) and due to environmental hazards (location on the river floodplain) and landownership (location on land owned by the Indian Railways). The evictees have been relocated in resettlement housing built under BSUP. These relocations of recent years have been different in that residents are relocated in flats and would be extended formal tenure after they pay the beneficiary amount. While at first glance it may seem that since relocation has happened in flats, new informal squatter settlements would not emerge, this is not necessarily the case. In many cities, slum notification, a cut-off date and "proof" documents have determined whether displacees are given alternate houses or not, and the exclusions that occur as a result of these eligibility criteria have led to the emergence of new informal settlements. In Nanded, however, the reasons for their emergence have been different.

NWCMC relaxed the Maharashtra-wide cut-off date of January 1, 1995 and also did not place much emphasis on proof documents. Instead, it carried out a survey in the to-be-demolished slums to identify all the households, all of whom were considered eligible for resettlement flats built under BSUP. However, it appears that an inaccurate survey led to the exclusion of some families. As a result, at the time of our research, about 20 families who had not been given resettlement housing were living in huts made out of tin sheets on the edge of the resettlement site, thus having created a new informal settlement. They had no running water or sanitation facilities. Some of these excluded families had election cards showing the demolished slum as their place of residence. While NWCMC argued that these families were not on its survey because they had moved away to live elsewhere but without transferring their election cards, the families claimed that they had been away at work or their village during the survey and their election cards were proof of their residence and the legitimacy of their claims. Squatter settlements thus get made, demolished and remade in interaction with state policies and practices.

Gunthewari Layouts

Gunthewari layouts refer to unauthorised layouts formed on the periphery of towns and cities of Maharashtra through the subdivision, sale and development of privately-owned land without taking permission for Non-Agricultural (NA) use and/or acquiring the necessary planning permissions. The term *gunthewari* comes from *guntha*, which is a unit of land measurement in Maharashtra.[5] In these layouts, since approvals have not been obtained, the local government is also not required to provide any infrastructure in these areas. All of this creates cheaper plots for sale which are (or were) bought by poor and low-income families. Since the plot sizes are (or were) around 1,000 sq.ft. (approx. 1 *guntha*), which is less than the acceptable norm of 3,000 sq.ft. in Maharashtra (Bhide, 2014), this too makes (made) land affordable to poor and low-income groups. Building construction in these plots may or may not be as per building bylaws, but since the layout is unauthorised, building permissions are also not taken and, therefore, construction on the plot is also unauthorised.

In Nanded, as in many other cities of Maharashtra, gaining access to land and housing through these *gunthewari* layouts—known as "informal subdivisions" in the international literature (*see* Payne, 1989)—has become widespread. Scholars have begun to trace the political-economy of the emergence of *gunthewari* layouts in some cities and towns. In Sangli and Miraj, the emergence of *gunthewaris* has been traced to the 1980s when landowners, threatened with losing their "surplus" land under the Urban Land Ceiling and Regulation Act (ULCRA) and to reservations under the Development Plan, responded by subdividing their lands into small residential plots and selling them off to make quick money (Bhide 2014). In Solapur also, *gunthewaris* were found to be developed by landowners trying to make some profits from their lands before it was acquired as "surplus" under ULCRA (Kamath and Deekshit, 2014). There were also plenty of buyers since the state had established an industrial estate but not workers' housing nor space for small factories, which, therefore, created a demand for land. Later, municipal limit extensions led to large number of land reservations for public amenities and here too landowners were found to respond by informally plotting their lands and making some money of this before their lands were acquired. In Aurangabad, a couple of processes including the 1988 riots which became an impetus for movement away from the city to fringe areas, were found to lead to *gunthewari* development (Bhide, 2014). In Nanded, we have not yet traced the processes that spurred the emergence of these layouts but the aforementioned research provides a window into how *gunthewari* development in Maharashtra might be tied into local economic dynamics, planning legislations and policies and their subversion, and even socio-spatial shifts due to urban conflicts. Furthermore, unauthorised layouts are also sometimes created by landowners, who wish to maximize their profits by developing their land without paying betterment charges to the planning authority without following planning norms since this would result in losing some land to open space, and without obtaining planning approvals since this is time-consuming and can impact financial gains. It is, however, not yet clear what set of practices and motivations spurred *gunthewari* layouts in Nanded.

In terms of the buyers, that is, plot owners, we find that many in Nanded possess recognized documentary proof of purchase. This legal ownership does not, however, mean that they have formal tenure. Durand-Lasserve and Selod (2007) define tenure as the rights individuals and communities have with regard to land—namely the right to occupy, to use, to develop, to inherit and to transfer land—based on various rules governing land use and land ownership. What this means is that tenure is not simply about ownership and the right to transfer land legally but about the rights that people have with respect to what they can do with this land. Since plot owners in *gunthewari* layouts occupy, use and develop the land in contravention of existing planning and building rules, their tenure rights are informal. However, due to recognized purchase/ownership, their tenure security is generally high since they cannot be easily dispossessed of their land like residents of squatter settlements. As explained later, a legislation enacted in Maharashtra in 2001 for the *gunthewari* layouts has increased their tenure security. But, it also seems that in many layouts, plot owners do not have recognized proof of purchase, and, with the legislation's implementation, it remains to be seen whether this leads to low tenure security for them at some point.

In 2006, there were about 205 *gunthewari* layouts in Nanded, with a total of about 25,000 plots.[6] This means that the *gunthewari* layouts house about 20 per cent of Nanded's population.[7] In other cities, the proportion of population living in *gunthewari* layouts has been found to vary between 20 per cent to 40 per cent (Bhide, 2014). In Nanded, plot sizes in some layouts are as small as 600 sq.ft. However, many plots are also larger than 2,000 sq.ft. in area.[8] In the older layouts, land prices have shot up, putting any new sales in the layout out of reach of a poor and even low-income family. For instance, in Gulshan Colony, a 1200 sq.ft. plot, which sold for Rs.16,000 in the mid-1990s was priced at Rs. 7.5 lakh in early 2013. Both the larger plot sizes and the rising land prices are likely to be linked to a legislation enacted in 2001 for regularising these layouts (discussed later). While many of the layouts in Nanded were thus initially inhabited by large numbers of urban poor and low-income families, with rising land prices and high demand for land and housing amongst higher-up socio-economic groups, they are increasingly going out of reach of poor and low-income groups. Nonetheless, many layouts in the city still comprise a socio-economic diversity.

The most visible effect of informal tenure in the *gunthewari* layouts is that the municipal government is not required to provide the layouts with infrastructure and basic services. There is no data regarding the overall status of housing quality or level of basic services and infrastructure in Nanded's *gunthewari* layouts. Our observations show that housing quality varies since there is a socio-economic diversity in many of the layouts. Where the plot owners are poor, the houses are ground-floor *katcha* structures; many of the plot owners are also middle-class and upper-middle class and live in well-made *pucca* houses. While the municipal government is not required to provide infrastructure to these localities, as with squatter settlements, here too infrastructure provision and improvements sometimes happen through political mobilisation and patronage. This often involves construction of roads and provision of municipal water through water tankers by the municipal councillor. Improvement and development also takes place through individual self-help, with plot-owners digging their own bore-wells and septic tanks if they can afford this.

An important state intervention with respect to the *gunthewari* layouts is the Maharashtra State Government's Gunthewari Developments (Regularisation, Upgradation and Control) Act, 2001. It was legislated to allow for regularisation of the layouts and extending infrastructure and services to them. As of December 2012, NWCMC's Gunthewari Department had received applications for regularisation of 12,000 plots and had approved regularisation for 7,500 of them. Regularisation under the Act is supposed to translate into adequate basic services and infrastructure. However, this has not been realised so far since this is supposed to be financed by the regularisation fees, which are quite low.[9] Moreover, response to the Act has been low and in most layouts not even 10 per cent of the plots have been regularised yet, which means that the fees collected per layout are totally insufficient for financing infrastructure provision.

Furthermore, the tenure security of many residents could be negatively affected by the Act. Firstly, the regularisation is contingent upon furnishing recognized proof of purchase. Plot owners who lack this recognized proof are not eligible for regularisation. Out of 12,000 applications for regularisation, those of about 2,100 plot owners have been pending due to this. Since the Act empowers NWCMC to acquire the plots that are not regularised and/or to demolish any construction on them, without offering any compensation or rehabilitation, it remains to be seen if such steps are taken in the future. Secondly, under the Act, even if the plot owners have recognized proof of purchase, regularisation can be denied if the plots are on government lands, ULC lands and reserved lands, and the municipal government can acquire these plots and/or demolish construction on them without offering any compensation or rehabilitation to the plot owners. Out of 12,000 applications for regularisation, those of about 2,000 plot owners have been already rejected due to this. It does not seem like many acquisitions or demolitions have taken place yet due to the political sensitivity of such actions. The only acquisitions that have been done are for roads (since no data is available on this, it is not clear how many have been impacted by this). This also means that the open spaces needed for improving public amenities in the layouts have not been created, and thus besides the lack of adequate finances, this is another reason why improvements are unlikely to be realized in the layouts through the Act.

Here, Bhide's (2014) findings from a study of the Act's provisions as well as its implementation and impacts in three cities—Sangli-Miraj, Akola and Aurangabad—are worth some consideration. She finds that the impact of regularisation is limited in terms of improving the quality of life and converging with planning standards. This is similar to our findings from Nanded. Bhide also argues that the move towards regularisation has enhanced the sense of security and led to an appreciation in prices. While the latter is probably true in Nanded, as already explained, the former might not be the case since not all plot holders' applications are being approved and the Act has provisions for demolishing construction on non-regularised plots without compensation/rehabilitation. However, this would need to be explored through ground-level studies. Such studies would also need to interrogate whether certain groups are able to negotiate the threat of non-regularisation (and thus, the threat of reduced tenure security) through subversions and how class and vulnerability determine the possibilities of such negotiations. For instance, the threat of non-regularisation due to inadequate documents might be negotiated by buying bogus documents [Bhide (2014) points towards the existence of such practices] and the threat of non-regularisation due to location on reserved lands might be politically negotiated in ways that lead to de-reservation [Kamath and Deekshit (2014) point to how de-reserving and cancelling of reservations are negotiable processes in Solapur].

Bhide (2014) further observes that the maximum impact of regularisation is being seen in encouraging the development of new *gunthewaris* which is becoming a highly organised activity, all of which is changing the nature of *gunthewaris*, and rather than representing affordable housing for the working class, they have become a strategy for the well-off. This is again likely to be also true in Nanded. Based on this, Bhide critiques the move towards regularisation, arguing that the Act has contrary aims: to regularise and develop existing *gunthewari* settlements and to control the growth of new ones. She argues that the regularisation "is an attempt to create a constant state of exception… It enables the abdication of state responsibility towards public housing and planning, while engaging in tokenistic exercises of welfare without substance" (p. 93). Interestingly in Nanded, BSUP, an intervention for slum improvement, was implemented in many *gunthewari* layouts as well. The implication of this for the improvement of living conditions and tenure security in the *gunthewari* layouts, particularly for its low-income residents, is discussed in the next section.

State Intervention for Slum Improvement: Basic Services for the Urban Poor (BSUP)

While individual and collective self-help as well as political mobilisation and patronage have played an important role in the improvement of informal settlements in Nanded, more recently a Central Government-sponsored government housing programme has been crucial in attempting to improve housing conditions in the city's informal settlements. Here, I describe the approach that the local state took towards this programme in Nanded, the processes through which it implemented this programme and the interventions this led to, and the implications for improvement in housing conditions, including tenure security, in both squatter settlements and *gunthewari* layouts.

The Government of India launched the Jawaharlal Nehru National Urban Renewal Mission (JNNURM) in December 2005. This Mission comprised two sub-missions, Basic Services for the Urban Poor (BSUP) and Urban Infrastructure and Governance (UIG). The Mission began in 2005-06 and ended in March 2014, and targeted 65 cities across India. Central Government assistance was in the form of a grant, with the grant share depending on the category of city.[10] Since, Nanded is a city with less than one million population and was placed in the category of cities with historic/cultural significance, the Central Government's share was 80 per cent and State Government's share was 10 per cent. In Nanded, the remaining 10 per cent was to be paid by the beneficiaries of the BSUP programme. Cities were required to prepare Detailed Project Reports (DPRs) and funding was made available after the DPR was sanctioned by the State Government and then the Central Government. As already mentioned, when the NWCMC began formulating its approach to BSUP, it passed a resolution to identify any housing cluster or settlement with more than 25 houses and lack of adequate infrastructure as a slum for BSUP. As a result, the number of settlements identified as slums increased from 58 to 252 as almost 200 *gunthewari* layouts were identified as slums since they were characterised by a lack of or inadequate basic services and comprised many *katcha* houses. BSUP implementation began in 2009 and 11 DPRs were sanctioned by 2012-end, covering a total of 132 settlements and 27,985 dwelling units.[11]

Government housing programmes in slums in India have always deployed some kind of eligibility criteria to determine the basis on which individual families would be included in them. As per a January 2007 resolution of the Housing Department, Government of Maharashtra, the electoral list was to be primarily referred to while deciding the eligibility of a slum dweller for BSUP, but if the name of resident was not in the electoral list, then electricity bill, telephone bill and ration card or the proof document prescribed by the local government could be accepted. NWCMC considered a range of documents in order to identify beneficiaries: municipal corporator's *olakh-patra* (letter proving identity), municipal corporation tax receipt, registry of sale deed (only for *gunthewari* layouts), electoral card, electricity bill, school certificate with house address, ration card, PAN card, and passport. The Government of Maharashtra had a cut-off date of January 1, 1995 to determine eligibility. However, NWCMC decided not to follow any cut-off date.

The NWCMC took three approaches to BSUP: (i) *in-situ* redevelopment on municipal and State Government lands through demolition and reconstruction as a new layout comprising low-rise (ground floor or G + 1) clusters; (ii) *in-situ* redevelopment on municipal lands and in *gunthewari* layouts through demolition and reconstruction on the existing plot footprint; and (iii) relocation from a few municipal and Central Government lands due to road widening, proximity to railway tracks, location in flood prone areas and location on airport land. What is noteworthy is that the first and second approach evolved out of a process involving NWCMC's interaction with ground realities. Most of the DPRs submitted by the NWCMC for BSUP had proposed an *in-situ* redevelopment approach in which the entire settlement would be demolished, following which it would be reconstructed as per a new layout of clusters of medium-rise buildings. As explained below, NWCMC abandoned this medium-rise cluster approach due to people's oppositions, evolving the first and second approach mentioned above.

The Local State's Evolving Approach to BSUP

At the time of the first DPR's preparation, 20-30 staff from the Public Works Department (PWD) were brought in by the NWCMC to go house-to-house in the slums to create awareness about the BSUP scheme. Forms were distributed in the slums and people were asked to fill them if they were interested in the scheme. The DPR was submitted along with this expression of people's interest to the Ministry of Housing and Urban Poverty Alleviation (MoHUPA), Government of India, and was sanctioned by it. However, when the NWCMC attempted to begin implementation, people were unwilling to vacate their houses.[12] Media Matters, a theatre group that works on social issues, was therefore invited by the NWCMC to conduct participative theatre workshops in the slums and discuss various issues of BSUP with the people (Vinayak, 2011). NWCMC also began construction of four houses by paying the beneficiary share itself and, according to a municipal official, people began to show real interest in the scheme only after this. However, in the midst of these awareness activities, NWCMC also found that people opposed the new layouts proposed in the DPRs. In some slums, elected representatives tried to persuade people of these new layouts which involved making medium-rise clusters. But the opposition continued following which the NWCMC developed a new approach to try and take into account people's concerns and demands. This was the approach of *in-situ* redevelopment on the existing plot footprint. This approach was taken not only in many *gunthewari* layouts where new layouts with medium-rise clusters would have been unfeasible since most residents had recognized proof of purchase for their plots of land (for which, nonetheless, DPRs proposing new layouts had been prepared), but also on many municipal and State Government lands. The entire process leading up to actual implementation thus led the NWCMC to deviate from what had been proposed in most of the sanctioned DPRs and change its approach.[13]

Under *in-situ* redevelopment on the existing plot footprint, only *katcha* houses were demolished and reconstructed as *pucca* houses. Since the plot area could be larger or smaller in area than the government's norm for a BSUP unit (i.e. carpet area of 269 sq.ft.), thirteen design models (M-1 to M-13) were prepared for a house. When a person applied for a

BSUP house and their eligibility was approved, they could choose from these 13 designs depending on their plot size and shape as well as their preference. This was an innovative, demand-driven housing design, rather than a design imposed on people. In a few settlements, which had more or less organized layouts and where most of the houses were *katcha*, a slightly different approach was taken—this was *in-situ* redevelopment into a new layout comprising low-rise (ground floor or G+1) clusters. Here, all the houses were demolished and reconstructed as clusters comprising rows of houses with shared walls, conforming more or less to the same plot footprints.

In the midst of BSUP implementation, people expressed other concerns and desires, and the NWCMC often tried to engage with these. For instance, the NWCMC had initially decided to give one BSUP unit to one household. But later, municipal officials realized that one household might actually comprise more than one family. For example, there were households in which 2-3 brothers, each with his own family, lived together in one structure. As conflicts arose amongst families within one household over the BSUP unit, some people asked NWCMC to consider each family as a separate beneficiary. NWCMC then began to consider a maximum of two beneficiaries from households with multiple families (which meant that each family would pay a separate beneficiary contribution). Since BSUP construction had already started, the second BSUP unit was built as a first-floor addition to the ground-floor BSUP unit, with an external staircase leading up so that it was an independent dwelling unit.

A sub-approach within the approach of *in-situ* redevelopment on the existing plot footprint was also evolved in 2012 when municipal officials encountered many beneficiaries complaining to them about the quality of construction by the contractor appointed by the NWCMC. In this, NWCMC gave people the option to construct their houses themselves rather than through the contractor. Under this self-construction approach, NWCMC would release the non-beneficiary share (that is, the Central Government and State Government's share towards house construction) to the beneficiary in four stages of construction: foundation level, completion of the building envelope, construction of the roof and completion of finishing. As a result, on the one hand, NWCMC no longer needed to take on the burden of collecting the beneficiary contribution (and dealing with the non-recovery of this, which they were facing), while on the other hand, the beneficiaries were free to reduce their share of the contribution, for example, by reusing building materials from their previous dwelling structure and contributing their own labour. 10,551 dwelling units were approved for this self-construction. Some of these beneficiaries were building their dwelling units as per their aspirations since they were also not required to follow any of NWCMC's 13 design models.

The final DPR was prepared by learning from the previous experience. The DPR proposed *in-situ* redevelopment on the existing plot footprint, converting the *katcha* houses into *pucca* houses. It also proposed to improve the amenities in the settlement by recommending that some of the open plots in the unauthorised layout can be bought by NWCMC to create open spaces. At the time of research, implementation of this last DPR had just begun.

The Mixed Story of BSUP in Nanded

Nanded presents a mixed story with regard to the processes and outcomes of state intervention to improve informal housing. NWCMC engaged with the residents of the city's informal settlements in some manner, modifying and evolving its BSUP approach to address people's concerns, demands and desires. This included ignoring the layout proposed in the sanctioned DPRs and moving to a new approach of *in-situ* redevelopment on the existing plot footprint; evolving various house designs from which residents could choose; approving two BSUP houses for large households with more than one family; and allowing residents to build their own BSUP house (self-construction) since many were not satisfied with the quality of construction by the contractor. This seems to have led to not just improvement in terms of converting *katcha* houses to *pucca* houses, but satisfaction amongst many residents. Many residents, especially in the *gunthewari* layouts, were also extending their BSUP house with their own money and in both types of informal settlements those who opted for self-construction were even creating their own house designs to suit their needs and desires.

However, there have also been limitations in terms of the outcomes. Since *in-situ* redevelopment on the existing plot footprint means that the settlement's overall layout remains the same, it means that BSUP has not really led to improvements at the settlement level. While complete convergence with planning norms may not be required to realize settlement-level improvements, some settlement-level re-planning may be required at times. However, since this was not done, open spaces or spaces for other public amenities have not been created. The built-up density was high in many of the settlements and since many of the BSUP houses are two-storied (either because the plot was so small that a single BSUP house had to be built as a two-storey structure as per design model M-13, or because a second BSUP house has been built on the first floor), some of the settlements seem to have become denser. In Nagpur, where a similar approach began later on, one government official termed this as a "concretization of slums." In some settlements where an approach of *in-situ* redevelopment into a new layout comprising of low-rise (ground floor or G+1) clusters has been taken, the layout designs have involved poor positioning of sewer lines and sewer manholes, which has created wasted and difficult-to-maintain spaces. Since the houses are quite small, many residents also continue to use the pathways in front of their houses as washing spaces, but the drainage infrastructure has not been planned to accommodate such usage, thus creating open drains in the middle of the pathways.

While the approach taken in the DPRs conformed to all planning norms but was impractical and rejected by people, the approach taken on the ground seems to be the path of least resistance which has, therefore, not allowed for the provision of any public amenities, including open space and social infrastructure like health centre, childcare centre, etc. One wonders whether it might have been possible to evolve an approach somewhere in the middle of these two extremes, taking into consideration settlement-level planning; people's concerns, demands and desires; and people's patterns of using their house and immediate open spaces.

Furthermore, at the time of our research, BSUP house construction had almost been completed in many settlements but most settlements still had inadequate physical infrastructures like road, sewerage, drainage and water. The infrastructure had been laid in many settlements but connection to city networks was not done yet as city-wide infrastructure projects were still ongoing under the JNNURM. Municipal officials stated that the work was in progress. However, this non-synchronization of construction of dwelling units and physical infrastructures had led to various problems for residents. Municipal officials informed us that in some settlements residents do not always use the toilets that are built as part of the house and continue to defecate in the surrounding fields. They stated that the NWCMC had tried several times to create awareness about sanitation but had not succeeded in many cases and people's sanitation practices were not transformed through provision of a house with a toilet or even with NWCMC's awareness activities on the issue. While transforming sanitation behaviour is challenging, our research revealed that the difficulty was not confined to the question of behaviour alone, but, drainage and sewerage infrastructures were also not functional in some of the settlements. Therefore, in certain cases, residents could not use the toilets inside their BSUP house and had even built their own makeshift toilet or toilet with septic tank to cope with the lack of sewerage. One of the reasons for continuing open defecation in some settlements might, therefore, be that while toilets were built in the BSUP houses and awareness activities were carried out, the infrastructure was simply not adequate to accommodate better and safer sanitation practices.

We carried out fieldwork in February 2013 and the BSUP scheme was to end in March 2014. It is not clear whether the NWCMC was able to provide the required physical infrastructure in the short time between our research visit and BSUP's end. It might be that the provision of this infrastructure has taken place relatively more smoothly in the *gunthewari* layouts than in the squatter settlements since the existing plots in the former are quite orderly and while planning norms are not followed in either, the layouts are more spacious than the squatter settlements, often (though not always) allowing for more easy intervention in terms of putting in physical infrastructures like water, sewerage and drainage. It is also important to recognize that under the new approach, the NWCMC mainly identified households having *katcha* houses as beneficiaries. However, those with *pucca* houses could have benefited from the infrastructure provision at the settlement level. However, this had not happened extensively and thus the BSUP, despite the innovations of NWCMC, seemed to have become a house construction scheme rather than a scheme to improve the informal settlements of the poor and low-income groups. One wishes that more emphasis had been put on the physical infrastructure component in the settlements.

In many settlements, the NWCMC had also organized vermiculture workshops with community groups. However, except for a couple of settlements with pre-existing strong community groups which made vermiculture a regular part of their activities and transformed solid waste management in their neighbourhoods through this, nothing long-term could be achieved in most of the settlements. It was thus also difficult to transform communities and improve neighbourhoods and living conditions without sustained engagement with the communities.

Beneficiaries had to pay approximately Rs. 28,000 as their share towards the construction of their BSUP house. About Rs. 25,000 was to be paid on a monthly basis over six months. Many were, however, unable to afford these instalments. Initially, 200-300 households were offered loans through the Bombay Mercantile Cooperative Bank. However, the interest rate was too high (14% per annum) so people did not take the loans. Some municipal officials argued that political leaders discouraged beneficiaries from paying their share, promising them that the government would forgive their due payments. They also reported that people did not behave properly with officials who tried to collect the beneficiary contribution from them. Due to these and other reasons, including the fact that the NWCMC did not attempt a heavy-handed approach towards people for collecting their contribution, cost recovery was poor. While this is likely to benefit families with low affordability, it is not clear whether this is financially sustainable, especially if the NWCMC is left to cover this cost. This could have repercussions for future efforts by the NWCMC towards housing programmes for the urban poor.

The many delays in BSUP implementation, which occurred due to the NWCMC, the contractors as well as the residents, also created problems, some of which affected outcomes. The NWCMC required that the contractor finish each BSUP house in four months. However, our research revealed that construction often took between 6 months to one year. In Ambedkar Nagar, residents reported that the work was delayed by 2-3 years due to localized political reasons. Labour shortfall during certain times of the year was also cited as a reason for delays by the contractor. Delays also occurred because many residents did not vacate their house quickly after the contractor was awarded the tender. The NWCMC's approach of *in-situ* redevelopment on the existing plot footprint meant that converting each beneficiary's *katcha* house to a *pucca* house became a project in itself, and its progress was susceptible to that of beneficiary's expectations and interventions. This also created delays many a time. Contractors found it difficult to deal with long delays since the tender cost remained the same while the cost of building material and labour increased over time. For residents, delays after the construction of their house was started, led to longer periods of living elsewhere, either on rent or by squatting somewhere nearby. While the NWCMC began to give beneficiaries the option of building their BSUP house through self-construction rather than through a contractor appointed by the NWCMC, it did not provide the government's share of the cost (which, as earlier mentioned, was to release to the beneficiary in four instalments) easily and timely. As a result, many beneficiaries were unable to build their house quickly. The reason for the slow progress of self-construction was also that some families who depended on daily earnings were unable to even smoothly raise the funds for their share of the cost.

A final point of consideration for the implications of BSUP for the improvement and further development of (existing) informal settlements is whether this intervention enhanced tenure security. Beneficiaries are be given a *taba paavti* (a house possession document) after they finish paying their beneficiary contribution. Thus, house tenure is formalised but land tenure is not. The document mentions various conditions regarding the transfer of the house. Beneficiaries cannot rent out the house and cannot sell the house for the next 20 years. NWCMC has also made a provision for residents in the *gunthewari* layouts who are BSUP beneficiaries to regularize their plots under the Gunthewari Act by paying much lower regularization charges than other residents of these layouts. The rationale for this is that a high proportion of the regularization charges are meant for financing the provision of infrastructure in the layout, but since infrastructures are to be provided/improved through BSUP funding in the settlements selected under BSUP, the BSUP beneficiary should not be required to pay towards this infrastructure. Despite this, at the time of our research in early 2013, hardly any BSUP beneficiaries had come forward to regularize their plots under the Act. The reason for this is likely to be the fact that there is no perceived need to regularize since BSUP implementation and formal house tenure has given high tenure security as it is. It remains to be seen whether and how BSUP implementation in the *gunthewari* layouts transforms these informal settlements over time, given the processes of gentrification discussed earlier with respect to these layouts.

Conclusion

This chapter has sketched out a broad picture of informal settlements in Nanded, a mid-sized city in central India. We find that between 23 to 28 per cent of the city's residents live in slums that are mostly squatter settlements. We also find that about 20 per cent of the city's residents live in *gunthewari* layouts, which are unauthorized layouts. This means that almost 50 per cent of the city's population lives in informal settlements. This must not, however, be confused with the urban poor and low-income groups, since many *gunthewari* layouts also have an increasing number of well-off residents. It is also quite possible that many low-income residents also live in the historic core of the city which is quite congested, however, we have not done any research on this housing and the question of its informality remains unexplored.

For the two types of informal settlements that we have studied, this chapter has outlined their characteristics and the processes through which they have emerged, are improving (or which are placing obstacles in their improvement) and developing further. These processes include self-help (individual and collective); political mobilisation and political patronage; and government policies, legislations and programmes. The changing urban political economy which shapes land markets and demands for land/housing is also beginning to play a crucial role in how *gunthewari* layouts are developing and transforming in Nanded, although this aspect has not been explored in any depth by us.

The chapter has also discussed BSUP, a recent state-led intervention aimed at improving slums, to consider the approach taken at the local level and whether and how this has improved housing conditions in both these types of informal settlements. The mixed story of improvement—when one considers all three aspects: housing, infrastructure and tenure security—has been discussed which provides numerous insights into the challenges around housing interventions for the urban poor, particularly around *in-situ* redevelopment and upgradation of informal housing.

NOTES

1. This chapter is based on a research study funded at the Centre for Urban Equity (CUE), CEPT University, by SNPUPR (Support to National Policies for Urban Poverty Reduction), a Ministry of Housing and Urban Poverty Alleviation (MoHUPA) and DFID partnership. This funding was part of a programme for Strengthening National Resource Centers for supporting states and cities in developing pro-poor urban policies and programme implementation. I would like to thank Aseem Mishra and Kaushal Jajoo who were involved in the study as research associates.
2. The case-studies were selected based on tenure (squatter settlements and *gunthewari* layouts), landownership (NWCMC, State Government, Central Government, etc.), and BSUP approach (the three approaches are explained later in the paper).
3. Interview with Mr. Ratnakar Waghmare, Deputy Municipal Commissioner, NWCMC, February 2013.
4. Religious place of Sikhs.
5. 1 acre (43,560 sq.ft.) equals 40 *guntha*.
6. Interview with Mr. Sonsale S.G., Deputy Engineer, Gunthewari Department, NWCMC, February, 2013.

7. This does not take into account the fact that there are some vacant plots in many of the layouts.
8. http://nwcmc.gov.in/files/unicodedata.pdf, Accessed last on August 19, 2014.
9. NWCMC calculates regularization fees based on compounding fees (Rs. 15 per sq.mt. for the plot and nil for built-up area of FSI 1 / Rs. 100 per sq.mt. for built-up area exceeding FSI 1) and development fees (Rs. 88 per sq.mt. for the plot area and Rs.55 per sq.mt. for the built-up area). Thus, for a 900 sq.ft. plot with built-up area of FSI 1, the regularization fee would be Rs. 8,611, while for a 2000 sq.ft. plot with a built-up of FSI 1, the fee would be Rs. 29,388.
10. The large funding that Nanded was able to secure for JNNURM, including BSUP, came out of a number of inter-related dynamics. Nanded is an important holy place for adherents of the Sikh faith and the Gur ta Gaddi Tercentenary Celebrations in October 2008, to commemorate the 300th year of the holy events of Sikhism led to funding assistance to the city by the Central Government through Nanded's inclusion in JNNURM as a city with historic and cultural importance. The fact that Dr. Manmohan Singh, the then Former Prime Minister of India, is Sikh, is said to have played a part in this. Moreover, Ashok Chavan, the chairman of the centenary celebration committee, was from the same political party as Singh and was also a state-level minister at this time. Subsequently, Chavan became Maharashtra's Chief Minister from 2008-end to 2010-end, and his Lok Sabha constituency during this period was Bhokar, a town in Nanded district. All this is also said to have secured the State Government's interest in Nanded during this period.
11. The criteria used to select these settlements is not clear. 15 of the 25 notified slums were covered under BSUP. Besides that, it is not known how many of the 132 settlements were proposed-to-be-notified slums and how many were *gunthewari* layouts. As of January 2013, of the 27,985 dwelling units, 10,175 dwelling units were completed, 4,615 dwelling units were under construction and 13,195 were yet to be started. It is not known if the latter were started and completed.
12. Interview with municipal official, NWCMC, February 2013.
13. The first two DPRs were sanctioned by the Central Government in 2006-07, while DPR-3 to DPR-9 were sanctioned in January 2009 (JNNURM Project Cell-NBO 2012). The change in approach seems to have emerged after this.

9

From Land Tenure Regularization to Mass Housing in Bhopal

An Assessment

Darshini Mahadevia[1] and *Abhijit Datey*

Introduction

Housing programmes in India have moved forward from "one size fits all" mass housing provided by public housing agencies, such as the housing or slum clearance boards to people-driven approaches such as slum upgrading or redevelopment or sites and services with tenure regularization, to again mass housing by the public agencies under the Valmiki Ambedkar Awas Yojana (VAMBAY) and the Basic Services for Urban Poor (BSUP) component of the Jawaharlal Nehru National Urban Renewal Mission (JNNURM). In-between, since 2000 in all India and since 1995 in Mumbai, Slum Redevelopment Scheme (SRS), a builder-driven housing programme under a generic approach called Public-Private Partnership (PPP) for the existing slums has been implemented. The Rajiv Awas Yojana (RAY), introduced in 2009-10, and discontinued in 2014, was an approach that introduced the idea of a contextual case-to-case basis approach to slum redevelopment, with the understanding that one-size does not fit all. Often, a development option for a slum has been linked to the policy and programme guidelines of a funding agency, largely external ones, which have to be followed by the city governments receiving these funds. This chapter discusses the case of Bhopal city, which has been at the receiving end of the different approaches to slum development in India. The city slums first benefited from the Tenure Regularization Policy of 1984 of the Government of Madhya Pradesh, the state whose capital city Bhopal is, followed by people-driven slum upgrading under the Department for International Development (DFID) programme and then mass housing under the BSUP. The experience of the city, therefore, provides valuable learning lessons for those interested in the urban housing programmes in India.

The study covers two aspects. The first is to understand the efficacy of earlier slum upgrading approaches, firstly on account of extension of tenure and then followed by a donor-funded programme. The second is to understand whether mass housing solution has been beneficial, however, through applying a 'Social Audit' methodology. The first aspect has been analysed using comprehensive city level data to calculate the coverage of each of the slum upgrading programmes supported by household surveys.

Bhopal: An Overview

The city of Bhopal is the capital of the state of Madhya Pradesh since 1956. The decadal population growth rate of Bhopal was 117.8 per cent in 1951-61, followed by 70 per cent growth in the next two decades till 1981. The population growth rate has more or less stabilized in the last decade and remained at 31.2 per cent in 2001-11 decade. The main driver of city's population growth has been setting up of large public and private industries, mainly Bharat Heavy Electricals Limited (BHEL) and state government offices. The city's area expanded from 71.2 square kilometres in 1975 to 285 square kilometres by 1999. The city's gross population density of 63 persons per hectare (ha) is very low and even if the 38 square kilometres of lake area is deducted the net density still remains low at 73 persons per ha. The city is characterised by sparse low rise development with large areas as green spaces and hills. The Bhopal Municipal Corporation (BMC) consists of 14 zones and 66 wards.

Slum Profile of Bhopal

The first squatter settlements of Bhopal were the construction worker's camps in wake of spurt in the construction activity in the mid-fifties. By the early sixties, some settlements even housed people other than construction workers. The first official survey of squatters in T.T. Nagar recorded seven *jhuggi* clusters with a total of 1,741 households (HHs) (Mitra, 1988). By 1972-73, the number of squatter settlements sharply increased to 33 and majority slums were in the new centre of the capital town. These 33 settlements occupied 34.2 ha and accommodated a population of 18,150 persons, 4.7 per cent of the city's population. In between 1973-1984, Bhopal's squatter population saw a nine-fold increase. In 1984, there were 163 squatter settlements housing 31,277 households or about 178,000 people, roughly 26.5 per cent of the city's population (Mitra, 1988).

The census figures of slum populations are available only from 1981, according to which the slum population of the city increased from 41,763 to 3,99,662 from 1981 to 1991, which is staggering decadal increase of 857 per cent or annual growth rate of 25.3 per cent. According to the Census 2001, the slum population of Bhopal was 1,25,720 persons which is 8.7 per cent of the total population of Bhopal. The figure seems to be highly under-reported if compared to 1991 Census data. In 2000, another survey conducted by a team of consultants advising on "Slum Networking Project (SNP)" for Bhopal, estimated 4,68,606 people (32.6 per cent of total population) living in 266 slum settlements (Table 9.1). This list included slums from the Urban Welfare Department list[2] and the BMC slums. A new survey conducted by the BMC in November 2005 estimated 1.83 lakh households, that is, 9.36 lakh people, living in 380 identified slums in Bhopal.

Table 9.1: Population and slum population of BMC

Year	*Population*	*Slum population*	*Slum population (%)*	*Growth rate per decade (%)*
1971	384,859	19,050	4.95	—
1981	671,018	41,763	6.22	119.23
1991	1,062,771	399,662	37.61	856.98
2001	1,437,354	*468,606	*32.60	*17.25

* Census 2001 figures for slum population were much under reported therefore figures from [Himanshu Parikh, *Consulting Engineers & Youth for Unity and Voluntary Action* (YUVA) 2001)] have been substituted.

Source: Census of India 2001.

A zone-wise distribution of slum population in Bhopal (Table 9.2) shows that zones 1, 3, 5, 11 and 14 each house near about 10 per cent of the city's slum population. The highest numbers of slum pockets are located in Zone 1, which has 45 slum pockets. Of the 266 slums, 61 per cent are on state government lands, 17 per cent on central public sector and military lands, 19 per cent on private and disputed lands and 3 per cent on unknown ownership lands (Himanshu Parikh, *Consulting*

Engineers and YUVA, 2001). This makes it easier to extend tenure security under the slum development programmes of the State government.

Table 9.2: Zone-wise distribution of slum pockets and slum population, Bhopal

Zone No.	*Number of Slum Pockets*	*Total Population*	*Total Number of Households*	*Households Below Poverty Line*	*% Slum Population*
1.	45	97,658	18,655	9,205	10.4
2.	26	69,335	12,995	4,413	7.4
3.	25	96,180	19,196	15,542	10.3
4.	16	23,850	2,383	526	2.5
5.	15	89,335	20,010	13,150	9.5
6.	24	33,519	9,230	3,086	3.6
7.	22	73,581	12,477	6,919	7.9
8.	28	56,235	11,052	7,325	6.0
9.	16	63,275	12,763	5,218	6.8
10.	21	76,777	15,378	4,989	8.2
11.	46	98,753	19,946	3,234	10.5
12.	29	29,309	5,859	2,652	3.1
13.	31	40,975	8,045	1,800	4.4
14.	36	87,284	16,000	8,649	9.3
Total	380	936,066	183,989	86,708	100.0

Source: Bhopal City Development Plan 2020, p. 80.

Chronology of Housing Programmes and Policies in Madhya Pradesh

Madhya Pradesh has proactively promoted slum development through number of programmes, from the Patta Act of 1984 to implementing the BSUP schemes. But, the policies and programmes have often been marred by poor implementation or management. As per Census 2001, 24.8 per cent of the total population of Madhya Pradesh was living in urban areas which increased to 27.6 per cent in 2011. In 2001, there were nearly 2.4 million persons residing in slums in Madhya Pradesh, which was almost 15 per cent of the total urban population of the state and 4 per cent of that of the entire state (Government of Madhya Pradesh, 2007). The large number of slum population was in the cities of Indore, Bhopal, Jabalpur, and Gwalior. The Urban Housing shortage in Madhya Pradesh is estimated to be 1.29 million housing units [Ministry of Housing and Urban Poverty Alleviation (MoHUPA) 2008] and the last major national estimation of poverty in 1999-2000 revealed that 38.5 per cent of urban residents in

Madhya Pradesh were Below Poverty Line (BPL) amounting to nearly 8.1 million persons. The cities like Bhopal and Indore had a decadal growth rate of 34 per cent and 42 per cent respectively. The State Housing and Habitat Policy (SHHP) of 2007 mentioned that the increase in urban population of Madhya Pradesh was six times in last half century and the reason was inmigration, which led to increase in population residing in slums (Government of Madhya Pradesh, 2008). Our assessment is that slum population increases not just due to migration but also due to lack of affordable housing supply.

The state was the first to create a state-wide legislation for providing land tenure to slum residents, called the Patta Act of 1984.[3] This was followed by infrastructure upgradation programmes in the slums that were given *patta*. The state also has an active Housing Board, the Madhya Pradesh Housing and Infrastructure Development Board (MPHIDB), which has constructed 1,66,853 Dwelling Units (DUs) and developed 1,53,698 plots since its inception in 1973[4]. 69 per cent out of these DUs, which is 1,15,612 units, were for EWS/LIG sector[5]. Urban Development Authorities (UDAs) have also constructed large number of DUs. The state released first of its kind "State Population Policy"[6] in the year 2000 for improving family welfare programmes and SHHP in the year 2007.[7]

A state-wide programme for providing basic services to slums settlement, called Madhya Pradesh Urban Services for Poor (MPUSP), was started in 2006, which was later labelled as "Project Utthan". It was a five-year programme (2006-2011) funded by a grant from DFID, United Kingdom (UK), and aimed at four major cities of Bhopal, Indore, Jabalpur and Gwalior. The state also received a grant from UN-HABITAT and Water Aid for building a slum-level basic services database for cities of Indore and Bhopal and to undertake basic services infrastructure improvement in few settlements under the programme Slum Environment Sanitation Initiative (SESI). The state through its "Single Light Electricity" connection scheme entitled slum households with *patta* an access to metered electricity connections. BSUP and Integrated Housing and Slum Development Programme (IHSDP) under the JNNURM were also undertaken and 41,446 DUs under BSUP and 22,510 DUs under IHSDP[8] were sanctioned to be constructed till January 2012.

All the above programmes were need of the hour, as the state was dealing with the most abysmal performance in the area of water and sanitation. The 58th round of National Sample Survey Organisation (NSSO) of 2002[9] indicated that 70 per cent of households in urban slums and squatter settlements had no household-level water source, and it was

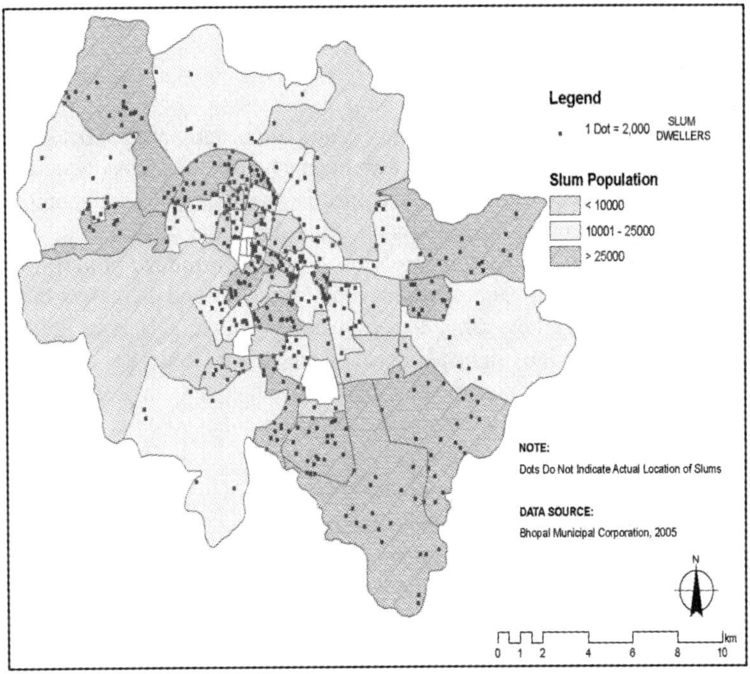

Source: Bhopal City Development Plan 2020, p. 80.
Exhibit 9.1: Location of Slums on Bhopal Map

within 0.5 km from the housing unit. 33 per cent of urban households and 70 per cent of slum households had no acccss to latrine (National Sample Survey Organisation, 2004, pp. 50,52). Consecutive survey in the 65th round revealed that only 66.8 per cent urban households had access to tap, 58.9 per cent had a water source within premises and just 75.3 per cent households got sufficient water from the first water source. 24.3 per cent households had no access to latrine and just 55 per cent had it for exclusive use.

This research has mainly looked at the city-wide implementation of four programmes mainly the Patta Act, MPUSP, SESI and BSUP in the city of Bhopal. Housing programmes like BSUP, based on mass housing construction, have started becoming a regular norm and are seen as best alternatives to housing problems. This research also looks at the complexities of such programmes by using social audit methodology in two settlements rehabilitated under BSUP.

A City-wide Assessment of Programmes

Patta Act

The security of tenure is known to be one of the most important steps leading to housing investments in low income households. It is frequently asserted that secure formal land tenure is an efficacious tool for the alleviation of poverty, especially in urban informal settlements. The conventional view is that secure tenure works to reduce poverty by increasing the security of households against eviction and increasing their access to credit markets using their property as collateral (Payne, 2002). Tenure regularization can be achieved by providing Land titles or rights. Land rights exist as a part of other rights in society as a whole and one cannot be changed easily without the change in others (Payne, 1997).

The Government of Madhya Pradesh decided to take the land tenure security route in the year 1984, when a special legislation for granting land tenure to slum households was enacted called the Patta Act 1984. A new department of urban welfare was set up under the revenue department for the implementation of this act, with power vested with the district collector to authorize *patta* granting. The Madhya Pradesh Slum Clearance Board (MPSCB) was brought directly under the ambit of department of urban welfare and the responsibility of carrying out slum surveys in the city was delegated to it. A list of slum settlements was prepared by MPSCB with exact land ownership status. In a record time of 4 months the work of slum survey and granting *pattas* was completed. A beneficiary household living in the surveyed household had to present an address proof issued before the cut-off date to be eligible to receive a *patta*.

Two kinds of *patta* could be issued: (i) permanent *patta* (referred to as Form-B) or temporary *patta* (referred to as Form-C). The slums with temporary *patta* could be relocated through any government housing scheme if the slum's land was required for public purpose. The type of *patta* a slum settlement was qualified to receive was decided by the officer in charge based on ownership of the particular land. It was easier to grant *patta* to slums on state government land, while it was not possible to give *patta* to slum on a private land or even Central Government and military lands. Therefore, lands other than state or municipal government ownership were out this Act's ambit and hence 39 per cent did not get its benefit. The process of decision of granting permanent or temporary *patta* was also not very transparent and many settlements earmarked for resettlement were given permanent *patta* for reasons unknown (Mitra

1988). BHEL which is a public sector organisation of Government of India owning vast amount of lands in Bhopal, also declined the proposal of granting *patta* on its land. The issue of land security for the poor on privately owned and central government land, therefore, remained unsolved (Banerjee, 2002).

In 2001 according to a survey by the consultants, only 177 out of 266 slums had *patta*, with 29 per cent (23,195) slum households having permanent *patta*, 12 per cent (10,541) households getting temporary *patta* and remaining 59 per cent (44,375) had no *patta* (Himanshu Parikh, Consulting Engineers and Youth for Unity and Voluntary Action (YUVA), 2001). Observed zone-wise (Table 9.3), a few zones benefited more from

Table 9.3: Zone-wise coverage of *patta*, Bhopal

Zone No.	*Ward Nos.*	*% Wards covered by patta*	*% Slums covered by patta*	*% HHs covered by patta (Perm. + Temp.)*	*% HHs covered by Perm. patta*	*% HHs without patta*
1.	1, 2, 3, 4	100	66	56.0	50.5	44.0
2.	5, 6, 7, 8, 9, 10, 13	71	60	25.6	15.0	74.4
3.	11, 12, 14, 15, 16	100	56	44.4	44.4	55.6
4.	17, 18, 19, 20, 21, 22	17	43	25.9	16.6	74.1
5.	23, 24, 25, 26, 27, 34	67	43	44.7	41.8	55.3
6.	28, 29, 30, 31	100	77	60.6	42.0	39.4
7.	35, 36, 37, 38, 43, 44	67	43	11.9	4.6	88.1
8.	45, 46, 47, 64	100	77	52.7	11.8	47.3
9.	32, 33, 48, 49, 50	100	81	65.3	37.9	34.7
10.	54, 55, 56, 57, 58, 59	50	50	9.8	8.1	90.2
11.	60, 61, 62, 63	100	53	29.0	26.6	71.0
12.	65, 66	100	100	83.4	72.5	16.6
13.	39, 40, 41, 42	75	55	36.4	20.5	63.6
14.	51, 52, 53	100	65	73.0	46.1	27.0
	Grand Total	**77**	**67**	**43.2**	**29.7**	**56.8**

Source: Collector's Survey of Slums 2000 [Himanshu Parikh, Consulting Engineers and Youth for Unity and Voluntary Action (YUVA) 2001] and Zone-wise calculation by Datey, 2010.

the Patta Act while others were left out. For example, zones 12 and 14 had the maximum coverage of *patta*, which was 83.4 and 73 per cent respectively, while the least coverage was in Zone 10. Also, Zone 1 with most slums had 44 per cent slum households without *patta*.

An important loophole in the *patta* distribution process was that the poor were on the mercy of surveyors and had to wait to get discovered and included in the slum list. The act did not prescribe any mechanism by which slum residents could approach the department of urban welfare as a community to ask for *patta*. The approach was very much top down and also favoured all kinds of political pressures to include or exclude a settlement.

A provision within the Patta Act enabled slum households to get basic services from the urban local body (ULB). The act commanded ULBs to extend basic services to all *patta*-settlements. A minimal lease rent of Rs. 1/sq.mt. for the purpose was also prescribed, but this meagre amount was never collected.

Our intention here was also to check if provision of *patta* has brought any betterment in the provision of basic services in the city slums. One slum with *patta* provision and another without *patta* provision was selected from each zone housing more than 10 per cent of city slums. Availability of basic services was then compared between the two.

Slums with *patta* were found to be having better linkages to the city-level basic services like water supply and sewerage. They also had lower households dependent on a single common tap and had larger penetration of household-level water connection and toilets. The first major reason the Act itself envisaged was extending these services in the slum. Further, the *patta* gives household an address to receive services from the local government and also other subsidy schemes from the government, such as for constructing toilets and many others including city-level programmes for betterment of basic services. Garbage disposal was found to be a major problem across slums, but one with *patta* had better collection and disposal.

Almost 28 years have passed since the enactment of the Patta Act, but the benefits of the programme have remained patchy. There are still many slums in the city which do not have access to basic services at household level and this is an urgent need to be addressed. Slums with *patta* have legal right to get connected to city-level basic services, and it is the duty of the municipal corporation to make capital investments for better access to basic services.

Table 9.4[10]: Basic services availability in *patta* slums *vis-à-vis* non-*patta* slums, Bhopal

Indicators	*Zone-1*		*Zone-3*		*Zone-5*		*Zone-11*		*Zone-14*	
	P	*NP*	*P*	*NP*	*P*	*NP*	*P*	*NP*	*P*	*NP*
Name of the Settlement	Dhobi Ghat	CRP Jhuggi	J.P. Nagar	Shakti Nagar	Roshanpura	Hasnat Nagar	Arjun Nagar	Bijli Nagar	Saibaba Nagar	Ishvar Nagar
No. of Households	1,000	400	1,230	335	3,000	3,200	400	400	1,650	1,609
Households per public stand post	67	100	38	84	300	320	67	80	33	80
% household level water tap	70	20	8	0	0	0	0	0	2	0
% household toilets	50	25	65	48	53	38	50	38	70	10
% disposing waste in open drains, septic tanks and sewage networks	95	50	51	50	60	56	100	43	90	50
% with access to secondary container	100	72	49	30	50	0	0	0	0	0

*P-*Patta*, NP-non-*Patta*

Source: Poverty Pockets Situation Analysis Data from Water Aid. Analysis by indicators from Datey, 2010.

MPUSP and SESI

MPUSP and SESI were both based on the basic services enhancement approach for slums. While MPUSP was a big programme with adequate funding, SESI was a comparatively smaller project with very limited coverage. The MPUSP was funded by a DFID support of £41[11] million for five years (2006-2011) and implemented in partnership with the BMC. The SESI had very limited funding from the partners like WaterAid and UN-HABITAT. But, its main objective of creating a slum database in the city with details of basic services was useful and was extensively used by the BMC and other allied agencies for slum development programmes. This database is titled Poverty Pockets Situation Analysis (PPSA). The MPUSP also relied on the same database for selection of slums for implementation. Thus, the SESI did not have any direct impact on slum households.

The MPUSP's main objective was to directly reduce proportion of poor without access to safe drinking water and sanitation and leading to infant mortality reduction. The programme aimed to target 25 per cent of the poorest households, which were selected by using a 3×3 matrix method, allotting scores to settlements to prioritize investments. The BMC set up a project cell in their office for the implementation of the project. In 2009, MPUSP programme identified 44 settlements for implementation, which consisted of the following steps:

1. **Initial Desk Screening**: Selection of slums was undertaken by 3×3 Matrix. A survey was undertaken to rectify data gaps, verify exact number of households, identify households with *patta*, area of the settlement, land ownership details and reservation of land in Master plan.
2. **Technical Screening**: Technical screening involved site survey to gauge the availability of trunk infrastructure, land slope and other technical aspects necessary for creating comprehensive maps.
3. **Community Organisation**: Community organisation involved participatory meetings to explain the people about the programme. A Basti Vikas Samiti (BVM) was formed consisting of a volunteer from every lane of the settlement, with a ratio of one volunteer for 20-40 households. Women were encouraged to be the volunteers of BVM. A volunteer per lane was appointed.
4. **Micro-Planning:** The volunteer, with the participation of households in the lane created maps of the lane, showing existing infrastructure in black and marking required infrastructure red colour. The volunteer was trained to sketch the map of the lane with symbols decided for each infrastructure. All the lane maps were then joined to form a complete map of the settlement.
5. **Technical Assessment:** The plan's cost was estimated and the proposal sent to Municipal Committee, MPUSP Cell and Urban Administration and Development Department (UADD) for

approval. A Detailed Project Report (DPR) was then formulated after which the work commenced.

MPUSP's settlement-level volunteers were trained to monitor construction quality. The overall mechanism of planning and implementation was very participatory in nature and community was involved at every stage of the process.

MPUSP covered only 12 per cent of slums and merely 8 per cent of the city's slum households (Table 9.5). Most of these households were located in the zones with high proportion of slum households. A major drawback of the MPUSP programme was that only slums situated on state government land were eligible for selection under the programme and slums on private or disputed lands were left out, even if they were qualifying according to the 3×3 matrix. The benefit, therefore, went to slums which already had *patta* provision and were anyways eligible to get city level services.

The SESI was a joint programme between the UN-HABITAT, the WaterAid and the BMC. It aimed at creating replicable models of provision of basic services in slums. SESI was implemented in the project

Table 9.5: Zone-wise coverage of MPUSP, Bhopal

Zone No.	Ward Nos.	Wards	% ward covered	% HHs covered	% slums covered
1.	1, 2, 3, 4	4	100	17	22
2.	5, 6, 7, 8, 9, 10, 13	7	14	0	4
3.	11, 12, 14, 15, 16	5	80	12	24
4.	17, 18, 19, 20, 21, 22	6	17	3	6
5.	23, 24, 25, 26, 27, 34	6	0	0	0
6.	28, 29, 30, 31	4	25	3	8
7.	35, 36, 37, 38, 43, 44	6	17	3	9
8.	45, 46, 47, 64	4	100	11	14
9.	32, 33, 48, 49, 50	5	40	5	13
10.	54, 55, 56, 57, 58, 59	6	83	18	24
11.	60, 61, 62, 63	4	75	1	7
12.	65, 66	2	50	14	10
13.	39, 40, 41, 42	4	0	0	0
14.	51, 52, 53	3	67	18	14
	Grand Total	**66**	**44**	**8**	**12**

Source: Project Data by BMC, PPSA Data from Water Aid and Zone, Ward and HH-wise tabulation by Datey 2010.

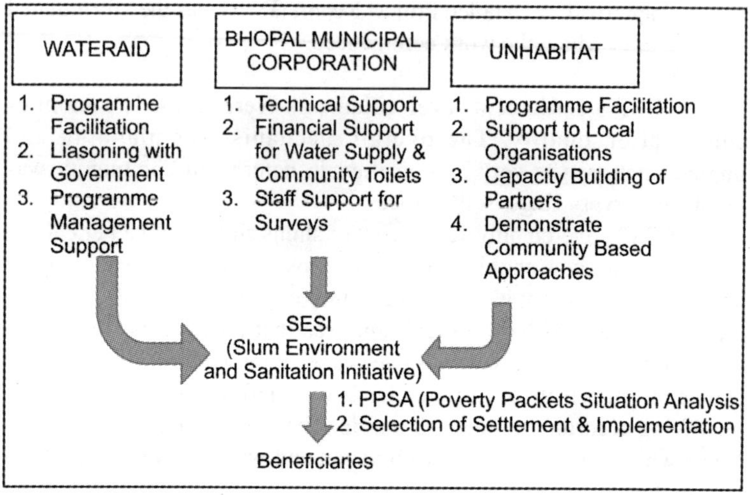

Source: Datey 2010.

Exhibit 9.2: SESI partners and implementation

cities in a tri-partite partnership model (Exhibit 9.2), bringing together either resources or expertise from the UN-HABITAT, WaterAid India and its local NGO partners and the four municipal corporations of Madhya Pradesh of Bhopal, Gwalior, Indore and Jabalpur. The programme undertook survey of all the poverty pockets in the city collecting information about level of basic services in slum pockets and published PPSA 2005. The BMC undertook upgrading of 16 slums, selected from the PPSA survey, by providing the households with individual water connections, community toilets (wherever space for individual toilets was not available), sewerage network, road and street lights. BMC also implemented pilot community solid waste management and low-cost sanitation projects. SESI benefited just 8,290 households. The work undertaken under the programme was not even completed at many places due to lack of community involvement and monitoring. The programme ended up covering just 5 per cent households in the city and just 4 per cent of city's slums (Table 9.6).

BSUP

The first project under the BSUP in Bhopal was sanctioned by the Government of India (GoI) in 2006. Since then a total of 16 projects having 23,609 DUs have been sanctioned. The programme was to be

Table 9.6: Zone-wise coverage of SESI, Bhopal

Zone No.	Ward No's	Wards	% ward covered	% HHs covered	% slums covered
1.	1, 2, 3, 4	4	50	6	7
2.	5, 6, 7, 8, 9, 10, 13	7	14	13	8
3.	11, 12, 14, 15, 16	5	40	6	8
4.	17, 18, 19, 20, 21, 22	6	0	0	0
5.	23, 24, 25, 26, 27, 34	6	0	0	0
6.	28, 29, 30, 31	4	0	0	0
7.	35, 36, 37, 38, 43, 44	6	0	0	0
8.	45, 46, 47, 64	4	25	7	11
9.	32, 33, 48, 49, 50	5	0	0	0
10.	54, 55, 56, 57, 58, 59	6	17	13	5
11.	60, 61, 62, 63	4	25	6	7
12.	65, 66	2	50	11	7
13.	39, 40, 41, 42	4	0	0	0
14.	51, 52, 53	3	0	0	0
	Grand Total	**66**	**14**	**5**	**4**

Source: MPUSP Project Data by BMC, PPSA Data from Water Aid and Zone, Ward and HH-wise tabulation by Datey 2010.

jointly implemented by the BMC and Bhopal Development Authority (BDA) in their respective areas. The responsibility of the BMC was to construct 18,542 housing units in various parts of the city. Till April 2011, BMC was able to start work at four sites. Construction had started on 5,692 housing units, 2,172 housing units were completed and allotment was completed for 1,113 housing units (Table 9.7).[12]

A decision of *in-situ* rehabilitation was taken, but required temporary relocation during construction period. The beneficiary selection under the scheme was highly centralized without any logic behind the selection of settlements. *Prima facie* it appears that settlements on prime urban lands owned by the government were selected for implementation. The households were asked to present a proof of residence of last three years. Election cards, ration cards and also *patta* documents were accepted as proof. Large number of households had *patta*, as BSUP was implemented only on state government lands. Thirty settlements were chosen for the scheme, and most of them were ones already covered under the Patta Act.

In BSUP, a Central Government grant of 50 per cent is provided and rest has to be borne by the state, city and the beneficiaries. In case of

Bhopal, the city's share was funded by Housing and Urban Development Corporation (HUDCO) as loan and the beneficiary-share was envisaged as loan by public sector banks. The loan instalment was kept to be Rs. 910 per month to be paid for 15 years at eight per cent rate of interest, which would remain floating. This instalment was seen as a big burden by the beneficiaries, including the extra burden on them put by electricity charges, maintenance charges and property taxes also. The norms envisaged EWS household's income to be Rs. 3,300 per month in 2009-11, the instalment thus coming to more than 25 per cent of the income, which is considered unaffordable. Our discussion with the households revealed that most of them were not regularly paying instalments and therefore, there were clear signs of housing falling apart in absence of maintenance. There was also a fear that the banks would forfeit the units due to non-repayment.

Table 9.7: BSUP Projects, Bhopal

Sl. No.	*BSUP DPRs*	*Sanction date*	*Units approved*	*Units allotted*[13]
1.	Shyam Nagar & Rishi Nagar	March 31, 2006	1,440	124
2.	Indrapuri & Kalpna Nagar	March 31, 2006	212	164
3.	Kotra (Weekly market) Housing units for Shabri Nagar & Bapu Nagar	March 31, 2006	512	0
4.	Rehabilitation of Baba Nagar, Shahpura	December 14, 2006	1,872	0
5.	Rehabilitation of Ganga Nagar & Aradhana Nagar	December 14, 2006	1,848	0
6.	Rehabilitation of Indira Nagar Phase-I	December 29, 2006 and February 2, 2007	1,216	0
7.	Indira Nagar Phase-II	February 2, 2007	896	0
8.	Rehabilitation of Bajpainagar, Police Line, Atal Ayub Nagar etc.	December 29, 2006	3,328	0
9.	Rehabilitation of Arjun Nagar, Bhim Nagar, Madrasi Colony	February 14, 2006	3,528	196
10.	Roshanpura	March 31, 2006	3,600	0

Source: BMC 2009.

An evident bias is visible towards Zone 6, as it was most centrally located and slums were located on high value lands (Table 9.8). 61 per cent of slum households in Zone 6 were covered under BSUP scheme where 44 per cent households already had permanent *patta*. The situation was similar in Zones 2, 14 and 9 which proves that households with *patta* were mainly able to access the benefits of BSUP. The programme in total covered just 10 per cent of the city's slum households.

Table 9.8: Zone-wise coverage of BSUP

Zone No.	*Ward Nos.*	*No. of wards*	*% ward covered*	*% HHs covered by permanent patta*	*% HHs covered by BSUP*
1.	1, 2, 3, 4	4	0	50.5	0
2.	5, 6, 7, 8, 9, 10, 13	7	14	15.0	24
3.	11, 12, 14, 15, 16	5	20	44.4	9
4.	17, 18, 19, 20, 21, 22	6	0	16.6	0
5.	23, 24, 25, 26, 27, 34	6	17	41.8	7
6.	28, 29, 30, 31	4	75	42.0	61
7.	35, 36, 37, 38, 43, 44	6	0	4.6	0
8.	45, 46, 47, 64	4	0	11.8	0
9.	32, 33, 48, 49, 50	5	40	37.9	28
10.	54, 55, 56, 57, 58, 59	6	0	8.1	0
11.	60, 61, 62, 63	4	25	26.6	1
12.	65, 66	2	0	72.5	0
13.	39, 40, 41, 42	4	0	20.5	0
14.	51, 52, 53	3	33	46.1	21
	Grand Total	**66**	**15**	**29.7**	**10**

Source: BSUP Project Data by BMC, Zone, Ward and HH-wise tabulation by Datey 2010.

Household Level Assessment of Programmes

A detailed primary survey was carried out to assess the programmes' services coverage and people's satisfaction with them. Total 384 household questionnaires were canvassed in nine settlements, one in each ward. Three each were under the MPUSP and BSUP programme, two under the Patta Act and one under the SESI (Table 9.9).

Settlement-level analysis of availability of basic services was also made and it was quite evident that solid waste management services were not available in most of the settlements (Table 9.10). The household-level data showed that the MPUSP and *patta* slums were enjoying better quality of basic services, where 40 per cent and 26 per cent of households had access to household-level water tap in MPUSP and *patta* settlements respectively (Table 9.11). Availability of household-level toilets stood at 75 per cent and 55 per cent respectively. Household-level solid waste collection was non-existent in most of the slums, as the solid waste management was in a sorry state everywhere irrespective of the housing

Table 9.9: Details of surveyed slums, Bhopal

Zone No.	*Ward No.*	*Programme name*	*Settlement name*	*No. of HH*	*Sample %*	*Sample size*
3	11	MPUSP	Durga Nagar	240	15	30
12	66	MPUSP	Timer Market ki Jhuggi	150	15	22
3	11	MPUSP	Harijan Basti (Nariyal Khera)	128	15	20
2	9	SESI	Bharat Mata Nagar ki Jhuggi	1,300	10	130
7	35	Patta Act	Om Nagar	400	10	40
9	32	Patta Act	Shiv Nagar	450	10	45
9	49	BSUP	Shyam Nagar	124	20	25
8	46	BSUP	Madrasi Colony	196	20	40
13	65	BSUP	Kalpana Nagar	164	20	32
			Total	**3,152**		**384**

Source: Primary Survey.

Table 9.10: Basic services profile of surveyed settlements, Bhopal

Ward No.	*Settlement name*	*Water supply*	*Toilets*	*SWM*
11	Durga Nagar	Alternate 30 min.	Household-level	No collection
66	Timer Market ki Jhuggi	Daily 30 min.	Household-level	Secondary container
11	Harijan Basti (Nariyal Khera)	Daily 30 min	Household-level	No collection
9	Bharat Mata Nagar ki Jhuggi	Variable 30 Min.	Community toilet	No collection
35	Om Nagar	Alternate 3 Hours	No toilet	No collection
32	Shiv Nagar	Daily 2 Hours	One community toilet	Secondary container
49	Shyam Nagar	Daily 20 Min.	Household level	No collection
46	Madrasi Colony	Daily 30 Min.	Household level	No collection
65	Kalpana Nagar	Daily 15 Min.	household level	Secondary container

Source: Primary Survey.

Table 9.11: Basic services status of surveyed households, Bhopal

Sl. No.	*Programme*	*Water supply source %*		*Toilet availability %*			*SWM %*
		HH tap	*Community level tap*	*HH level*	*Community*	*Open*	*Secondary container*
1.	BSUP*	100	0	100	0	0	72
2.	MPUSP	40	60	75	1	24	38
3.	SESI	13	87	5	58	36	1
4.	Patta Act	26	74	55	2	42	58
	All Programmes	43	57	53	21	26	38

Source: Primary Survey.

programmes. A large number of households used settlement-level garbage containers to dispose their solid waste, except in SESI settlements where 99 per cent households resorted to threw garbage on nearby empty plots.

Just 8 per cent households lived in *katcha* house whereas overwhelming 63 per cent lived in semi-*pucca* and 29 per cent in *pucca* DUs (Table 9.12). In *patta* slums, 40 per cent DUs were *pucca* and another 56 per cent semi-*pucca*, which showed that provision of *patta* did lead to housing investments by households and thus there were improvements in tune with the theories of land security. However, it is surprising to note that settlements covered under the MPUSP programme were also found to be having similar characteristics; 43 per cent houses in them were already *pucca*, which indicates that something went wrong in selecting the slums under the MPUSP programme and the 3×3 matrix method did not lead to the right choices. There can be two reasons for the same. One, the slums which were selected under MPUSP may have enjoyed a higher political patronage than the others and second that the BSUP was implemented on only state government slums, which already had *patta* and hence a better housing quality. Higher political patronage can also be assessed from the fact that only 49 per cent of households in MPUSP slums were actually EWS. On the whole, 60 per cent households in our study area were EWS. Further, 83 per cent of households in MPUSP already had *patta* leading to better housing conditions. The households covered under BSUP already had access to *patta*; 87 per cent had permanent *patta* before owning a BSUP house, one per cent had temporary *patta* and 51.6 per cent already owned a *pucca* house. This proves how the sole purpose of BSUP programme got defeated due to wrong selection of the beneficiaries. Thus, there has been duplication of benefits for some of the *patta* slums; firstly, they were covered under the MPUSP and then under the BSUP!

Table 9.12: Income, housing type and *patta* status of surveyed households, Bhopal

Sl. No.	*Programme Name*	*Income group %*			*Housing type %*			*Permanent patta %*
		EWS	*LIG*	*MIG*	*Katcha*	*Pucca*	*Semi-pucca*	
1.	BSUP	61	36	3	—	—	—	—
2.	MPUSP	49	46	6	4	43	53	83
3.	SESI	64	35	2	12	14	74	60
4.	Patta Act	61	38	1	4	40	56	81
	All Programmes	60	38	3	8	29	63	72

Source: Primary Survey.

One part of the survey was also to capture people's own assessment of the housing programme they benefited from. The questions were dealt with satisfaction with the quality of water supply, sanitation and public works in the programmes. The BSUP households were also asked about the construction quality of houses. None of the programmes were able to satisfy people to the fullest, but MPUSP which covered mostly better-off households and had a more participatory nature of planning stood out specifically (Table 9.13).

Table 9.13: Level of dissatisfaction with basic services, Bhopal

Sl. No.	*Programme Name*	*% dissatisfied HH*			
		Water supply	*Sanitation*	*Public works*	*Construction quality*
1.	BSUP	84	66	56	87
2.	MPUSP	30	100	78	—
3.	SESI	63	81	7	—
4.	Patta Act	44	62	60	—
	All Programmes	53	79	55	—

Source: Primary Survey.

Although dissatisfaction with water supply was a general phenomenon across slums due to very limited and irregular water supply available, the level of dissatisfaction was the highest in BSUP programme where 84 per cent of households were dissatisfied by the water supply and 66 per cent were dissatisfied by the level of sanitation. 79 per cent people in all settlements were dissatisfied with the sanitation provided and 52 per cent of them complained of chocking drains while other 33 per cent claimed the construction to be faulty. 87 per cent of the BSUP households totally rejected the construction quality of their houses.

Inadequate Planning and Implementation

Bhopal is one of the rare cities in India, where almost all major kinds of housing and infrastructure provision programmes for urban poor have been undertaken. The city has done a gamut of programmes from land tenure regularization to housing construction, and many of these are still running parallel. These programmes have undoubtedly benefited many, but still have remained insufficient to change much for the poor households. As high as 65 per cent of the city's slum households still depend on public taps for water; only 31 per cent have access to piped water supply and 42 per cent of the people resort to open defecation. Over 40 per cent of the poverty pockets report the incidence of water logging (UN-HABITAT, BMC and Water Aid, 2006). Programmes were started with great enthusiasm, but the implementation slackened as the time went by. *Patta* only penetrated to 29 per cent of the total slum households, while the city's housing shortage by 2012 was estimated to reach 4.4 lakh (BMC, 2005). On the whole, just 35 per cent slum hosueholds have benefitted from all these programmes (Table 9.14). What lies behind is inability to converge all these programmes by integrating them into a larger city context through comprehensive planning. Bhopal's city development plan also claimed that the government interventions implemented towards betterment of the slum community were lot in number but they lacked the integrated approach. Ironically, one slum benefitted from number of programmes while large number were left out. If those who have benefitted twice are taken out then (12.6% households), on the whole, just 22.6 per cent households have benefitted from all the programmes together.

Implementation of any programme should usually start from surveying the settlements. Slum lists in Bhopal were repeatedly made,

Table 9.14: Households benefitted, Bhopal

Name of programme	*No. of Households benefitted*	*% to total slum households*
Patta Act	23,195	12.6
SESI	8,290	4.5
MPUSP	14,649	8.0
BSUP	18,542	10.1
Total	64,676	35.2
Benefited more than once	23,097	12.6
Actual benefitted	41,580	22.6

Source: Compiled from the BMC data.

for different purposes and each new programme did its own survey and formulated a new list instead of enriching and updating the prior one. Three surveys were done in the city, one by the Census of 2001, which has been discarded for all practical purposes. In 2000, Himanshu Parikh and YUVA consultants did the first verification of slums, by taking the district collector's list as the base list and matching it with the slum list of BMC. The study estimated 266 slum pockets housing 4.68 lakh people. In 2005, PPSA survey was conducted by UN-HABITAT, WatcrAid and BMC to implement SESI concluded that there were 380 slum pockets in Bhopal housing 9.6 lakh population. The slum population doubled in just 5 years! Finally, the dust on the slum estimates in Bhopal has settled down and PPSA survey figures have been finally adopted. The newly made Bhopal Master Plan 2021 quotes the PPSA survey figures.

The base was not accurately drawn, due to which many programmes overlapped each other and ended up benefiting same set of beneficiaries. In most of the new programmes such as BSUP and MPUSP, the PPSA slum list was used which had no mention of the land status of slums. This was the major reason that all the 30 settlements considered for BSUP already had full or partial access to *patta*, and *patta* was also in the list of eligibility documents required to get BSUP dwelling unit. This was completely bizarre, as BSUP ended up giving security of tenure to those, who already had it. Five settlements were considered for both SESI and MPUSP and one settlement featured in both MPUSP and BSUP's list. This overlap was found to be decreasing the number of households benefitted by 12.6 per cent, from 35.2 per cent to just 22.6 per cent.

Problems also emerged due to fragmented institutional arrangements. There were three major state government departments involved in these schemes. Department of Revenue (DoR) was involved in deciding the slums to be given *patta* and also during the allotment of land for construction of houses for the poor. The other two departments involved were Department of Urban Development and Department of Housing and Environment. The BMC did not own any land in the city and hence was not the partner in implementing the Patta Act. The funding agencies like UN-HABITAT and DFID influenced the BMC in selection of slums for programmes, resulting in the BMC's inability to converge all these programmes into a city-level strategy. This was also visible in the way BSUP beneficiaries were selected. The list had to be first approved by the Municipal Council and then by the District Collector for verification of *patta* document. A lot of time was consumed in transferring the land

Table 9.15: A Summary of findings, Bhopal slum development programme

Provisions	*BSUP*	*MPUSP*	*SESI*	*Patta Act*
	Housing and basic services	*Basic services*	*Basic Services*	*Land*
Budget for programme (Rs. Crores)	200.04	21.00	1.40	N.A.
Total beneficiary HHs.	18,542	14,649*	8,290	23,195**
Land status coverage	*In-situ upgradation* covers slums on State Govt. lands. *Relocation* covers slums on other lands	Covers slums on State Govt. land only	Covers slums on State Govt. Lands only.	Covers slums on State Govt. land only.
De-notification clause	Available	Not-available	Not-available	Not-available
Beneficiary selection Approval***	BMC, DoR and UADD	BMC, DFID and UADD	BMC & UADD	DoUW & UADD
Participation	Not participatory	Very participatory	Participatory	Not participatory
Formation of resident welfare society satisfaction levels	Yes	Yes	Yes	Yes
9.1 Water supply	16%	38%	70%	56%
9.2 Construction	0%			
9.3 Public works	44%	93%	22%	40%
9.4 Sanitation	34%	19%	0%	38%

* Were expected to benefit in near future in 2010.
** Only permanent *patta* holders were considered as beneficiaries.
*** Department of Revenue (DoR), Urban Administration and Development Directorate (UADD), Department of Urban Welfare (DoUW).

Source: Datey 2010.

from *patta* beneficiaries to the Municipal Corporation and finally, deciding the list of beneficiaries.

It is intriguing that programmes with highest expenditure ended up dissatisfying people more and acquired lesser coverage. It is commendable that Bhopal repeatedly picked best approaches for improving housing and basic services for slums, as most of the BSUP projects taken up by BMC were *in-situ*. It also favoured participatory approach to plan under the MPUSP. But, unfortunately, the outcomes were not as desired. *Patta* was supposed to evoke better basic services and housing investments, but even if it was realized to some extent, the assets created were demolished by BMC to construct BSUP housing. The former *patta* (land) owners were converted into debtors through forcing people to borrow for the BSUP. During the BSUP construction, households were located to temporary sites. The process of construction dragged on due to land acquisition and contractual issues and many households converted their temporary dwellings into permanent abodes. On the temporary relocation sites, the housing quality and basic services availability worsened as compared to their original housing on *patta* sites!

BSUP was launched with great expectation and huge budget (Table 9.15) and subsidy. It was expected to be a better programme than its predecessors but it ended up disappointing even more. The abandoning of contextual multi-approach housing programmes for BSUP created an unwarranted mess and slum like high rise blocks. The possible reasons of apparent failure of the BSUP and its impact on slum households are discussed in the next section. The method adopted of assessment is the Social Audit.

Social Audit of Bhopal's BSUP: Methodology and Process

BSUP's components have a direct link to the urban poor households and the success of the programme, therefore, requires community mobilisation, participation and support from the slum dwellers for its timely and successful implementation. To minimize the effects of relocation and shifting to transit shelter during the construction phase, the 'beneficiary households' (the term used by the government), should participate in the process. Hence, we would like to call them 'participating households'. Thus, it is of importance that all the decisions on BSUP housing are taken in consultation with the community. A people-centric evaluation of programmes such as BSUP is a necessity to understand the positive and negative dimensions of the implementation so that better evaluation mechanisms are evolved and there is a possibility of introducing programme corrective mechanisms while the implementation is on-going.

Social Audit is an independent and participatory evaluation tool for evaluating the performance of a public agency or a programme or scheme. It is an evaluation by the civil society in general, and the 'beneficiary households' in particular, of the programme or scheme delivery. Social Audit enables the civil society to assess whether the agency lives up to the shared values and objectives it is committed to. Social Audit also helps to rectify the deficiencies in a programme and to redesign the objectives, focus and mode of implementation. The key objectives of Social Audit are:

1. To ensure proper implementation of the scheme under audit;

2. To ensure accountability in implementing the scheme;
3. To ensure participation of all the stakeholders;
4. To ensure community participation and help them to realize their rights and entitlements; and
5. To identify and resolve gaps and mismanagement.

It is extremely important that Social Audits are undertaken in collaboration with state and city governments, as it helps to generate a transparent dialogue between people and the authorities. These audits need to be facilitated by Non-governmental Organisations (NGOs), Community-based Organisations (CBOs) and research institutions, by innovating better and effective methodologies. Their involvement is also required to make the process structured and transparent. The Social Audit of the BSUP projects in Bhopal is based on a methodology developed by the team of Unnati, a NGO with very rich experience in conducting Social Audits of National Rural Employment Guarantee Scheme (NREGS) in Gujarat and Centre for Urban Equity (CUE), CEPT University.[14] Subsequently, the methodology evolved during the actual exercise in response to the needs.

The focus of the whole exercise remained on generating people-centric, participatory mechanisms to create an environment where people feel free to talk, suggest and complain about the project in a structured way, so that grievances are heard and addressed by the city authorities. The exercise also dwelt on creating a common platform which brought together people, NGOs and city government to create a fruitful dialogue and discussion about the implementation of the programme, which in turn would be helpful to evoke possible post-project rectification in a step-by-step manner.

The process undertaken had three phases, namely the pre-audit process, social audit and public consultation and post-audit process. The pre-audit process involved collection of initial information of the BSUP project and gathering documents listed in Exhibit 9.3. The officials of the concerned city were informed about the Social Audit methodology and a round of meetings were held with them to understand various stages involved in beneficiary selection process and implementation mechanisms. The relevant data was then collected and analysed to select the settlements for Social Audit. A visit to all the implemented BSUP sites was also undertaken to finalize the settlements to be taken for the audit. A second meeting was then held with the people in the selected settlements to explain the concept and need of Social Audit. The dates of the audit were decided through

Exhibit 9.3: List of documents required for the social audit process

No.	Document	Contents	Role in the process
1.	Latest Monthly Progress Report (MPR)	1. No. of city-wide projects, project cost, funding shares, no. of approved dwelling units. 2. Completed, Allotted, Under-progress housing units. 3. No. of instalments (Central/State/ULB/ beneficiary) received by the corporation in sanctioned projects. 4. Expenditure incurred in projects.	1. Selection of settlements for Social Audit.
2.	Detailed Project Reports (DPRs)	1. Layout details (Drawings) 2. List of amenities 3. Building quality specifications. 4. Costing	1. To covert the technical information into Janta Information System (JIS) or Public Information System so that people themselves can assess. 2. To assess deviation in approved DPRs.
3.	Beneficiary Lists	1. Contains names of people surveyed, with their eligibility criteria and list of documents held. In Bhopal the list also had their *patta* number.[15]	1. To assess criteria for allotment to people. 2. To assess the level of exclusion and wrong inclusions while listing.
4.	Allotment Lists	1. List of beneficiaries with allotted house numbers	1. To check whether all eligible beneficiaries have been included in allotment lists. 2. Deviation of allotted from beneficiaries (favouritism).
5.	Notifications and Regulations	1. Notifications and regulations regarding procedure of beneficiary selection. 2. Other implementation related documents, like waiver of stamp duties, beneficiary share, etc.	1. To understand process of beneficiary selection. 2. State initiatives and provisions for smooth implementation.

Source: Mahadevia *et al.*, 2013.

consultations with the people. They were asked to form committees of 10-15 members to carry out the process. These were called Social Audit Committees (SAC). The main roles of SACs were the following:

(i) To understand the process of Social Audit through trainings, and facilitate dialogue by talking to people, thereby creating better public participation in the process.
(ii) To understand the issues of the settlement in the purview of the existing DPR and raise them on behalf of the people in the public consultations.
(iii) To help the team to register complaints, filling household questionnaire forms and setting up space for training and consultations.

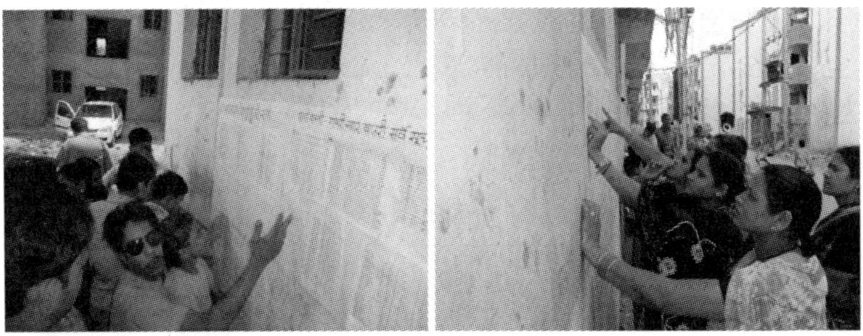

Photo Credit: CUE.
Exhibit 9.4: Making all information public and people reading the information about BSUP

It was evident to the researchers after the first few meetings that people had very little knowledge about the BSUP project or its deliverables. The DPR was never discussed with them, beneficiary selection process was opaque and they had no access to this information either. Therefore, the first part of the audit process was to translate all the information collected into the local language and make things easily available for the people to understand. The team visited each settlement everyday and a display of the whole information from the beneficiary lists, DPRs and drawings of the projects was shared with the people in the form of a wall (Exhibit 9.4). Interactive displays in formats like the one shown in Exhibit 9.5 were also adopted and people were asked to write their comments and submit complaints.

A trustworthy relationship was built with the SACs, who helped the team of researchers to set the time for training and public consultations.

They also helped the team to set up the display wall, and fill complaint forms and collect them. Large number of people came with great enthusiasm to see the display, verify names in the beneficiary lists and allotment lists, ask questions about the DPRs and register complaints. The counter was also kept open on Saturday and Sunday from morning to evening so that more people had access to the information. Rounds of discussions were undertaken for a week in each settlement, and a public consultation with the designated officials of the municipal corporation was held to make the problems heard (Exhibit 9.6). The result of the one week long process was that the people were much more informed, and asked straightforward questions to the officials without deviating into asking about provisions which were not part of the DPRs.

BSUP Implementation in Bhopal and Projects Picked for Social Audit

The team of researchers visited all the four sites. The two settlements of Madrasi Colony and Shabari Nagar were selected to conduct the Social Audit.

Table 9.16: The status of BSUP projects as on April 2011, Bhopal

No.	*BSUP Project Name*	*Approved dwelling units*	*Completed dwelling units*	*Allotted dwelling units*
1.	Redevelopment of Shyam Nagar	1,440	792	454
2.	Redevelopment of Kotra Weekly Market (Shabari Nagar)	512	512	304
3.	Redevelopment of Kalpana Nagar	212	164	163
4.	Redevelopment of Rahul Nagar, Madrasi Nagar, Bhim Nagar and Arjun Nagar	3,528	704	192
	Total	5,692	2,172	1,113

Source: BMC.

BSUP Housing at Shabari Nagar

The DPR for the development of Shabari Nagar was titled 'Redevelopment of Kotra Market by Relocation of Existing Slums'. A slum called Bapu Nagar was situated on the land reserved to build a weekly market for the Kotra area. The DPR proposed to relocate this slum to a site approximately a kilometre away, which had another slum called Shabari Nagar. The result was a proposal of a housing complex consisting of 512 houses, with all the

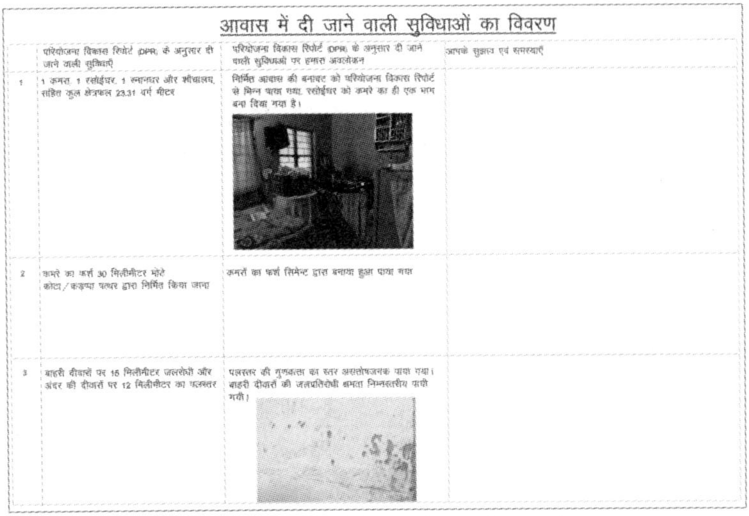

आवास में दी जाने वाली सुविधाओं का विवरण

	परियोजना विकास रिपोर्ट (DPR) के अनुसार दी जाने वाली सुविधाएँ	परियोजना विकास रिपोर्ट (DPR) के अनुसार दी जाने वाली सुविधाओं पर हमारा अवलोकन	आपके सुझाव एवं समस्याएँ
1	1 कमरा, 1 रसोईघर, 1 स्नानघर और शौचालय, सहित कुल क्षेत्रफल 23.31 वर्ग मीटर	निर्मित आवास की बनावट को परियोजना विकास रिपोर्ट से भिन्न पाया गया, रसोईघर को कमरे का ही एक भाग बना दिया गया है।	
2	कमरे का फर्श 30 मिलीमीटर मोटे कोटा/कड़प्पा पत्थर द्वारा निर्मित किया जाना	कमरों का फर्श सिमेन्ट द्वारा बनाया हुआ पाया गया	
3	बाहरी दीवारों पर 15 मिलीमीटर जलरोधी और अंदर की दीवारों पर 12 मिलीमीटर का पलस्तर	पलस्तर की गुणवत्ता का स्तर असंतोषजनक पाया गया। बाहरी दीवारों की जलप्रतिरोधी क्षमता निम्नस्तरीय पायी गयी।	

Exhibit 9.5: Format for displaying information and gathering comments

Photo Credit: CUE.

Exhibit 9.6: Social Audit public consultation with government officials in Madrasi Colony (left) and Shabari Nagar (right)

necessary amenities like water, sanitation, open spaces, boundary walls, etc. Therefore, this was part *in-situ*, part-relocation project.

During the process of Social Audit, the research team asked people to write their complaints about the housing and submit these in a complaint box, which was placed on the site. The research team received a total of 385 complaints from the residents regarding many different issues. Sixty-four per cent of these complaints were about quality of construction and water and sanitation, which are two major pillars to make any housing programme successful. 12.7 per cent complaints were regarding allotment issues.

BSUP Housing at Madrasi Colony

Madrasi Colony settlement was part of a larger DPR which covered four settlements of Arjun Nagar, Bheem Nagar, Madrasi Nagar and Rahul Nagar. A total of 3,528 housing units were sanctioned under the DPR, which had the breakup as given in Table 9.17.

Table 9.17: Slums included in the Madrasi Colony DPR, Bhopal

No.	*Settlement Name*	*Dwelling Units*
1.	Arjun Nagar	352
2.	Madrasi Colony	180
3.	Bhim Nagar	968
4.	Rahul Nagar	2,028
	Total	3,528

Source: BMC.

The DPR proposed *in-situ* rehabilitation of slum households by constructing apartments. Interestingly, a large number of households had a *patta* earlier, which shows that they were already enjoying a high security of tenure. Till April 2011, only 192 units were constructed and allotted under this DPR.

Unfolding the BSUP Housing Process and Underlying Errors

The Social Audit of BSUP projects in Bhopal raised large many intriguing questions, and also formed a set of learnings regarding mechanisms to create a successful housing programme. The first and the foremost problem with the BSUP projects were that they were trying to construct houses and not to create liveable habitat. Housing is not just the house alone, but it is also a bundle of goods and services. The two projects, as discussed above, took the two best approaches in literature suggested for slum rehabilitation but still failed miserably. Shabari Nagar was relocation of slum households within the radius of one km from the previous housing site and Madrasi Colony was *in-situ* rehabilitation of slum households by housing reconstruction. This section will unfold in detail the processes that went wrong with the housing projects and rendered them worthless even after the pursuance of what might seem to be the best approach. There are certain crucial steps which are important to undertake to make any housing project successful and when it is about a slum rehabilitation project, it becomes even more crucial to give attention to detail in each and every step of a project.

Selection of Settlements for BSUP

The first and the most crucial step in starting any slum housing project is the selection of the settlements for housing intervention. Looking at the past history of many housing projects in Bhopal, selection of settlements was one of the most crucial aspect, which was not taken up very seriously. *Prima facie* it seems that slums on most prominent land parcels were chosen for redevelopment. The Madrasi Colony slum which was part of Social Audit was one such slum which was located on the main link road. The other slum was on the land which was reserved for constructing a space for weekly street market of Kotra. The DPR combined the two aspects of housing and livelihood by relocating Bapu Nagar to a nearby location and using its space as a market space for street vendors, who otherwise were sitting on the street causing traffic congestion. As there was no comprehensive information available for slum settlements, and no methodology available for slum selection, most of the slums chosen for the BSUP already had *patta* under the Patta Act, which also means that they were enjoying very high tenure security, and did not require housing support from the BSUP in the first place. Most of these families owned good quality houses, with larger areas, and had heavily invested in their houses over time. In fact, ironically, *patta* was used as one of the identity/eligibility documents for being a BSUP beneficiary.

Re-providing Tenure Security: Turning from Owners to Borrowers

The faulty selection of settlements for BSUP intervention intentionally converted beneficiaries from land owners to loan borrowers. Even though the BSUP housing was heavily subsidized, it was targeted at those who did not require this subsidy as they already had relatively good houses and high tenure security. Moreover, the additional cost of housing construction due to delays was also passed on to the beneficiaries without any prior consultation. The beneficiary share was initially decided to be Rs. 35,000 per household which was manageable for most of the households. As the project progressed, the beneficiary share was increased to Rs. 57,000 in Shabari Nagar and Rs. 90,000 in Madrasi Colony. After people's protest, a financial institution was brought on board to give loans to people. The beneficiaries of Madrasi Colony were asked to pay Rs. 910

per month as instalment, which was not affordable to most of them. The house was also kept as a collateral by the bank. Earlier, these households also enjoyed various other subsidies by the State Government which were now removed. Households living in slums, prior to the BSUP project, paid lower water and property taxes to the BMC as compared to the new site and there were no maintenance charges collected then. Even the electricity was subsidized under the *Ekal batti* (individual light) connection scheme by the government. BSUP housing meant an end to all these subsidies, increasing unexpected expenditures for people.

The association of banks with the housing scheme also brought a new problem of exclusion of female headed households, disabled and old people due to their perceived low creditworthiness. A woman from the settlement of Madrasi Colony said something very poignant during the discussion: "*Everybody starting from central to state and city government paid for my house, then why should my house be mortgaged and why should I be at the mercy of a bank? If I really wanted a loan, I could have taken it on my patta for improving my existing house*". The process on one hand created duplication of benefits for people of Madrasi Colony and increased financial burdens for people in Shabari Nagar on the other. Both these situations were not expected as an outcome of the project.

A Mess in Beneficiary Selection and Identification

The list of beneficiaries was not finalized before the commencement of construction which created a lot of confusion amongst the people. The constructed buildings of Shabari Nagar remained vacant for a long time, waiting to be allotted to the inhabitants as the beneficiary list could not be finalized. Subsequently, the houses were badly vandalized, and finally people, frustrated at the allotment process, forcefully entered the houses and occupied them. There were also few anti-social elements and also political elements who illegally occupied the houses.

In Madrasi Colony, many claimed to have been left out during the beneficiary selection process in absence of proper documents. The team found almost 17 such families who were excluded in the process of allotment. Many houses were allotted to the people who neither lived in the settlement nor were below poverty line.

Although the officials of the corporation claimed that a very comprehensive process was followed in selection of beneficiaries and many re-checks were done before finalizing the list, but no one from the settlement agreed to these claims. A problem with the procedure was the involvement of the Revenue Department too, as the beneficiaries lived on *patta* land. The beneficiary list had also passed many hands from the city-level departments to the state-level causing delays. This was a major reason why beneficiaries could not be decided before the commencement of construction and their contribution to the site planning, design or quality control was non-existent.

Non-Participatory and Arbitrary Site Planning and Design

It was evident that the site planning of most of the BSUP housing schemes was done without even visiting the site, leave aside meeting with the beneficiaries. Sites were not measured properly before making plans. Many details like existing open drains and *nallahs* were ignored. This is what happens when the government abdicates its responsibilities to the consultants!

The housing plan was faulty, with silly mistakes which were not culturally acceptable to the people. The housing type for Shabari Nagar was planned to be a one-room and kitchen unit, which was not suitable. The plan was later changed and two rooms were accommodated in the same amount of space, making rooms very small and unusable (Exhibit 9.7). The room at the back was just 4.4 sq.mt., insufficient to even keep

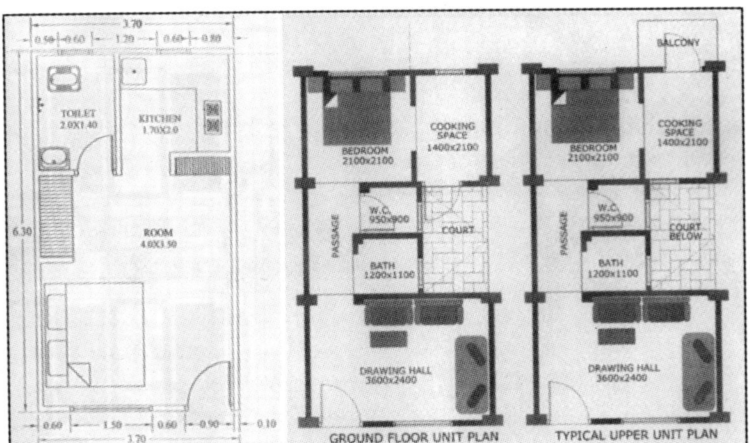

Source: From the BMC records.

Exhibit 9.7: Unit Plan proposed initially (left) and Unit Plan changed to accommodate two rooms and kitchen in the same area (right)

a single bed. The net liveable area in the last plan was 23.21 sq.mt., which was reduced to mere 20.8 sq.mt, way lower than the BSUP standard of 25 sq.mt.

Site plans were sketchy, which led to many changes in the middle of the construction cycle. In Shabari Nagar, the BMC, at the time of construction, realized that the site was not even properly measured and had a low-lying open drain flowing from the middle, which reduced the size of the site. This drain could also have caused flooding of houses beside it. This in turn led to a complete change in the site plan, reducing the planned open space, leaving unusable triangular unplanned open spaces (Exhibit 9.8). The initial plan also had no contours to denote the slope of the site. This was later added in the changed plan. It was found that the site had a very high slope towards the drain; the cost of filling the site and making it flat was also not properly counted in the initial estimates. This led to unusual cost increase in filling the site and making it flat. A convenient shopping space designed in the initial plan was very conveniently deleted.

These changes were done without telling the community or taking their approval on anything. In the end when people shifted to the houses, they were horrified and shocked at the state of affairs. Staircases did not reach to the top of the building where water tanks were kept, there was no space in the houses to accommodate a single family with all belongings,

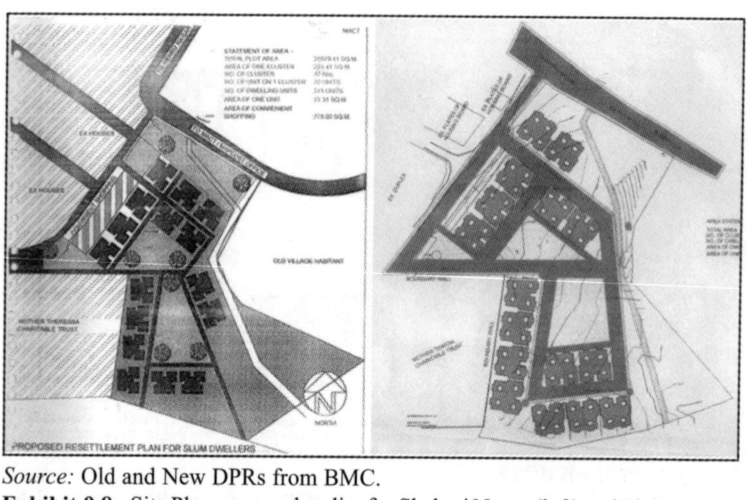

Source: Old and New DPRs from BMC.

Exhibit 9.8: Site Plan proposed earlier for Shabari Nagar (left) and Plan actually implemented at the site (right)

there was no parapet wall on the roof and an useless duct-like courtyard was connected to the ground-floor flats carrying sewage pipes and housing a sewage chamber. There were no glass panes on the windows, front doors opened in dark tunnel-like corridors (Exhibit 9.9) and unusable open spaces were taken up by electricity transformers and accommodating buildings from nearby BSUP projects sanctioned later. There were also no boundary walls and no fixed entrance to the site. This mess was going to cost the people Rs. 57,000 each, excluding the stamp duty and other connection charges to the utilities like electricity and water. The housing looked like a shabby dilapidated cluster of windows and small balconies (Exhibit 9.9).

Photo Credit: CUE.

Exhibit 9.9: A row of buildings in Shabari Nagar (left) and a tunnel-like entrance corridor with useless windows (right)

The DPR for Madrasi Colony actually consisted of a proposal of *in-situ* rehabilitation of four slum settlements, as mentioned above. The total numbers of housing units sanctioned were 3,528. The site planning of this settlement was also done without getting an actual plan of the land and the process followed was bizarre. The people were slowly moved from their place to a transit shelter and then few buildings were constructed. There was a site plan, but it was so sketchy that following it was almost impossible. An overhead water tank and community hall was also planned, but it was nowhere to be seen during our social audit process, as there was no space left to build it. An existing temple was not taken care of while site planning, nor was the open drain passing from the site. The buildings abruptly ended at an open drain beside where an unattended temple stood dilapidated. Entry and exits were not planned and an extremely high boundary wall separated the settlement from the main road, while there was no boundary wall on the other sides of the plot, allowing access to all. Many households had small shops in the existing slum settlement, for which no provision was made in the DPR, causing loss of livelihood for many.

The housing situation in Madrasi Colony was a little better, but extreme callousness in project execution and management was still visible. Here the design of the housing unit had a toilet adjacent to the kitchen, which was completely unacceptable by the people. The people complained of toilet odours entering into the kitchen. The staircase landing was so low (at four and a half feet), that it was impossible to pass beneath it to access the courtyard in the centre of each of the three connected buildings. Many households also complained that the housing size was small. A lady during a public meeting said that she owned a larger plot of land with *patta* and now it was difficult for her whole family to manage in such a small size house.

Worsening State of Basic Services

The state of basic services in these settlements was absolutely appalling and unfortunately this state was created by using funds from a programme which was intended to improve the state of basic services as its first priority! Shabari Nagar had very poor state, where there were separate water tanks for each flat, but the installed water mains were actually garden hose pipes, which hanged unclamped from the damp walls (Exhibit 9.10). Many were not connected to the kitchen and toilets. The water supply was for half an hour every evening and people resorted to climbing up on a parapet-less terrace using a dangerous bamboo ladder to fill water in buckets. There was a signboard by the corporation regarding the timings for a water tanker (Exhibit 9.10), which means that sometimes water supply was also through tankers. People confirmed this during the focus group discussions (FGDs) and said that higher-floor residents had to climb all the way up with buckets full of water, or they resorted to filling water by pulling buckets of water tied to strings from their balconies. It was also reported that a young girl fell down from the terrace and died in attempt to fill water from the roof-top tanks.

The distance to water in the slums was at least horizontal to a public tap, but the BSUP housing made it vertical. In Madrasi Colony, the water supply system was even more bizarre. The Municipal Corporation decided it would not construct an overhead water tank so as to avoid daily quarrels of the residents regarding the water distribution. They decided to instead build an elevated storage reservoir of a larger capacity for the whole

Photo Credit: CUE.

Exhibit 9.10: Women filling water from the terrace (left), dangling water mains (middle) and water tanker timings (right)

housing scheme. But this was never built due to the space crunch. Each household was given just one 200 litres water tank to be kept inside the house. People kept this below the kitchen platform (Exhibit 9.11). No tap was provided in the kitchen in both the settlements, and daily need of drinking water also had to be filled from the toilet which is culturally unacceptable. In Madrasi Colony, the toilet's entry was from the kitchen (Exhibit 9.11). The taps were useless except for 30 minutes in the morning when there was water supply in the settlement. Even at this time, water did not always reach the upper floors due to lack of sufficient water pressure. The water for use in the toilets had to be stored in the kitchen!

Each house had individual toilet, which however did not function well due to lack of water, specifically running water. It also led to serious sewage blockages in Shabari Nagar, where unfortunately the sewage inspection chamber was in the courtyard of the ground-floor apartment

Photo Credit: CUE.

Exhibit 9.11: Water tank kept below kitchen platform and entry to toilet from kitchen (left) and dilapidated state of main valve (right)

Photo Credit: CUE.

Exhibit 9.12: Open drain beside Madrasi Colony (left) and sewage chamber connected to the ground-floor apartment (right)

(Exhibit 9.12). It filled the courtyard with sewage and also sometimes the house. In the first few months of residence in Shabari Nagar, the ground-floor residents paid a hefty amount to get the sewage chambers cleaned every month. After few months of constant struggle with the badly constructed sewage system, they either closed their doors and windows, turning them into a permanent wall, resulting in non-ventilated room or made high door sills to prevent sewage from overflowing into their rooms.

Solid Waste Management (SWM) was the most neglected of the basic services and was completely missing in Shabari Nagar. There were heaps of garbage everywhere in Shabari Nagar, and it seemed to have taken over all the remaining open spaces (Exhibit 9.13). Daily sweeping and garbage collection happened in Madrasi Colony, which owed this to its location on a main road.

Photo Credit: CUE

Exhibit 9.13: Solid waste scattered all across in Shabari Nagar

Photo Credit: CUE.

Exhibit 9.14: A web of wires in Shabari Nagar (left) and a transformer very close to the window in Madrasi Colony (right)

The provision of electricity was also not properly done. Transformers were kept very near the buildings. High tension wires were directly clamped on the walls and a very low quality of wiring was used, which led to fire-like situation in one of the buildings. In Madrasi Colony no electricity meters were put and people paid average bills in fear that they would get inflated bills afterwards. In Shabari Nagar, houses were allotted without the provision of electricity. People themselves used wires and illegally connected their units to the transformer, forming a web of dangerous wires and a fire safety hazard (Exhibit 9.14).

Transit Housing: A Matter Left Unattended

Transit housing is an important component of any housing project where *in-situ* reconstruction is proposed. Construction is a time consuming activity, and it leads to a temporary relocation of households. Unfortunately, the DPRs for *in-situ* BSUP Projects in Bhopal did not take transit accommodation or costs allied to it as a serious matter of concern. In Madrasi Colony people were gradually removed cluster by cluster, emptying spaces for buildings which were constructed one after another without any plan of action, and at another BSUP site of Rahul Nagar, all the households were moved to a nearby site while the construction continued for two years, creating a new settlement (Exhibit 9.15).

The site for relocation was extremely rocky and sloping on one side. Households were dumped on the site which had individual land parcels demarcated by lime powder, and four tor steel bars at the corners. People invested a whole lot of money in constructing a transit house (Exhibit 9.15). As the span of stay increased, people kept on investing smaller

Photo Credit: CUE.

Exhibit 9.15: Transit housing on sloping rocky terrain (right), filtering water from water mains (middle) and toilets (right)

amounts to make them more liveable. Households who were dependent on smaller shops reopened them in transit shelters too. Most of the expenditure was done on flooring and the terrain was not habitable. Households transported the bricks from their demolished house to build these transit shelters and no financial help was provided to them. The state of basic services in these sites was also appalling and clean drinking water was not readily available. There were just five toilets for 500 households and one water tap in every lane of more than 50 households. Clearly the provision of transit housing was unattended in the whole scheme of BSUP.

People's Perception of the Programme

> *"It is a zoo and we are now been treated as animals, who have been filled in these cage-like houses with bad construction quality and without proper amenities. We are poor. What could we do? Whom to believe?"*

> *"We have never seen the houses we were going to get. We were dumped here in scorching sun without any facilities on the name of resettlement. We cooked in open, lived under the sky. Slowly we have consumed all our savings to build this house; from where would we bring money for the new flat?"*

> *"They (Authorities) expect us to pay money for these houses which will not even stand for four-five years. We can pay, but only for better quality houses. How can they shift us to such unplanned, amenity-less houses forcefully, and then have courage to ask for money."*

> *"We were better off in the slum settlement. We had water supply, sanitation and we used to keep our pathways clean."*
>
> *"We don't think these buildings will stand for more than one-two years. These are threat to life and may collapse anytime. This place would become our grave."*

The above statements are useful for judging people's perceptions of the housing they got under BSUP. These were not just statements arising out of the problems created by the housing as an end product, but also a satirical take on flawed processes and decisions which failed to work.

In his book *Housing by People*, Turner (1976) writes that deficiencies and imperfections in one's housing are infinitely more tolerable if they are one's own responsibility than if they are somebody else's. It is one of the three laws of Turner. He suggests that if decision and control systems governing the supply and use of personal services such as housing is the primary responsibility of the users, then housing economy and equity can be achieved if householders and their local communities are responsible for what is built and how it is used and maintained. As the above discussions suggest, something very similar was seen in Bhopal. End users were detached from the decisions which were taken to shape their living space. They were pushed into a completely new living environment, rather than guided. In this case beneficiaries were not consulted regarding any decisions, from planning and design to location of dwelling units and even the share to be paid by them. Changes were constantly brought into the project without their consent.

As a result, people could not accept or attach themselves to this new housing asset they received, which in many cases was worse than prior one. People also compared the housing they received with the other beneficiaries in the city. Specifically in the case of Shabari Nagar, it so happened that the housing size provided to them was smaller than to the BSUP beneficiaries in the rest of the city.

Lessons Learnt: Towards Housing where People Matter

Housing in itself is a broader concept and a housing project may or may not involve construction of houses. Housing is creating a liveable habitat for people for their well-being. Housing is related to health, physical and mental; it is related to livelihoods and the distance to access those livelihoods. Housing is also a subject of personal choice and requires engagement by the person who lives or is going to live in the habitat. A house cannot be seen detached from all other virtues like access to basic services and social services. In Bhopal, the BSUP housing experiment missed these vital linkages to be taken into consideration, out of which most important was the residents' engagement. Architects and planners did not involve the community in planning and decision making.

Ad hoc planning and decision making lead to big project delays, and cost escalations lead to omission of many compulsory and significant components (e.g. permanent water pipes were omitted from Shabari Nagar, and a complete elevated water reservoir including a community hall was omitted from the Madrasi Colony site). Bhopal's BSUP became a case of good approach—in the sense of carrying out nearby resettlement or *in-situ* redevelopment—and worst implementation.

(i) Innumerable discussions show that there are certain necessities in managing, planning and implementation of any successful housing project and it is also important that these activities are done in a meaningful sequence without skipping any step.
(ii) Selection of settlement for housing intervention.
(iii) Building community trust in the project, beneficiary selection and listing.
(iv) Community consultations to decide housing options, site planning, housing design, amenities, transit housing, beneficiary share etc.
(v) Preparation of DPRs, administrative approvals and funding.
(vi) Commencement of work and managing transit housing.
(vii) Allotment process.
(viii) Post-project maintenance.

A huge amount of money is spent in large programmes for housing the urban poor. This housing is always greatly subsidized, with a prime goal of constructing houses. But these programmes, more often than not, completely ignore the real requirements which may make the existing settlement habitable. Constructing afresh is always the easiest approach to take, but it may not be always required. *In-situ* upgradation and redevelopment is always the best approach but requires much more detailing to avoid delays and ensure smoother implementation. In case of Bhopal, we also saw that the officials of the municipal corporation were uninterested and unperturbed by the perils of bad housing on the people. Their attitude towards these settlements was insensitive. Therefore, there is also a great need to create sensitivity in consultants and government officials dealing with such programmes. The last and the most important lesson is the addition of grievance redressal systems in the projects to avoid exclusions.

Multiple programmes running simultaneously in the city require an integrated planning strategy at the city level to create maximum benefit for the slum households. Many institutions working on the same issues in Bhopal ended up creating immense duplication of benefits, ultimately resulting in decreased effectiveness of the programmes. Haphazard implementation in Bhopal has resulted in chaos, created distrust in governance, worsened the state of basic services, snatched right to land and has converted owners into borrowers, which is the least expected outcome of any housing improvement programme.

The government was very optimistic about RAY, and it seems that in terms of the process, a lot of learning has penetrated into the programme document. Being a more open programme, RAY counted on community participation and in provision of many options to the cities to make them more habitable. Looking at the case studies presented in this chapter, one can only hope that the remaining projects under the RAY will not also be taken away by private interests of construction and will facilitate a more structured view to slum upgradation and redevelopment.

While more programmes for housing the poor are being launched such as Sardar Patel Urban Housing Mission in the quest of housing for all, the major emphasis still seems to be creation of more mass housing. In this, we could only hope that the learnings till now would not get wasted by such interventions of the government and housing solutions would be able to come out of the box of mass housing.

NOTES

1. Authors would like to thank the Secretary, Department of Local Self Government, Government of Madhya Pradesh, Officials of the Bhopal Municipal Corporation, Officials of the JNNURM Cell at State and City level and Officials of the Town and Country Planning Department for their immense cooperation. The authors would like to convey their gratitude to the people, especially women from the settlements of Shabari Nagar and Madrasi Nagar for their valuable time, enthusiasm and active participation. The Social Audit was not possible without the help of the enthusiastic team

from NGO partners Unnati, Samarthan and our colleague Aseem Mishra from Centre for Urban Equity (CUE), CEPT University.

2. The list used for providing leasehold titles under the *Patta Act*.
3. The legislation is called *Madhya Pradesh Nagariya Kshetron Ke Bhoomihin Vyakti (Pattadhruti Adhikaron Ka Pradan Kiya Jana) Adhiniyam*, 1984 which translates into "The Act for "Providing Tenure Rights" to Landless Persons of the Urban Madhya Pradesh. 1984". It is called as the Patta Act of 1984 in different literature as "*Patta*" means the land tenure right.
4. Details are available on the website of the Madhya Pradesh Housing and Infrastructure Development Board (MPHIDB) at *http://www.mphousing.in/achievements.asp* accessed on October 2, 2014.
5. Details are available on the website of the Madhya Pradesh Housing and Infrastructure Development Board (MPHIDB) at *http://www.mphousing.in/achievements.asp* accessed on October 2, 2014.
6. The state population policy was released in the year 2000. The full text is available on *http://dit.mp.gov.in/documents/10180/08bee5d4-a917-468a-a21d-d976bad5034a*, accessed on October 24, 2014.
7. In 2007, the state released the housing policy for Madhya Pradesh called as *"Avas evam Paryavas Neeti 2007"* on the lines of "National Urban Housing and Habitat Policy 2007". The text in Hindi is available on *http://mphed.nic.in/Housing%20Policy%20Oct-2007-Final.pdf* accessed on November 11, 2010.
8. Ministry of Housing and Urban Poverty Alleviation (MoHUPA) keeps state-wise monthly data for sanctioned housing units under BSUP and IHSDP at www.jnnurm.nic.in.
9. 58th Round of the National Sample Survey Organisation (NSSO) was carried out from July 2002-December 2002, in which 2160 urban sample households were surveyed. The report text can be found on *http://mospi.nic.in/Mospi_New/upload/488_final.pdf* accessed on October 7, 2012.
10. All tables are taken from Datey 2010, unless otherwise mentioned.
11. This information is from the Ministry of Housing and Urban Poverty Alleviation website *http://mhupa.gov.in/programs/housing/bilateral.htm* accessed on 2.11.2014.
12. This information was gathered from BMC's Monthly Progress Report (MPR) for the month of April 2011.
13. The status of units allotted as on January 31, 2010.
14. See Mahadevia *et al.*, 2013.
15. The BSUP projects were taken up in only the slums that had *patta* (tenure guarantee) under the Madhya Pradesh Patta Act.

Bibliography

Acharya, S.K. and S. Parikh (2002). "Slum Networking in Ahmedabad: An Alternate Approach," in A. Kundu and D. Mahadevia (eds.) *Poverty and Vulnerabilities in a Globalizing Metropolis: Ahmedabad*, Delhi: Manak Publishers, pp. 349-72.

Al Sayyad, N. (2004). "Urban Informality as a 'New' Way of Life," in Roy and Al Sayyad (eds.) *Urban Informality, Transnational Perspectives from the Middle East, South Asia and Latin America*, Lanham, MD: Lexington Books. pp. 7-30.

Angotti, T. (2005). "New Anti-Urban Theories of the Metropolitan Region: "Planet of Slums" and Apocalyptic Regionalism", Paper presented at the Conference of the Association of Collegiate School of Planners, Missouri accessed on October 27, 2005, (*http://www.scribd.com/doc/288301/00101Tom AngottiNew-AntiUrban-Theories*).

ASAG (1992). *Census of Poverty Pockets in Ahmedabad*, unpublished study sponsored by the Ahmedabad Municipal Corporation, Ahmedabad: ASAG.

Ballestores, M. (2004). "*Rental Housing for Urban Low-income Households in Philippines,*" Discussion Paper Series No. 2004-47, Philippines Institute for Development Studies, December.

Banerjee, B. (2002). "Security of Tenure in Indian Cities", in A. Durand-Lasserve & L. Rayston (ed.) *Holding Their Ground: Secure Land Tenure for Urban Poor in Developing Countries*, London: Earth Scan Publications, pp. 37-58.

Bardhan, K. (1985). "Women's Work, Welfare and Status Force of Tradition and Change in India," *Economic and Political Weekly*, Vol. XX No. 50, December 14.

Bayat, A. (2000). "From 'Dangerous Classes' to 'Quiet Rebels': The Politics of the Urban Subaltern in the Global South," *International Sociology,* 15(3), pp. 533-57.

Bayat, A. (2007). "Radical Religion and the Habitus of the Dispossessed: Does Islamic Militancy have an Urban Ecology?," *International Journal of Urban and Regional Research,* 31(3), pp. 579-90.

Benjamin, S. (2005). "Touts Pirates and Ghosts" in *SARIA Reader 05: Bare Act*, Sarai, New Delhi.

Benjamin, S. (2008). "Occupancy Urbanism: Radicalizing Politics and Economy Beyond Policy and Programmes," *International Journal of Urban and Regional Research,* 32(3), pp. 719-29.

Benjamin, S. R. Bhuvaneswari, P. Rajan and Manjunath (2008). "'Fractured' Terrain, Spaces Left-over or Contested: A Closer Look at the IT-Dominated Territories in East and South Bangalore", in D. Mahadevia (ed.) *Inside the Transforming Urban Asia—Processes, Policies and Public Actions*, New Delhi: Concept Publishing Company Pvt. Ltd., pp. 239-85.

Bhan, G. (2014). "Planned Illegalities: Housing and the 'Failure' of Planning in Delhi," *Economic and Political Weekly*, Vol. XLVIII, No. 24, pp. 58-70.

Bhan, G. and S. Shivanand (2013). "(Un)Settling the City: Analysing Displacement in Delhi from 1990 to 2007," *Economic and Political Weekly*, 48(13), pp. 54-61.

Bhide, A. (2014). "The Regularising State," *Economic and Political Weekly*, Vol. XLIX, No. 22, pp. 92-100.

Bhopal Municipal Corporation (2005). *Bhopal City Development Plan,* Bhopal.

Bhopal Municipal Corporation (2009). *JNNURM: Perspectives from Bhopal City*, Bhopal.

Blood, R. and D. Wolfe (1960). *Husbands and Wives: The Dynamics of Married Living*, New York: The Free Press.

Buckley, R.M., Mahavir Singh, and J. Kalarickal (2007). *Strategizing Slum Improvement in India—A Method to Monitor and Refocus Slum Development Programmes, Global Urban Development Magazine,* 3(1).

Census of India (2001). *Slum Population, Series-1*, Office of the Registrar General and Census Commissioner, India, New Delhi.

Census of India (2011). *Houselisting and Housing Census Data Highlights—2011*, Office of the Registrar General and Census Commissioner, India, New Delhi, accessed on February 15, 2014 (*http://www.censusindia.gov.in/2011census/hlo/hlo_highlights.html*).

Chatterjee, P. (2004). *The Politics of the Governed: Reflections on Popular Politics in Most of the World*, New York: Columbia University Press.

Christian, J.W. (1995). *Housing Finance for Developing Countries*. Illinois, Chicago.

Clemens, M. and T. Moss (2005). *What's Wrong with the Millennium Development Goals*?, Centre for Global Development, accessed on December 1, 2010 (*www.cgdev.org/files/3940_file_WWMGD.pdf*).

Coccato, M. (1996). Alternatives to Home Ownership: Rental and Shared Sub-markets in Informal Settlements, Resistencia, Argentina, Canada:

MCHG School of Architecture, McGill University, Master of Architecture Thesis.

Coelho, K. and N. Raman (2010). "Salvaging and Scapegoating: Slum Evictions on Chennai's Waterways," *Economic and Political Weekly*, 45(21), pp. 19-23.

Centre of Housing Rights and Eviction (COHRE) (2003). *Annual Report 2002*, Appendix 2, Constitutional Sources of Housing Rights, Geneva: COHRE.

Das, B. (2006). *Slum Dwellers in Indian Cities: The Case of Surat in Western India*, QEH Working Paper Number 7, Oxford Department of International Development, University of Oxford, accessed on June 22, 2010 (*www.qeh.ox.ac.uk/pdf/qehwp/qehwps07.pdf*).

Datey, A. (2010). *An Assessment of "Housing and Infrastructure" Provision Programmes for Urban Poor: A Case of Bhopal*, Ahmedabad: CEPT University, Unpublished Thesis.

Davis, M. (2004). *Planet of Slums*, London: Verso.

Dayal, R. (1960). *Community Programme in India,* Delhi: Kitab Mahal Publisher.

De Soto, H. (2003). *The Mystery of Capital—Why Capitalism Triumphs in the West and Fails Elsewhere*, New York: Basic Books.

De Wandeler, K. And A. Khanaiklang (1992). "Low Income Rental and Rent Free Housing," in Y.K. Sheng (eds.) *Low-income Housing in Bangkok: A Review of Some Housing Sub-Markets*, Bangkok: Asian Institute of Technology, pp. 115-131.

De Wit, J. (1997). *Poverty, Policy, and Politics in Madras Slums: Dynamics of Survival, Gender, and Leadership*, Delhi: Sage.

Desai, R. and D. Mahadevia, (2013). *Land and Housing Development Processes as Determinants of Rental Housing for the Urban Poor: The Case of Guwahati City*, Working Paper 19, Centre for Urban Equity, CEPT University, Ahmedabad, August.

Desai, R. (2014). *Municipal Politics, Court Sympathy and Housing Rights: A Post-Mortem of Displacement and Resettlement under the Sabarmati River front Project, Ahmedabad*, Working Paper 23, Centre for Urban Equity, CEPT University, Ahmedabad, May.

Desai, R. and K. Jajoo (2014). *Tenure Policies and Politics in Informal Settlements: A Study of Nagpur and Nanded*, Maharashtra, Research Report, Centre for Urban Equity, CEPT University, Ahmedabad, January.

Dey, C.K. (1962). *Community Development*, Delhi: Kitab Mahal Publisher.

Dubey, A. and D.Mahadevia (2001). "Poverty and Inequality in Indian Metropolises," *The Indian Journal of Labour Economics,* 44(2), pp. 223-42.

Dubey, A., Gangopadhyay, S. and Wadhwa, W. (2001). "Occupational

Structure and Incidence of Poverty in Indian Towns of Different Sizes," *Review of Development Economics*, 5, pp. 49-59.

Durand-Laserve, A. and H. Selod (2007). *The Formalisation of Urban Land Tenure in Developing Countries*, Background paper prepared for The World Bank's 2007 Urban Research Symposium, Washington DC, May 14-16.

Durand-Laserve, Alain and Lauren Rayston (2002). *Holding Their Ground*, London: Earth Scan Publications.

Dutta, S.S. (2002). "Partnership for Urban Poverty Reduction: A Review of Experience," in A. Kundu and D. Mahadevia (eds.) *Poverty and Vulnerabilities in a Globalizing Metropolis: Ahmedabad*, Delhi: Manak Publishers, pp. 237-67.

Echanove, M. and R. Srivastava (2009). "Taking the Slum out of 'Slumdog'," *The New York Times,* 21 February, A 21.

Edwards, M. (1983). "Residential Mobility in a Changing Housing Market: The Case of Bucaramnaga, Columbia," *Urban Studies*, 20, pp. 131-45.

Esser, D. (2009). *Development as Fiction: The Failure of the MDGs,* Danielesser blogs, accessed on November 30, 2010 (*http://danielesser.org/2009/07/13/development-as-fiction-the-failure-of-the-mdgs/*).

Gangrade, K.D. (1971). *Community Organisation in India,* Mumbai: Popular Prakashan.

Ghertner, A. (2008). "Analysis of New Legal Discourse behind Delhi's Slum Demolitions," *Economic and Political Weekly,* 43(20), pp. 57-66.

GHMC and NCPE Infrastructure (2013). *Slum Free City Plan of Action for Greater Hyderabad Municipal Corporation*, submitted to MoHUPA, GoI, Greater Hyderabad Municipal Corporation, accessed on August 15, 2014 (*http://mhupa.gov.in/ray/SFCPoAs/Hyd_AP_sfcp.pdf*).

Gidwani, V.K. (2006). "Subaltern Cosmopolitanism as Politics," *Antipode*, 38(1), pp. 7-21.

Gilbert, A. (1983). "The Tenants of Self-Help Housing: Choice and Constraint in the Housing Markets of Less Developed Countries," *Development and Change*, 14 (3), pp. 449-77.

Gilbert, A. (2001). *On the Mystery of Capital and the Myths of Hernando De Soto: What Difference Does Legal Title Make*, accessed on March 20, 2009 (*http:/www.n-aerus.net/web/sat/workshops/2001/papers/gilbert.pdf*).

GoI (1997). *Ninth Five Year Plan of India (1997-2002)*, Government of India, Vol. 2, (3.2), accessed on December 1, 2012 (*http://planningcommission.nic.in/plans/planrel/fiveyr/9th/vol2/v2c3-2.htm*).

GoI (2002). *Tenth Five Year Plan of India (2002-2007)*, Government of India, Vol. 2, (6.2), pp. 636, accessed on December 1, 2012 (*http://*

planningcommission.nic.in/plans/planrel/fiveyr/10th/volume2/v2_ch6_2.pdf).

Government of Madhya Pradesh. (2007). *Madhya Pradesh Human Development Report.* New Delhi : Oxford University Press.

Government of Madhya Pradesh. (2008). *Madhya Pradesh Housing and Habitat Policy*, Bhopal.

Hamer, A. M. (1985). *Bagota's Unregulated Subdivisions: The Myths and Realities of Incremental Housing Construction*, World Bank Staff Working Paper No. 734. Washington DC: The World Bank.

Hansen, E. and J. Williams (1988). "Economic Issues and the Progressive Housing Development Model", in C.V. Patton (eds.) *Spontaneous Shelter—International Perspectives and Prospects,* Temple University Press, Philadelphia, pp. 303-25.

Hasan, A., S. Patel and D. Satherthwaite (2005). "How to Meet the Millennium Development Goals (MDGs) in Urban Areas," *Environment and Urbanization*, 17(3), pp. 3-19.

Himanshu Parikh (2001). Consulting Engineers and Youth for Unity and Voluntary Action (YUVA). Project Framework Report: Slum Networking of Bhopal for Government of Madhya Pradesh.

Hirway, I. and D. Mahadevia (2005). *The Gujarat Human Development Report, 2004*, Ahmedabad: Mahatma Gandhi Labour Institute.

Hirway, I., A. Shah and G. Shah (eds.) (2014). *Growth or Development—Which Way is Gujarat Going*, New Delhi: Oxford University Press.

Holston, J. (2007). *Insurgent Citizenship: Disjunctions of Democracy and Modernity in Brazil*, Princeton: Princeton University Press.

Howard, G.L. and G. Snetro, (2003). *How to Mobilize Communities for Health and Social Change,* Baltimore, MD: Health Communication Partnership, USAID, accessed on March 13, 2009 *(pdf.usaid.gov/pdf_docs/PNADI338.pdf).*

Howard, G. and J. Bartram (2003). *Domestic Water Quantity, Service, Level and Health.* Geneva : World Health Organisation (WHO).

HPEC (2011). *Report on Indian Urban Infrastructure and Services,* New Delhi: High Powered Expert Committee (HPEC), Ministry of Urban Development (MoUD), Government of India, March.

JNNURM (2006). *Surat City Development Plan 2006-2012*, New Delhi: Jawaharlal Nehru National Urban Renewal Mission, Government of India, pp. 7-10, accessed on June 22, 2010 (*http://jnnurmmis.nic.in/toolkit/SuratCdp/Surat_CDP.PDF*).

JNNURM Project Cell-NBO (2012). "Status of DPRs received under Basic Services for the Urban Poor (Sub-Mission II) from Mission Cities," January 2, 2012.

Joshi, R. (2002). "Integrated Slum Development: Case of Pravinnagar-

Guptanagar", in A. Kundu and D. Mahadevia (eds.) *Poverty and Vulnerabilities in a Globalizing Metropolis: Ahmedabad*, Delhi: Manak Publishers, pp. 268-308.

Joshi, R., P. Shah, K. Nazareth and D. Mahadevia (2010). *From Basic Services Delivery to Policy Advocacy-Community Mobilisation in Pravinnagar-Guptanagar, Ahmedabad*, Working Paper No. 6, Centre for Urban Equity, CEPT University.

Kamath, L. and P. Deekshit (2014). "Planning as Practice: Governing Conjunctures and Informal Urbanisation in Solapur Town," *Economic and Political Weekly*, 49(22), pp. 72-81.

Kamau, P.K. (2002). *Enhancing Housing Development and Ownership: Prospects for Individual Housing Development in Nairobi, Kenya*, Japan: University of Tsukuba, Doctoral Programme in Policy and Planning Sciences Thesis.

Kavoori, J.C. (1974). "Objectives of Community Development and Democratic Growth," Seminar paper in NR Inamdar (eds.) *Community Development and Democratic Growth*, Mumbai: Popular Prakashan, pp. 1-8.

Keare, D., H. and S. Parris (1982). *Evaluation of Shelter Programmes for the Urban Poor*, World Bank Staff Working Paper No. 547, Washington DC : The World Bank.

Kombe, W.J. (1995). *Formal and Informal Land Management in Tanzania, The Case of Dar-Es-Salaam City*, Spring Research Series No. 13, University of Dortmund, Dortmund, Germany.

Konduri, V. (2009). Right to Housing: Context and Trends in Contemporary Debates: Struggles for Homestead Land in Andhra Pradesh", accessed on November 30, 2010 (*http://indiacurrentaffairs.org/right-to-housing-context-and-trends-in-contemporary-debates-struggle-for-homestead-land-in-andhra-pradesh-veeraiah-konduri/*).

Kreibich, V. and W.J. Kombe (2002), *Informal Land Management in Tanzania*, Spring Research Series, Vol. 29, University of Dortmund, Dortmund, Germany.

Kumar, S. (2001). *Social Relations, Rental Housing Markets and the Poor in Urban India*, Report prepared for the Infrastructure and Urban Development Department, London: Department for International Development (DFID).

Lal, R. (1963). *Community Development: Principles, Practice and Problems* (*With special reference to state of Bihar*), Patna: Bookland Pvt. Ltd.

Leckie, S. (2004). *Framing the Discussion about Housing Rights*, Mimeo, Geneva: COHRE.

Lim, G.C. (1987). "Housing Policies for Urban Poor in Developing Countries," *APA Journal*, Vol. 53, pp. 176-83.

Mahadeva, M. (2006). "Reforms in Housing Sector in India: Impact on

Housing Development and Housing Amenities," *Habitat International,* 30, pp. 412-433.

Mahadevia, D. (2002a). "Changing Economic Scenario: Informalisation and Increased Vulnerability" in A. Kundu and D. Mahadevia (eds.) *Poverty and Vulnerability in a Globalising Metropolis: Ahmedabad*, Delhi: Manak Publishers, pp. 30-79.

Mahadevia, D. (2002b). "Interventions in Development: A Shift towards a Model of Exclusion" in A. Kundu and D. Mahadevia (eds.) *Poverty and Vulnerability in a Globalising Metropolis: Ahmedabad*, Delhi: Manak Publishers, pp. 80-132.

Mahadevia, D. (2003). *Globalisation, Urban Reforms and Metropolitan Response: India*, Delhi: Manak.

Mahadevia, D. (2007). "A City with Many Borders—Beyond Ghettoisation in Ahmedabad", in Annapurna Shaw (ed.) *Indian Cities in Transition*, Hyderabad: Orient Longman, pp. 315-40.

Mahadevia, D. (2008). "Metropolitan Employment in India, in Darshini Mahadevia (ed.), *Inside the Transforming Urban Asia: Policies, Processes and Public Actions*, New Delhi: Concept Publishing Copmany Pvt. Ltd., pp. 56-93.

Mahadevia, D. (2010): "Tenure Security and Urban Social Protection Links: India," *IDS Bulletin*, 41 (4), pp. 52-62.

Mahadevia, D. (2011a). "Branded and Renewed? Policies, Politics and Processes of Urban Development in the Reform Era", *Economic and Political Weekly*, 46 (31), pp. 56-64.

Mahadevia, D. (2011b). *Shelter Security and Urban Social Protection—Findings and Policy Implications in India*, Chronic Poverty Research Centre, CPRC Publication, accessed on November 30, 2010 (*http://www.chronicpoverty.org/publications/details/shelter-security-and-urban-social-protection*).

Mahadevia, D. and Brar, H. (2008). "Basic Infrastructure, Public Finance and Slum Dwellers: Ahmedabad," in D. Mahadevia (eds.) *Inside the Transforming Urban Asia: Processes, Policies and Public Actions,* New Delhi: Concept Publishing Company Pvt. Ltd., pp. 361-90.

Mahadevia, D. and P. Shah (2010). *Welfare Extension by Local State and Social Protection: Surat*, Working Paper 11, Centre for Urban Equity, CEPT University, Ahmedabad.

Mahadevia, D., A. Datey and A. Mishra (2013). *Foisting Mass Housing on the Poor: Lessons from the Social Audit of BSUP*, Working Paper 21, Centre for Urban Equity, CEPT University, Ahmedabad, accessed on October 20, 2014.

Mahadevia, D., A. Mishra and S. Vyas (2014). *Home-Based Workers in Ahmedabad, India*, Informal Economy Monitoring Study, Women in

Informal Employment: Globalizing and Organizing (WIEGO), Manchester UK, April.

Mahadevia, D., Liu and Yuan (2010). "Housing Options and Mobility of Urban Migrants in India and China", *Environment and Urbanization, ASIA*, 3(1), pp. 143-63.

Mathur, O.P. (2009). *Slum Free Cities: A New Deal for the Urban Poor,* Delhi: NIPFP, (*www.nipfp.org.in/opm_files/../Final%20Poverty%20Rep.pdf*).

Mehta, D. and M. Mehta (1989). *Metropolitan Housing Market: A Study of Ahmedabad*, New Delhi: Sage Publications.

Mehta, U. (1974). "Gandhi and Community Development," Seminar paper in NR Inamdar, N.R. (eds.) *Community Development and Democratic Growth*, Mumbai: Popular Prakashan, pp. 8-11.

Mitra, B.C. (1988). *Impact of Land Tenure Regularisation and Environmental Upgrading Programmes on Shelter Consolidation in Squatter Settlements in Bhopal*. New Delhi: HSMI.

MoHUPA (2006). *Report of the Technical Group on the Estimation of Urban Housing Shortage, 11th Five Year Plan 2007-2012*, National Building Organisation (NBO), Ministry of Urban Poverty and Alleviation, New Delhi: Government of India.

MoHUPA (2008). *Annual Report 2008-09,* Ministry of Housing and Urban Poverty Alleviation, New Delhi: Government of India.

MoHUPA (2009). *Modified Guidelines for Sub-Mission on Basic Services for the Urban Poor (BSUP)*. Ministry of Housing and Urban Poverty Alleviation, New Delhi: Government of India, February.

MoHUPA (2009). *Toolkit for Financial Support for Comprehensive Capacity Building for Improved Urban Governance and Poverty Alleviation of JNNURM; Annexure-VII*, To the minutes of 65th CSMC (Central Sanctioning and Monitoring Committee) dated July 15, 2009, Ministry of Housing and Urban Poverty Alleviation, Government of India, New Delhi, accessed on December 17, 2009 (https://jnnurmmis.nic.in/jnnurm_hupa/jnnurm/Toolkit%20for%20Capacity%20Buildings.pdf).

MoHUPA (2010). *Report of the Committee on Slum Settlement*, National Building Organisation (NBO), Ministry of Urban Poverty and Alleviation, New Delhi: Government of India. (*mohupa.gov.in/W_new/Slum_Report_NBO.pdf*)

MoHUPA (2012). *Report of the Technical Group (TG-12) on Urban Housing Shortage (2012-17)*, National Building Organisation (NBO), Ministry of Housing and Urban Poverty Alleviation, New Delhi: Government of India.

Mooya, M.M., and C.E. Cloete (2008). *Land Tenure and Urban Poverty Alleviation: Theory, Evidence and New Direction.*

Neuwirth, R. (2005). *Shadow Cities: A Billion Squatters, A New Urban World*, New York: Routledge.

NIUA (1989). *Modelling a Rental Housing Market: A Conceptual Framework*, Research Study Series No. 36, National Institute of Urban Affairs, New Delhi.

NSSO (2004). *Housing Stock and Constructions 58th Round 2002, Report No. 488 (58/1.2/1), NSS 58th Round (July 200-December 2002),* National Sample Survey Organisation, Ministry of Statistics and Programme Implementation, March, New Delhi: Government of India.

NSSO (2010). *Housing Condition and Amenities in India, 2008-09, Report No. 535 (65/1.2/1), NSS 65th Round (July 2008-June 2009),* National Sample Survey Organisation, Ministry of Statistics and Programme Implementation November, New Delhi: Government of India.

NWCMC (2006). *City Development Plan 2006-25*, Prepared with technical assistance from IL&FS and Fortress Financial Services Ltd., July.

NWCMC (not dated). *BSUP Project Proposal for Nanded DPR VII*. Nanded: Nanded Waghala City Municipal Corporation.

NWCMC (not dated). *BSUP Project Proposal for Nanded DPR XI*. Nanded: Nanded Waghala City Municipal Corporation.

Oakley, P. (1991). *Projects with People: The Practice of Participation in Rural Development*, Geneva: International Labour Organisation.

Oberlander, P. (1985). *Land: The Central Human Settlement Issue*, Vancouver, Canada: University of British Columbia Press.

Okoro, E. (2000). *Quantitative Techniques in Urban Analysis,* Ibadan: Kraft Books Ltd.

Our Inclusive Ahmedabad (2010). *Report of the Public Hearing on Habitat and Livelihood Displacements*, Ahmedabad: Our Inclusive Ahmedabad.

Payne, G. (1989). *Informal Housing and Land Subdivisions in Third World Cities: A Review of the Literature*, Oxford: Centre for Emergency and Development Practice.

Payne, G. (1997). *Urban Land Tenure and Property Rights in Developing Countries*. London: Intermediate Technology Publications.

Payne, G. (2000). *Urban Land Tenure Policy Options: Titles or Rights?*, Virginia, USA: World Bank Urban Forum.

Payne, G. (2005). *Reviewing Titling and Other Tenure Options*, Global Land Tool Network Meeting, Sweden.

Planning Commission (2009). *Report of the Expert Group to Review the Methodology for Estimation of Poverty,* New Delhi: Government of India, November.

Planning Commission (2012). *Press Note on Poverty Estimates, 2009-10*, March, New Delhi: Government of India.

Reddy, R. (2002). *Empowerment of Women and Ecological Development*, New Delhi: Serials Publications.

Roy, A. (2009). "Why India Cannot Plan Its Cities: Informality, Insurgence and Idiom or Urbanization," *Planning Theory*, 8, pp. 76-87.

Roy, A. (2011). "Slumdog Cities: Rethinking Subaltern Urbanism", *International Journal of Urban and Regional Research*, 35 (2), pp. 223-38.

Roy, A. and N. Al Sayyad (2004). *Urban informality: transnational perspectives from the Middle East, Latin America, and South Asia.* Lanham: Lexington Books.

Sen, A. (2000). *Development as Freedom,* New Delhi: Oxford University Press.

Shah, G. (1997). *Public Health and Urban Development: The Plague in Surat*, New Delhi: Sage Publications.

Sharma, U. (1983). *Women's Work and Poverty in North West India*, Delhi: Tavistock Publications.

Sivam, A. *et al.,* (2001). "An approach to improved housing delivery in large cities of less developed countries," *Habitat International*, Vol. 25, pp. 99-113.

Soliman, A. (2004). *A Possible Way Out: Formalizing Housing Informality in Egyptian Cities*, Lanham: USA: University Press of America.

Struyk, R. and R. Lynn (1983). "Determinants of Housing Investments in Slum Area," *Land Economics*, 59(4), pp. 444-54.

Swamy, S., A. Vyas and S. Narang (1997). *Transformation of Surat: From Plague to Second Cleanest City of India*, Urban Management Programme for Asia and the Pacific, New Delhi: All India Institute of Local Self Government.

Thakur-Joshi, S. (1999). *Women and Development*, New Delhi: Mittal Publications.

Thorbek, S. (1994). *Gender and Slum Culture in Urban Asia*, New Delhi: Vistaar Publications—A division of Sage Publications India Private Limited.

Tiwari, P. (2001). "Housing and Development Objectives in India," *Habitat International,* Vol. 25, pp. 229-53.

Topfer, K. (2002). *Re-assessment of Urban Planning and Development Regulations in Africa Cities*, Nairobi: Habitat.

Turner, J.F.C. (1967). "Barriers and Channels for Housing Development in Modernizing Countries," *Journal of American Institute of Planners*, May, pp. 167-81.

Turner, J.F.C. (1968). "Housing Priorities, Settlement Patterns, and Urban Development in Modernizing Countries," *Journal of American Institute of Planners*, November, pp. 354-63.

Turner, J.F.C. (1976). *Housing by People*, London: Marion Boyars.

UNCHS (1996). *An Urbanising World—Global Report on Human*

Settlements: Nairobi: United Nations Centre for Human Settlements (Habitat).

UN-HABITAT (2003). "Rental Housing: An Essential Option for the Urban Poor in Developing Countries," Nairobi: UN-HABITAT.

UN-HABITAT, BMC and WaterAid. (2006). *A Situational Analysis of Poverty Pockets in Bhopal*, Bhopal: BMC.

Unni, J. (1999). *Urban Informal Sector: Size and Income Generation Processes in Gujarat*, Gujarat Institute of Development Research, GIDR and Self-employed Women's Association, SEWA.

Unni, J. and Uma Rani (2007). "Informal Workers in Ahmedabad City", in Annapurna Shaw (ed.), *Indian Cities in Transition*, Hyderabad: Orient Longman, pp. 217-37.

UNRISD (2010), *Combating Poverty and Inequality: Structural Change, Social Policy and Politics,* Geneva: United Nations Research Institute for Social Development (UNRISD).

Vinayak, N. (2011). "Inclusive Cities and Participative Development: A Case for Discussion," accessed on May 4, 2013. (http://www.slideshare.net/shruthipeddinti/case-study-nanded-community-participation).

Weinstein, L. (2008). "Mumbai's Development Mafias: Globalization, Organized Crime and Land Development," *International Journal of Urban and Regional Research,* 32 (1), pp. 22-39.

World Bank (1993). *Housing: Enabling Markets to Work*, World Bank Policy Paper, Washington DC: The World Bank.

Yuen, B. (2007). "Squatters No More: Singapore Social Housing," *Global Urban Development (GUD) Magazine*, 3(1), November. (*www.globalurban.org/GUDMag07Vol3Iss1/MagHome.htm*).

Index